SECOND EDITION

CRIMINOLOGY THEORY

Selected Classic Readings

Frank P. Williams III
California State University—San Bernardino

Marilyn D. McShane
Northern Arizona University

anderson publishing co.
p.o. box 1576
cincinnati, oh 45201-1576
(513) 421-4142

since 1887

Criminology Theory: Selected Classic Readings, Second Edition

Copyright © 1993, 1998
    Anderson Publishing Co.
    2035 Reading Rd.
    Cincinnati, OH 45202

Phone 800.582.7295 or 513.421.4142
Web Site www.andersonpublishing.com

Library of Congress Cataloging-in-Publication Data

Williams, Franklin P.
   Criminology theory : selected classic readings / Frank P.
Williams, III, Marilyn D. McShane. -- 2nd ed.
      p.   cm.
   Includes bibliographical references and indexes.
   ISBN 0-87084-201-3 (pbk.)
   1. Criminology. I. McShane, Marilyn D., 1956- . II. Title.
HV6018.W48 1998
364--dc21   97-48646
                                          CIP

Cover design by Edward Smith Design/New York, NY

EDITOR Gail Eccleston
ASSISTANT EDITOR Elizabeth A. Shipp
ACQUISITIONS EDITOR Michael C. Braswell

Preface

This anthology is a set of readings featuring major criminological perspectives. Except for two articles in the final section, all readings represent the staples of criminological theory. There is no attempt to include "interesting" readings, or excerpts from major works not directly associated with those theories commonly covered in textbooks and in courses in criminology. In part, this approach is derived from our own frustration, and that of several of our colleagues, with existing anthologies. The common approach seems to be for editors to excerpt from the major articles and then include a series of each editor's own "favorite" articles. We generally found that the excerpted materials left out enough of the originals that we had to add pages and materials so that students could gain a fuller appreciation of the theorists' work. Where the "favorite" articles are concerned, we often found ourselves telling students that these would not be used (in effect, informing students that one-half of the money they spent for the book was wasted). Thus, we decided that there should be a reader with only the core materials in criminological theory. This is that product.

The readings in this anthology are all from the original sources. We made every attempt to ensure their accuracy. We did, in some cases, correct misspellings and grammatical errors. In the case of the Beccaria reading, for instance, we used the earliest English-language version of the text we could find. The reader may be surprised by the difference in passion and intensity between our 1814 source and the Bobbs-Merrill/Paolucci translation commonly used in courses; and the text is, after all, a protest piece. In two other cases (Lombroso and Reckless), we used sources other than the "usual" ones because we felt they better reflected the "average" position of the theoretical perspective and would be more comprehensible for a first-time reader.

The two final selections were chosen for reasons other than the fact that they might be favorite pieces. The Cohen and Felson routine-activities article presaged the current emphasis on rationalistic theory and is fast becoming a classic. In order to make it more intelligible to undergraduate readers, we excerpted the theoretical thrust of the article and eliminated the empirical materials and the statistical analysis and discussion. The Klein article is also a classic—representing the first of the feminist critiques of male-dominated theorizing. In addition, it serves to help students appreciate the shortcomings of classic theories. While it is true that gender-based critiques and theories have come a long way since the Klein article was published, none have yet been ascribed the status of a "classic."

This edition of the anthology includes two new readings, requested by those who are using it in their courses. The two additions are excerpts from the works of Jeremy Bentham and Richard Quinney. The Bentham excerpt is drawn from an old version of his *Introduction to the Principles of Morals and Legislation*. We purposefully left old spellings and grammatical idiosyncracies in the excerpt because we believe they add to the sense of reaching into the past (we did, however, eliminate the various footnotes). Bentham had much more to say about crime than we were able to capture here, but students reading the material will certainly be able to ascertain the general approach to crime and crime prevention of his day.

Richard Quinney's *Social Reality of Crime*, on the other hand, was not a difficult selection to excerpt. The core presentation of the book is concisely outlined with six propositions in the first chapter. Those who have been exposed to Quinney's theory, largely through textbook commentary, may be surprised to find out just how integrative it was. He used concepts from virtually all of the major theories of the day and wove them into a pluralist conflict perspective with an eye toward the importance of media in society. This selection was omitted from the first edition not because it was not worthy, but because we were concerned with space. Those who are familiar with the "Lone Ranger" know the importance we place on Quinney's work. We now rectify that omission.

Even with these two additions, instructors will still find that there are a few of their favorite theory articles that are omitted. This anthology purposefully serves only as a core for a course in criminological theory. We still believe that this approach offers the best compromise to placing readings on reserve and using only one-half of the selections in a more general anthology. Instructors can easily place other articles on reserve in the library or use one of the many photocopying services to add a package of supplementary materials for their specific course objectives. Our goal was to help keep the reserve reading list to a minimum.

One other point should be made in regard to instructor preferences. "Classification" of the theories into the various sections is a rather arbitrary process. Different texts and instructors classify the theories differently depending upon their assumptions, chronological order, relationship with other theories, and so forth. We used two criteria for categorizing theories: first, we used a logical order of similarity in presenting theoretical materials to students and, second, we used chronological order where appropriate. Thus, we placed Akers' learning theory after its intellectual father, differential association, in order to continue the logical threads. Similarly, Miller's focal concern theory, even though it was a conflict-based theory, was included with subculture theories because it was an important part of the subcultural delinquency literature of the 1950s. Instructors with other preferences should mix the readings in whatever fashion matches their teaching style. *And to students of those instructors—we want you to know that your instructor is just as correct in his or her categorization of theories as the scheme we used in this book.* There is simply no one correct way to classify theories.

Finally, we wish to express our appreciation to our many students and colleagues who assisted through the years in identifying the core set of readings we include here. Many of you are teaching criminological theory courses and, in one sense, this anthology was constructed especially for you. We also wish to thank those colleagues who have used this anthology and written to us with comments and suggestions. All were read, and where they were not implemented, it is quite obvious that we cannot recognize superior advice. The instructor's manual that was constructed to be used in conjunction with this new edition was, in part, due to the efforts of Aimee Cassiday and she deserves thanks for that work. And, last but not least, we wish to express thanks to Mickey Braswell and Gail Eccleston of Anderson Publishing Co. Mickey had the amazing foresight to see some value in what we wanted to do and Gail made working with Anderson a pleasure.

Frank Williams and Marilyn McShane

Contents

Section I
THE FOUNDATIONS OF
MODERN CRIMINOLOGY

Introduction

This section contains three major writings. All are excerpted from longer sources and are representative of schools of criminological thought originating in the eighteenth and nineteenth centuries, respectively. More than just being "theories" of crime or criminality, these three writings helped to change the criminal justice system and the study of criminals into what they are today.

The Classical School

The first selection, from *An Essay on Crimes and Punishment*, written in 1764 by an Italian, Cesare Beccaria, was one of the most powerful documents of its day. Until the time of Beccaria's essay, European criminal justice systems bore little resemblance to ours today. Laws were made by the aristocracy, often at whim. Law could be retroactive, it did not have to be written, it rarely applied to members of the aristocracy, and no one even had to know about the law until it was applied. There was no "due process" as we think of it today, evidence was not particularly reliable (confessions under torture were considered excellent evidence of guilt), and an accused could be kept imprisoned for as long as the magistrate required. Punishment was determined on a case-by-case basis with no thought to fairness or equity and large numbers of "offenses" were punishable by death. In short, the European criminal justice system prior to 1750 was an arbitrary and capricious one run largely for the benefit of the aristocracy and the church.

A new era was already at hand by the time Beccaria wrote his essay. Merchants (the soon-to-be new middle class) were seeking power, science was challenging the church as a source of knowledge, the new protestant reformation was under way, and philosophies of human nature were changing to characterize all humans as rational, capable persons with *free will* (not just the aristocracy and clergy). Equally as important, a philosophy of government called the *social contract* was growing in popularity. Under social contract philosophy, governments existed to serve the people, not the other way around. All people had certain rights and the primary function of a government was to ensure that those rights were protected. Thus, a government existed as a result of a social contract with its citizens, whereby it was agreed that individual citizens would give up only the minimal amount of their freedom and rights required for government to protect the majority of society. The *utilitarian* phrase "the greatest good for the greatest number" became the essence of social contract governments. These, and many more thoughts and ideas, were generally referred to as the "Classical School."

Beccaria's essay expressed all of these thoughts and applied them to criminal justice, and did it passionately. The essay itself is really a protest piece written anonymously at first and only acknowledged by its author three years after its first publication. Seemingly, Beccaria was concerned that there would be retaliation by the rulers of his day.

The essay begins with an acknowledgment of the importance of humanist and rationalist philosophies of human nature and goes on to argue against the "excesses" of the criminal justice system. Beccaria takes the reader on a tour through that criminal justice system, from legislation and law-making through arrest and trial to punishment. In each case, Beccaria argues against what is, presents an alternative form of criminal justice system, and argues for it. These alternative forms of doing justice laid the foundation for today's system. In fact, our founding fathers constructed the United States Constitution and Bill of Rights on the basic concepts of the Classical School. Some of the ideas put into place were a right to a speedy trial, jury of one's peers, separation of executive and judicial functions (law-making and law-judging), the use of standards of evidence, written laws, no retroactive laws, and punishment fitting the crime. In short, most of the content of procedural law, or due process, is directly related to legal reforms attributable to the Classical School, and to the writing of Beccaria.

One other idea also was important to the Classical School: a concept of humans as rational individuals who were governed by *hedonism*. In other words, people were thought to behave according to rational calculations of pleasure and pain they expected to receive as a product of their actions. Jeremy Bentham, another major writer in the Classical School, had perhaps the most to say here, and his work is exemplified in the second reading in this section. Applied to the criminal justice context, the hedonistic principle meant that punishment could be used to *deter* individuals from committing crimes and transgressing on the rights of others. As a reader can tell from the excerpt of Bentham's work, the concept of a rational person was a powerful one for philosophers in the late eighteenth and nineteenth centuries. Bentham elaborated on the different rationales of various classes of offenders, all with the idea that punishment had to be carefully crafted to be a convincing force to prevent crime.

Thus, a calculated punishment was to be designed for each crime so that the gain from the crime would be offset by the punishment. Since punishment was viewed as a scarce resource, however, only the amount of pain necessary to cancel the gain from the crime should be used. Bentham spent a good deal of effort in attempting to devise a *hedonistic calculus* of the exact amount of pain to be applied to each offense. If no pleasure were to be gained from a crime, Classical theorists assumed that an individual would rationally consider that fact and therefore not commit the crime. If a crime was committed, the offender had to be punished in order to make an example, and thereby deter, others. The *speed* and *certainty* of punishment were both more important than the *severity* because they created the greatest efficiency in punishment resources.

Bentham's style was to create classifications of the different aspects of crime—from motivation to act to punishment. He carefully analyzed and enumerated the pertinent details of each class, and then developed a rationale for dealing with it. Bentham also echoed the comments of Beccaria in arguing the purpose of punishment and law, and by being careful to avoid placing government in the position of a heartless despot, particularly in those cases where punishment could be seen as unnecessary.

In sum, Beccaria, Bentham, and the other writers of the Classical School emphasized not so much the criminal, but crime and legal structure. They focused on law-making and the way the criminal justice system should process accused persons, the rights of those persons, justice, and fairness. They also strongly believed that the only justification for punishing criminals was deterrence, which served to correct a wrong to the social contract.

The Positive School

After most of the ideas of the Classical School had been implemented, the need for concern about the creation of law and political structures diminished. A little more than 100 years after Beccaria wrote, people had put aside discussions of the political nature of crime and justice and another Italian, Cesare Lombroso, began to study and advance new ideas about criminals. His was a world of *science*, where systematic study and new discoveries had created amazing advances in industry, medicine, and engineering. Most people felt that a scientific approach to the study of human societies could be used to solve social ills. In fact, there was a good deal of optimism that almost any social problem could be treated and corrected through the positive application of science (thus the name "positivism").

Lombroso was a medical doctor, used to looking for symptoms and diagnosing diseases. When he looked at prisoners, he saw symptoms—characteristics and features that suggested criminals were different from "normal" people. He also had the assistance of a new social science called anthropology where people studying primitive tribes and other non-western cultures were making interesting observations. It seemed that the primitives they described were more like the criminals he knew than "civilized" Europeans. Moreover, the popularity of Darwin's work in evolution had some people looking for connections between different cultures and highly-evolved species. Therefore, Lombroso reasoned, criminals must represent a more primitive form of human. He began to make systematic measurements of the physical features of prisoners and criminals and came to the conclusion that criminals were indeed different from normal, civilized people.

Lombroso was not the first writer and theorist to systematically study criminals; he was not even the first to conclude that there were physical differences. Others had already examined criminal physiognomy (della Porte in the 1500s) and phrenology (the examination of skull shapes, contours, and "bumps" on the head) was popular some 50 years before Lombroso began to write (Gall and Spurzheim in the 1820s and 1830s). Lombroso, however, had the advantage of the new tools of science and the mood of treatment and prevention of his day.

His theory was that criminals had a criminal personality and were largely a more primitive form of human than were non-criminals. He talked of sloping foreheads, heavy brow ridges, jutting jaws, and the like. He also described criminals as lacking in moral development and having sensory impairment. He found enough physical anomalies in criminals, and enough similarities to primitive human types, to characterize them as *atavistic* types or throwbacks to an earlier species of human. He also believed that there were similarities between criminals and epileptics. Where there were no marked physical anomalies, Lombroso determined that criminals had begun life normally but, for some reason, had *degenerated* internally into a primitive state. When criminals exhibited only a few of the characteristics he expected to see, they were "criminaloids"—or pseudo-criminals. Thus, he saw two basic forms of criminality—the atavist and the degenerate.

After much examination of criminals and after others had criticized his work, Lombroso added other categories of criminality. One was the criminally insane. A second was the "occasional criminal"—a class of criminals with few of the characteristics of common criminals. Other offenders, such as members of the nobility who engaged in (illegal) duels, really had nothing wrong with them and were "criminals by passion." Finally, in his later work Lombroso acknowledged the contributions of social and psychological factors, but always indicated that they were less important in causing criminality than the biological ones.

Other writers followed Lombroso. In Italy, Raffaele Garofalo and Enrico Ferri elaborated on his ideas and the three became known as the "Italian Triumvirate." Others wrote on all manner of causes of crime and the Positivist School became the foundation of modern criminology. The essence of this school of criminology is not so much an emphasis on biological causes as it is an emphasis on the study of criminal *behavior*, the use of *scientific methodology*, the assumption of *pathology*, *classification* of criminal types, *prediction* of criminality, and *treatment* of criminals (or the problem factors, whatever they may be). From this perspective, most of today's sociological, psychological, economic, and biological theories of criminality are positivistic.

BIBLIOGRAPHY

Allen, Francis A. (1972). "Raffaele Garofalo," in Hermann Mannheim (ed.) *Pioneers in Criminology*, 2nd ed. Montclair, NJ: Patterson Smith, 318-40.

Atkinson, Charles (1905). *Jeremy Bentham: His Life and Work*. Westport, CT: Greenwood (reprinted 1970).

Beirne, Piers (1991). "Inventing criminology: The 'science of man' in Cesare Beccaria's *De Delitti e Delle Pene (1964)*," *Criminology* 29: 777-820.

Bentham, Jeremy (1843). *The Works of Jeremy Bentham*. Vol. I. *An Introduction to the Principles of Morals and Legislation*. Published under the superintendence of his executor, John Bowring. Edinburgh: William Tait.

Ferri, Enrico (1881). *Criminal Sociology*. Trans. Joseph Killey and John Lisle. Boston: Little, Brown (reprinted 1917).

Garofalo, Raffaele (1885). *Criminology*. Trans. Robert W. Millar. Boston: Little, Brown (reprinted 1914).

Geis, Gilbert (1955). "Jeremy Bentham," *Journal of Criminal Law, Criminology, and Police Science* 46: 159-71.

Goddard, Henry H. (1914). *Feeblemindedness, Its Causes and Consequences*. New York: Macmillan.

Jeffery, C. Ray (1972). "The historical development of criminology," in Hermann Mannheim (ed.) *Pioneers in Criminology*, 2nd ed. Montclair, NJ: Patterson Smith, 458-98.

Kaplan, Abraham (1968). "Positivism," in David L. Sills (ed.) *International Encyclopedia of the Social Sciences*, Vol. 12. New York: Macmillan, 389-95.

Lombroso, Cesare (1876). *L'Uomo Delinquente* (The Criminal Man). Milano: Hoepli.

Maestro, Marcello T. (1973). *Cesare Beccaria and the Origins of Penal Reform*. Philadelphia: Temple University Press.

Maestro, Marcello T. (1942). *Voltaire and Beccaria as Reformers of Criminal Law.* New York: Columbia University Press.

Mannheim, Hermann (ed.) (1973). *Pioneers in Criminology*, 2nd ed. Montclair, NJ: Patterson Smith.

Monachesi, Elio D. (1955). "Cesare Beccaria," *Journal of Criminal Law, Criminology, and Police Science* 46: 439-49.

Phillipson, Coleman (1923). *Three Criminal Law Reformers: Beccaria, Bentham and Romilly.* Montclair, NJ: Patterson Smith (reprinted 1972).

Savitz, Leonard D. (1972). "Introduction to the Reprint Edition," in Gina Lombroso-Ferrero, *Criminal Man: According to the Classification of Cesare Lombroso,* reprinted ed. Montclair, NJ: Patterson Smith, v-xx.

Sellin, Thorsten (1972). "Enrico Ferri," in Hermann Mannheim (ed.) *Pioneers in Criminology*, 2nd ed. Montclair, NJ: Patterson Smith, 361-84.

Tarde, Gabriel (1890). *Penal Philosophy.* Trans. Rapelje Howell. Boston: Little, Brown (reprinted 1912).

Wolfgang, Marvin E. (1972). "Cesare Lombroso," in Hermann Mannheim (ed.) *Pioneers in Criminology*, 2nd ed. Montclair, NJ: Patterson Smith, 232-91.

Cesare Beccaria (1738-1794)

Beccaria was born in Milan, Italy, the son of a minor aristocrat. He was educated by Jesuits and received a degree in law in 1758 from the University of Pavia. In 1768, he took a position at the Palatine School in Milan, and accepted the chair in political economy and commerce, remaining for only two years. Appointed to the Supreme Ecomomic Council of Milan in 1771, he spent the remainder of his life as a public official. His full title was Cesare Bonesana, Marchese di Beccaria.

On Crimes and Punishments[*]
Cesare Beccaria

INTRODUCTION

IN every human society, there is an effort continually tending to confer on one part the height of power and happiness, and to reduce the other to the extreme of weakness and misery. The intent of good laws is to oppose this effort, and to diffuse their influence universally and equally. But men generally abandoned the care of their most important concerns to the uncertain prudence and discretion of those whose interest it is to reject the best and wisest institutions; and it is not till they have been led into a thousand mistakes in matters the most essential to their lives and liberties, and are weary of suffering, that they can be induced to apply a remedy to the evils with which they are oppressed. It is then they begin to conceive and acknowledge the most palpable truths, which, from their very simplicity, commonly escape vulgar minds, incapable of analysing objects, accustomed to receive impressions without distinction, and to be determined rather by the opinions of others than by the result of their own examination.

If we look into history we shall find that laws, which are, or ought to be, conventions between men in a state of freedom, have been, for the most part the work of the passions of a few, or the consequences of a fortuitous or temporary necessity; not dictated by a cool examiner of human nature, who knew how to collect in one point the actions of a multitude, and had this only end in view, *the greatest happiness of the*

---

*Source: Cesare Bonesana, Marquis Beccaria, 1819. *An Essay on Crimes and Punishments,* trans. from the Italian by M.D. Voltaire, trans. from the French by Edward D. Ingraham. 2nd American ed. Philadelphia: Philip H. Nicklin. (Original published in 1764.)

greatest number. Happy are those few nations that have not waited till the slow succession of human vicissitudes should, from the extremity of evil, produce a transition to good; but by prudent laws have facilitated the progress from one to the other! And how great are the obligations due from mankind to that philosopher, who, from the obscurity of his closet, had the courage to scatter among the multitude the seeds of useful truths, so long unfruitful!

The art of printing has diffused the knowledge of those philosophical truths, by which the relations between sovereigns and their subjects, and between nations are discovered. By this knowledge commerce is animated, and there has sprung up a spirit of emulation and industry, worthy of rational beings. These are the products of this enlightened age; but the cruelty of punishments, and the irregularity of proceedings in criminal cases, such principal parts of the legislation, and so much neglected throughout Europe, have hardly ever been called in question. Errors, accumulated through many centuries, have never yet been exposed by ascending to general principles; nor has the force of acknowledged truths been ever opposed to the unbounded licentiousness of ill-directed power, which has continually produced so many authorized examples of the most unfeeling barbarity. Surely, the groans of the weak, sacrificed to the cruel ignorance and indolence of the powerful, the barbarous torments lavished, and multiplied with useless severity, for crimes either not proved, or in their nature impossible, the filth and horrors of a prison, increased by the most cruel tormentor of the miserable, uncertainty, ought to have roused the attention of those whose business is to direct the opinions of mankind.

The immortal Montesquieu has but slightly touched on this subject. Truth, which is eternally the same, has obliged me to follow the steps of that great man; but the studious part of mankind, for whom I write, will easily distinguish the superstructure from the foundation. I shall be happy if, with him, I can obtain the secret thanks of the obscure and peaceful disciples of reason and philosophy, and excite that tender emotion in which sensible minds sympathize with him who pleads the cause of humanity.

CHAP. I.
Of the Origin of Punishments

LAWS are the conditions under which men, naturally independent, united themselves in society. Weary of living in a continual state of war, and of enjoying a liberty, which became of little value, from the uncertainty of its duration, they sacrificed one part of it, to enjoy the rest in peace and security. The sum of all these portions of the liberty of each individual constituted the sovereignty of a nation and was deposited in the hands of the sovereign, as the lawful administrator, But it was not sufficient only to establish this deposit; it was also necessary to defend it from the usurpation of each individual, who will always endeavour to take away from the mass, not only his own portion, but to encroach on that of others. Some motives therefore, that strike the senses were necessary to prevent the despotism of each individual from plunging society into its former chaos. Such motives are the punishments established against the infractors of the laws. . . .

CHAP. II.
Of the Right to Punish

EVERY punishment which does not arise from absolute necessity, says the great Montesquieu, is tyrannical. A proposition which may be made more general thus: every act of authority of one man over another, for which there is not an absolute necessity, is tyrannical. It is upon this then that the sovereign's right to punish crimes is founded; that is, upon the necessity of defending the public liberty, entrusted to his care, from the usurpation of individuals; and punishments are just in proportion, as the liberty, preserved by the sovereign, is sacred and valuable. . . .

No man ever gave up his liberty merely for the good of the public. Such a chimera exists only in romances. Every individual wishes, if possible, to be exempt from the compacts that bind the rest of mankind.

The multiplication of mankind, though slow, being too great, for the means which the earth, in its natural state, offered to satisfy necessities which every day became more numerous, obliged men to separate again, and form new societies. These naturally opposed the first, and a state of war was transferred from individuals to nations.

Thus it was necessity that forced men to give up a part of their liberty. It is certain, then, that every individual would choose to put into the public stock the smallest portion possible, as much only as was sufficient to engage others to defend it. The aggregate of these, the smallest portions possible, forms the right of punishing; all that extends beyond this is abuse, not justice.

Observe that by *justice* I understand nothing more than that bond which is necessary to keep the interest of individuals united, without which men would return to their original state of barbarity. All punishments which exceed the necessity of preserving this bond are in their nature unjust. We should be cautious how we associate with the word *justice* an idea of anything real, such as a physical power, or a being that actually exists.

CHAP. III.
Consequences of the Foregoing Principles

THE laws only can determine the punishment of crimes; and the authority of making penal laws can only reside with the legislator, who represents the whole society united by the social compact. No magistrate then, (as he is one of the society,) can, with justice, inflict on any other member of the same society punishment that is not ordained by the laws. But as a punishment, increased beyond the degree fixed by the law, is the just punishment with the addition of another, it follows that no magistrate, even under a pretence of zeal, or the public good, should increase the punishment already determined by the laws.

If every individual be bound to society, society is equally bound to him, by a contract which, from its nature equally binds both parties. This obligation, which descends from the throne to the cottage, and equally binds the highest and lowest of mankind, signifies nothing more than that it is the interest of all, that conventions, which are useful to the greatest number, should be punctually observed. The violation of this compact by any individual is an introduction to anarchy.

The sovereign, who represents the society itself, can only make general laws to bind the members; but it belongs not to him to judge whether any individual has violated the social compact, or incurred the punishment in consequence. For in this case there are two parties, one represented by the sovereign, who insists upon the violation of the contract, and the other is the person accused, who denies it. It is necessary then that there should be a third person to decide this contest; that is to say, a judge, or magistrate, from whose determination should consist of a simple affirmation or negation of fact.

CHAP. IV.
Of the Interpretation of Laws

JUDGES, in criminal cases, have no right to interpret the penal laws, because they are not legislators. They have not received the laws from our ancestors as a domestic tradition, or as the will of a testator, which his heirs and executors are to obey; but they receive them from a society actually existing, or from the sovereign, its representative. Even the authority of the laws is not founded on any pretended obligations, or ancient convention; which must be null, as it cannot bind those who did not exist at the time of its institution; and unjust, as it would reduce men in the ages following, to a herd of brutes, without any power of judging or acting. The laws receive their force and authority from an oath of fidelity, either tacit or expressed, which living subjects have sworn to their sovereign, in order to restrain the intestine fermentation of the private interest of individuals. From hence springs their true and natural authority. Who then is their lawful interpreter? The sovereign, that is the representative of society, and not the judge, whose office is only to examine if a man has or has not committed an action contrary to the laws. . .

The disorders that may arise from a rigorous observance of the letter of penal laws are not to be compared with those produced by the interpretation of them. The first are temporary inconveniences which will oblige the legislature to correct the letter of the law, the want of preciseness and uncertainty of which has occasioned these disorders; and this will put a stop to the fatal liberty of explaining, the source of arbitrary and venal declamations. When the code of laws is once fixed, it should be observed in the literal sense, and nothing more is left to the judge than to determine whether an action is or is not conformable to the written law.

CHAP. V.
Of the Obscurity of Laws

IF the power of interpreting laws is an evil, obscurity in them must be another, as the former is the consequence of the latter. This evil will be still greater if the laws are written in a language unknown to the people; who, being ignorant of the consequences of their own actions, become necessarily dependent on a few, who are interpreters of the laws, which instead of being public and general, are thus rendered private and particular. What must we think of mankind when we reflect, that such is the established custom of the greatest part of our polished and enlightened Europe? Crimes will be less frequent in proportion as the code of laws is more universally read and understood; for there is no doubt but that the eloquence of the passions is greatly assisted by the ignorance and uncertainty of punishments.

The necessity of uniting in society being granted, together with the conventions which the opposite interests of individuals must necessarily require, a scale of crimes may be formed, of which the first degree should consist of those which immediately tend to the dissolution of society, and the last of the smallest possible injustice done to a private member of that society. Between these extremes will be comprehended all actions contrary to the public good which are called criminal, and which descend by insensible degrees, decreasing from the highest to the lowest. If mathematical calculations could be applied to the obscure and infinite combinations of human actions, there might be a corresponding scale of punishments, descending from the greatest to the least; but it will be sufficient that the wise legislator mark the principal divisions, without disturbing the order, left to crimes of the *first* degree be assigned punishments of the *last.*

Pleasure and pain are the only springs of actions in beings endowed with sensibility. Even amongst the motives which incite men to acts of religion, the invisible legislator has ordained rewards and punishments. From a partial distribution of these will rise that contradiction, so little observed, because so common, I mean that of punishing by the laws the crimes which the laws have occasioned. If an equal punishment be ordained for two crimes that injure society in different degrees, there is nothing to deter men from committing the greater as often as it is attended with greater advantage. . . .

CHAP. VII.
Of Estimating the Degree of Crimes

THE foregoing reflections authorize me to assert that crimes are only to be measured by the injury done to society.

They err, therefore, who imagine that a crime is greater or less according to the intention of the person by whom it is committed; for this will depend on the actual impression of objects on the senses, and on the previous disposition of the mind; both which will vary in different persons, and even in the same person at different times, according to the succession of ideas, passions, and circumstances. Upon that system it would be necessary to form, not only a particular code for every individual, but a new penal law for every crime. Men, often with the best intention, do the greatest injury to society, and, with the worst, do it the most essential services. . . .

CHAP. XII.
Of the Intent of Punishments

FROM the foregoing considerations it is evident that the intent of punishments is not to torment a sensible being, nor to undo a crime already committed. Is it possible that torments and useless cruelty, the instrument of furious fanaticism or the impotency of tyrants, can be authorized by a political body, which so far from being influenced by passion, should be the cool moderator of the passions of individuals? Can the groans of a tortured wretch recall the time past, or reverse the crime he has committed?

The end of punishment, therefore, is no other than to prevent the criminal from doing further injury to society, and to prevent others from committing the like offense. Such punishments, therefore, and such a mode of inflicting them, ought to be chosen, as will make the strongest and most lasting impressions on the minds of others, with the least torment to the body of the criminal. . . .

CHAP. XV.
Of Secret Accusations

SECRET accusations are a manifest abuse, but consecrated by custom in many nations, where, from the weakness of the government, they are necessary. This custom makes men false and treacherous. . . .

Public accusations, says Montesquieu, are more conformable to the nature of a republic, where zeal for the public good is the principal passion of a citizen, than of a monarchy, in which, as this sentiment is very feeble, from the nature of the government, the best establishment is that of commissioners, who, in the name of the public, accuse the infractors of the laws. But in all governments, in a republic as well as in a monarchy, the punishment due to the crime of which one accuses another ought to be inflicted on the informer.

CHAP. XVI.
Of Torture

THE torture of a criminal during the course of his trial is a cruelty consecrated by custom in most nations. It is used with an intent either to make him confess his crime, or to explain some contradictions into which he had been led during his examination, or to discover his accomplices, or for some kind of metaphysical and incomprehensible purgation of infamy, or, finally, in order to discover other crimes of which he is not accused, but of which he may be guilty.

No man can be judged a criminal until he is found guilty; nor can society take from him the public protection until it has been proved that he has violated the conditions on which it was granted. What right, then, but that of power, can authorize the punishment of a citizen so long as there remains any doubt of his guilt? This dilemma is frequent. Either he is guilty, or not guilty. If guilty, he should only suffer the punishment ordained by the laws, and torture becomes useless, as his confession is unnecessary. If he is not guilty, you torture the innocent; for, in the eye of the law, every man is innocent whose crime has not been proved. Besides, it is confounding all relations to expect that a man should be both the accuser and accused; and that pain should be the test of truth, as if truth resided in the muscles and fibres of a wretch in torture. By this method the robust will escape, and the feeble be condemned. . . .

It is not difficult to trace this senseless law to its origin; for an absurdity, adopted by a whole nation, must have some affinity with other ideas established and respected by the same nation. This custom seems to be the offspring of religion, by which mankind, in all nations and in all ages, are so generally influenced. We are taught by our infallible church, that those stains of sin contracted through human frailty, and which have not deserved the eternal anger of the Almighty, are to be purged away in another life by an incomprehensible fire. No infamy is a stain, and if the punishments and fire of purgatory can take away all spiritual stains, why should not the pain of torture take away those of a civil nature? . . .

It would be superfluous to confirm these reflections by examples of innocent persons who, from the agony of torture, have confessed themselves guilty: innumerable instances may be found in all nations, and in every age. How amazing that mankind has always neglected to draw the natural conclusion! . . .

CHAP. XIX.
Of the Advantage of Immediate Punishment

THE more immediately after the commission of a crime a punishment is inflicted, the more just and useful it will be. It will be more just, because it spares the criminal the cruel and superfluous torment of uncertainty, which increases in proportion to the strength of his imagination and the sense of his weakness; and because the privation of liberty, being a punishment, ought to be inflicted before condemnation but for as short a time as possible. Imprisonment, I say, being only the means of securing the person of the accused until he is tried, condemned, or acquitted, ought not only to be of as short duration, but attended with as little severity as possible. The time should be determined by the necessary preparation for the trial, and the right of priority in the oldest prisoners. The confinement ought not to be closer than is requisite to prevent his flight, or his concealing the proofs of the crime; and the trial should be conducted with all possible expedition. Can there be a more cruel contrast than that between the indolence of a judge and the painful anxiety of the accused; the comforts and pleasures of an insensible magistrate, and the filth and misery of the prisoner? In general, as I have before observed, *the degree of the punishment, and the consequences of a crime, ought to be so contrived as to have the greatest possible effect on others, with the least possible pain to the delinquent.* If there be any society in which this is not a fundamental principle, it is an unlawful society; for mankind, by their union, originally intended to subject themselves to the least evils possible.

An immediate punishment is more useful; because the smaller the interval of time between the punishment and the crime, the stronger and more lasting will be the association of the two ideas of *crime and punishment;* so that they may be considered, one as the cause, and the other as the unavoidable and necessary effect. . . .

It is, then, of the greatest importance that the punishment should succeed the crime as immediately as possible, if we intend that, in the rude minds of the multitude, the seducing picture of the advantage arising from the crime should instantly awake the attendant idea of punishment. Delaying the punishment serves only to separate these two ideas, and thus affects the minds of the spectators rather as being a terrible sight than the necessary consequence of a crime, the horror of which should contribute to heighten the idea of punishment.

There is another excellent method of strengthening this important connection between the ideas of crime and punishment as analogous as possible to the nature of the crime, in order that the punishment may lead the mind to consider the crime in a different point of view from that in which it was placed by the flattering idea of promised advantages.

Crimes of less importance are commonly punished either in the obscurity of a prison, or the criminal is *transported,* to give by his slavery an example to societies which he never offended; an example absolutely useless, because distant from the place where the crime was committed. Men do not, in general, commit great crimes deliberately, but rather in a sudden gust of passion; and they commonly look on the punishment for a great crime as remote and improbable. The public punishment, therefore, of small crimes will make a greater impression, and, by deterring men from the smaller, will effectually prevent the greater.

CHAP. XXVII.
Of the Mildness of Punishments

. . . Crimes are more effectually prevented by the *certainty* and the *severity* of punishment. Hence, in a magistrate, the necessity of vigilance, and in a judge of implacability, which, that it may become a useful virtue, should be joined to a mild legislation. The certainty of a small punishment will make a stronger impression than the fear of one more severe, if attended with the hopes of escaping; for it is the nature of mankind to be terrified at the approach of the smallest inevitable evil, whilst hope, the best gift of Heaven, hath the power of dispelling the apprehension of a greater, especially if supported by examples of impunity, which weakness or avarice too frequently afford.

If punishments be very severe, men are naturally led to the perpetration of other crimes, to avoid the punishment due to the first. . .

That a punishment may produce the effect required, it is sufficient that the *evil* it occasions should exceed the *good* expected from the crime, including in the calculation the certainty of the punishment, and the privation of the expected advantage. All severity beyond this is superfluous, and therefore tyrannical. . .

There are yet two other consequences of cruel punishments which counteract the purpose of their institution, which was to prevent crimes. The *first* arises from the impossibility of establishing an exact proportion between the crime and punishment; for though ingenious cruelty hath greatly multiplied the variety of torments, yet the human frame can suffer only to a certain degree, beyond which it is impossible to proceed, be the enormity of the crime ever so great. The *second* consequence is impunity. Human nature is limited no less in evil than in good. Excessive barbarity can never be more than temporary, it being impossible that it should be supported by a permanent system of legislation; for if the laws be too cruel, they must be altered, or anarchy and impunity will succeed. . . .

CHAP. XXIX.
Of Imprisonment

. . . Imprisonment is a punishment which differs from all others in this particular, that it necessarily precedes conviction; but this difference does not destroy a circumstance which is essential and common to it with all other punishments, viz. that it should never be inflicted but when ordained by the law. The law should therefore determine the crime, the presumption, and the evidence sufficient to subject the accused to imprisonment and examination. Public report, his flight, his extrajudicial confession, that of an accomplice, menaces, and his constant enmity with that person injured, the circumstances of the crime, and such other evidence, may be sufficient to justify the imprisonment of a citizen. But the nature of this evidence should be determined by the laws, and not by the magistrates, whose decrees are always contrary to political liberty, when they are not particular applications of a general maxim of the public code. . .

CHAP. XXX.
Of Prosecution and Prescription

THE proofs of the crime being obtained, and the certainty of it determined, it is necessary to allow the criminal time and means for his justification; but a time so short as not to diminish that promptitude of punishment, which, as we have shown, is one of the most powerful means of preventing crimes. A mistaken humanity may object to the shortness of the time, but the force of the objection will vanish if we consider that the danger of the innocent increases with the defects of the legislation.

The time for inquiry and for justification should be fixed by the laws, and not by the judge, who, in that case, would become legislator. With regard to atrocious crimes, which are long remembered, when they are once proved, if the criminal has fled, no time should be allowed; but in less considerable and more obscure crimes, a time should be fixed, after which the delinquent should no longer be uncertain of his fate; for, in the later case, the length of time in which the crime is almost forgotten prevents the example of impunity, and allows the criminal to amend, and become a better member of society. . . .

CHAP. XXXIX.
Of a Particular Kind of Crimes

I write only of *crimes* which violate the laws of nature and the social contract, and not of *sins,* even the temporal punishments of which must be determined from other principles than those of limited human philosophy. . . .

CHAP. XLI.
Of the Means of Preventing Crimes

IT is better to prevent crimes than to punish them. This is the fundamental principle of good legislation, which is the art of conducting men to the *maximum* of happiness, and to the *minimum* of misery, if we may apply this mathematical expression to the good and evil of life.

Would you prevent crimes? Let the laws be clear and simple, let the entire force of the nation be united in their defense, let them be intended rather to favor every individual than any particular classes of men, let the laws be feared, and the laws only. . . .

CHAP. XLII.
Of the Sciences

WOULD you prevent crimes? Let liberty be attended with knowledge. As knowledge extends, the disadvantages which attend it diminish and the advantages increase. A daring impostor, who is always a man of some genius, is adored by the ignorant populace, and despised by men of understanding. Knowledge facilitates the comparison of objects, by showing them in different points of view. When the clouds of ignorance are dispelled by the radiance of knowledge, authority trembles, but the force of the laws remains immovable. Men of enlightened understanding must necessarily approve those useful conventions which are the foundation of public safety; they compare with the highest satisfaction, the inconsiderable portion of liberty of which they are deprived with the sum total sacrificed by others for their security; observing that they have only given up the pernicious liberty of injuring their fellow-creatures, they bless the throne, and the laws upon which it is established. . . .

CHAP. XLIII.
Of Magistrates

ANOTHER method of preventing crimes is to make the observance of the laws, and not their violation, the interest of the magistrate. . . .

The greater the number of those who constitute the tribunal, the less is the danger of corruption; because the attempt will be more difficult, and the power and temptation of each individual will be proportionately less. If the sovereign, by pomp and the austerity of edicts, and by refusing to hear the complaints of the oppressed, accustom his subjects to respect the magistrates more than the laws, the magistrates will gain indeed, but it will be at the expense of public and private security. . . .

CHAP. XLIV.
Of Rewards

Yet another method of preventing crimes is to reward virtue. Upon this subject the laws of all nations are silent. If the rewards proposed by academies for the discovery of useful truths have increased our knowledge, and multiplied good books, it is not probable, that rewards, distributed by the beneficent hand of a sovereign, would also multiply virtuous actions. The coin of honor is inexhaustible, and is abundantly fruitful in the hands of a prince who distributes it wisely. . . .

CHAP. XLV.
Of Education

Finally, the most certain method of preventing crimes is to perfect the system of education.

CHAP. XLVII.
Conclusion

I conclude with this reflection, that the severity of punishments ought to be in proportion to the state of the nation. Among a people hardly yet emerged from barbarity, they should be most severe, as strong impressions are required; but, in proportion as the minds of men become softened by their intercourse in society, the severity of punishments should be diminished, if it is intended that the necessary relation between the object and the sensation should be maintained. . . .

From what I have written results the following general theorem, of considerable utility, though not conformable to custom, the common legislator of nations: *That a punishment may not be an act of violence, of one, or of many, against a private member of society, it should be public, immediate, and necessary, the least possible in the case given, proportioned to the crime, and determined by the laws.* . . .

Jeremy Bentham (1748-1832)

Bentham was born in London, England. He attended Westminster School until enrolling at Queen's College, Oxford, at the age of 12 and received his degree at the age of 15. Thereafter, Bentham studied law at Lincoln's Inn, but ultimately decided not to pursue law as a career. As a well-to-do and self-made scholar, Bentham wrote prolifically in philosophy, economics, and law. He was the earliest proponent of utilitarianism. Upon his death, per his instructions, his body was embalmed and fitted with a wax head likeness and then placed in a glass-fronted case on display at University College, London.

Introduction to the
Principles of Morals and Legislation*
Jeremy Bentham

CHAPTER I.
OF THE PRINCIPLE OF UTILITY

I.

Nature has placed mankind under the governance of two sovereign masters, *pain* and *pleasure*. It is for them alone to point out what we ought to do, as well as to determine what we shall do. On the one hand the standard of right and wrong, on the other the chain of causes and effects, are fastened to their throne. They govern us in all we do, in all we say, in all we think: every effort we can make to throw off our subjection, will serve but to demonstrate and confirm it. In words a man may pretend to abjure their empire: but in reality he will remain subject to it all the while. *The principle of utility* recognizes this subjection, and assumes it for the foundation of that system, the object of which is to rear the fabric of felicity by the hands of reason and of law. Systems which attempt to question it, deal in sounds instead of sense, in caprice instead of reason, in darkness instead of light.

But enough of metaphor and declamation: it is not by such means that moral science is to be improved.

---

*Source: Jeremy Bentham, 1843. *The Works of Jeremy Bentham.* Volume I. *An Introduction to the Principles of Morals and Legislation.* Published under the superintendence of his executor, John Bowring. Edinburgh: William Tait. Original spelling retained.

II.

The principle of utility is the foundation of the present work: it will be proper therefore at the outset to give an explicit and determinate account of what is meant by it. By the principle of utility is meant that principle which approves or disapproves of every action whatsoever, according to the tendency which it appears to have to augment or diminish the happiness of the party whose interest is in question: or, what is the same thing in other words, to promote or to oppose that happiness. I say of every action whatsoever; and therefore not only of every action of a private individual, but of every measure of government.

CHAPTER III.
OF THE FOUR SANCTIONS OR SOURCES OF PAIN AND PLEASURE

I.

It has been shown that the happiness of the individuals, of whom a community is composed, that is, their pleasures and their security, is the end and the sole end which the legislator ought to have in view: the sole standard, in conformity to which each individual ought, as far as depends upon the legislator, to be *made* to fashion his behaviour. But whether it be this or any thing else that is to be *done*, there is nothing by which a man can ultimately be *made* to do it, but either pain or pleasure. Having taken a general view of these two grand objects (*viz.* pleasure, and what comes to the same thing, immunity from pain) in the character of *final* causes; it will be necessary to take a view of pleasure and pain itself, in the character of *efficient* causes or means.

II.

There are four distinguishable sources from which pleasure and pain are in use to flow: considered separately, they may be termed the *physical*, the *political*, the *moral*, and the *religious:* and inasmuch as the pleasures and pains belonging to each of them are capable of giving a binding force to any law or rule of conduct, they may all of them be termed *sanctions*.

III.

If it be in the present life, and from the ordinary course of nature, not purposely modified by the interposition of the will of any human being, nor by any extraordinary interposition of any superior invisible being, that the pleasure or the pain takes place or is expected, it may be said to issue from, or to belong to, the *physical sanction*.

IV.

If at the hands of a particular person or set of persons in the community, who under names correspondent to that of *judge*, are chosen for the particular purpose of dispensing it, according to the will of the sovereign or supreme ruling power in the state, it may be said to issue from the *political sanction*.

V.

If at the hands of such chance persons in the community, as the party in question may happen in the course of his life to have concerns with, according to each man's spontaneous disposition, and not according to any settled or concerted rule, it may be said to issue from the *moral or popular sanction*.

VI.

If from the immediate hand of a superior invisible being, either in the present life, or in a future, it may be said to issue from the religious sanction.

VII.

Pleasures or pains which may be expected to issue from the *physical, political,* or *moral* sanctions, must all of them be expected to be experienced, if ever in the present life: those which may be expected to issue from the religious sanction, may be expected to be experienced either in the *present* life or in a *future*.

VIII.

Those which can be experienced in the present life, can of course be no others than such as human nature in the course of the present life is susceptible of: and from each of these sources may flow all the pleasures or pains of which, in the course of the present life, human nature is susceptible. With regard to these, then (with which alone we have in this place any concern), those of them which belong to any one of those sanctions, differ not ultimately in kind from those which belong to any one of the other three: the only difference there is among them lies in the circumstances that accompany their production. A suffering which befals a man in the natural and spontaneous course of things, shall be styled, for instance, a *calamity*; in which case, if it be supposed to befal him through any imprudence of his, it may be styled a punishment issuing from the physical sanction. Now this same suffering, if inflicted by the law, will be what is commonly called a *punishment;* if incurred for want of any friendly assistance, which the misconduct, or supposed misconduct, of the sufferer has occasioned to be withholden, a punishment issuing from the *moral* sanction; if through the immediate interposition of a particular providence, a punishment issuing from the religious sanction.

IX.

A man's goods, or his person, are consumed by fire. If this happened to him by what is called an accident, it was a calamity: if by reason of his own imprudence (for instance, from his neglecting to put his candle out), it may be styled a punishment of the physical sanction: if it happened to him by the sentence of the political magistrate, a punishment belonging to the political sanction—that is, what is commonly called a punishment: if for want of any assistance which his *neighbour* withheld from him out of some dislike to his *moral* character, a punishment of the *moral* sanction: if by an immediate act of *God's* displeasure, manifested on account of some sin committed by him, or through any distraction of mind, occasioned by the dread of such displeasure, a punishment of the *religious* sanction.

X.

As to such of the pleasures and pains belonging to the religious sanction, as regard a future life, of what kind these may be, we cannot know. These lie not open to our observation. During the present life they are matter only of expectation: and, whether that expectation be derived from natural or revealed religion, the particular kind of pleasure or pain, if it be different from all those which lie open to our observation, is what we can have no idea of. The best ideas we can obtain of such pains and pleasures are altogether unliquidated in point of quality. In what other respects our ideas of them *may* be liquidated, will be considered in another place.

XI.

Of these four sanctions, the physical is altogether, we may observe, the ground-work of the political and the moral: so is it also of the religious, in as far as the latter bears relation to the present life. It is included in each of those other three. This may operate in any case (that is, any of the pains or pleasures belonging to it may operate) independently of *them:* none of *them* can operate but by means of this. In a word, the powers of nature may operate of themselves; but neither the magistrate, nor men at large, *can* operate, nor is God in the case in question *supposed* to operate, but through the powers of nature.

XII.

For these four objects, which in their nature have so much in common, it seemed of use to find a common name. It seemed of use, in the first place, for the convenience of giving a name to certain pleasures and pains, for which a name equally characteristic could hardly otherwise have been found: in the second place, for the sake of holding up the efficacy of certain moral forces, the influence of which is apt not to be sufficiently attended to. Does the political sanction exert an influence over the conduct of mankind? The moral, the religious sanctions, do so too. In every inch of his career are the operations of the political magistrate liable to be aided or impeded by these two foreign powers: who, one or other of them, or both, are sure to be either his rivals or his allies. Does it happen to him to leave them out in his calculations? He will be sure almost to find himself mistaken in the result. Of all this we shall find abundant proofs in the sequel of this work. It behoves him, therefore, to have them continually before his eyes; and that under such a name as exhibits the relation they bear to his own purposes and designs.

CHAPTER IV.
VALUE OF A LOT OF PLEASURE OR PAIN,
HOW TO BE MEASURED

I.

Pleasures then, and the avoidance of pains are the *ends* which the legislator has in view: it behoves him therefore to understand their *value.* Pleasures and pains are the *instruments* he has to work with: it behoves him therefore to understand their force, which is again, in another point of view, their value.

II.

To a person considered *by himself*, the value of a pleasure or pain considered *by itself*, will be greater or less according to the four following circumstances:

1. Its *intensity*
2. Its *duration*
3. Its *certainty or uncertainty*
4. Its *propinquity or remoteness*

III.

These are the circumstances which are to be considered in estimating a pleasure or a pain considered each of them in itself. But when the value of any pleasure or pain is considered for the purpose of estimating the tendency of any *act* by which it is produced, there are two other circumstances to be taken into the account; these are,

5. Its *fecundity*, or the chance it has of being followed by sensations of the *same* kind: that is, pleasures, if it be a pleasure: pains, if it be a pain.

6. Its *purity*, or the chance it has of *not* being followed by sensations of the *opposite* kind: that is, pains, if it be a pleasure: pleasures, if it be a pain.

These two last, however, are in strictness scarcely to be deemed properties of the pleasure or the pain itself; they are not, therefore, in strictness to be taken into the account of the value of that pleasure or that pain. They are in strictness to be deemed properties only of the act, or other event, by which such pleasure or pain has been produced; and accordingly are only to be taken into the account of the tendency of such act or such event.

IV.

To a *number* of persons, with reference to each of whom the value of a pleasure or a pain is considered, it will be greater or less, according to seven circumstances: to wit, the six preceding ones; *viz.*

1. Its *intensity*
2. Its *duration*
3. Its *certainty or uncertainty*
4. Its *propinquity or remoteness*

5. Its *fecundity*
6. Its *purity*

And one other; to wit:

7. Its *extent;* that is, the number of persons to whom it *extends;* or (in other words) who are affected by it.

V.

To take an exact account, then of the general tendency of any act, by which the interests of a community are affected, proceed as follows. Begin with any one person of those whose interests seem most immediately to be affected by it: and take an account,

1. Of the value of each distinguishable *pleasure* which appears to be produced by it in the *first* instance.

2. Of the value of each *pain* which appears to be produced by it in the *first* instance.

3. Of the value of each pleasure which appears to be produced by it *after* the first. This constitutes the *fecundity* of the first *pleasure* and the *impurity* of the first *pain.*

4. Of the value of each *pain* which appears to be produced by it after the first. This constitutes the *fecundity* of the first *pain* and the *impurity* of the first pleasure.

5. Sum up all the values of all the *pleasures* on the one side, and those of all the pains on the other. The balance, if it be on the side of pleasure, will give the *good* tendency of the act upon the whole, with respect to the interests of that *individual* person; if on the side of pain, the *bad* tendency of it upon the whole.

6. Take an account of the *number* of persons whose interests appear to be concerned; and repeat the above process with respect to each. *Sum up* the numbers expressive of the degrees of *good* tendency, which the act has, with respect to each individual, in regard to whom the tendency of it is good upon the whole: do this again with respect to each individual, in regard to whom the tendency of it is *good* upon the whole: do this again with respect to each individual, in regard to whom the tendency of it is *bad* upon the whole. Take the *balance;* which, if on the side of *pleasure,* will give the general *good tendency* of the act, with respect to the total number or community of individuals concerned; if on the side of pain, the general *evil tendency,* with respect to the same community.

VI.

It is not to be expected that this process should be strictly pursued previously to every moral judgment, or to every legislative or judicial operation. It may, however, be always kept in view: and as near as the process actually pursued on these occasions approaches to it, so near will such process approach to the character of an exact one.

VII.

The same process is alike applicable to pleasure and pain, in whatever shape they appear; and by whatever denomination they are distinguished: to pleasure, whether it be called *good* (which is properly the cause or instrument of pleasure), or *profit* (which is distant pleasure), or *convenience*, or *advantage, benefit, emolument, happiness,* and so forth: to pain, whether it be called *evil* (which corresponds to *good*), or *mischief*, or *inconvenience*, or *disadvantage,* or *loss*, or *unhappiness,* and so forth.

VIII.

Now is this a novel and unwarranted, any more than it is a useless theory? In all this there is nothing but what the practice of mankind, wheresoever they have a clear view of their own interest, is perfectly conformable to. An article of property, an estate in land, for instance, is valuable: on what account? On account of the pleasures of all kinds which it enables a man to produce, and what comes to the same thing, the pains of all kinds which it enables him to avert. But the value of such an article of property is universally understood to rise or fall according to the length or shortness of the time which a man has in it: the certainty or uncertainty of its coming into possession: and the nearness or remoteness of the time at which, if at all, it is to come into possession. As to the *intensity* of the pleasures which a man may derive from it, this is never thought of, because it depends upon the use which each particular person may come to make of it; which cannot be estimate till the particular pleasures he may come to derive from it, or the particular pains he may come to exclude by means of it, are brought to view. For the same reason, neither does he think of the *fecundity* or *purity* of those pleasures.

Thus much for pleasure and pain, happiness and unhappiness, in *general*. We come now to consider the several particular kinds of pain and pleasure.

CHAPTER V.
PLEASURES AND PAINS, THEIR KINDS

I.

Having represented what belongs to all sorts of pleasures and pains alike, we come now to exhibit, each in itself, the several sorts of pains and pleasures. Pains and pleasures may be called by one general word, interesting perceptions. Interesting perceptions are either simple or complex. The simple ones are those which cannot any one of them be resolved into more: complex are those which are resolvable into diverse simple ones. A complex interesting perception may accordingly be composed either, 1. Of pleasures alone: 2. Of pains alone: or, 3. Of a pleasure or pleasures, and a pain or pains together. What determines a lot of pleasure, for example, to be regarded as one complex pleasure, rather than as diverse simple ones, is the nature of the exciting cause. Whatever pleasures are excited all at once by the action of the same cause, are apt to be looked upon as constituting all together but one pleasure.

II.

The several simple pleasures of which human nature is susceptible, seem to be as follows: 1. The pleasures of sense. 2. The pleasures of wealth. 3. The pleasures of skill. 4. The pleasures of amity. 5. The pleasures of a good name. 6. The pleasures of power. 7. The pleasures of piety. 8. The pleasures of benevolence. 9. The pleasures of malevolence. 10. The pleasures of memory. 11. The pleasures of imagination. 12. The pleasures of expectation. 13. The pleasures dependent on association. 14. The pleasures of relief.

III.

The several simple pains seem to be as follows: 1. The pains of privation. 2. The pains of the senses. 3. The pains of awkwardness. 4. The pains of enmity. 5. The pains of an ill name. 6. The pains of piety. 7. The pains of benevolence. 8. The pains of malevolence. 9. The pains of memory. 10. The pains of the imagination. 11. The pains of expectation. 12. The pains dependent on association.

CHAPTER VII.
OF HUMAN ACTIONS IN GENERAL

I.

The business of government is to promote the happiness of the society, by punishing and rewarding. That part of its business which consists in punishing, is more particularly the subject of penal law. In proportion as an act tends to disturb that happiness, in proportion as the tendency of it is pernicious, will be the demand it creates for punishment. What happiness consists of, we have already seen: enjoyment of pleasure, security from pains.

II.

The general tendency of an act is more or less pernicious, according to the sum total of its consequences: that is, according to the difference between the sum of such as are good, and the sum of such as are evil.

III.

It is to be observed, that here, as well as henceforward, wherever consequences are spoken of, such only are meant as are *material*. Of the consequences of any act, the multitude, and variety must needs be infinite: but such of them only as are material are worth regarding. Now among the consequences of an act, be they what they may, such only, by one who views them in the capacity of a legislator, can be said to be material, as either consist of pain or pleasure, or have an influence in the production of pain or pleasure.

IV.

It is also to be observed, that into the account of the consequences of the act, are to be taken no such only as might have ensued, were intention out of the question, but such also as depend upon the connexion there may be between these first-mentioned consequences and the intention. The connexion there is between the intention and certain consequences is, as we shall see hereafter, a means of producing other consequences. In this lies the difference between rational agency and irrational.

V.

Now the intention, with regard to the consequences of an act, will depend upon two things: 1. The state of the will or intention with respect to the act itself. And, 2. The state of the understanding, or perceptive faculties, with regard to the circumstances which it is, or may appear to be, accompanied with. Now with respect to these circumstances, the perceptive faculty is susceptible of three states: consciousness, unconsciousness, and false consciousness. Consciousness, when the party believes precisely those circumstances, and no others, to subsist, which really do subsist: unconsciousness, when he fails of perceiving certain circumstances to subsist, which however, do subsist: false consciousness, when he believes or imagines certain circumstances to subsist, which in truth do not subsist.

VI.

In every transaction, therefore, which is examined with a view to punishment, there are four articles to be considered: 1. The *act* itself, which is done. 2. The *circumstances* in which it is done. 3. The *intentionality* that may have accompanied it. 4. The *consciousness*, unconsciousness, or false consciousness, that may have accompanied it.

VII.

There are also two other articles on which the general tendency of an act depends: and on that, as well as on other accounts, the demand which it creates for punishment. These are, 1. The particular *motive* or motives which gave birth to it. 2. The general *disposition* which it indicates.

VIII.

Acts may be distinguished in several ways, for several purposes.

They may be distinguished, in the first place, into *positive* and *negative*. By positive are meant such as consist in motion or exertion: by negative, such as consist in keeping at rest; that is, in forbearing to move or exert one's self in such and such circumstances. Thus, to strike is a positive act: not to strike on a certain occasion, a negative one. Positive acts are styled also acts of commission; negative, acts of omission or forbearance.

IX.

Such acts, again, as are negative, may either be *absolutely* so, or *relatively*: absolutely, when they import the negation of all positive agency whatsoever; for instance, not to strike at all: relatively, when they import the negation of such or such a particular mode of agency; for instance, not to strike such a person or such a thing, or in such a direction.

X.

It is to be observed, that the nature of the act, whether positive or negative, is not to be determined immediately by the form of the discourse made use of to express it. An act which is positive in its nature may be characterized by a negative expression: thus, not to be at rest, is as much as to say to move. So also an act, which is negative in its nature, may be characterized by a positive expression: thus, to forbear or omit to bring food to a person in certain circumstances, is signified by the single and positive term *to starve*.

XI.

In the second place, acts may be distinguished into *external* and *internal*. By external, are meant corporal acts; acts of the body: by internal, mental acts; acts of the mind. Thus, to strike is an external or exterior act: to intend to strike, an internal or interior one.

XII.

Acts of *discourse* are a sort of mixture of the two: external acts, which are no ways material, nor attended with any consequences, any farther than as they serve to express the existence of internal ones. To speak to another to strike, to write to him to strike, to make signs to him to strike, are all so many acts of discourse.

XIII.

Third, acts that are external may be distinguished into *transitive* and *intransitive*. Acts may be called transitive, when the motion is communicated from the person of the agent to some foreign body: this is, to such a foreign body on which the effects of it are considered as being *material*; as where a man runs against you, or throws water in your face. Acts may be called intransitive, when the motion is communicated to no other body, on which the effects of it are regarded as materi-al, than some part of the same person in whom it originated; as where a man runs, or washes himself.

CHAPTER XV.
1. General View of Cases unmeet for Punishment

I.

The general object which all laws have, or ought to have, in com-mon, is to augment the total happiness of the community; and there-fore, in the first place, to exclude, as far as may be, every thing that tends to subtract from that happiness: in other words, to exclude mis-chief.

II.

But all punishment is mischief: all punishment in itself is evil. Upon the principle of utility, if it ought at all to be admitted, it ought only to be admitted in as far as it promises to exclude some greater evil.

III.

It is plain, therefore, that in the following cases, punishment ought not to be inflicted.

1. Where it is *groundless*; where there is no mischief for it to prevent; the act not being mischievous upon the whole.

2. Where it must be *inefficacious;* where it cannot act so as to prevent the mischief.

3. Where it is *unprofitable,* or *too expensive;* where the mischief it would produce would be greater than what it would prevent.

4. Where it is *needless*; where the mischief may be prevented, or cease of itself, without it; that is, at a cheaper rate.

2. *Cases in which Punishment is groundless*

IV.

These are, 1. Where there has never been any mischief; where no mischief has been produced to any body by the act in question. Of this number are those in which the act was such as might, on some occasions, be mischievous or disagreeable, but the person whose interest it concerns gave his *consent* to the performance of it. This consent, provided it be free, and fairly obtained, is the best proof that can be produced, that, to the person who gives it, no mischief, at least no immediate mischief, upon the whole, is done. For no man can be so good a judge as the man himself, what it is gives him pleasure or displeasure.

V.

2. Where the mischief was *outweighed*: although a mischief was produced by that act, yet the same act was necessary to the production of a benefit which was of greater value than the mischief. This may be the case with any thing that is done in the way of precaution against instant calamity, as also with any thing that is done in the exercise of the several sorts of powers necessary to be established in every community, to wit, domestic, judicial, military, and supreme.

CHAPTER XVI.
OF THE PROPORTION BETWEEN PUNISHMENTS AND OFFENCES

I.

We have seen that the general object of all laws is to prevent mischief, that is to say, when it is worth while; but that, where there are no other means of doing this than punishment, there are four cases in which it is *not* worth while.

II.

When it *is* worth while, there are four subordinate designs or objects, which, in the course of his endeavours to compass, as far as may be, that one general object, a legislator, whose views are governed by the principle of utility, comes naturally to propose to himself.

III.

1. His first, most extensive, and most eligible object, is to prevent, in as far as it is possible, and worth while, all sorts of offences whatsoever: in other words, so to manage, that no offence whatsoever be committed.

IV.

2. But if a man must needs commit an offence of some kind or other, the next object is to induce him to commit an offence *less* mischievous, *rather* than one *more* mischievous: in other words, to choose always the *least* mischievous, of two offences that will either of them suit his purpose.

V.

3. When a man has resolved upon a particular offence, the next object is to dispose him to do *no more* mischief than is *necessary* to his purpose: in other words, to do as little mischief as is consistent with the benefit he has in view.

VI.

4. The last object is, whatever the mischief be, which it is proposed to prevent, to prevent it at as *cheap* a rate as possible.

VII.

Subservient to these four objects, or purposes, must be the rule or canons by which the proportion of punishments to offences is to be governed.

VIII.

Rule 1.—1. The first object, it has been seen, is to prevent, in as far as it is worth while, all sorts of offences: therefore,

The value of the punishment must not be less in any case than what is sufficient to outweigh that of the profit of the offence.

If it be, the offence (unless some other considerations, independent of the punishment, should intervene and operate efficaciously in the character of tutelary motives) will be sure to be committed notwithstanding: the whole lot of punishment will be thrown away: it will be altogether inefficacious.

IX.

The above rule has been often objected to, on account of its seeming harshness: but this can only have happened for want of its being properly understood. The strength of the temptation, *caeteris paribus*, is as the profit of the offence: the quantum of the punishment must rise with the profit of the offence: *caeteris paribus*, it must therefore rise with the strength of the temptation. This there is no disputing. True it is, that the stronger the temptation, the less conclusive is the indication which the act of delinquency affords of the depravity of the offender's disposition. So far, then, as the absence of any aggravation, arising from extraordinary depravity of disposition, may operate, or at the utmost, so far as the presence of a ground of extenuation, resulting from the innocence or beneficence of the offender's disposition, can operate, the strength of the temptation may operate in abatement of the demand for punishment. But it can never operate so far as to indicate the propriety of making the punishment ineffectual, which it is sure to be when brought below the level of the apparent profit of the offence.

The partial benevolence which should prevail for the reduction of it below this level, would counteract as well those purposes which such a motive would actually have in view, as those more extensive purposes which benevolence ought to have in view: it would be cruelty not only to the public, but to the very persons in whose behalf it pleads in its effects, I mean, however opposite in its intention. Cruelty to the public, that is, cruelty to the innocent, by suffering them, for want of an adequate protection, to lie exposed to the mischief of the offence: cruelty even to the offender himself, by punishing him to no purpose, and without the chance of compassing that beneficial end, by which alone the introduction of the evil of punishment is to be justified.

X.

Rule 2. But whether a given offence shall be prevent in a given degree by a given quantity of punishment, is never any thing better than a chance; for the purchasing of which, whatever punishment is employed, is so much expended in advance. However, for the sake of giving it the better chance of outweighing the profit of the offence,

The greater the mischief of the offence, the greater is the expense, which it may be worth while to be at, in the way of punishment.

XI.

Rule 3. The next object is, to induce a man to choose always the least mischievous of two offences: therefore,

Where two offences come in competition, the punishment for the greater offence must be sufficient to induce a man to prefer the less.

XII.

Rule 4. When a man has resolved upon a particular offence, the next object is, to induce him to do no more mischief than what is necessary for his purpose: therefore,

The punishment should be adjusted in such manner to each particular offence, that for every part of the mischief there may be a motive to restrain the offender from giving birth to it.

XIII.

Rule 5. The last object is, whatever mischief is guarded against, to guard against it at as cheap a rate as possible: therefore,

The punishment ought in no case to be more than what is necessary to bring it into conformity with the rules here given.

XIV.

Rule 6. It is further to be observed, that owing to the different manners and degrees in which persons under different circumstances are affected by the same exciting cause, a punishment which is the same in name will not always either really produce, or even so much as appear to others to produce, in two different persons the same degree of pain: therefore,

That the quantity actually inflicted on each individual offender may correspond to the quantity intended for similar offenders in general, the several circumstances influencing sensibility ought always to be taken into account.

XV.

Of the above rules of proportion, the four first, we may perceive, serve to mark out the limits on the side of diminution; the limits below which a punishment ought not to be diminished: the fifth, the limits on the side of increase; the limits above which it ought not to be increased. The five first are calculated to serve as guides to the legislator: the sixth is calculated, in some measure, indeed, for the same purpose; but principally for guiding the judge in his endeavours to conform, on both sides, to the intentions of the legislator.

Cesare Lombroso (1835-1909)

Lombroso was born in Verona, Italy. Educated by the Jesuits, Lombroso received degrees in medicine in 1858 from the University of Pavia and in surgery in 1859 from the University of Genoa. He served as an army physician and was in charge of the insane at several hospitals. Returning to university, he held positions at the University of Turin including professor of legal medicine and public hygiene (1876), professor of psychiatry and clinical psychiatry (1896), and professor of criminal anthropology (1906).

Crime: Its Causes and Remedies*
Cesare Lombroso

§199 Atavism and Epilepsy
in Crime and Punishment

All that I have set forth in the present book and in those which preceded it (Vol. I and II of the "Homme Criminel") proves clearly the
insecurity of the ancient criminological scaffolding. Have I succeeded in
substituting a more solid edifice? If pride in a long and painful task has
not blinded me, I think that I can answer in the affirmative. The fundamental proposition undoubtedly is that we ought to study not so much
the abstract crime as the criminal.

§200 Atavism

The born criminal shows in a proportion reaching 33% numerous
specific characteristics that are almost always atavistic. Those who
have followed us thus far have seen that many of the characteristics
presented by savage races are very often found among born criminals.
Such, for example, are: the slight development of the pilar system; low
cranial capacity; retreating forehead; highly developed frontal sinuses;
great frequency of Wormian bones; early closing of the cranial sutures;
the simplicity of the sutures; the thickness of the bones of the skull;
enormous development of the maxillaries and the zygomata; prog-
nathism; obliquity of the orbits; greater pigmentation of the skin; tufted

---

*Source: Cesare Lombroso, 1918. *Crime: Its Causes and Remedies.* Boston: Little, Brown, and
Company.

and crispy hair; and large ears. To these we may add the lemurine appendix; anomalies of the ear; dental diastemata; great agility; relative insensibility to pain; dullness of the sense of touch; great visual acuteness; ability to recover quickly from wounds; blunted affections; precocity as to sensual pleasures;[1] greater resemblance between the sexes; greater incorrigibility of the woman (Spencer); laziness; absence of remorse; impulsiveness; physiopsychic excitability; and especially improvidence, which sometimes appears as courage and again as recklessness changing to cowardice. Besides these there is great vanity; a passion for gambling and alcoholic drinks; violent but fleeting passions; superstition; extraordinary sensitiveness with regard to one's own personality; and a special conception of God and morality. Unexpected analogies are met even in small details, as, for example, the improvised rules of criminal gangs; the entirely personal influence of the chiefs;[2] the custom of tattooing, the not uncommon cruelty of their games; the excessive use of gestures; the onomatopoeic language with personification of inanimate things; and a special literature recalling that of heroic times, when crimes were celebrated and the thought tended to clothe itself in rhythmic form.

This atavism explains the diffusion of certain crimes, such as the pederasty and infanticide, whose extension to whole companies we could not explain if we did not recall the Romans, the Greeks, the Chinese, and the Tahitians, who not only did not regard them as crimes, but sometimes even practiced them as a national custom. Garofalo has admirably summed up the psychical characteristics of the born criminal as being the absence of the feelings of shame, honor, and pity, which are those that are lacking in the savage also.[3] We may add to these the lack of industry and self-control.

To those who, like Reclus and Krapotkin, object that there are savage peoples who are honorable and chaste, we must reply that a certain degree of density of population and of association among men is necessary for crimes to develop. It is not possible for example, to steal when property does not exist, or to swindle when there is no trade. But the proof that these tendencies exist in germ in the savage, is that when they begin to pass from their stage of savagery and take on a little civilization they always develop the characteristics of criminality in an exaggerated form. As Ferrero has pointed out to us, even when honor, chastity, and pity are found among savages, impulsiveness and laziness are never wanting. Savages have a horror of continuous work, so that for them the passage to active and methodical labor lies by the road of selection or of slavery only. Thus, according to the testimony of Tacitus, the impulsiveness of the ancient Germans frequently resulted in the murder of slaves, committed in a fit of anger, an act which was not regarded as culpable. Tacitus notes also their lack of capacity for work.

"They have," he says, "large bodies, effective for sudden effort, but they lack the patience necessary for regular work. When they are not at war they do nothing . . . they sleep and eat. The strongest and most warlike live in idleness, leaving the care of the house and the field to the women, the old men, and the weak, becoming themselves, brutalized in sloth."

At times, on the other hand, impulsiveness, rather than sluggishness, seems to ally itself with a ceaseless need of movement, which asserts itself in savage peoples in a life of incessant vagabondage. Thus the Andaman Islanders, as Hovelacque tells us, have so restless a disposition that they remain not more than two or three days in the same place, and their wanderings have no other reason than the need of movement. This attitude seems to be the result of a passage between physiopsychic inertia and an intermittent need of violent and unrestrained physical and moral excitation, which always goes with inertia and impulsiveness. Thus it is that those peoples who are normally most lazy and indolent have the most unrestrained and noisy dances, which they carry on until they get into a kind of delirium, and fall down utterly exhausted. "When the Spaniards," writes Robertson "first saw the American Indians, they were astonished at their mad passion for dancing, and at the dizzy activity which this people, almost always cold and passive, displayed when they gave themselves up to this amusement." "The negroes of Africa," writes Du Chaillu, "dance madly when they hear the sound of the tom-tom, and lose all command of themselves." "It is," says Letourneau, "a real dancing madness, which makes them forget their troubles, public or private."

We may add that the atavism of the criminal, when he lacks absolutely every trace of shame and pity, may go back far beyond the savage, even to the brutes themselves. Pathological anatomy helps prove our position by showing in the case of the criminal a greater development of the cerebellum, a rarer union of the calcarine fissure with the parietooccipital, the absence of folds in the passage of Gratiolet, the gutter-like shape of the nasal incisure, the frequency of the olecranial foramen, extra ribs and vertebrae, and especially the histological anomalies discovered by Roncoroni in the cortex of the cerebrum of criminals, that is to say, the frequent absence, of granular layers and the presence of nerve cells in the white matter, and immense pyramidal cells. In seeking for analogies beyond our own race we come upon the explanation of the union of the atlas with the occipital bone, the prominence of the canine teeth, the flattening of the palate, and the median occipital fossa, occurring among criminals as with the lemurs and rodents;[4] as also the prehensile foot, the simplicity of the lines of the palm, motor and sensory left-handedness. We recall also the tendency to cannibalism even without desire for vengeance and still more that form of sanguinary ferocity, mingled with lubricity, of which examples are furnished us by Gille, Verzeni, Legier, Bertrand, Artusio, the Marquis of Sade, and others, with whom atavism was accompanied by epilepsy, idiocy, or general paralysis, but who always recall the pairing of animals, preceded by ferocious and sanguinary contests to overcome the reticence of the female or to conquer rivals.[5]

✗ These facts prove clearly that the most horrible crimes have their origin in those animal instincts of which childhood gives us a pale reflection. Repressed in civilized man by education, environment, and the fear of punishment, they suddenly break out in the born criminal without apparent cause, or under the influence of certain circumstances, such as sickness, atmospheric influences, sexual excitement, or mob influence. We know that certain morbid conditions, such as injuries to the head, meningitis, and chronic intoxication, or certain physiological conditions such as pregnancy and senility, produce derangements in the nutrition of the nervous centers, and in consequence atavistic retrogressions. We can see, then, how they may facilitate the tendency to crime, and when we take into account the short distance that separates the criminal from the savage, we come to understand why convicts so easily adopt savage customs including cannibalism, as was observed in Australia and Guiana.[6] When we note, further, how children, until they are educated, are ignorant of the difference between vice and virtue and steal, strike, and lie without the least compunction, we easily understand the great precocity in crime, and see why it is that the majority of abandoned children and orphans end by becoming criminals.[7] Further, atavism shows us the inefficacy of punishment for born criminals and why it is that they inevitably have periodic relapses into crime, so that the greatest variation shown by the number of crimes against persons is not more than 1/25, and by those against property not more than 1/50.[8] We see, as Maury very truly remarks, that we are governed by silent laws, which never fall into desuetude and rule society much more surely than the laws inscribed in the codes.

§201 Epilepsy

The same phenomena which we observe in the case of born criminals appear again in the rare cases of moral insanity,[9] but may be studied minutely, and on a large scale, in epileptics, criminal or not.[10] Not one of the atavistic phenomena shown by criminals is lacking in epilepsy; though epileptics show also certain purely morbid phenomena, such as cephalea, atheroma, delirium, and hallucination. In born criminals also we find, besides the atavistic characteristics, certain others that appear to be entirely pathological, or which at first sight seem more nearly allied to disease than to atavism. Such are, for example, in the anatomical field, excessive asymmetry, cranial capacity and face too large or too small, sclerosis, traces of meningitis, hydrocephalous forehead, oxycephaly, acrocephaly, cranial depressions, numerous osteophytes, early closing of the cranial sutures, thoracic asymmetry, late grayness of hair, late baldness, and abnormal and early wrinkles; in the biological field alterations of the reflexes and pupillary inequalities. To these we may add peripheral scotomata of the visual field which one never finds in savages, with whom, on the contrary the field of vision is remarkably wide and regular, as we see in the case of the Dinkas. There is [al]so to be added the alteration of hearing, taste, and smell, the predilection for animals, precocity in sexual pleasures, amnesia, vertigo, and maniac and paranoiac complications. These abnormalities, which are found in greater proportion among idiots, cretins, and degenerates in general, are to be explained by the fact that in these cases alcoholic intoxication is added to the effect of atavism, and still more to that of epilepsy.

However, the participation of epilepsy in producing the effect does not exclude atavism, since they equally involve characteristics at once atavistic and pathological, like macrocephaly, cranial sclerosis, Wormian bones, rarity of beard; and in the biological field, left-handedness, analgesis, obtuseness of all senses except that of sight, impulsiveness, pederasty, obscenity sluggishness, superstition, frequent cannibalism, choleric and impetuous disposition, tendency to reproduce the cries and actions of animals; and especially the histological anomalies of the cortex, which we have noted among criminals, and which reproduce the conditions of the lower animals; and finally anomalies of the teeth. These latter might appear to have no connection with the brain, but are, on the contrary, intimately connected with it, since the teeth proceed from the same embryonic membrane as the brain does.[11]

We may recall here that Gowers, having often noted in epileptics acts peculiar to animals, such as biting, barking, and mewing, concludes from this "that these are manifestations of that instinctive animalism which we possess in the latent state."[12]

If fully developed epileptic fits are often lacking in the case of the born criminal, this is because they remain latent, and only show themselves later under the influence of the causes assigned (anger, alcoholism), which bring them to the surface. With both criminals and epileptics there is to be noted an insufficient development of the higher centers. This manifests itself in a deterioration in the moral and emotional sensibilities, in sluggishness, physiopsychic hyperexcitability, and especially in a lack of balance in the mental faculties, which, even when distinguished by genius and altruism, nevertheless always show gaps, contrasts, and intermittent action.

§202 Combination of Morbid Anomalies with Atavism

Very often, moreover, certain common characteristics of criminals and epileptics have been classified as abnormal or morbid and not as atavistic, entirely because of the insufficiency of our embryological and phylogenetic knowledge. Many of the characteristics are atavistic and morbid at the same time, such as microcephaly, cranial sclerosis, etc. Facial asymmetry would also appear to be atavistic when we recall, for example, the flat-fishes (Penta); so likewise the abnormally wrinkled face, taking us back to the Hottentots and the apes. Hernia, also, as Feré rightly remarks, recalls conditions that are normal in the lower vertebrates and in the embryo.

Very often morbidity and atavism go back to a common cause, as Wagner[13] observes in a magnificent dissertation.

> "The idea," he writes, "that the atavism of criminals is associated with some specific disease of the foetus has been completely confirmed by the discoveries of Ettinghausen. If, for example, we freeze the roots of an oak so as partly to kill it, the following year it will put out leaves that are not like the leaves of the modern oak, but like those of the oak of the tertiary period. This fact explains the reappearance of inter-mediate and indistinct fossil forms. We see very clearly, then, that influences capable of producing a disease can bring about atavistic morphological retrogressions."

The epileptic background upon which the clinical and anatomical picture of the moral lunatic and the born criminal is drawn (a picture that would otherwise be lost in vague semijuridical, semi-psychiatric hypotheses) explains the instantaneousness, periodicity, and paradoxical character of their symptoms, which are doubtless their most marked characteristics. Note, for example, in this class, the coexistence and interchange of kindness and ferocity, of cowardice and the maddest recklessness, and of genius and complete stupidity.

§203 The Criminaloid

Criminaloids, while quite separable from born criminals, do not lack some connection with epilepsy and atavism. Thus there are more epileptics among them (10% among pickpockets) than among normal men, and a greater proportion of criminal types (17%), but there are also certain specific anomalies, such as left-handedness, common among swindlers.[14]

In the biology of the criminaloid we observe a smaller number of anomalies in touch, sensibility to pain, psychometry, an especially less early baldness and grayness, and less tattooing. But, on the other hand, we meet with a larger number of strictly morbid anomalies, depending upon the abuse of alcoholic drinks, such as atheromata, paresis, and scars. Psychic anomalies are especially less frequent with the criminaloid, who has not the cynicism of the born criminal nor the passion for doing evil for its own sake; he confesses his fault more easily and with more sincerity, and repents more often. But he is more lascivious, and more often given to alcoholism; and the criminaloid women are more susceptible to suggestion. The criminaloid is more precocious and relapses oftener—at least this is the case with pickpockets and simple thieves. They are often drawn into crime by a greater opportunity, although the lack of self-control which makes the epileptic commit crime without reason is sometimes also found in the criminaloid. We may recall how Casenova confessed that when he committed a fraud he never premeditated it, but "seemed to yield to a superior will." A pickpocket said to me, "When the inspiration comes to us we cannot resist." Dostojevsky depicts smugglers of the prison as carrying on their occupation almost without returns, notwithstanding the grave risks they run and in spite of repeated promises not to relapse. Mendel and Benedict describe the impulsive nature of the vagabond, which keeps him moving without object and without rest.

Criminaloids, then, differ from born criminals in degree, not in kind. This is so true that the greater number of them having become habitual criminals, thanks to a long sojourn in prison, can no longer be distinguished from born criminals except by the slighter character of their physical marks of criminality.

Still less different from born criminals are those latent criminals, high in power, whom society venerates as its chiefs. They bear the marks of congenital criminality, but their high position generally prevents their criminal character from being recognized. Their families, of which they are the scourges, may discover it; or their depraved nature may be revealed all too late at the expense of the whole country, at the head of which their own shamelessness, seconded by the ignorance and cowardice of the majority, has caused them to be placed. Even this strange species of criminal monomaniac, who seems to differ from the epileptic in the motive of his crime and the manner of carrying it out,[15] shows nevertheless the epileptic and atavistic origin of his criminality by obsessions, interrupted periods of ideation, lack of self-control, exaggerated importance given to certain details, exhaustion after his criminal crises, fondness for symbolism, excessive and intermittent activity, and finally by hereditary stigmata.

§204 Criminal Insane

Even among the true insane criminals those forms predominate which we may call the hypertrophy of crime, the exaggeration of the born criminal, not only in bodily and functional characteristics but also in the manner of committing the crime and in conduct afterward.[16] These serve to explain to us the extent of the impulsive, obscene, and cruel tendencies of the criminal insane, who are almost always obscure epileptics or born criminals upon whom melancholia and monomania have grafted themselves, according to the natural tendency of different forms of psychic disorders to take root together upon the corrupted soil of degeneracy. We have seen, likewise, how hysterical persons, alcoholics, dipsomaniacs, pyromaniacs, kleptomaniacs, the temporarily insane, reproduce many of the characteristics of the epileptic. Even the mattoid, who on account of his habitual calm and the absence of signs of degeneracy and heredity, seems far removed from epilepsy, yet shows at times this epileptic form, which we have seen to be the kernel of crime.[17]

§205 Criminals by Passion

Criminals of this class form a species apart, and are in complete contrast with the born criminal, both in the harmonious lines of the body, the beauty of the soul, and great nervous and emotional sensitiveness, as well as in the motives of their crimes, always noble and powerful, such as love or politics. Nevertheless they show some points of resemblance with epileptics, such as their tendency to excesses, impulsiveness, suddenness in their outbreaks, and frequent amnesia.[18]

§206 Occasional Criminals

Occasional criminals, or better, pseudo-criminals, are those who do not seek the occasion for the crime but are almost drawn into it, or fall into the meshes of the code for very insignificant reasons. These are the only ones who escape all connection with atavism and epilepsy; but, as Garafalo observes, these ought not, properly speaking, to be called criminals.

§207 Causes

The study of the causes of crime does not lessen the fatal influence to be assigned to the organic factor, which certainly amounts to 35% and possibly even 40%; the so-called causes of crime being often only the last determinants and the great strength of congenital impulsiveness

the principal cause. This we have proved in some cases by the continual
relapses occasioned by very small causes, or even without causes, when
not only the economic environment has been changed, but when all the
circumstances that might encourage crime have been removed; and we
have proved it especially by the increasing recidivism in London,
notwithstanding the great efforts made by Great Britain to suppress the
causes which produce crime. Finally, we have seen that certain circumstances have so strong an action upon criminaloids that they are equivalent to organic causes, and we may even say that they become organic.
Among these circumstances should be noted the effect of excessive heat
upon rapes, assaults, assassinations, and revolts, and the effect of alcohol and heredity upon the whole gamut of crime; and to these must be
added the effect of race, which in Italy through the Semitic race, and in
France through the Ligurian race, increases the crimes of blood.

A fact of the greatest importance is that the same causes which
diminish certain crimes increase others, making it difficult for the statesman to devise a remedy. Thus we have seen that education and wealth
cause a decrease in certain brutal crimes especially homicides and assassinations, but at the same time increase others, or even create new
crimes, such as bankruptcy and swindling. And if, for example, too
great a density is the cause of many crimes, such as frauds and thefts, a
sparse population, in its turn, favors brigandage and crimes of blood.
Scarcity favors thefts from the forests, forgeries, insurrections and incen-
diary fires, while cheapness of grain multiplies the rapes, homicides, and
crimes against persons generally.

Alcohol, which next to heat is the most powerful crime-producer,
increases, when it is cheap, all the crimes against persons and against the
public administration; and if it is dear, all the crimes against property.
Yet it presents this strange contradiction, that the more serious crimes
are least numerous where alcohol is most abused, doubtless because this
abuse takes place in just those localities where there is a higher degree of
civilization, and this, by favoring inhibition, decreases the more barbarous crimes.

The school, likewise is a cause of crime, but where education is
most general it diminishes the number and seriousness of the crimes.

§208 Necessity of Crime

Statistics as well as anthropological investigations show us crime,
then, as a natural phenomenon—a phenomenon (some philosophers
would say) as necessary as birth, death, or conception.

This idea of the necessity of crime, however bold it may appear, is
nevertheless not so new nor so heterodox as one might believe at first
sight. Centuries ago Casaubon expressed the same truth when he said,

"Man does not sin, but he is coerced in various degrees"; and St. Bernard likewise said, "Which one of us, however experienced he may be, can distinguish among his own wishes the influence of the morbus serpentis from that of the morbus mentis?" And further: "The sin is less in our heart, and we do not know whether we ought to ascribe it to ourselves or to the enemy: it is hard to know what the heart does and what it is obliged to do." St. Augustine is still more explicit when he says: "Not even the angels can make the man who wills evil will the good." The boldest and most ardent defender of this theory is a fervent Catholic and a priest of the Tyrol, Ruf.[19]

The defenders of theories quite opposed to our own also affirm it indirectly by the contradictions into which they fall in their definitions. If we compare the different attempts at criminal codes we see how difficult it is for the legal expert to fix the theory of irresponsibility and to find an exact definition for it. "The whole world knows what a good or a bad action is, but it is difficult, even impossible, to tell whether the depraved act has been committed with a full, or only an incomplete, knowledge of the evil," says Mittermayer. Way[20] writes: "We have not yet any scientific knowledge of responsibility." And Mahring says:[21] "Irresponsibility is a matter which criminal justice cannot decide with certainty in any special case." In fact, there are men who are afflicted with incipient insanity or are so profoundly predisposed to it that the slightest cause may make them fall into it. Others are driven by heredity to eccentricity or to immoral excesses. "Knowledge of the act," says Delbruck, "with an examination of the body and the mind before and after it, is not enough to clear up the question of responsibility; it is necessary to know the life of the criminal from the cradle to the dissecting table."[22] Now as long as the criminal is living it is hardly possible to dissect him. Carrara presumes "absolute responsibility where both intellect and will combine in the accomplishment of a criminal action," but he adds immediately afterward, "upon the condition that the action of the will has not been lessened by physical, intellectual, or moral causes." Now we have seen that there is no crime in which these causes are lacking.

ENDNOTES

1   "Homme Criminel," Vol. I, pp. 136 to 579.

2   Tacitus, "Germ.," VII.

3   "Criminologie," 2d ed., 1895.

4   "Homme Criminel," Vol. I, pp. 160, 217, 276, 282.

5   "Homme Criminel," Vol. I, pp. 449, 513; Vol. II, pp. 95, 96, 123, 139, 144, 147.

6   Bouvier, "Voyage á la Guyane," 1866.

7   "Homme Criminel," Vol. I, pp. 92 to 108.

8   Maury, "Mouvemente Moral de La Société," Paris, 1860.

9   "Homme Criminel," Vol. II, pp. 2-13.

10   "Homme Criminel," Vol. II, pp. 50-210.

11   "Homme Criminel," Vol. I, p. 232, n.

12   "Epilepsy," London, 1880.

13   Wagner von Jauregg, "Antrittsvorlesung an der Psychiatrischen Klinik," Vienna, 1895.

14   "Homme Criminel," Vol. II, pp. 216, 514, 518.

15   "Homme Criminel," Vol. II, pp. 94, 97, 418.

16   "Homme Criminel," Vol. I, pp. 34-228; Vol. II, p. 213

17   "Homme Criminel," Vol. II, p. 646.

18   "Homme Criminel," Vol. II, p. 226.

19   G. Ruf, "Die Criminaljustiz, ihre Widerspruche und Zukunft," Innsbruck, 1870.

20   "Die strafrechtliche Zurechnung," 1851.

21   "Die Zukunft der peinlichen Rechtspflege," p. 188.

22   "Zeitschrift fur Psychiatrie," 1864, p. 72.

Essay/Discussion Questions for Section I

Note to the student: If you are able to provide thorough responses to all of the following questions, you have mastered excellent comprehension of the classic readings presented in this section.

1. Why do you think the Classical School happened? That is, to what events or practices in the criminal justice system of the times were they reacting? (From the section introduction.)

2. What was the *essence* of the Classical School? (From the section introduction.)

3. How did the Classical School and the Positive School differ? (From the section introduction.)

4. What does Beccaria seem to be doing with his treatise? How is what he has to say important to the times in which he lived? What did he contribute to today's criminal justice system? (From the Beccaria reading.)

5. Bentham is a moral philosopher. What points can you make to demonstrate this? (From the Bentham reading.)

6. What does Bentham say about punishment? When is it justified? Is there ever a case when it is *not* justified? (From the Bentham reading.)

7. How does Lombroso describe criminals? Is this used in his reasons for criminal behavior? (From the Lombroso reading.)

8. How does Lombroso feel about the place of biological and social causality in criminal behavior? Is either one more important? (From the Lombroso reading.)

Section II
THE CHICAGO SCHOOL
AND DERIVATIVES

Introduction

The positivist criminological writings in the first two decades of the twentieth century tended toward biological and psychological causality. Theorists wrote about poor genetic structures, lack of intelligence, and emotional trauma, to name but a few of the directions taken by those studying criminals. In the United States, the emergence of sociological concerns about crime chiefly came from a group of social scientists working at the University of Chicago. This group became collectively known as the *Chicago School*.

Their ideas can be grouped under four main headings: ecological theory, culture conflict, symbolic interactionism, and differential association. A close examination of general criminological theory since that time yields the conclusion that these ideas are woven throughout most major theories. Further, the methods the Chicago School developed to study crime and criminals—life histories, ethnography, and the use of official statistics—remain the dominant ways we do research today. The Chicago School clearly had a profound effect on the study of crime and criminals. The four readings in this section are typical examples of the ways in which members of the Chicago School, and their heirs, looked at the causes of crime. Symbolic interactionism, while used as a foundation of the readings in this section, will not directly appear until the section on labeling theory.

Ecological Theory

The beginnings of the sociological study of crime in America are found in what came to be known as ecological theory. Its origins lie in

53

(1) the literature on plant and animal ecology (life systems) around the early part of this century and (2) the emergence of social data, collected by governmental agencies, on Chicago. Biological ecology provided notions of how land was used, with ideas about dominant uses, invasion and encroachment by new uses, and finally succession and new land use. Two Chicago sociologists, Robert Park and Ernest Burgess, used these ideas in an ecological study of the city.

Where Chicago was concerned, the theorists saw a series of *concentric circles* radiating out from a central core. Each concentric circle represented a form of land use. The core was the *central business district* where few people lived and where factories and businesses dominated. The zone around that core was the *zone of transition* where residential areas were mixed with the encroaching business district. Thus, it was a zone undergoing a transition in land use from residential to business. This zone was an undesirable place to live and the residences were poorly maintained and inexpensive. The next zone was the *zone of workingmen's homes* where people could live close to the factories and businesses in which they worked. It, too, was not particularly desirable as a residence area, but at least it had very little encroachment. Other zones radiating outward were increasingly more expensive places to live.

When social statistics were examined for these zones, it became obvious that social ills decreased with distance from the core. This meant rates of tuberculosis, infant mortality, various diseases, delinquency, and crime all increased with proximity to the central business district. Shaw and McKay collected as much data as they could, and they all fit the same pattern. Investigating the areas and zones with the highest crime and delinquency rates, Chicago School researchers noted that they were characterized by relationships that were impersonal, superficial, and transitory. Family life was poor and, in short, all primary social relationships were weak. Where these conditions existed, Chicago School researchers decided the areas were socially disorganized. From this, they concluded that *social disorganization* caused crime and delinquency. Shaw and McKay exemplify this perspective in a reading from the final chapter of their classic book *Juvenile Delinquency and Urban Areas*.

Culture Conflict Theory

The next problem was to determine what created social disorganization. For Chicago School scholars steeped in German sociology where conflict was assumed to be a normal part of life, the answer was obvious. Conflicting values and norms were common to Chicago because of several waves of immigrants and new immigrants were most likely to live in the problem zones of the city. They reasoned that one's cultural lifestyles, beliefs, and values were critical to behavior. W.I. Thomas, an important member of the Chicago School, introduced a concept called *definition of the situation*. By that term he meant that there are various norms and values (definitions) governing everyday life, but those norms and values vary from situation to situation. If an individual misunderstood a situation, or did not know the proper response, his or her behavior would likely conflict with the norms and values of that situation. Other Chicago scholars, such as Louis Wirth (1931) and Edwin Sutherland (1929), expounded on the ideas of cultural conflicts and conflicting values and related them to crime and delinquency. It was left to Thorsten Sellin, a scholar from outside the Chicago School, to put these ideas together.

Sellin's culture conflict theory (published in 1938) borrows directly from Wirth's *conduct norms* (rules that govern behavior). One grows up with cultural values about proper behavior, the content of which varies from culture to culture. Sellin saw two forms of values: one is cultural and the other is subcultural.* The first form makes up the laws and definitions of crimes for a particular area. The second governs behavior within another culture. When people obey their own conduct norms but come into conflict with other's conduct norms, culture conflict exists. When the conduct norms are legal norms, delinquent or criminal behavior exists.

Two types of culture conflict arise. The first, *primary conflict*, happens when the legal norms of one culture apply to people brought up in a different culture—for example, when an immigrant moves into Chicago or when one country conquers another in war. The second type, *secondary conflict*, happens when members of smaller cultures existing within a larger culture develop values in opposition to the legal norms. The basic idea of culture conflict is that members of subcultures and "other" cultures will follow their own familiar conduct norms. In doing so, they are more likely to do something that would bring them into conflict with the legal norms. Thus, they are more likely to be arrested.

Differential Association

Edwin Sutherland is perhaps best known for his popular theory of differential association, published first in 1939 and in its final version in 1947. In this theory, he brings together the thoughts of the Chicago School in a straightforward manner and states the theory in nine propositions.

---

*The use of the term "subcultural" here is ours. Sellin did not use the word and it was not widely used in criminology until the 1950s. We believe it best describes to today's readers what he meant when discussing secondary conflict.

First, he casts off biological and psychological explanations of criminal behavior for a sociological version. He declares that all behavior is *learned* in social settings, where people *communicate and interact* with each other. This means that criminal and non-criminal behavior is learned the same way. The major part of this learning happens in settings with people who are very close to the individual (*intimate personal groups . . .*). Second, Sutherland describes the kinds of things that are learned: behavioral techniques and definitions for behavior. *Techniques* are a necessary part of learning because one has to know *how* to do some behaviors. Some behaviors require special techniques that are hard to acquire, but others only require a general knowledge that is shared among several common behaviors. *Definitions*, on the other hand, are values and rationalizations that allow techniques to be used. Here, Sutherland is referring to conduct norms and definitions of the situation.

The third component of differential association is the most important one and is embodied in proposition number six. Sutherland says that criminal behavior occurs because a person has an *excess of definitions favorable to law violation*. This excess occurs because the definitions against law violation do not carry as much weight as the criminal ones. The weight differential is not a simple matter of counting the number of definitions; instead, it is determined by the importance, length, and intensity (*frequency, intensity, duration, and priority . . .*) of association with those from whom one receives definitions.

It should be noted that Sutherland was not saying that mere association with those who engage in criminal behavior will cause an individual to become criminal. Instead, the problem is to determine the strength and weight of the various definitions a person receives. As Sutherland noted, criminal definitions can even come from a non-criminal parent.

Social Learning Theory

The final reading in this section is Ron Akers' reworking of differential association into a behaviorally oriented theory that is more testable than Sutherland's original version. Drawing from Sutherland's statement that criminal behavior is learned, Akers takes psychological versions of learning theories, particularly from Skinner and Bandura, and reformulates differential association. In fact, the first version of the theory (in 1966 with Robert Burgess) was called a *"differential association-reinforcement"* theory. He assumes, as did Sutherland, that the primary learning of definitions occurs in various social settings, some of which are subcultural. When social definitions for behavior are learned in subcultural situations, the probability of conflict with legal norms increases.

The principle concepts of Akers' theory are derived from operant-based social learning theories. They are reinforcement, punishment, discriminative stimuli, imitation and modeling, and conditioning. *Reinforcement* increases the probability of a particular behavior occurring; *punishment* (aversive stimuli) decreases the probability of occurrence. *Discriminative stimuli* allow an individual to associate a certain setting or situation with reinforcement or punishment probabilities and pattern their behavior accordingly. *Imitation and modeling* allow an individual to see the consequences of another's behavior and learn from it. *Conditioning* occurs when behaviors are shaped by reinforcement or punishment consequences, or by watching the consequences occurring to others.

Social learning theory basically states that all behaviors are the result of conditioning, a process continuing throughout our lives. The type of conditioning, however, varies with the environment in which we live and the consequences attached to alternative behaviors. Whether one behavior will be rewarded (or punished) over another is *differential reinforcement*. Associated with the behavior, and learned also, is an *evaluative definition* or value to be placed on the behavior. This evaluative definition is a form of discriminative stimuli and suggests that the behavior will be rewarded. If an individual associates a positive evaluative definition with a behavior, he or she is more likely to engage in that behavior. Rewards from primary associates are most important to an individual because these people provide the great bulk of behavioral consequences. Deviant behavior is more likely when *primary associates* provide definitions rewarding that form of behavior more than alternative behaviors.

Epilogue

The Chicago School influence is literally everywhere in criminological theory. While the field is moving away from the direct theoretical propositions of these scholars, the methodologies and ideas they formulated continue to provide the foundation for criminology. In some cases, one can even make an argument that the Chicago School is enjoying a resurgence, particularly in the areas of environmental design, routine activities, and geographic criminology. Even more directly, there are some scholars who are studying the importance of changes over time in communities as an important ingredient in explaining both crime and delinquency (see Bursik and Webb, 1982; Reiss, 1986; Sampson, 1986; Schuerman & Kobrin, 1986).

BIBLIOGRAPHY

Adams, Reed L. (1974). "The adequacy of differential association theory," *Journal of Research in Crime and Delinquency* 11: 1-8.

Adams, Reed L. (1973). "Differential association and learning principles revisited," *Social Problems* 20: 458-70.

Akers, Ronald L., Marvin D. Krohn, Lonn Lanza-Kaduce, and Marcia Radosevich (1979). "Social learning and deviant behavior: A specific test of a general theory," *American Sociological Review* 44: 636-55.

Anderson, Nels (1923). *The Hobo*. Chicago: University of Chicago Press.

Bandura, Albert (1977). *Social Learning Theory*. Englewood Cliffs, NJ: Prentice-Hall.

Bandura, Albert (1969). *Principles of Behavior Modification*. New York: Holt, Rinehart and Winston.

Bulmer, Martin (1984). *The Chicago School of Sociology*. Chicago: University of Chicago Press.

Burgess, Robert L. and Ronald L. Akers (1966a). "A differential association-reinforcement theory of criminal behavior," *Social Problems* 14: 128-47.

Burgess, Robert L. and Ronald L. Akers (1966b). "Are operant principles tautological?" *The Psychological Record* 16: 305-12.

Bursik, Robert J., Jr. and Jim Webb (1982). "Community change and patterns of delinquency," *American Journal of Sociology* 88: 24-42.

Chiricos, Theodore G. (1967). "The concept of cause: A developmental analysis of the theory of differential association," *Issues in Criminology* 3: 91-99.

Cohen, Albert K., Alfred Lindesmith, and Karl Schuessler (eds.) (1956). *The Sutherland Papers*. Terre Haute: Indiana University Press.

Conger, Rand (1976). "Social control and social learning models of delinquency: A synthesis," *Criminology* 14: 17-40.

Cressey, Donald R. (1979). "Fifty years of criminology," *Pacific Sociological Review* 22: 457-80.

Cressey, Donald R. (1966). "The language of set theory and differential association," *Journal of Research in Crime and Delinquency* 3: 22-26.

Cressey, Donald R. (1964). *Delinquency, Crime and Differential Association*. Hague, Netherlands: Martinus Nijhoff.

Cressey, Donald R. (1960a). "The theory of differential association: An introduction," *Social Problems* 8: 2-6.

Cressey, Donald R. (1960b). "Epidemiology and individual conduct: A case from criminology," *Pacific Sociological Review* 3: 47-58.

Cressey, Donald R. (1954). "The differential association theory and compulsive crimes," *Journal of Criminal Law and Criminology* 45: 49-64.

Cressey, Donald R. (1953). *Other People's Money*. New York: Free Press.

DeFleur, Melvin L. and Richard Quinney (1966). "A reformulation of Sutherland's differential association theory and a strategy for empirical verification," *Journal of Research in Crime and Delinquency* 3: 1-22.

Farris, Robert E.L. (1970). *Chicago Sociology: 1920-1932*. Chicago: University of Chicago Press.

Gaylord, Mark S. and John Galliher (1988). *The Criminology of Edwin Sutherland*. New Brunswick, NJ: Transaction.

Glaser, Daniel (1962). "The differential association theory of crime," in Arnold Rose (ed.) *Human Behavior and Social Process*. Boston: Houghton Mifflin, 425-42.

Glaser, Daniel (1960). "Differential association and criminological prediction," *Social Problems* 8: 6-14.

Glaser, Daniel (1956). "Criminality theories and behavioral images," *American Journal of Sociology* 61: 433-44.

Glueck, Sheldon (1956). "Theory and fact in criminology: A criticism of differential association," *British Journal of Delinquency* 7: 92-109.

Gold, David (1957). "On description of differential association," *American Sociological Review* 22: 448-50.

Homans, George C. (1961). *Human Behavior: Its Elementary Forms*. New York: Harcourt, Brace & World.

Jeffery, C. Ray (1965). "Criminal behavior and learning theory," *Journal of Criminal Law, Criminology, and Police Science* 54: 294-300.

Kobrin, Solomon (1959). "The Chicago Area Project—A 25-year assessment," *Annals of the American Academy of Political and Social Science* 322: 19-29.

Matsueda, Ross (1988). "The current state of differential association theory," *Crime and Delinquency* 34:277-306.

Matza, David (1969). *Becoming Deviant*. Englewood Cliffs, NJ: Prentice-Hall.

McKay, Henry D. (1960). "Differential association and crime prevention: Problems of utilization," *Social Problems* 8: 25-37.

McKenzie, Roderick D. (1924). "The ecological approach to the study of the human community," *American Journal of Sociology* 30: 287-301.

Mead, George H. (1934). *Mind, Self, and Society*. Charles W. Morris (ed.). Chicago: University of Chicago Press.

Park, Robert E. and Ernest Burgess (eds.) (1925). *The City*. Chicago: University of Chicago Press.

Park, Robert E. and Ernest Burgess (1924). *Introduction to the Science of Sociology*, 2nd ed. Chicago: University of Chicago Press.

Reiss, Albert J., Jr. (1986). "Why are communities important to understanding crime?" in A. Reiss and M. Tonry (eds.) *Communities and Crime. Crime and Justice: A Review of Research*, Vol. 8: 271-311. Chicago: University of Chicago Press.

Sampson, Robert J. (1986). "Crime in cities: The effects of formal and informal social control," in A. Reiss and M. Tonry (eds.) *Communities and Crime. Crime and Justice: A Review of Research*, Vol. 8: 1-33. Chicago: University of Chicago Press.

Schuerman, Leo and Solomon Kobrin (1986). "Community careers in crime," in A. Reiss and M. Tonry (eds.) *Communities and Crime. Crime and Justice: A Review of Research*, Vol. 8: 67-100. Chicago: University of Chicago Press.

Schuessler, Karl (ed.) (1973). *Edwin H. Sutherland: On Analyzing Crime*. Chicago: University of Chicago Press.

Sellin, Thorsten (1938). *Culture Conflict and Crime*. New York: Social Science Research Council, Bulletin No. 41.

Shaw, Clifford R. (1930). *The Jackroller*. Chicago: University of Chicago Press.

Shaw, Clifford R. and Henry D. McKay (1931). *Social Factors in Juvenile Delinquency*. Vol. II of *Report on the Causes of Crime*. National Commission on Law Observance and Enforcement, Report No. 13. Washington, DC: U.S. Government Printing Office.

Skinner, B.F. (1971). *Beyond Freedom and Dignity*. New York: Knopf.

Skinner, B.F. (1953). *Science and Human Behavior*. New York: Macmillan.

Snodgrass, Jon (1976). "Clifford R. Shaw and Henry D. McKay: Chicago criminologists," *British Journal of Criminology* 16: 1-19.

Snodgrass, Jon (1973). "The criminologist and his criminal: The case of Edwin H. Sutherland and Broadway Jones," *Issues in Criminology* 8: 2-17.

Snodgrass, Jon (1972). *The American Criminological Tradition: Portraits of the Men and Ideology in a Discipline*. Doctoral dissertation: University of Pennsylvania.

Sorentino, Anthony (1972). *Organizing Against Crime: Redeveloping the Neighborhood*. New York: Human Sciences Press.

Sutherland, Edwin H. (1956). "Development of the theory," in Albert K. Cohen et al. (eds.), *The Sutherland Papers*. Bloomington, IN: Indiana University Press, 13-29.

Sutherland, Edwin H. (1949). *White Collar Crime*. New York: Dryden.

Sutherland, Edwin H. (1947). *Principles of Criminology*, 4th ed. Philadelphia: Lippincott.

Sutherland, Edwin H. (1939). *Principles of Criminology*, 3rd ed. Philadelphia: Lippincott.

Sutherland, Edwin H. (1937). *The Professional Thief: By a Professional Thief*. Chicago: University of Chicago Press.

Sutherland, Edwin H. (1929). "Crime and the conflict process," *Journal of Juvenile Research* 13: 38-48.

Sutherland, Edwin H. and Donald R. Cressey (1978). *Criminology*, 10th ed. Philadelphia: Lippincott.

Thomas, William I., and Florian Znaniecki (1918). *The Polish Peasant in Europe and America*. Chicago: University of Chicago Press.

Thrasher, Frederick M. (1927). *The Gang*. Chicago: University of Chicago Press.

Turner, Jonathan H. (1988). "The mixed legacy of the Chicago School of sociology," *Sociological Perspectives* 31: 325-38.

Vasoli, Robert H. and Dennis A. Terzola (1974). "Sutherland's professional thief," *Criminology* 12: 131-54.

Vold, George B. (1951). "Edwin Hardin Sutherland: Sociological criminologist," *American Sociological Review* 16: 3-9.

Volkman, Rita and Donald R. Cressey (1963). "Differential association and the rehabilitation of drug addicts," *American Journal of Sociology* 69: 129-42.

Wirth, Louis (1931). "Culture conflict and misconduct," *Social Forces* 9: 484-92.

Clifford Robe Shaw (1896-1957)

Shaw was born in Luray, Indiana. He received an A.B. from Albion College in 1919 and an M.A. (sociology) from the University of Chicago in 1921. Shaw also did doctoral work at the University of Chicago but left in 1924 without completing his Ph.D. He worked as a parole officer for the Illinois State Training School for Boys from 1921-1923 and as a probation officer for the Cook County Juvenile Court from 1924-1926. In 1926, Shaw was appointed director of the new sociology department at the Institute for Juvenile Research and held the position until his death in 1957. He taught as an adjunct professor at George Williams College (Chicago) and the Central YMCA College (Chicago) from 1926-1941 and at the University of Chicago from 1941-1957.

Henry D. McKay (1899-1980)

McKay was born in Orient, South Dakota. He was educated at Dakota Wesleyan University (A.B., 1922) and at the University of Chicago in sociology (M.A., 1924). McKay taught at the University of Illinois in sociology from 1925-1926, returned to the University of Chicago for doctoral studies (1926-1929), but did not finish his Ph.D. He took a position with Shaw's sociology department at the Institute for Juvenile Research in 1927, and remained there until he retired.

Juvenile Delinquency and Urban Areas*
Clifford R. Shaw and Henry D. McKay

CONCLUSION

SUMMARY AND INTERPRETATION

IT IS clear from the data included in this volume that there is a direct relationship between conditions existing in local communities of American cities and differential rates of delinquents and criminals. Communities with high rates have social and economic characteristics which differentiate them from communities with low rates. Delinquency—particularly group delinquency, which constitutes a preponderance of all officially recorded offenses committed by boys and young men—has its roots in the dynamic life of the community.

It is recognized that the data included in this volume may be interpreted from many different points of view. However, the high degree of consistency in the association between delinquency and other characteristics of the community not only sustains the conclusion that delinquent behavior is related dynamically to the community but also appears to establish that all community characteristics, including delinquency, are products of the operation of general processes more or less common to American cities. Moreover, the fact that in Chicago the rates of delinquents for many years have remained relatively constant in the areas adjacent to centers of commerce and heavy industry, despite successive changes in the nativity and nationality composition of the population,

---

*Source: Clifford R. Shaw and Henry D. McKay, 1942. *Juvenile Delinquency and Urban Areas*. Chicago: The University of Chicago Press, pp. 435-441, 445-446. By permission of the publisher.

supports emphatically the conclusion that the delinquency-producing factors are inherent in the community.

From the data available, it appears that local variations in the conduct of children, as revealed in differential rates of delinquents, reflect the differences in social values, norms, and attitudes to which the children are exposed. In some parts of the city, attitudes which support and sanction delinquency are, it seems, sufficiently extensive and dynamic to become the controlling forces in the development of delinquent careers among a relatively large number of boys and young men. These are the low-income areas, where delinquency has developed in the form of a social tradition, inseparable from the life of the local community.

This tradition is manifested in many different ways. It becomes meaningful to the child through the conduct, speech, gestures, and attitudes of persons with whom he has contact. Of particular importance is the child's intimate association with predatory gangs or other forms of delinquent and criminal organization. Through his contacts with these groups and by virtue of his participation in their activities he learns the techniques of stealing, becomes involved in binding relationships with his companions in delinquency, and acquires the attitudes appropriate to his position as a member of such groups. To use the words of Frank Tannenbaum: "It is the group that sets the pattern, provides the stimulus, gives the rewards in glory and companionship, offers the protection and loyalty, and, most of all, gives the criminal life its ethical content without which it cannot persist."[1]

In these communities, many children encounter competing systems of values. Their community, which provides most of the social forms in terms of how their life will be organized, presents conflicting possibilities. A career in delinquency and crime is one alternative, which often becomes real and enticing to the boy because it offers the promise of economic gain, prestige, and companionship and because he becomes acquainted with it through relationships with persons whose esteem and approbation are vital to his security and to the achievement of satisfactory status. In this situation the delinquent group may become both the incentive and the mechanism for initiating the boy into a career of delinquency and crime and for sustaining him in such a career, once he has embarked upon it.

In cases of group delinquency it may be said, therefore, that from the point of view of the delinquent's immediate social world, he is not necessarily disorganized, maladjusted, or antisocial. Within the limits of his social world and in terms of its norms and expectations, he may be a highly organized and well-adjusted person.

The residential communities of higher economic status, where the proportion of persons dealt with as delinquents and criminals is relatively low, stand in sharp contrast to the situation described above. Here the norms and values of the child's social world are more or less uniformly and consistently conventional. Generally speaking, the boy who grows up in this situation is not faced with the problem of making a choice between conflicting systems of moral values. Throughout the range of his contacts in the community he encounters similar attitudes of approval or disapproval. Cases of delinquency are relatively few and sporadic. The system of conventional values in the community is sufficiently pervasive and powerful to control and organize effectively, with few exceptions, the lives of most children and young people.

In both these types of communities the dominant system of values is conventional. In the first, however, a powerful competing system of delinquency values exists; whereas in the second, such a system, if it exists at all, is not sufficiently extensive and powerful to exercise a strong influence in the lives of many children. Most of the communities of the city fall between these two extremes and represent gradations in the extent to which delinquency has become an established way of life.

It is important to ask what the forces are which give rise to these significant differences in the organized values in different communities. Under what conditions do the conventional forces in the community become so weakened as to tolerate the development of a conflicting system of criminal values? Under what conditions is the conventional community capable of maintaining its integrity and exercising such control over the lives of its members as to check the development of the competing system? Obviously, any discussion of this question at present must be tentative. The data presented in this volume, however, afford a basis for consideration of certain points which may be significant.

It may be observed, in the first instance, that the variations in rates of officially recorded delinquents in communities of the city correspond very closely with variations in economic status. The communities with the highest rates of delinquents are occupied by those segments of the population whose position is most disadvantageous in relation to the distribution of economic, social, and cultural values. Of all the communities in the city, these have the fewest facilities for acquiring the economic goods indicative of status and success in our conventional culture. Residence in the community is in itself an indication of inferior status, from the standpoint of persons residing in the more prosperous areas. It is a handicap in securing employment and in making satisfactory advancement in industry and the professions. Fewer opportunities are provided for securing the training, education, and contacts which facilitate advancement in the fields of business, industry, and the professions.

The communities with the lowest rates of delinquency, on the other hand, occupy a relatively high position in relation to the economic and social hierarchy of the city. Here, the residents are relatively much more secure; and adequate provision is offered to young people for securing the material possessions symbolic of success and the education, training, and personal contacts which facilitate their advancement in the conventional careers they may pursue.

Despite these marked differences in the relative position of people in different communities, children and young people in all areas, both rich and poor, are exposed to the luxury values and success patterns of our culture. In school and elsewhere they are also exposed to ideas of equality, freedom, and individual enterprise. Among children and young people residing in low-income areas, interests in acquiring material goods and enhancing personal status are developed which are often difficult to realize by legitimate means because of limited access to the necessary facilities and opportunities.

This disparity in the facilities available to people in different communities for achieving a satisfactory position of social security and prestige is particularly important in relation to delinquency and crime in the urban world. In the city, relationships are largely impersonal. Because of the anonymity in urban life, the individual is freed from much of the scrutiny and control which characterize life in primary-group situations in small towns and rural communities. Personal status and the status of one's community are, to a very great extent, determined by economic achievement. Superior status depends not so much on character as on the possession of those goods and values which symbolize success. Hence, the kind of clothes one wears, the automobile one drives, the type of building in which one lives, and the physical character of one's community become of great importance to the person. To a large degree, these are the symbols of his position—the external evidences of the extent to which he has succeeded in the struggle for a living. The urban world, with its anonymity, its greater freedom, the more impersonal character of its relationships, and the varied assortment of economic, social, and cultural backgrounds in its communities, provides a general setting particularly conducive to the development of deviations in moral norms and behavior practices.

In the low-income areas, where there is the greatest deprivation and frustration, where, in the history of the city, immigrant and migrant groups have brought together the widest variety of divergent cultural traditions and institutions, and where there exists the greatest disparity between the social values to which the people aspire and the availability of facilities for acquiring these values in conventional ways, the development of crime as an organized way of life is most marked. Crime, in this situation, may be regarded as one of the means employed by people to acquire, or to attempt to acquire, the economic and social values generally idealized in our culture, which persons in other circumstances acquire by conventional means. While the origin of this tradition of crime is obscure, it can be said that its development in the history of the community has been facilitated by the fact that many persons have, as a result of their criminal activities, greatly improved their economic and social status. Their clothes, cars, and other possessions are unmistakable evidence of this fact. That many of these persons also acquire influence and power in politics and elsewhere is so well known that it does not need elaboration at this point. The power and affluence achieved, at least temporarily, by many persons involved in crime and illegal rackets are well known to the children and youth of the community and are important in determining the character of their ideals.

It may be said, therefore, that the existence of a powerful system of criminal values and relationships in low-income urban areas is the product of a cumulative process extending back into the history of the community and of the city. It is related both to the general character of the urban world and to the fact that the population in these communities has long occupied a disadvantageous position. It has developed in somewhat the same way as have all social traditions, that is, as a means of satisfying certain felt needs within the limits of a particular social and economic framework.

It should be observed that, while the tradition of delinquency and crime is thus a powerful force in certain communities, it is only a part of the community's system of values. As was pointed out previously, the dominant tradition in every community is conventional, even in those having the highest rates of delinquency. The traditionally conventional values are embodied in the family, the church, the school, and many other such institutions and organizations. Since the dominant tradition in the community is conventional, more persons pursue law-abiding careers than careers of delinquency and crime, as might be expected.

In communities occupied by Orientals, even those communities located in the most deteriorated sections of our large cities, the solidarity of Old World cultures and institutions has been preserved to such a marked extent that control of the child is still sufficiently effective to keep at a minimum delinquency and other forms of deviant behavior. As Professor Hayner has pointed out in his chapter on five cities of the Pacific Northwest, the close integration of the Oriental family, the feeling of group responsibility for the behavior of the child, and the desire of these groups to maintain a good reputation in American communities have all been important elements in preserving this cultural solidarity.

It is the assumption of this volume that many factors are important in determining whether a particular child will become involved in delinquency, even in those communities where a system of delinquent and criminal values exists. Individual and personality differences, as well as differences in family relationships and in contacts with other institutions and groups, no doubt influence greatly his acceptance or rejection of opportunities to engage in delinquent activities. It may be said, however, that if the delinquency tradition were not present and the boys were not thus exposed to it, a preponderance of those who become delinquent in low-income areas would find satisfaction in activities other than delinquency.

In conclusion, it is not assumed that this theoretical proposition applies to all cases of officially proscribed behavior. It applies primarily to those delinquent activities which become embodied in groups and social organizations. For the most part, these are offenses against property, which comprise a very large proportion of all the cases of boys coming to the attention of the courts.

IMPLICATIONS FOR PREVENTION AND TREATMENT

The theoretical formulation set forth in the preceding pages has certain definite implications with regard to the task of dealing with the problem of delinquency in large American cities. Some of the more important ones may be stated as follows:

1. Any great reduction in the volume of delinquency in large cities probably will not occur except as general changes take place which effect improvements in the economic and social conditions surrounding children in those areas in which the delinquency rates are relatively high.

2. Individualized methods of treatment probably will not be successful in a sufficiently large number of cases to result in any substantial diminution of the volume of delinquency and crime.

3. Treatment and preventive efforts, if they are to achieve general success, should increasingly take the form of broad programs which seek to utilize more effectively the constructive institutional and human resources available in every local community in the city. Tannenbaum states this point vividly: "The criminal is a product of the community, and his own criminal gang is part of the whole community, natural and logical to it; but it is only part of it. In that lies the hope that the rest of the community can do something with the gang as such."[2] . . .

. . . the data in this volume provide a basis for the conclusion that programs for the prevention of delinquency in low income areas of American cities are not likely to succeed unless they can effect certain basic changes in the conditions of life surrounding children. As long as the present condition exists, little change in the volume of delinquency should be expected.

Year after year, decade after decade, large cities—and especially certain areas in large cities—send to the courts an undiminished line of juvenile offenders. Year after year, decade after decade, likewise, society continues to organize or construct new agencies or institutions designed to reduce the number of these offenders and to rehabilitate those who have already offended against the law. Perhaps the unsatisfactory results of these treatment and prevention efforts have been due, in part at least, to the fact that our attention has been focused too much upon the individual delinquent and not enough upon the setting in which delinquency arises.

James S. Plant, on the basis of many years' experience in a psychiatric clinic, arrives at somewhat the same conclusion. He states:

> Society is, and has been, aroused over its misfits and the mass of human breakdown that is in the wake of its progress. It has erected every conceivable type of agency to study, salvage, or merely sweep up this debris. As the wreckage mounts, new agencies are demanded or "better standards of service" asked of those existing. The folly of believing that happiness and goodness can be fabricated by machinery (agencies) will be exposed only when we understand that the ills, corruptions, and hypocrisies of a cultural pattern flow into the child and man and "become a part of him for the day, for the year, or for stretching cycles of years." If it is true that the triumphs and tragedies of the street flow into and become a part of the child, then all programs of personality change must manage somehow to change the street.[3]

Whether or not we care to admit it, most delinquent boys reflect all too accurately what they have learned in the process of living in their own communities. If we wish to have fewer delinquents, or if we wish to modify the mode of life of those who already are delinquent, a way must be found to modify those aspects of the community life which provide the appropriate setting for delinquency careers and which give to these careers the sanction and approbation on which all social behavior depends.

ENDNOTES

1   *Crime and the Community* (New York: Ginn & Co., 1938), p. 475.

2   *Op. cit.,* p. 474.

3   *Personality and the Cultural Pattern* (New York: Commonwealth Fund, 1937), p. 18.

Thorsten Sellin (1896-1994)

Sellin was born in Ornskoldsvik, Sweden. He attended elementary and secondary school in Sweden, moving to Fort William, Ontario, at the age of 17. Sellin received his B.A. in 1915 from Augustana College (Illinois), his M.A. in sociology in 1916 at the University of Pennsylvania, did part-time graduate study at the University of Minnesota and completed his Ph.D. in sociology in 1922 at the University of Pennsylvania. He taught in the secondary schools of Minneapolis (while doing part-time graduate work) and, upon receiving his Ph.D., took a position as instructor of sociology at the University of Pennsylvania. He remained there for 45 years, serving from 1944 to 1959 as chair of the department and retiring as professor emeritus in 1967.

The Conflict of Conduct Norms*
Thorsten Sellin

Culture Conflicts as Conflicts of Cultural Codes

. . . There are social groups on the surface of the earth which possess complexes of conduct norms which, due to differences in the mode of life and the social values evolved by these groups, appear to set them apart from other groups in many or most respects. We may expect conflicts of norms when the rural dweller moves to the city, but we assume that he has absorbed the basic norms of the culture which comprises both town and country. How much greater is not the conflict likely to be when Orient and Occident meet, or when the Corsican mountaineer is transplanted to the lower East Side of New York. Conflicts of cultures are inevitable when the norms of one cultural or subcultural area migrate to or come in contact with those of another. . . .

Conflicts between the norms of divergent cultural codes may arise:

1. when these codes clash on the border of contiguous culture areas;

2. when, as may be the case with legal norms, the law of one cultural group is extended to cover the territory of another; or

3. when members of one cultural group migrate to another.[1]

Speck, for instance, notes that "where the bands popularly known as Montagnais have come more and more into contact with Whites, their reputation has fallen lower among the traders who have known them

---

*Source: Thorsten Sellin, 1938. *Culture Conflict and Crime*. The Social Science Research Council Bulletin 41, pp. 63-70.

through commercial relationships within that period. The accusation is made that they have become less honest in connection with their debts, less trustworthy with property, less truthful, and more inclined to alcoholism and sexual freedom as contacts with the frontier towns have become easier for them. Richard White reports in 1933 unusual instances of Naskapi breaking into traders' store houses."[2]

Similar illustrations abound in the works of the cultural anthropologists. We need only to recall the effect on the American Indian of the culture conflicts induced by our policy of acculturation by guile and force. In this instance, it was not merely contact with the white man's culture, his religion, his business methods, and his liquor, which weakened the tribal mores. In addition, the Indian became subject to the white man's law and this brought conflicts as well, as has always been the case when legal norms have been imposed upon a group previously ignorant of them. Maunier[3] in discussing the diffusion of French law in Algeria, recently stated: "In introducing the *Code Penal* in our colonies, as we do, we transform into offenses the ancient usages of the inhabitants which their customs permitted or imposed. Thus, among the Khabyles of Algeria, the killing of adulterous wives is ritual murder committed by the father or brother of the wife and not by her husband, as elsewhere. The woman having been sold by her family to her husband's family, the honor of her relatives is soiled by her infidelity. Her father or brother has the right and the duty to kill her in order to cleanse by her blood the honor of her relatives. Murder in revenge is also a duty, from family to family, in case of murder of, or even in case of insults to, a relative: the vendetta, called the *rekba* in Khabylian, is imposed by the law of honor. But these are crimes in French law! Murder for revenge, being premeditated and planned, is assassination, punishable by death! . . . What happens, then, often when our authorities pursue the criminal, guilty of an offense against public safety as well as against morality: public enemy of the French order, but who has acted in accord with a respected custom? The witnesses of the assassination, who are his relatives, or neighbors, fail to lay charges against the assassin; when they are questioned, they pretend to know nothing; and the pursuit is therefore useless. A French magistrate has been able to speak of the conspiracy of silence among the Algerians'; a conspiracy aiming to preserve traditions, always followed and obeyed, against their violation by our power. This is the tragic aspect of the conflict of laws. A recent decree forbids the husband among the Khabyles to profit arbitrarily by the power given him according to this law to repudiate his wife, demanding that her new husband pay an exorbitant price for her—this is the custom of the *lefdi*. Earlier, one who married a repudiated wife paid nothing to the former husband. It appears that the first who tried to avail himself of the new law was killed for violating the old custom. The abolition of the ancient law does not always occur without protest or opposition. That which is a crime was a duty; and the order which we cause to reign is sometimes established to the detriment of 'superstition'; it is the gods and the spirits, it is believed, that would punish any one who fails to revenge his honor."

When Soviet law was extended to Siberia, similar effects were observed. Anossow[4] and Wirschubski[5] both relate that women among the Siberian tribes, who in obedience to the law, laid aside their veils and were killed by their relatives for violating one of the most sacred norms of their tribes.

We have noted that culture conflicts are the natural outgrowth of processes of social differentiation, which produce an infinity of social groupings, each with its own definitions of life situations, its own interpretations of social relationships, its own ignorance or misunderstanding of the social values of other groups. The transformation of a culture from a homogeneous and well-integrated type to a heterogeneous and disintegrated type is therefore accompanied by an increase of conflict situations. Conversely, the operation of integrating processes will reduce the number of conflict situations. Such conflicts within a changing culture may be distinguished from those created when different cultural systems come in contact with one another, regardless of the character or stage of development of these systems. In either case, the conduct of members of a group involved in the conflict of codes will in some respects be judged abnormal by the other group.

The Study of Culture Conflicts

In the study of culture conflicts, some scholars have been concerned with the effect of such conflicts on the conduct of specific persons, an approach which is naturally preferred by psychologists and psychiatrists and by sociologists who have used the life history technique. These scholars view the conflict as internal. Wirth[6] states categorically that a culture "conflict can be said to be a factor in delinquency only if the individual feels it or acts as if it were present." Culture conflict is mental conflict, but the character of this conflict is viewed differently by the various disciplines which use this term. Freudian psychiatrists[7] regard it as a struggle between deeply rooted biological urges which demand expression and the culturally created rules which give rise to inhibitive mechanisms which thwart this expression and drive them below the conscious level of the mind, whence they rise either by ruse in some socially acceptable disguise, as abnormal conduct when the inhibiting mechanism breaks down, or as neuroses when it works too well. The sociologist, on the other hand, thinks of mental conflict as being primarily the clash between antagonistic conduct norms incorporated in personality. "Mental conflict in the person," says Burgess in discussing the case presented by Shaw in *The Jack-Roller,* "may always be explained in terms of the conflict of divergent cultures."[8]

If this view is accepted, sociological research on culture conflict and its relationships to abnormal conduct would have to be strictly limited to a study of the personality of cultural hybrids. Significant studies could be conducted only by the life-history case technique applied to persons in whom the conflict is internalized, appropriate control groups being utilized, of course. . . .

The absence of mental conflict, in the sociological sense, may, however, be well-studied in terms of culture conflict. An example may make this clear. A few years ago a Sicilian father in New Jersey killed the sixteen-year-old seducer of his daughter, expressing surprise at his arrest since he had merely defended his family honor in a traditional way. In this case a mental conflict in the sociological sense did not exist. The conflict was external and occurred between cultural codes or norms. We may assume that where such conflicts occur, violations of norms will arise merely because persons who have absorbed the norms of one cultural group or area migrate to another and that such conflict will continue so long as the acculturation process has not been completed. . . . Only then may the violations be regarded in terms of mental conflict.

If culture conflict may be regarded as sometimes personalized, or mental, and sometimes as occurring entirely in an impersonal way solely as a conflict of group codes, it is obvious that research should not be confined to the investigation of mental conflicts, and that contrary to Wirth's categorical statement that it is impossible to demonstrate the existence of a culture conflict "objectively . . . by a comparison between two cultural codes,"[9] this procedure has not only a definite function, but may be carried out by researchers employing techniques which are familiar to the sociologist.

The emphasis on the life-history technique has grown out of the assumption that "the experiences of one person at the same time reveals the life activities of his group" and that "habit in the individual is an expression of custom in society."[10] This is undoubtedly one valid approach. Through it we may hope to discover generalizations of a scientific nature by studying persons who (1) have drawn their norms of conduct from a variety of groups with conflicting norms, or (2) who possess norms drawn from a group whose code is in conflict with that of the group which judges the conduct. In the former case alone can we speak of mental or internal culture conflict; in the latter, the conflict is external.

If the conduct norms of a group are, with reference to a given life situation, inconsistent, or if two groups possess inconsistent norms, we may assume that the members of these various groups will individually reflect such group attitudes. Paraphrasing Burgess, the experiences of a group will reveal the life activities of its members. While these norms can, no doubt, be best established by a study of a sufficient number of representative group members, they may for some groups at least be fixed with sufficient certainty to serve research purposes by a study of the social institutions, the administration of justice, the novel, the drama, the press, and other expressions of group attitudes. The identification of the groups in question having been made, it might be possible to determine to what extent such conflicts are reflected in the conduct of their members. Comparative studies based on the violation rates of the members of such groups, the trends of such rates, etc., would dominate this approach to the problem.

In conclusion, then, culture conflict may be studied either as mental conflict or as a conflict of cultural codes. The criminologist will naturally tend to concentrate on such conflicts between legal and nonlegal conduct norms. The concept of conflict fails to give him more than a general framework of reference for research. In practice, it has, however, become nearly synonymous with conflicts between the norms of cultural systems or areas. Most researches which have employed it have been done on immigrant or race groups in the United States, perhaps due to the ease with which such groups may be identified, the existence of more statistical data recognizing such groupings, and the conspicuous differences between some immigrant norms and our norms.

ENDNOTES

1   This is unfortunately not the whole story, for with the rapid growth of impersonal communication, the written (press, literature) and the spoken word (radio, talkie), knowledge concerning divergent conduct norms no longer grows solely out of direct personal contact with their carriers. And out of such conflicts grow some violations of custom and of law which would not have occurred without them.

2   Speck, Frank G. "Ethical Attributes of the Labrador Indians." *American Anthropologist.* N.S. 35:559-94. October-December 1933. P. 559.

3   Maunier, Reneé. "La diffusion du droit francais en Algerie." Harvard Tercentenary Publications, *Independence, Convergence and Borrowing in Institutions, Thought and Art.* Cambridge: Harvard University Press. 1937. Pp. 84-85.

4   Anossow, J.J. "Die volkstumlichen Verbrechen im Strafkodex der USSR." *Monatsschrist fur Kriminalpsychologie und Strafrechtsreform.* 24: 534-37. September 1933.

5   Wirschubski, Gregor. "Der Schutz der Sittlichkeit im Sowjetstrafrecht." *Zeitschrift fur die gesamte Strafrechtswissenschaft.* 51: 317-28. 1931.

6   Wirth, Louis. "Culture Conflict and Misconduct." *Social Forces.* 9: 484-92. June 1931. P. 490. Cf. Allport, Floyd H. "Culture Conflict versus the Individual as Factors in Delinquency." *Ibid.* Pp. 493-497.

7   White, William A. *Crimes and Criminals.* New York: Farrar & Rinehart. 1933. Healy, William. *Mental Conflict and Misconduct.* Boston: Little, Brown & Co. 1917. Alexander, Franz and Healy, William. *Roots of Crime.* New York: Alfred A. Knopf. 1935.

8   Burgess, Ernest W. in Clifford R. Shaw's *The Jack-Roller.* Chicago: University of Chicago Press. 1930. Pp. 184-197, p. 186.

9   Wirth, Louis. *Op. cit.* P. 490. It should be noted that Wirth also states that culture should be studied "on the objective side" and that "the sociologist is not primarily interested in personality but in culture."

10   Burgess, Ernest W. *Op. cit.* P. 186.

Edwin H. Sutherland (1883-1950)

Sutherland was born in Gibbon, Nebraska. He received his B.A. in 1904 from Grand Island College and his Ph.D. in sociology in 1913 from the University of Chicago. He taught at Sioux Falls College (1905-1906), Grand Island College (1908-1911), William Jewell College (1913-1919), the University of Illinois (1919-1926), the University of Minnesota (1926-1929), the University of Chicago (1930-1935), and Indiana University (1935-1950). He was head of the sociology department at Indiana from 1935 to 1949.

Differential Association*
Edwin H. Sutherland

The scientific explanation of a phenomenon may be stated either in terms of the factors which are operating at the moment of the occurrence of a phenomenon or in terms of the processes operating in the earlier history of that phenomenon. In the first case the explanation is mechanistic, in the second historical or genetic; both are desirable. The physical and biological scientists favor the first of these methods and it would probably be superior as an explanation of criminal behavior. Efforts at explanations of the mechanistic type have been notably unsuccessful, perhaps largely because they have been concentrated on the attempt to isolate personal and social pathologies. Work from this point of view has, at least, resulted in the conclusion that the immediate factors in criminal behavior lie in the person-situation complex. Person and situation are not factors exclusive of each other, for the situation which is important is the situation as defined by the person who is involved. The tendencies and inhibitions at the moment of the criminal behavior are, to be sure, largely a product of the earlier history of the person, but the expression of these tendencies and inhibitions is a reaction to the immediate situation as defined by the person. The situation operates in many ways, of which perhaps the least important is the provision of an opportunity for a criminal act. A thief may steal from a fruit stand when the owner is not in sight, but refrain when the owner is in sight, a bank burglar may attack a bank which is poorly protected, but refrain from attacking a bank protected by watchmen and burglar alarms. A corporation which manufactures automobiles seldom or never violates the

---

*Source: Edwin H. Sutherland, 1947. *Principles of Criminology*. Philadelphia: J.B. Lippincott Company, pp. 5-9. By permission of the Donald R. Cressey Estate.

Pure Food and Drug Law, but a meat-packing corporation could violate this law with great frequency.

The second type of explanation of criminal behavior is made in terms of the life experience of a person. This is a historical or genetic explanation of criminal behavior. This, to be sure, assumes a situation to be defined by the person in terms of the inclinations and abilities which the person has acquired up to that date. The following paragraphs state such a genetic theory of criminal behavior on the assumption that a criminal act occurs when a situation appropriate for it, as defined by a person, is present.

Genetic Explanation of Criminal Behavior

The following statement refers to the process by which a particular person comes to engage in criminal behavior.

1. *Criminal behavior is learned.* Negatively, this means that criminal behavior is not inherited, as such; also, the person who is not already trained in crime does not invent criminal behavior, just as a person does not make mechanical inventions unless he has had training in mechanics.

2. *Criminal behavior is learned in interaction with other persons in a process of communication.* This communication is verbal in many respects, but also includes "the communication of gestures."

3. *The principal part of the learning of criminal behavior occurs within intimate personal groups*. Negatively, this means that the impersonal agencies of communication, such as picture shows and newspapers, play a relatively unimportant part in the genesis of criminal behavior.

4. *When criminal behavior is learned, the learning includes (a) techniques of committing the crime, which are sometimes very complicated, sometimes very simple; (b) the specific direction of motives, drives, rationalizations, and attitudes.*

5. *The specific direction of motives and drives is learned from definitions of the legal codes as favorable or unfavorable.* In some societies an individual is surrounded by persons who invariably define the legal codes as rules to be observed, while in others he is surrounded by persons whose definitions are favorable to the violation of the legal codes. In our American society these definitions are almost always mixed and consequently we have culture conflict in relation to the legal codes.

6. *A person becomes delinquent because of an excess of definitions favorable to violation of law over definitions unfavorable to violation of law.* This is the principle of differential association. It refers to both criminal and anti-criminal associations and has to do with counteracting forces. When persons become criminal they do so because of contacts with criminal patterns and also because of isolation from anti-criminal patterns. Any person inevitably assimilates the surrounding culture unless other patterns are in conflict; a Southerner does not pronounce "r" because other Southerners do not pronounce "r." Negatively, this proposition of differential association means that associations which are neutral so far as crime is concerned have little or no effect on the genesis of criminal behavior. Much of the experience of a person is neutral in this sense, e.g., learning to brush one's teeth. This behavior has no negative or positive effect on criminal behavior except as it may be related to associations which are concerned with the legal codes. This neutral behavior is important especially as an occupier of the time of a child so that he is not in contact with criminal behavior during the time he is so engaged in the neutral behavior.

7. *Differential associations may vary in frequency, duration, priority, and intensity.* This means that associations with criminal behavior and also associations with anti-criminal behavior vary in those respects. "Frequency" and "duration" as modalities of associations are obvious and need no explanation. "Priority" is assumed to be important in the sense that lawful behavior developed in early childhood may persist throughout life, and also that delinquent behavior developed in early childhood may persist throughout life. This tendency, however, has not been adequately demonstrated, and priority seems to be important principally through its selective influence. "Intensity" is not precisely defined but it has to do with such things as the prestige of the source of a criminal or anti-criminal pattern and with emotional reactions related to the associations. In a precise description of the criminal behavior of a person, these modalities would be stated in quantitative form and a mathematical ratio would be reached. A formula in this sense has not been developed and the development of such a formula would be extremely difficult.

8. *The process of learning criminal behavior by association with criminal and anti-criminal patterns involves all of the mechanisms that are involved in any other learning.* Negatively, this means that the learning of criminal behavior is not restricted to the process of imitation. A person who is seduced, for instance, learns criminal behavior by association but this process would not ordinarily be described as imitation.

9. *While criminal behavior is an expression of general needs and val-ues, it is not explained by those general needs and values since non-criminal behavior is an expression of the same needs and values.* Thieves generally steal in order to secure money, but likewise honest laborers work in order to secure money. The attempts by many scholars to explain criminal behavior by general drives and values, such as the happiness principle, striving for social status, the money motive, or frustration, have been and must continue to be futile since they explain lawful behavior as completely as they explain criminal behavior. They are similar to respiration, which is necessary for any behavior but which does not differentiate criminal from noncriminal behavior.

It is not necessary, at this level of explanation, to explain why a person has the associations which he has; this certainly involves a complex of many things. In an area where the delinquency rate is high, a boy who is sociable, gregarious, active, and athletic is very likely to come in contact with the other boys in the neighborhood, learn delinquent behavior from them, and become a gangster; in the same neighborhood, the psychopathic boy who is isolated, introverted, and inert may remain at home, not become acquainted with the other boys in the neighborhood, and not become delinquent. In another situation, the sociable, athletic, aggressive boy may become a member of a scout troop and not become involved in delinquent behavior. The person's associations are determined in a general context of social organization. A child is ordinarily reared in a family; the place of residence of the family is determined largely by family income; and the delinquency rate is in many respects related to the rental value of the houses. Many other factors enter into this social organization, including many of the small personal group relationships.

The preceding explanation of criminal behavior was stated from the point of view of the person who engages in criminal behavior. It is possible, also, to state theories of criminal behavior from the point of view of the community, nation, or other group. The problem, when thus stated, is generally concerned with crime rates and involves a comparison of the crime rates of various groups or the crime rates of a particular group at different times. One of the best explanations of crime rates from this point of view is that a high crime rate is due to social disorganization. The term "social disorganization" is not entirely satisfactory and it seems preferable to substitute for it the term "differential social organization." The postulate on which this theory is based, regardless of the name, is that crime is rooted in the social organization and is an expression of that social organization. A group may be organized for criminal behavior or organized against criminal behavior. Most communities are organized both for criminal and anti-criminal behavior, and in that sense the crime rate is an expression of the differential group organization. Differential group organization as an explanation of a crime rate must be consistent with the explanation of the criminal behavior of the person, since the crime rate is a summary statement of the number of persons in the group who commit crimes and the frequency with which they commit crimes.

Ronald Louis Akers (1939-   )

Akers was born in New Albany, Indiana. He received his B.S. in 1960 at Indiana State College (now University), M.A. in 1961 at Kent State University, and Ph.D. in sociology in 1966 from the University of Kentucky. Akers taught at the University of Washington (sociology) from 1965-1972, Florida State University (criminology) from 1972-1974, University of Iowa (sociology) from 1974-1980 (Chair of the department from 1978-1980), and the University of Florida (sociology) from 1980-present (Chair of the department from 1980-1985). Since 1994, he has also been the director of the Center for Studies in Criminology and Law.

A Social Learning Perspective on Deviant Behavior*
Ronald L. Akers

A SOCIAL LEARNING THEORY: DIFFERENTIAL ASSOCIATION-REINFORCEMENT

We turn now . . . to the presentation of the social learning theory of deviant behavior, which is used throughout the rest of the book to explain each of the types of deviance. This theory integrates Edwin H. Sutherland's *differential association theory* of violations of social and legal norms with principles of modern learning theory. Sutherland's theory as he finally stated in 1947 is in the form of . . . nine declarative statements (Sutherland and Cressey, 1970:75-77).

Although the entire set of statements collectively make up the theory of differential association, the sixth statement was referred to by Sutherland as the "principle of differential association" and is seen as the heart of the theory; it is that *one commits criminal acts because his accepted "definitions" of law as something to violate are in "excess" of his accepted definitions of the law as something that can, must, or should be obeyed.* Thus, it is not a simple theory of associating with "bad companions"; rather, it is concerned with contact with criminal patterns and definitions (normative evaluations) *balanced against* contact with conforming definitions, whether this contact comes from association with those who commit crime or with those who are law-abiding (Cressey, 1960:49).

---

*Source: Ronald L. Akers, 1985. *Deviant Behavior: A Social Learning Approach*, 3rd edition. Belmont, CA: Wadsworth, pp. 39-67 (excerpted). By permission of the author.

Sutherland's theory states that criminal behavior is learned in a process of symbolic interaction with others, mainly in primary or intimate groups. These groups present the individual with both criminal and anti-criminal patterns, techniques, motivations, and definitions (normative meanings) of the legal norms. The balance of criminal and anti-criminal definitions determines whether one will conform to a given legal code. When one's definitions of the law as something to violate are in excess of definitions of the law as something that should be obeyed, criminal behavior is the result. This balance of law-abiding and law-violating definitions is the result of the frequency, duration, priority, and intensity with which one has been exposed to lawful and criminal patterns. If people are more exposed to law-violating definitions while being relatively isolated from law-abiding definitions, they will deviate from the law.

In an effort to provide a more behavioral specification of the learning process indicated in Sutherland's theory, I collaborated with Robert L. Burgess to produce a reformulation, which we called *differential association-reinforcement* (Burgess and Akers, 1966b). The set of principles we used in reformulating the theory is variously called operant conditioning, reinforcement, learning, or simply behavior theory.[1] By whatever name, these are very general and powerful behavior principles of precise learning mechanisms which have been worked out and verified in laboratory settings and which can be extended, applied to, and tested in more complex social situations.

Our revision was a reformulation of Sutherland's theory, but it was not intended as an alternative theory. Rather, of necessity, some ideas not intrinsic to differential association were introduced, and additions were made to the original propositions. The reformulation was a new, broader theory which integrated differential association with differential reinforcement; one could not arrive at it starting with reinforcement theory and ignoring differential association or by starting with differential association and ignoring reinforcement theory—hence the name of differential association-reinforcement. I now usually refer to the theory as a *social learning* theory, but the earlier designation as differential association-reinforcement is still appropriate. Although Burgess and I retained Sutherland's references to criminal and delinquent behavior in our reformulation, it was our intention that it apply to any form of deviant behavior. The remainder of this chapter presents the theory as extended to deviant behavior in general, and this social learning theory provides the unifying framework within which each form of deviance is examined. . .

By dropping the last statement and combining the first and eighth statements in Sutherland's theory, the Burgess-Akers reformulation reduced the theory to seven statements consistent with the principles of modern behavior:

1. Deviant behavior is learned according to the principles of operant conditioning.

2. Deviant behavior is learned both in nonsocial situations that are reinforcing or discriminating and through that social interaction in which the behavior of other persons is reinforcing or discriminating for such behavior.

3. The principal part of the learning of deviant behavior occurs in those groups which comprise or control the individual's major source of reinforcements.

4. The learning of deviant behavior, including specific techniques, attitudes, and avoidance procedures, is a function of the effective and available reinforcers and the existing reinforcement contingencies.

5. The specific class of behavior learned and its frequency of occurrence are a function of the effective and available reinforcers, and the deviant or nondeviant direction of the norms, rules, and definitions which in the past have accompanied the reinforcement.

6. The probability that a person will commit deviant behavior is increased in the presence of normative statements, definitions, and verbalizations which, in the process of differential reinforcement of such behavior over conforming behavior, have acquired discriminative value.

7. The strength of deviant behavior is a direct function of the amount, frequency, and probability of its reinforcement. The modalities of association with deviant patterns are important insofar as they affect the source, amount, and scheduling of reinforcement.[2]

These seven statements contain terms which need definition and present only an outline of the theory; reference to only these seven statements will not give the full substance of the theory. The remaining discussion in this chapter is to define and clarify terms; explain the theory more fully; present the way it has been developed, criticized, and tested; and show how it will be applied . . .

Operant behavior

An assumption of the theory is that deviant behavior does not differ *as behavior* from conforming conduct and that both, therefore, can be explained by the same general behavioral principles. These principles are referred to in statement 1 as operant conditioning principles, but they actually include propositions about respondent as well as operant behavior. *Operant behavior* is mediated primarily by the central nervous system and involves the large striated muscles, as contrasted with *respondent behavior,* which is controlled primarily by the autonomic nervous system and involves the smooth muscles. Operants are voluntary; respondents are reflex or involuntary responses. Respondents are contingent upon antecedent or eliciting stimuli. Operants, on the other hand, are capable of being influenced by stimulus events which follow them. Thus, respondents are unaffected by the outcome or change they produce in the individual's environment. Your hand will always withdraw from a hot stove (unless physically restrained or unless the reflex is operantly, and bravely, superseded) and will not be affected by changes caused by moving your hand. Depriving people of food will inevitably produce hunger pangs, and showing them food will make their mouths water (although they may for any number of reasons voluntarily refuse to eat the food). A puff of air or movement of an object which threatens to intrude into the eye makes the eyelid flutter or close. . .

. . . The form and rate with which operant behavior occurs, however, depends on *instrumental conditioning.* That is, the behavior is acquired or conditioned by the effects, outcomes, or *consequences* it has on the person's environment. Operants are not automatic responses to eliciting stimuli; instead, they are capable of developing a functional relationship with stimulus events. They are developed, maintained, and strengthened (or conversely are repressed or fail to develop), depending on the feedback received or produced from the environment. In this sense the stimulus following or *contingent* on an operant controls it; the preceding stimulus controls a respondent.

Any behavioral episode may be a complex combination or chain of both operant and respondent behavior. But social behavior (including deviant behavior) is predominantly operant. . .

. . . The theory does not explain how or why behavior based solely on some physiological condition or inherited attribute occurs. It does not account for why one has a physical deformity, disease, brain damage, or some other condition that produces a characteristic or behavior which is socially defined as deviant. The theory can explain why a person with such a condition responds to deviant labels and treatment by attempting to avoid the company of others, conceal the deviance or otherwise adapt to the deviant label. Internal biochemical and neurological processes obviously are involved in any behavior and interact with the environment to affect the individual's learning of behavior. Reference to them is compatible with (although not emphasized in) learning theory (M. Mahoney, 1974:263-65). However, accounting for these processes is outside the scope of the theory. Behavior explained by them without reference to effects on learning by the individual interaction with the environment is outside the scope of the theory.

The theory is also incapable of accounting for why anyone or anything is socially defined as undesirable. It is capable of accounting for the reactions of the one who is so stigmatized to the sanctions others apply to him. The theory does not say how or why the culture, structure, and social patterning of society sets up and implements certain sets and schedules of reactions to given behavior and characteristics. It does say what the impact of these reactions will be on the individual and what the impact of his counterreactions will be on others.

With these background comments in mind, let us turn now to a brief review of learning principles to which the theory refers. The two major processes in instrumental conditioning are *reinforcement and punishment.*

Reinforcement

. . . First, we may be motivated to continue the behavior because we have been rewarded for doing so. That is, our actions are followed by pleasant, pleasing, desirable, or enjoyable events. When these strengthen behavior, *positive reinforcement* has occurred. The pleasant consequences may be any of the positive social sanctions listed in the first chapter. They may be social approval or status; they may be symbols of approval such as a grade or a medal. The reward may be money. The positive reinforcer may be the effect of something physically consumed such as food, drink, or drugs. Whatever it is, it is defined as a positive reinforcer because it is added to rather than taken away from the environment.

The second type of reinforcement, *negative reinforcement,* is based on taking something away from the environment. That is, people may engage in some activity which enables them to remove or avoid unpleasant or painful stimuli, and this too will reinforce that activity. Behavior produced or maintained in this way is usually labeled *escape-avoidance behavior* because it allows one to avoid aversive events. In negative reinforcement we repeat an act not because we have been or expect to be rewarded for it but because it forestalls, mitigates, or removes something that otherwise would be punishing. Positive and negative reinforcement have the same behavioral effect; both increase the rate of behavior. But in positive reinforcement this effect is produced by the addition and in negative reinforcement by the removal or avoidance of some stimulus event. . . . Children who put away their bicycles every evening because in the past they have been spanked when they did not have had their behavior negatively reinforced; the ones who do so because in the past they have been given a treat have had their behavior positively reinforced.

Punishment

When the events following behavior have the effect of repressing or weakening it (technically decreasing the rate at which it is emitted), we say that punishment has occurred. As with reinforcement, punishment may be brought about by either the addition or subtraction of stimulus events. When the decrease in behavior is brought on by adding punishers as consequences of behavior it is defined as positive punishment. Removing a privilege or reward is negative punishment. The criminal who ceases to steal or cuts down after having been convicted and given harsh sentences in the past has been positively punished. The motorist who reduces his or her fast driving after having had his or her license and money (in fines) taken away has been negatively punished.

In the commonsense meanings it may seem a contradiction in terms to call receiving punishment "positive" or to say it is "negative" to escape punishment. But the terms are not used here as judgments of good and bad; they are used simply in the sense of plus and minus. The table below shows the way in which reinforcement and punishment are positive and negative.

Stimulus	Behavior increases—reinforcement	Behavior decreases—punishment
+	Positive Reinforcement (reward received)	Positive Punishment (punisher received)
−	Negative Reinforcement (punisher removed or avoided)	Negative Punishment (reward removed or lost)

Social and nonsocial reinforcement

What is likely or not likely to be reinforcing or punishing for what and for whom is not part of operant learning principles. Such predictions about the probable reinforcing or punishing relationship that a stimulus has with a class of behavior can be made from experimentation and observation. Predictions can also be made from existing knowledge about biological, psychological, and sociocultural variables. Through these observations substantive kinds and sources of reinforcement and punishment are incorporated into social learning.

At the physiological level, satisfaction of hunger, thirst, and sex drive tend to be reinforcing for all humans (as well as other organisms) who are in a state of deprivation of food, water, or sex. Also, approving responses, recognition, status, and acceptance from significant others are universal social reinforcers for humans. Within a society there are commonly valued rewards which have acquired such generalized value—money is the most obvious example—that they tend to reinforce any behavior that achieves them. There is also commonly valued behavior that is likely to produce positive social sanctions from others in that society. But within the society numerous subcultures may vary from the larger society in the kinds of behavior valued and the stimuli which are reinforcing for the participants. Ultimately, of course, each individual has a unique conditioning history. But a knowledge of group history, social structure, and cultural values enables us to make some predictions about what are likely to be available and effective reinforcers for members of specific groups. Through observation of individuals who are exposed to a given set of recurring stimuli, we can say something about what typically will happen when other individuals are exposed to the same stimuli. Finally, by observing an individual's behavior we can determine what specific parts of his or her behavior are under the control of what specific stimuli.

Unconditioned or intrinsically rewarding physiological stimuli mentioned above may be defined as nonsocial and are involved in shaping and maintaining behavior. Behavioral adaptations must be made to the physical environment. Also, individuals can and do acquire behavior more or less on their own without contact, directly or indirectly, with any of the other reinforcers listed above, and we can describe that learning also as nonsocial. However, most of the learning relevant to deviant behavior is the result of social interactions or exchange in which the words, responses, presence, and behavior of other persons make reinforcers available and provide the setting for reinforcement or are the behavior reinforcers. Many of the social rewards are highly symbolic and intangible and are reinforcing because they fulfill ideological, religious, political, or other goals. Even the more tangible rewards such as money and material goods gain their reinforcing value from the prestige and approval value they have acquired in society. One may be reinforced by these rewards for some particular pattern of behavior in a nonsocial context in the narrow sense that other people are not present at the time and do not respond directly to the behavior. But this is still social reinforcement in the sense that one finds the acquisition of these things reinforcing mainly because of their social desirability. Without social acceptance as a generalized medium of exchange for socially defined rewards, money would be so much paper and metal with no function as a reinforcing stimulus. People may reinforce or punish their own behavior even when alone. But this *self-reinforcement*[3] is still social in that one takes the role of others as if they were present, responding to one's own behavior as learned previously from others. In a well-fed society, the reinforcement coming from the consumption of food is mainly the conditioned reinforcement from association with the social setting in which food is customarily consumed. Moreover, symbolic rewards sometimes override nonsocial reinforcers—for instance, when one goes on a hunger strike to make a political point.

We recognize that learning can occur in connection with nonsocial rewards and punishment, but it is the power and centrality of the direct and symbolic social rewards in society which lead to labeling this theory *social learning*. This theory further proposes that the groups and individuals that comprise or control the major sources of the individual's reinforcement will have the greatest influence on his or her behavior. Usually these are primary groups, which Sutherland emphasized, but they can also be secondary or reference groups. They may be imaginary groups, persons, and situations portrayed through the books and the mass media. They may also be the more formal bureaucratic organizations like an individual's school or job, including agencies of social control and law enforcement.

Imitation and Modeling

In addition to their role in directly reinforcing behavior, these groups influence behavior by providing models for *imitation,* or modeling the behavior of others. Imitation is engaging in behavior after observation of similar behavior, but this observational learning is a more complicated process than "monkey see, monkey do." Whether models' behavior will be imitated is affected by several factors, including characteristics of the models and the observed behavior.

> Models can be real (bodily present) or symbolic (presented via books, movies, TV, or verbal descriptions). The observer can be a passive onlooker or an active participant in the model's activity. The observer may show behavior changes immediately after seeing the model's behavior, after a delay, or never. Observers tend to imitate modeled behavior if they like or respect the model, see the model receive reinforcement, see the model give off signs of pleasure, or are in an environment where imitating the model's performance is reinforced. There are times when an observer does the opposite from the model. This inverse imitation is common when an observer does not like the model, sees the model get punished, or is in an environment where conformity is being punished (Baldwin and Baldwin, 1981:187).

. . . There is persuasive evidence that the observation of salient models, not only in primary groups but also on television or other media, is important in learning normative definitions and affects both prosocial and deviant behavior (Rushton 1979, 1980). Whether imitation is a special learning process or part of the general class of instrumental processes, it is clear that modeling is an important part of social learning. It is more important in the initial acquisition and performance of novel behavior than in the maintenance of behavioral patterns once established, although as we have seen, that observation of models is also involved in the occurrence of already learned behavior.

Differential reinforcement

The specific process by which deviant behavior becomes dominant over conforming behavior in specified situations is *differential reinforcement*. In the simplest terms, differential reinforcement means that given two alternative acts, both of which produce and are reinforced by the same or similar consequences, the one which does so in the greatest amount, more frequently, and with higher probability will be maintained. In a sense the one that has been more successful in obtaining the desired payoffs will become dominant. Differential reinforcement operates when both acts are similar and both are rewarded, but one is more highly rewarded. But differential learning of this kind is most dramatic and effective when the alternatives are incompatible and one is rewarded while the other is unrewarded. One can be continued strongly and the other discontinued even more quickly and effectively if while the first is rewarded the other is punished, even mildly. *Amount* of reinforcement simply refers to the measurable quantities of the reinforcer— food, tokens, money, approval, and so on. Frequency and probability of reinforcement are based on *schedules of reinforcement,* of which there are basically two types, *continuous* and *intermittent.*[4]

On a continuous schedule each response is followed immediately by a reinforcing stimulus. For example, children who are given a penny or a piece of candy immediately each time they spell a word correctly would have their spelling behavior on a continuous reinforcement schedule. Any schedule of reinforcement which is discontinuous, which departs from this continuous pattern, is an intermittent schedule. Reinforcement can be intermittent in time; that is, there is an interval or lapse of time (either a fixed or variable length of time) between the act and its reinforcement. The person who must work a week before getting paid and the one who must work an entire month before getting paid are both on intermittent schedules, but the one who is paid every week has a higher *frequency* of reinforcement. Another type of intermittent schedule is based on the ratio of responses to reinforcement—the number of acts or the number of times one must repeat an act to achieve some reward. The burglar who breaks into three houses before he finds something worth stealing and then has to burglarize ten more before he scores again has a lower *probability* of reinforcement for burglary than the thief who is reasonably sure of making a score in at least every other house he breaks into. Continuous schedules are rare in society; nearly all patterning of social reinforcement is intermittent. The varied time intervals between performances and reward (or punishment) and the uncertainties connected with receiving social rewards give behavior much of its variety, complexity, and stability. . .

We know, of course, that the same behavior can be rewarded at one time and place and punished at another time and place. Whether others react to one's actions in such a way that they are reinforced depends on what is considered good, desirable, approved, necessary, important, or what have you, and this depends on the values of those with whom one customarily interacts. For this reason the frequency, duration, priority, and intensity of differential association with deviant and nondeviant cultural and behavioral patterns have an impact on reinforcement. They should affect whether deviant or conforming behavior is rewarded and, if so, in what amount, how frequently, and with what probability.

Definitions favorable to deviant behavior and discriminative stimuli

In the original differential association theory, Sutherland pointed to two things that are learned which are conducive to law violation: (1) learning techniques which make people able to commit crime and (2) learning definitions which motivate them or make them willing to violate the law. Both techniques and definitions are retained in the reformulated theory, differential association-reinforcement.

Obviously the necessary techniques to carry out deviant behavior must be learned before one can commit deviant acts; inability to perform them precludes commission. Many of the techniques, either simple or complex, are not novel to most of us. Rather, the required component parts or the complete skill is acquired in essentially conforming or neutral contexts to which many of us have been exposed—driving a car, shooting a gun, fighting with fists, signing checks, having sexual intercourse, and so on. Other skills are specific to given deviant acts—safe cracking, counterfeiting, pocket picking, jimmying and picking doors and locks, bringing off a con game, administering narcotics, and so forth—and most of us would not be able to perform them or at least would be initially very inept.

Definitions are normative meanings which are given to behavior; that is, they define an action as right or not right. Sutherland's conception was that the individual is exposed, through interaction with other people, to definitions that approve certain acts prohibited by law and to definitions that condemn the acts. If the approval definitions of the behavior are in excess, the person would be willing to commit the act and violate the law.

These definitions have been incorporated into the reformulated differential association-reinforcement theory by viewing them as verbal behavior (overt and subvocal), which can be reinforced, and by viewing them as included in the class of stimuli called *discriminative stimuli*. Discriminative stimuli are stimuli which become associated with reinforcement. In addition to the reinforcers, other stimuli are ordinarily present when behavior is reinforced—the physical surroundings, one's own feelings, others' behavior, one's own and others' spoken words, and so on. Those that customarily accompany reinforcement (or punishment) come to be associated with it; they set the stage or provide the *cues* for the reinforcement. In a sense discriminative stimuli signal the actor that when they are present he or she can expect reinforcement. In social interaction the place, the people, and what they say all act as cues which allow one to recognize situations in which certain behavior is appropriate and is apt to be rewarded or is not appropriate and is apt not to be rewarded. Through differential reinforcement we learn that some behavior is appropriate, approved, and likely to be rewarded in some situations and not in others.

Children who remain quiet and inactive while their parents are with other adults and are attempting to carry on a conversation will be rewarded and perhaps told later, "I was so proud of you." But the same children who behave the same way on the playground with other children will soon be excluded from the group; if they want the attention and approval of their playmates they must join in. After this happens a few times they learn that they will be positively reinforced for quietness when adults are around but not when adults are absent and other children are around. The presence of adults is discriminative for behaving quietly, whereas the presence of children is discriminative for playing. Discriminative stimuli thereby increase the probability that the behavior will recur beyond that provided by the reinforcing stimuli, although discriminative stimuli have no independent reinforcing value themselves. To the extent that the stimuli in one situation are similar to those of another in which the person has been reinforced for some behavior, he or she will behave similarly in both situations.

Among the most important of stimuli which can become discriminative in social interaction are verbal symbols. Social reinforcers typically consist of or are delivered through words, and verbal interaction often accompanies nonverbal reinforcement ("I love you," "That's nice"). A significant portion of these verbal stimuli are comprised of normative definitions which evaluate the behavior in question as good or bad, right or wrong, justified or unjustified. When social sanctions are applied to behavior something evaluative will probably be said ("Lying is not right," "Good little boys don't do that"). After a while these evaluative definitions associated with the reward and punishment of behavior become discriminative for the behavior.

Definitions favorable or unfavorable to behavior may be *general* beliefs, attitudes, or orientations. For instance, general religious or moral beliefs are unfavorable toward a range of deviant acts such as drug taking, theft, and violence, even though the beliefs do not specifically refer to these acts. Definitions may also be *specific* to an act or series of acts. Thus, one may believe that it is wrong to steal and that laws against theft should be obeyed but that it is all right to take drugs and violate laws against drug possession.

General and specific definitions can be either favorable or unfavorable to deviant behavior. Definitions favorable to deviant behavior are basically of two types. First, there are those which place the behavior in a positive light, *defining it as desirable* or permissible. These would be associated with positive reinforcement through the reactions of others who share a subculture. Within the subculture the behavior seems appropriate, and one who conforms automatically violates the notions of appropriate behavior held by other groups in society. Thus it would be analogous to learning conforming behavior defined as desirable in American society but which would be deviant in another society.

These positive verbalizations may be the "higher values" conception of some groups in conflict with the established order. Some deviant groups, such as homosexuals, may develop full-blown ideologies which define their behavior as contributing a positive good to the world. But although the existence of such groups can be established and such verbalizations can be identified, the type of definition which probably occurs more frequently is the second type.

This second type is comprised of definitions which are discriminative for deviant behavior by virtue of the fact that they *counteract or neutralize definitions of the behavior as undesirable.* They make the behavior, which others condemn and which the persons themselves may initially define as bad, seem all right, justified, excusable, necessary, the lesser of two evils, or not "really" deviant after all. This type of definition was first used by Cressey (1953) in analyzing deviance. He referred to "verbalizations," "rationalizations," and "vocabularies of adjustment and motives." Taking their lead from Cressey, Sykes and Matza (1957) laid out several "techniques of neutralization" used by delinquents to counter antidelinquent definitions and make delinquencies seem all right. These techniques function to make the delinquent acts seem justified and deflect social and self-disapproval. These neutralizing definitions are peculiar extensions of "defenses to crime" contained in the general conforming culture and incorporated into the criminal law. These defenses include "denial of responsibility," "denial of injury," "denial of the victim," and "condemnation of the condemners." Others have used terms such as "accounts" (Lyman and Scott, 1970:111-43) and "disclaimers" (Hewitt and Stokes, 1975).

Such definitions have probably originated primarily through the process of negative reinforcement. That is, they serve to defend against or to avoid the punishment that comes from social disapproval of the activity by oneself and others. Behavior has escaped or avoided punishment in the presence of these definitions and is punished in their absence.

For example, the child who has become accustomed to being punished for running over his little sister with his bicycle accidentally runs into her one time, and his parent, seeing that his bike went out of control, does not punish him, saying something like, "It was an accident, it wasn't your fault." On another occasion he runs into his sister intentionally and avoids a spanking by telling his dad, "It was an accident." This does not have to happen many times before he learns that if behavior is defined as his fault he is likely to be punished, but if it is defined as an accident he will probably escape punishment.

Some neutralizing definitions become incorporated into deviant subcultures (along with the positive definitions noted above). For persons participating in those subcultures then the neutralizations are reinforced in two ways: they are positively reinforced by gaining approval in the subculture and negatively reinforced by providing a defense against the blandishments of those outside the subculture. Examples of such neutralizations which have become part of subcultural ideologies include those employed by professional thieves: "Everybody has a racket," "All people have larceny in their hearts," "The thief is at least honest about his crookedness; the square john is hypocritical about his"; those used in the homosexual subculture: "I can't help myself, I was born this way"; and those used in prostitution: "Every wife is really a prostitute exchanging sexual favors for room and board," "Prostitution protects other women from attack by kooks."

However, most neutralizing definitions discriminative for deviant behavior are probably learned from carriers of conventional culture, including social control and treatment agencies themselves. For nearly every norm we have a norm of evasion; that is, there are accepted exceptions to or ways of getting around the moral imperatives in the norms and the reproach expected from violating the norms. Thus "Thou shalt not kill" is nearly always accompanied by implicit or explicit exceptions (except in time of war if the victim is the enemy, in self-defense, in the line of duty, to protect life and limb, and so on). The moral injunctions against physical aggression are suspended if the victim can be defined as the initial aggressor and therefore deserves to be attacked. Premarital and extramarital sexual behavior can go without negative social sanctions because, "After all they loved one another and established a meaningful relationship," "Temptations that great couldn't be resisted by anyone," "Married to someone like that, what would you do?" Some rationalizations, such as *nonresponsibility,* can be generalized to a wide range of disapproved behavior. "I couldn't help myself," "It wasn't my fault," "I am not responsible," "It was an accident," "She started it," "I was drunk and didn't know what I was doing," "I was so mad I just blew my top."

These types of definitions are often expressed as excuses for one's own and others' deviancy, and punishment which would otherwise follow is withheld or is considerably mitigated. The individual then learns the excuses her- or himself, either directly or through imitation, and uses them to lessen self-reproach and disapproval from others. They would therefore seem to be important in cases where initial moral abhorrence or obstacles to deviant acts must first be overcome by the individual before he or she can commit them.

This hypothesizes that an excess of one set of definitions over another in the sense of a cumulative ratio is not crucial for deviance, as Sutherland would have it. Rather, the deviant outcome is determined by differential reinforcement for and the relative discriminative stimulus value of one set of verbalizations over another. That is, the using of the definitions is an operant behavior which can be reinforced, but the definitions may in turn serve as discriminative stimuli for other behavior, provided that they accompany (at least occasionally) reinforcement of the behavior. Of course, deviant actions may be reinforced and may recur without being accompanied by definitions. However, insofar as that reinforcement is customarily accompanied by such definitions, it is more likely that the behavior will recur in situations to which the definitions can be applied. Typically these definitions are learned and applied to an act prior to one's committing or refraining from it (Andrews and Kandel, 1979; Minor, 1980). But it should be clear that the definitions are themselves affected by the reinforcement or punishment of the act after it has occurred.

Differential Association

In Sutherland's theory, as we have seen, the emphasis is on differential association as the process of being exposed to and taking on definitions favorable or unfavorable to conforming or deviant behavior. However, the reference by Sutherland to learning in intimate (primary) groups and to learning in interaction or communication with others indicates that differential association has both a behavioral aspect and a definitional aspect. That is, differential association means not only associating (directly or indirectly) with people who engage in certain kinds of acts but also being exposed to different normative patterns. This conception of differential association is retained in the social learning approach here. The original statement of differential-association theory by Burgess and Akers (1966b) referred to these groups with which one is in differential association mainly with reference to reinforcement. Nevertheless, the foregoing discussion should make it clear that these different groups provide the major social contexts in which all the learning mechanisms operate as aspects of the same learning process.

The variations in associations with individuals and groups are important in two ways. First, they provide the deviant or conforming definitions and models to which one is exposed. Second, they influence the amount, frequency, and probability of reinforcement for deviant or conforming behavior and verbalizations as well as the probability that the definitions will become discriminative for deviance.

CRITIQUE OF AND RESEARCH ON THE SOCIAL LEARNING THEORY OF DEVIANT BEHAVIOR

The Burgess and Akers article on differential association-reinforcement began not long after its publication in 1966 to attract "attention from sociologists and criminologists, being quoted, referenced, and reprinted" (Adams, 1973:447). By 1974, Cressey viewed it as a promising theoretical development (Sutherland and Cressey, 1974), and the article began to be reprinted in collections of readings (see Cressey and Ward, 1969; Farrell and Swigert, 1978). It was among the most frequently nominated by criminologists in one study as among the "best twenty" articles in the criminological theory and research literature published from 1945 to 1972 (Wolfgang et al., 1978:90). The first two editions of Deviant Behavior have also been cited in the professional and pedagogical literature in the sociology of deviance and crime. Social learning as an approach to deviant behavior is now included in many textbooks on deviance, delinquency, criminology, and general sociology.[5]

There is therefore some recognition of the differential association-reinforcement theory as having relevance for deviant behavior. This recognition is not, however, equivalent to acceptance and does not by itself establish the validity of the theory. Indeed, much of the attention to the theory in the literature has not been approving but instead has been critical, pointing to perceived empirical and logical inadequacies of the theory.

One criticism of the basic learning principles is that they are *tautological*. That is, unless one is careful with the way terms are defined and propositions are stated, the principles become true by definition and therefore are not capable of being tested. Burgess and I offered a resolution to this problem. We carefully separated definitions from propositions in behavior theory and proposed that repeated findings of no reinforcing stimulus would have to be taken as falsification of the principle, at least for the class of behavior on which the findings were obtained (Burgess and Akers, 1966a). This resolution has been discussed in the literature as one reasonable approach to the tautology issue (Chadwick-Jones, 1976; Molm, 1981). But it may not be wholly satisfactory, because we could not offer concrete guidelines beyond "extended and systematic analysis" for deciding when enough exceptions to the principles had been found to render the theory false.

Some theorists contend that tautologies may have value in social theory (Chadwick-Jones, 1976), and Liska (1969) offers a powerful resolution to the issue. His argument is that the basic operant principle of reinforcement and punishment is a prime example of useful tautologies found in social science. Although they cannot themselves be tested, they provide good grounds for devising nontautological propositions. They are "open concepts" which are untestable but from which one can develop testable hypotheses. Emerson (1972) takes a similar approach in arguing that the operant conditioning principles should be taken as nonproblematic assumptions on which testable propositions in social exchange theory are based.

This is basically the approach I have taken here and in previous editions of this book. Tautology is not much of a problem as the theory is applied here. Substantive sources and kinds of stimuli are located and specified as reinforcing specific forms of behavior, which avoids circularity. For instance, the hypothesis that marijuana use has been differentially rewarded by approval from and acceptance by drug-using friends and is not inhibited by informal sanctions of parents and friends or by fear of legal sanctions is testable. Testable hypotheses have been derived from the theory and tested in experimental field studies. . .

Social learning theory (differential association-reinforcement) has also been criticized for incorrectly and incompletely incorporating operant conditioning principles and for not adequately dealing with the importance of nonsocial reinforcement (Adams, 1973). On the other hand, the very inclusion of nonsocial reinforcement and the integration of behavioral concepts with Sutherland's theory have been strongly criticized (Taylor et al., 1973:131-33). The issue seems mainly semantic and is resolved simply by making plain what one means by "social."

"Social" reinforcement is broadly conceived of here as involving not just the direct reactions of others present while an act is performed but also the whole range of tangible and intangible rewards valued in society and its subgroups. Nonsocial contingencies are more narrowly confined to unconditioned physiological and physical stimuli. This conception of social reinforcement neither violates the spirit of Sutherland's theory nor is inconsistent with basic learning theory, which is uninterested in the substantive nature of stimuli. . .

SUMMARY OF THE THEORY AND HOW IT WILL BE USED

The theory may be summarized as follows: Social behavior is learned by conditioning, primarily instrumental or operant, in which behavior is shaped by the stimuli that follow or are consequences of the behavior and by imitation or modeling of others' behavior. Behavior is strengthened by reward (positive reinforcement) and avoidance of punishment (negative reinforcement) or weakened (punished) by aversive stimuli (positive punishment) and lack of reward (negative punishment). Whether deviant or conforming behavior persists depends on the past and present rewards and punishments and on the rewards and punishments attached to alterative behavior—differential reinforcement. The person learns evaluative definitions (attitudes, orientations, knowledge) of the behavior as good or bad, right or wrong, which are favorable to the behavior on the one hand or unfavorable on the other. These definitions are themselves verbal (vocal and subvocal) and cognitive behavior which can be directly reinforced and can also act as cue or discriminative stimuli for other behavior. The more individuals define the behavior as good (positive definitions) or at least justified or excusable (neutralizing) rather than as undesirable (negative definitions), the more likely they are to engage in it.

The reinforcers can be nonsocial (as in the direct physiological effects of drugs or in unconditioned reinforcers such as food). But the theory posits that the principal behavioral effects come from interaction in or under the influence of those groups with which one is in differential association and which control sources and patterns of reinforcement, provide normative definitions, and expose one to behavioral models. The most important of these are primary groups such as peer and friendship groups and the family, but they also include work, school, church, and other membership and reference groups.

Deviant behavior can be expected to the extent that it has been differentially reinforced over alternative behavior (conforming or other deviant behavior) and is defined as desirable or justified when the individual is in a situation discriminative for the behavior. Although all the mechanisms of learning are recognized, the emphasis in the following chapters is on differential association, definitions favorable or unfavorable to the deviant behavior, and differential reinforcement.

The theory is applied to deviant behavior in the following ways:

1. The sources, content, and impact of differential reinforcement, positive and negative reinforcement and punishment, conditioning, imitation, and other behavioral processes are identified on the basis of available research findings and reasonable inferences from them.

Positive reinforcement is identified in the descriptions of most types of deviant behavior. For instance, the preaddictive use of opiates in a drug subculture and the use of hallucinogenic drugs are rewarded by the recognition and approval of drug-using peers. Moderate drinking by adolescents is socially reinforced in some families and peer groups, and excessive drinking is positively reinforced in some drinking groups. Social rewards are also attached to playing a homosexual role in the homosexual community. Prostitution is economically more rewarding than conventional jobs for some women, and the prostitute builds reinforcing relationships with others in the life. Occupational crimes are financially rewarding, and having the good opinion of and acceptance by co-workers and supervisors also influences the participation of some executives in corporate crimes. The professional thief finds crime remunerative and is also reinforced for criminal activity by the prestige and acceptance with fellow thieves. Suicidal behavior and mental illness can be reinforced by increased social attention following self-injurious behavior or "psychotic" episodes. In addition to social reinforcement, taking drugs is conditioned by the reinforcement of the effects of the drugs; drinking may continue because of the positive effects and good taste of the alcoholic beverage; and deviant sexual behavior may be chosen because of the greater sexual pleasure derived from it than from conventional sexual behavior. The effects of these activities may be intrinsically pleasurable, but they are also conditioned to be so by their association with social reinforcement.

Negative reinforcement is identified in opiate addiction; one motivation of the addict is to avoid or escape the sickness which accompanies abstinence, and drug taking may become a general response to other unpleasant conditions. In addition to the positive support received from some groups for heavy drinking, many alcoholics drink large quantities of alcohol in order to deal with anxiety and problems. Negative reinforcement is intertwined with positive inducements in other forms of deviance. For example, in some cases suicidal behavior is an attempt to resolve unbearable problems; the prostitute remains in the business partly because she fears what her pimp would do if she left; embezzlement is the white collar worker's resolution of a problem.

2. The sources and nature of the definitions (the verbalizations and rationalizations discussed previously) and other discriminative stimuli conducive to the deviant behavior will be located and described.

Positive definitions are favorable to deviance because they evaluate the behavior positively and tend to be learned by participating in deviant subcultures. Illustrations are the "cool" view of opiate use and the personal and intellectual benefits attributed to hallucinogenic drugs in drug subcultures, the glorification of homosexual behavior in the homosexual community, and the "prostitution helps keep the sex freaks from your daughters" ideology in prostitution.

The subcultures also offer definitions that characterize the behavior as not necessarily desirable but as excusable, justified, not really bad, or not the fault of the individual. These *neutralizing or justifying definitions* are more plentiful than positive definitions. They are found both in subcultures and in the general culture. For example, subcultural addicts and physician addicts both neutralize their initially unfavorable definition of opiates (because they are addictive) by saying, "I can control it." The physician addicts also justify their use of opiates as necessary to combat their ailments and to allow them to be effective despite fatigue from overwork. Initially negative definitions of homosexual behavior are overcome and homosexual acts justified as "not really queer." Later, homosexuals rationalize their continued homosexual behavior by thinking, "This is just the way I am." Prostitutes and professional thieves may justify their behavior by condemning the immorality and hypocrisy of the "straight" world: "Others are doing much the same thing, but they don't get caught and aren't honest enough to admit it." Corporate executives who violate restraint of trade laws try to rationalize their actions with the belief that such action is not really criminal or harmful to society. Embezzlers also define their theft as not really stealing, as only borrowing or at least as justified in a particular case. People who lash out with savage violence and seriously injure or kill others may account for their actions by saying, "They deserved it," or "I just couldn't help myself; I blew my stack and didn't know what I was doing." People may justify their suicide attempts by blaming others or by believing suicide is the only way out of suffering a tragic loss or critical illness.[6]

3. As the above should make clear, in examining both the definitions and the reinforcing processes the primary aim in each case is to locate the patterns of *differential association* which provide the individual with the group contexts and sources of *social reinforcement*. However, nonsocial, physical, and physiological stimuli are recognized and incorporated into the explanation where appropriate.

4. *Differential reinforcement and definitions* are identified. However, the analysis focuses on the positive and negative reinforcers for the deviant behavior. Less attention is paid to comparison of these with the punishing consequences of the behavior and the counteracting reinforcement and punishment of conforming alternatives. For example, this comparison is made in showing the differential reinforcement of professional crime. Sometimes it is a major part of the analysis—for instance, in the relative pleasure derived by homosexuals from homosexual and heterosexual alternatives. But even when it is not stated explicitly, the understood requirement is that deviant behavior results from greater reinforcement *on balance over* the probability of punishment and the contingencies on other behavior.

Similarly, more space is devoted to showing the kinds of positive and neutralizing definitions favorable to deviance than to showing the anti-deviant definitions over which they have ascended. However, the guiding principle throughout is that the definitions favorable to deviance are conducive to deviance because on balance they have been reinforced more and have acquired greater discriminative value than unfavorable definitions. This is explicitly stated in discussing definitions that overcome original inhibiting definitions—overcoming initial distaste for drugs, neutralizing abhorrence of homosexuality, and overcoming learned definitions of embezzlement as criminal. Even so, the principle holds even where it is left implicit.

5. The usual result of the analysis is to spell out a typical process or processes through which a person progresses from conforming to deviant behavior—a "natural history" of becoming a homosexual, an addict, an alcoholic, and so on. . .

The process is a complex one with reciprocal and feedback effects, and the sequence of events is variable. Nevertheless, the typical process envisioned by the theory is that through differential association in which individuals interact and identify with different groups (mainly between family and peer groups), they are exposed to models, norms, and reinforcement patterns tending toward continued conforming to or refraining from particular deviant acts or toward committing those acts. The balance of definitions favorable to deviant acts combined with imitation of deviant models and the anticipated balance of reinforcement (gained from direct consequences of conforming and perhaps observation of consequences of the deviant behavior by others) produces the initial deviant acts. After the initial acts, imitation becomes less important (although facilitative effects of modeling may remain) while the effects of the definitions continue (themselves now affected by the consequences of initial deviant acts). Once the acts have been performed, the actual consequences (social and nonsocial reinforcers and punishers) of the specific behavior come into play to affect the chances that the deviant behavior will be continued and at what level. The actual social sanctions and other effects of engaging in the behavior may be perceived differently, but to the extent that they are more rewarding than alternative behavior, then the deviant behavior will be repeated again under similar circumstances. Progression into more frequent or sustained patterns of deviant behavior is promoted so that reinforcement, exposure to deviant models, and definitions are not offset by negative formal and informal sanctions and definitions.

Initial acts may and do occur in the absence of definitions favorable to them; rather, the definitions get applied retroactively to excuse or redefine the initial deviant acts. To the extent that they successfully mitigate others' or self-punishment, they become discriminative for repetition of the deviant acts and, hence, precede the future commission of the acts. Association with others engaging in or supporting particular deviant acts typically precedes the individual's committing the acts. Those associations are most often formed on bases other than coinvolvement in the deviant behavior. However, after the deviant activity has begun and the consequences accompanying it are experienced, the associational patterns may themselves in turn be altered so that the fact that one is drawn to or chooses further interaction with others is based, at least in part, on whether they too are involved in the deviant activity and to what degree.

6. The emphasis throughout is on *learning to do* something that is defined by others as deviant. Obviously, however, deviant behavior can also result from learning failures. Failure to learn the proper conforming responses either may be defined directly as deviant—that is, behavioral deficits such as in mentally retarded people—or may allow the development of other deviant behavior. . .

BEHAVIORISM, SYMBOLIC INTERACTIONISM AND SOCIAL LEARNING

. . . The social learning theory presented . . ., then, draws from behaviorally oriented theories in psychology while retaining social interaction and normative emphases in differential association theory from sociology. As such it uses certain aspects of *behaviorism* and *symbolic interactionism;* thus, it is appropriate to review how this perspective relates to them. . .

The predominant social psychological orientation in sociology is symbolic interactionism. This perspective is traced back to the early writings of Cooley (1902) and Mead (1934). As it has come to be practiced in sociology, symbolic interactionism stresses the exchange of meanings communicated in face-to-face interaction through verbal and gestural symbols and the effect this interaction has on the individual's self-concept and identity. Symbolic interactionism stresses the symbolic rather than the concrete in social interaction. It makes no use (or only incidental use) of reinforcement or other behavioristic concepts, relies heavily on nonexperimental "naturalistic" observations and qualitative data, and tends not to be environmentally deterministic (Blumer, 1969).

Operant conditioning theory, as formulated by Skinner (1953) and developed by those who work in the Skinnerian tradition, is strongly behavioristic. Skinner did not reject all interest in "internal states," but he saw them as effects rather than independent or intervening variables affecting behavior. In the strict behavioral approach only directly observable, overt behavior and external environmental stimuli can be studied scientifically. Hence the only propositions worthy of consideration are those about the relationship between overt behavioral response and observable stimuli. There is no reference to behavior resulting from or mediated by mental or emotional events. Operant behaviorism recognizes two major forms this relationship can take: (1) a stimulus elicits a reflex or response; when other stimuli are paired with it they come to elicit the same response (referred to as respondent conditioning, classical conditioning, or Pavlovian conditioning); (2) a behavior, by operating on the environment, produces or is followed by a stimulus which feeds back upon the behavior and conditions its future occurrence (operant conditioning or instrumental conditioning). In earlier times, behaviorism was based entirely on the first kind of stimulus-response relationship (Watson, 1930). Modern behavioral learning theory, even though it may be referred to as operant conditioning theory, includes both respondent and operant conditioning. Laboratory experimentation with animal and human subjects is the primary research strategy of behavioral psychology, and experimental behaviorism is a major part of psychology.[7]

The reformulation of differential association by Burgess and Akers (1966b) was one of the early efforts in a movement of behavioral theory into sociology which has developed over the past two decades. Some trace this movement to George Homans (1961, 1974), the first prominent sociologist to make use of Skinnerian theory; a recent collection of essays on behavioral theory in sociology was rendered in honor of Homans (Hamblin and Kunkel, 1977). Other sociologists also began years ago incorporating operant principles to analyze concepts and problems of long-standing interest to sociologists. Notable among these were Burgess and Bushell (1969) and others who applied behavioral theory to such problems as social change and social problems (Kunkel, 1970,1975), socialization (Scott, 1971), criminal behavior (Jeffery, 1965), and cultural diffusion (Hamblin and Miller, 1976). A behavioral perspective in sociology is most apt to be found in social exchange theory and research (Emerson, 1972, 1981; Burgess and Nielsen, 1974; Chadwick-Jones, 1976; Molm and Wiggins, 1979). . .

The behavioral and symbolic interaction perspectives are not as incompatible as many believe. Later interpretations of symbolic interactionism diverged from Mead (1934), but he referred to his own perspective as "social behaviorism" (McPhail and Rexroat, 1979; see Blumer's 1980 dispute of this and McPhail and Rexroat's 1980 response). Indeed, there are many similarities between Mead's theory and modern behaviorism in such concepts as meaning, self-awareness, self-control, and intention (Baldwin 1981). Present-day behaviorism is not a totally mechanistic perspective. . .

Learning psychology has a long tradition of reinforcement theories using cognitive concepts which have developed somewhat independently and somewhat in interaction with operant theory. These differ from strict behaviorism in making explicit theoretical use of notions about cognitive and symbolic processes such as self-reinforcement, anticipation of reinforcement, and vicarious reinforcement. These have continued to develop and are now recognized as a major behavioral perspective. (See the review of various traditional and contemporary theories in Swenson, 1980.) They are compatible with symbolic interactionism.

The prime example of this type of theory is Bandura's social learning theory (Bandura, 1969, 1973, 1977). There is also the social behaviorism of Staats (1975), the social learning theory of Rotter (1954), the psychosocial "problem behavior" theory of Jessor and Jessor (1977), and the applications of the social learning theory of Rushton (1980) and the cognitive behaviorism of Rachman and Teasdale (1970) and Mahoney (1974). A number of these theorists maintain that much research evidence (including findings of experimental studies) is inconsistent with a strict behavioristic model focusing only on external events. They argue that internal, cognitive processes operate in both operant and respondent behavioral conditioning (Bandura, 1969, 1977; Staats, 1975; Mahoney, 1974; Rachman and Teasdale, 1970). . . . Subjective phenomena, choice, values, feelings are increasingly recognized as real phenomena and incorporated into modern behaviorism (Baldwin and Baldwin, 1978; Baldwin, 1981). Bandura (1969:45) reminds us, however, that reinforcement and external environmental events are very important and that "internal symbolic control" is just one element in learning. An overemphasis on internal, mental processes can lead to almost mystical constructions about what is going on in people's heads.

The social learning theory of deviant behavior developed and applied here more closely resembles the theories of Bandura, Rotter, Staats, and others than it resembles theories of a "purer" Skinnerian or radical behaviorism. Social learning then may be seen as "soft" behaviorism. Much attention is paid in the following pages to behavior and its relation to external environmental stimuli. But there is no effort to avoid connotations of cognition in the concept of definitions or other concepts such as anticipated reinforcement.[8]

THE RELATIONSHIP OF SOCIAL LEARNING TO STRUCTURAL PERSPECTIVES

. . . The basic premise of the social learning approach is that both conforming and deviant behavior are learned in the same way; the substance and direction of the learning is different, but the general process is the same for both conforming and deviant behavior. This theory is not that persons become deviant because they are certain kinds of people or that the deviance is merely a manifestation of an intrapsychic trauma or disturbance. Rather, the theory is that they have simply learned to respond to the environment and their human makeup in ways that others (and perhaps they too) define as deviant.

This learning proposition has been widely accepted in sociology and is quite consistent with the structural approaches to deviance. None of these approaches denies that normal learning processes are involved in the acquisition of deviant behavior. All would agree that the individual's behavior is shaped by the situations experienced in life. In fact, as has been shown, the burden of these structural theories is to show what kinds of situations and structures lead to deviant behavior.

But none of them adequately specifies the process by which social structure shapes individual behavior. The structural theories refer to the structure of learning environments likely to produce deviant behavior—breakdowns in social control, growing up in disorganized areas of the city, participation in deviant groups and subcultures or in groups in conflict with the established order, deprivation of legitimate opportunities, exposure to anomic conditions, or being labeled deviant—but they do not specify *how* they produce deviant behavior. However, the learning perspective does specify the process by which social structure produces individual behavior. Thus, social learning is complementary to, not competing with, the structural theories. The deviance-producing environments have an impact on individual conduct through the operation of learning mechanisms.

The connection between social structure and the mechanisms of learning which shape individual conduct can be viewed in this way: the general culture and structure of society and the particular groups, subcultures, and social situations in which individuals participate provide learning environments in which the norms define what is approved and disapproved, and the reactions of others (for example, in applying social sanctions) attach different reinforcing or punishing consequences to individuals' behavior. In a sense, then, social structure is an arrangement of sets and schedules of reinforcement contingencies.

Some groups and segments of society have higher rates of some kinds of deviant behavior than other groups. For every form of deviance on which we have information, the level of deviance varies systematically by such factors as age, sex, religion, ethnic classifications, race, occupation, socioeconomic status, and place of residence. These social characteristics indicate the individuals' location in the structure of society, the particular groups of which they are likely to be members, with whom they interact, and how others are apt to respond to them and their behavior. Therefore, these characteristics reflect which behavioral and normative patterns the individuals will be exposed to and which behavior is likely to be approved and rewarded or disapproved and punished. . .

ENDNOTES

1   What follows in this chapter is an overview of the particular version of social learning theory applied to deviant behavior throughout this book. It is not intended and will not serve as a complete introduction to the full set of concepts, propositions, and issues in learning theory. For the reader interested in pursuing the issue further, the behavioral principles are presented in the literature as operant conditioning, learning, reinforcement, behavior analysis, and behavior modification. For expositions of basic principles by psychologists see Skinner (1953, 1959), Staats (1964, 1975), Ullman and Krasner (1969), Bandura (1969, 1977), M. Mahoney (1974), Craighead et al. (1976), and Millenson and Leslie (1979). There are also many psychology textbooks and introductions to learning theory. See Catania (1979), Chance (1979), or Swenson (1980). Also see the publications in journals such as *Journal of Experimental Analysis of Behavior, Journal of Applied Behavior Analysis, Behavior Modification,* and *Behavior Research and Therapy.*

   As I shall note in the next chapter, learning perspectives have become incorporated into sociology. See Homans (1974), Burgess and Bushell (1969), Scott (1971), Kunkel (1970), Hamblin and Kunkel (1977), and Emerson (1981). Also, there are now some very good introductions to behavioral theory for sociology students, such as Baldwin and Baldwin (1981) and Tarter (1979).

2   See Burgess and Akers 1966b. In the original Burgess-Akers statement the words *criminal behavior* were used where the words *deviant behavior* appear here. Also, statements 5, 6, and 7 are worded somewhat differently here than they were in the 1966 statement.

3   *Self-reinforcement,* or *self-control,* has come into increased prominence in behavior theory and modification but not without some debate and controversy. See the exchange among Goldiamond (1976); Mahoney (1976); and Thoresen and Wilbur (1976).

4   These and the following comments refer only to reinforcement, but the concepts of amount, frequency, probability, and schedules also apply to punishment.

5   For earlier examples see Mauss (1975), social problems, and Quinney (1975), criminology. For more recent examples see Vold (1979), Reid (1979), Barlow (1984), Thomas and Hepburn (1983), criminology; Jensen and Rojek (1980), Gibbons (1981), delinquency; Liska (1981), Farrell and Swigert (1982), Orcutt (1983), deviance; DeFleur et al. (1981), Robertson (1981), sociology.

6   The point of these examples is that there are neutralizing definitions for various types of deviant behavior, not that all are equally condemned or that all involve neutralization to the same extent.

7   Even clinical psychology, which for so long has been in conflict with experimental psychology, has developed treatment procedures based on behavorial learning theory. The clinical application has tended to be referred to in general as *behavior therapy* or *behavior modification.* Some of this is classical conditioning, some is strictly Skinnerian, and some is a combination of these, with some reliance on notions about intrapsychic processes. See Ullmann and Krasner (1964), Bandura (1969), Mahoney (1974), and Craighead et al. (1976).

8   This statement of the position of the social learning theory of deviant behavior on cognitive concepts was included in both the first (1973) and second (1977) editions of this book. Yet many years later some critics mistakenly continue to characterize the theory as the "mere claim that criminal behavior is operant conditioning behavior" and reject it on the grounds that it thereby dismisses all mentalistic concepts, some of which may be useful in predicting behavior (Halbasch, 1979). It should be clear from this section that this is an entirely incorrect description of the theory. The theory also continues to be criticized by strict behaviorists who believe that no social or cognitive variables should be included in explaining human behavior (Jeffery, 1977).

REFERENCES

Adams, Reed. 1973. "Differential association and learning principles revisited." *Social Problems* 20:447-58.

Andrews, Kenneth H. and Kandel, Denise B. 1979. "Attitude and behavior: A specification of the contingent consistency hypothesis." *American Sociological Review* 44:298-310.

Baldwin, John D. 1981. "George Herbert Mead and modern behaviorism." *Pacific Sociological Review* 24:411-40.

Baldwin, John D. and Baldwin, Janice I. 1978. "Behaviorism on verstehen and eklaren." *American Sociological Review* 43:335-47.

Baldwin, John D. and Baldwin, Janice I. 1981. *Behavior principles in everyday life.* Englewood Cliffs, N.J.: Prentice-Hall.

Bandura, Albert. 1969. *Principles of behavior modification.* New York: Holt, Rinehart, and Winston.

Bandura, Albert. 1973. *Aggression: A social learning analysis.* Englewood Cliffs, N.J.: Prentice-Hall.

Bandura, Albert. 1977. *Social learning theory.* Englewood Cliffs, N.J.: Prentice-Hall.

Barlow, Hugh. 1984. *Introduction to criminology.* 3d ed. Boston: Little-Brown.

Blumer, Herbert. 1969. *Symbolic interactionism: Perspective and method.* Englewood Cliffs, N.J.: Prentice-Hall.

Blumer, Herbert. 1980. "Mead and Blumer: The convergent methodological perspectives of social behaviorism and symbolic interactionism." *American Sociological Review* 45:409-19.

Burgess, Robert L. and Akers, Ronald L. 1966a. "Are operant principles tautological?" *Psychological Record* 16:305-12.

Burgess, Robert L. and Akers, Ronald L. 1966b. "A differential association-reinforcement theory of criminal behavior." *Social Problems* 14:128-47.

Burgess, Robert and Bushell, Don, eds. 1969. *Behavioral sociology.* New York: Columbia University Press.

Burgess, Robert L. and Nielsen, Joyce M. 1974. "An experimental analysis of some structural determinants of equitable and inequitable exchange relations." *American Sociological Review* 39:427-43.

Catania, A. Charles. 1979. *Learning.* Englewood Cliffs, N.J.: Prentice-Hall.

Chadwick-Jones, J.K. 1976. *Social exchange theory: Its structure and influence in social psychology.* London: Academic Press.

Chance, Paul. 1979. *Learning and behavior.* Belmont, Calif.: Wadsworth.

Cooley, Charles Horton. 1902. *Human nature and the social order.* New York: Scribner.

Craighead, W. Edward, Kazdin, Alan E., and Mahoney, Michael J., eds. 1976. *Behavior modification: Principles, issues, and applications.* Boston: Houghton Mifflin.

Cressey, Donald R. 1953. *Other people's money.* Glencoe, Ill.: Free Press.

Cressey, Donald R. 1960. "Epidemiology and individual conduct: A case from criminology." *Pacific Sociological Review* 3:47-58.

Cressey, Donald R. and Ward, David, eds. 1969. *Delinquency, crime, and social process.* New York: Holt, Rinehart, and Winston .

DeFleur, Melvin, Williams, V. D'Antonio, and DeFleur, Lois B. 1981. *Sociology: Human society.* 3d ed. Glenview, Ill.: Scott, Foresman.

Emerson, Richard N. 1972. "Exchange theory, part I: A psychological basis for social exchange." In *Sociological theories in progress* Vol 2, ed. Joseph Berger et al. Boston: Houghton Mifflin.

Emerson, Richard N. 1981. "Social exchange theory." In *Social psychology,* ed. Morris Rosenberg and Ralph Turner, pp. 30-65. New York: Basic Books.

Farrell, Ronald and Swigert, Victoria, eds. 1978. *Social deviance.* Chicago: Lippincott.

Farrell, Ronald and Swigert, Victoria. 1982. *Deviance and social control.* Glenview, Ill.: Scott, Foresman.

Gibbons, Don. 1981. *Delinquent behavior.* 3d ed. Englewood Cliffs, N.J.: Prentice-Hall.

Goldiamond, Israel. 1976. "Self-reinforcement." *Journal of Applied Behavior Analysis* 9:509- 14.

Halbasch, Keith. 1979. "Differential reinforcement theory examined." *Criminology* 17:217-29.

Hamblin, Robert L. and Kunkel, John H., eds. 1977. *Behavioral theory in sociology: essays in honor of George C. Homans.* New Brunswick, N.J.: Transaction Books.

Hamblin, Robert L. and Miller, Jerry L. 1976. "Reinforcement and the origin, rate and extent of cultural diffusion." *Social Forces* 54:743-49.

Hewitt, John P. and Stokes, Randall. 1975. "Disclaimers." *American Sociological Review* 40:1-11.

Homans, George C. 1961. *Social behavior: Its elementary forms.* New York: Harcourt Brace Jovanovich.

Homans, George C. 1974. *Social behavior: Its elementary forms.* Revised ed. New York: Harcourt Brace Jovanovich.

Jeffery, C.R. 1965. "Criminal behavior and learning theory." *Journal of Criminal Law, Criminology, and Police Science* 56:294-300.

Jeffery, C.R. 1977. *Crime prevention through environmental design.* 2d ed. Beverly Hills, Calif.: Sage.

Jensen, Gary F. and Rojek, Dean. 1980. *Delinquency.* New York: Heath.

Jessor, Richard and Jessor, Shirley L. 1977. *Problem behavior and psychosocial development.* New York: Academic Press.

Kunkel, John H. 1970. *Society and economic growth: A behavioral perspective of social change.* New York: Oxford University Press.

Kunkel, John H. 1975. *Behavior, social problems, and change.* Englewood Cliffs, N.J.: Prentice-Hall.

Liska, Allen E. 1969. "Uses and misuses of tautologies in social psychology." *Sociometry* 33:444-57.

Liska, Allen E. 1981. *Perspectives on deviance.* Englewood Cliffs, N.J.: Prentice-Hall.

Lyman, Stanford M., and Scott, Marvin B. 1970. *A sociology of the absurd.* New York: Appleton-Century-Crofts.

McPhail, Clark and Rexroat, Cynthia. 1979. "Mead vs. Blumer: The divergent methodological perspectives of social behaviorism and symbolic interactionism." *American Sociological Review* 44:449-67.

McPhail, Clark and Rexroat, Cynthia. 1980. "Ex cathedra Blumer or ex libris Mead?" *American Sociological Review* 45:420-30.

Mahoney, Michael J. 1974. *Cognition and behavior modification.* Cambridge, Mass.: Ballinger.

Mahoney, Michael J. 1976. "Terminal terminology: A self-regulated response to Goldiamond." *Journal of Applied Behavior Analysis* 9:515-17.

Mauss, Armand L. 1975. *Social problems and social movements.* Philadelphia: J.B. Lippincott.

Mead, George Herbert. 1934. *Mind, self, and society.* Chicago: University of Chicago Press.

Millenson, J. R. and Leslie, Julian C. 1979. *Principles of behavior analysis.* New York: Macmillan.

Minor, W. William. 1980. "The neutralization of criminal offense." *Criminology* 18:103-20.

Molm, Linda D. 1981. "The legitimacy of behavioral theory as a sociological perspective." *American Sociologist* 16:153-65.

Molm, Linda D. and Wiggins, James A. 1979. "A behavioral analysis of the dynamics of social exchange in the dyad." *Social Forces* 57:1157-79.

Orcutt, James D. 1983. *Analyzing deviance.* Homewood, Ill.: Dorsey.

Quinney, Richard. 1975. *Criminology.* Boston: Little, Brown.

Rachman, Stanley and Teasdale, John. 1970. *Aversion therapy and behavior disorders.* Coral Gables, Fla.: University of Miami Press.

Reid, Sue Titus. 1979. *Crime and criminology.* 2d ed. New York: Holt, Rinehart, and Winston.

Robertson, Ian. 1981. *Sociology.* 2d ed. New York: Worth.

Rotter, Julian. 1954. *Social learning and clinical psychology.* Englewood Cliffs, N.J.: Prentice-Hall.

Rushton, O. Phillippe. 1979. "Effects of prosocial television and film material on the behavior of viewers." In *Advances in experimental social psychology,* ed. Leonard Berkowitz, pp. 321-51. New York: Academic Press.

Rushton, O. Phillippe. 1980. *Altruism, socialization, and society.* Englewood Cliffs, N.J.: Prentice-Hall.

Scott, John Finley. 1971. *Internalization of norms: A sociological theory of moral commitment.* Englewood Cliffs, N.J.: Prentice-Hall.

Skinner, B.F. 1953. *Science and human behavior.* New York: Macmillan.

Skinner, B.F. 1959. *Cumulative record.* New York: Appleton-Century-Crofts.

Staats, Arthur. 1964. *Human learning.* New York: Holt, Rinehart, and Winston.

Staats, Arthur. 1975. *Social behaviorism.* Homewood, Ill.: Dorsey.

Sutherland, Edwin H. and Cressey, Donald R. 1970. *Criminology.* 8th ed. Philadelphia: J.B. Lippincott.

Swenson, Leland C. 1980. *Theories of learning: Traditional perspectives/contemporary developments.* Belmont, Calif.: Wadsworth.

Sykes, Gresham and Matza, David. 1957. "Techniques of neutralization: A theory of delinquency." *American Journal of Sociology* 22:664-70.

Tarter, Donald E. 1979. *Turning behavior inside out.* Washington, D.C.: University Press of America.

Taylor, Ian, Walton, Paul, and Young, Jock. 1973. *The new criminology.* New York: Harper and Row.

Thomas, Charles W. and Hepburn, John R. 1983. *Crime, criminal law, and criminology.* Dubuque, Iowa: Wm. C. Brown.

Thoresen, Carl E. and Wilbur, S. Wilbur. 1976. "Some encouraging thoughts about self-reinforcement." *Journal of Applied Behavior Analysis* 9:518-20.

Ullman, Leonard P. and Krasner, Leonard. 1969. *A psychological approach to abnormal behavior.* Englewood Cliffs, N.J.: Prentice-Hall.

Vold, George B. 1979. *Theoretical criminology.* 2d ed. Prepared by Thomas J. Bernard. New York: Oxford University Press.

Watson, J.B. 1930. *Behaviorism.* 2d ed. Chicago: University of Chicago Press.

Wolfgang, Marvin E., Figlio, Robert M. and Thornberry, Terence P. 1978. *Evaluating criminology.* New York: Elsevier.

Essay/Discussion Questions for Section II

Note to the student: If you are able to provide thorough responses to all of the following questions, you have mastered excellent comprehension of the classic readings presented in this section.

1. What is different about the Chicago School when compared to the Positive School? (From the section introduction.)

2. What was the *essence* of the Chicago School? (From the section introduction.)

3. What is the concept of *concentric circles* and how does this help to explain rates of delinquency? (From the section introduction.)

4. How does culture conflict help explain the findings of ecological criminology? (From the section introduction.)

5. Explain the connections between ecological, culture conflict, differential association, and social learning theories. (From the section introduction.)

6. How do communities contribute to crime and delinquency? (From the Shaw & McKay reading.)

7. What are "conduct norms" and why is conflict important? (From the Sellin reading.)

8. What are the key components of differential association theory and why is the interpretation that the theory just says "delinquent peers cause delinquency" incorrect? (From the Sutherland reading.)

9. How does social learning theory differ from differential association theory? What does it add? (From the Akers reading.)

Section III
STRAIN AND
SUBCULTURE THEORIES

Introduction

An alternative, and competing position, to the Chicago School approach was a theory developed by Robert Merton in 1938. This theory is commonly called anomie theory. Instead of postulating that social disorganization led to culture conflict and crime, Merton (and other strain[1] theorists) worked from a larger picture of society. He wanted to explore the effects of social structure on *rates* of deviance in society. As a result, strain theories are commonly known as *structural* theories (but they can be individual-level theories as well). Other theories followed Merton's popular formulation and many of them attempted to reconcile his version of social disorganization with that of the Chicago School.

Anomie Theory

In the 1892 book titled *The Division of Labor in Society*, the French sociologist Emile Durkheim put forth the concept of anomie. He used it as a way of explaining the normlessness created when societies are somehow disrupted by various events such as economic or political upheaval. Anomie, then, is a disruption or breakdown of norms in a society. Durkheim noted that one of the products of anomie (he also used the term "deregulation") was a higher crime rate. He compared societies in various states of social disorganization and found that rates of deviance varied according to the degree of anomie they were experiencing. He also explained that as societies have evolved from a primitive, uncomplicated form to a modern, complex form the probability of disorganization has increased. As a result, a modern society could always have some degree of anomie present.

Robert K. Merton wrote a classic article in 1938 in which he further developed and extended anomie theory. His concept of a disorganized society was one where too much emphasis was placed on common cultural success-*goals* and where the societally approved *means* to reach those goals were not equally distributed among its members. This *disjuncture between goals and means*, or a lack of access to the means by which to achieve the goals, is anomie. He postulated that a state of anomie would increase deviance, particularly among groups who were especially disadvantaged in the availability of means.

Merton theorized that there were five *modes of adaptation* to anomie. First was *conformity*. If a person remained conforming in the face of anomie, then conformity itself was a type of deviance. The second mode he called *innovation*. In this deviant adaptation, an individual would continue to find the goals attractive and work toward them, but would reject the normal means for achieving those goals in favor of deviant means. An example of this mode is a person who pursues the goal of making a fortune, has no legitimate avenues open, and decides to sell drugs. The third mode was *ritualism*. Here, the goals are rejected as unobtainable but the means are kept and pursued as if they were the goals. Bureaucrats ("red-tape") and religious fanatics are both examples of people who have fallen into this mode of adaptation. A fourth mode was *retreatism* in which both the goals and the means are rejected. Hermits and other societal "drop-outs" are good examples of retreatism. Finally, there was *rebellion*. Under this mode, both the goals and the means are not only rejected, but other goals and means are substituted for them. Obviously, rebels and revolutionaries are the types of individuals in this mode.

Merton's theoretical formulation was so popular that it is almost taken as a truism today. Two major criminological theories followed in the 1950s. Both attempted to merge the structural approach of anomie with the Chicago School's explanations of the process of becoming deviant. Those two theories were Cohen's subculture theory and Cloward and Ohlin's differential opportunity theory. A resurgence of interest in the late 1980s and early 1990s led to two major additions to Merton's theory. Robert Agnew (1985, 1989, 1992) added the more individual-level concept of avoidance of painful (or negative) situations. Just as an individual's goals can be positively blocked (Merton's anomie), so can the ability to avoid undesirable things or stressful life events. When both positive blockage and negative avoidance are combined, the stress levels suggest that we can expect the highest rates of delinquency or deviance. The second contemporary adaptation of anomie theories is that of Steven Messner and Richard Rosenfeld (1994), who add institutional strain to the mix. They argue that an entire level of non-economic institutions (family, schools, religion, and law) has been omitted. For anomie to work, not only is a dysjunction of goals and means necessary, but social institutions must also be weakened.

Subculture Theory

Perhaps the only person who was a student of both Merton and Sutherland, Albert K. Cohen set about the process of reconciling both theories in a book titled *Delinquent Boys: The Culture of The Gang*, published in 1955. The result was a theory of the creation and evolution of delinquent subcultures. Cohen began by reviewing the existing evidence on delinquency. He noted that delinquency was largely a *male, urban, lower-class, gang* phenomenon. Delinquency was characterized by an emphasis on short-run hedonism, a viewpoint that stressed the here-and-now rather than the future. He also said that delinquency was associated with a *negativistic, malicious, and non-utilitarian* approach to behavior. By that, Cohen meant that delinquents possessed anti-middle class values, enjoyed being "bad," and engaged in behaviors with no meaningful purpose. These characteristics of delinquency, he said, needed explaining in any theory of delinquency. Cohen posited that the values of delinquency were transmitted through a delinquent subculture. The task was to explain the emergence of the delinquent subculture.

Cohen used the Mertonian scheme of a disorganized society where an unequal distribution of means existed. This inequality created problems for lower-class children, particularly when they entered school. Cohen theorized that the goal sought by almost everyone, adult and child alike, was *status*. Lower-class children tend to be unprepared when they enter school; middle-class children have already been to preschool, parents have already taught them how to behave (and compete) in school, and so forth. Problems also exist because schools are based on middle-class values, and children are evaluated according to a *middle-class measuring rod*. Lower-class children are relatively disadvantaged in gaining status in school and *status-deprivation* brings *frustration*.

The problem of what to do about this frustration ultimately results in the development of a subculture. Cohen used the Chicago School's symbolic interactionist approach and postulated that subcultures develop out of a collective need for a solution to a common problem. Lower-class children, experiencing the problem of status-deprivation, begin seeking a solution. This occurs individually at first. Later, as they recognize their common plight, the youths begin sharing their frustrations and tentative solutions. Over time these tentative solutions spread to more children and begin to be treated as standard solutions. Once enough children are involved, a subculture is formed. As long as lower-class children continue to experience status-deprivation in school, the subculture continues as a ready-made solution to their problems.

Cohen explained that the collective solution is a system of values in opposition to middle-class values. He described the opposition values as part of a psychological *reaction formation* process in which frustration from status-deprivation is resolved by a value-inversion. Once middle-class values are turned upside-down, the subculture becomes a delinquent one focused on negativistic, malicious, and non-utilitarian behavior. In this way, lower-class children can gain status in the delinquent subculture they have created.

Differential Opportunity Theory

Richard Cloward and Lloyd Ohlin also attempted a merger of the work of Sutherland and Merton. Their theory, published in a 1960 book titled *Delinquency and Opportunity: A Theory of Delinquent Gangs*, borrowed heavily from an earlier article written by Cloward. In that article Cloward extended Merton's notion of a legitimate opportunity structure (the societally approved means to reach the goals). He argued there was another opportunity structure in existence, but an illegal one (i.e., organized crime). In short, individuals without access to the legitimate means did not have to invent new means to reach their success-goals—those means existed. The problem was the degree to which individuals had access to those means (the *illegitimate opportunity structure*) as well.

Cloward and Ohlin attempted to reconcile the problem of access to a dual opportunity structure with the development of different types of gangs. As opposed to Cohen who described one general delinquent subculture, Cloward and Ohlin decided there were three subcultural forms of gangs: criminal, conflict, and retreatist. The form of gang subculture, they said, depended on (1) the type of opportunities available in the community and (2) the degree to which the two opportunity structures were *integrated* (shared similar interests). When both legitimate and illegitimate opportunity structures were in a community, and when they were well-integrated, gangs developed as a criminal subculture. The *criminal gang* served as a sort of apprenticeship training for "jobs" in the illegitimate opportunity structure. Surprisingly, such an integrated community exerted a great deal of control over the juveniles and violent behavior was kept to a minimum. It seems that neither conventional people nor organized crime wanted violence in the streets—it was bad for business and created poor living conditions.

A non-integrated community, or one in which the illegitimate opportunity structure was not available, precipitated a subculture with a *conflict gang*. Without the double control of both opportunity structures, delinquents had no particular reason to use the gang for apprenticeship training. Instead they used the gang for status and personal needs. This led to a subculture much like the one described by Cohen and a gang that fostered violent, unfocused activity.

The remaining form of gang subculture, the *retreatist gang*, developed when juveniles were "double failures." That is, those who were unsuccessful in both the legitimate and illegitimate structures. These gangs focused on drug use. Though they might engage in theft or other money-producing activities, their main purpose of the activity was to purchase drugs.

Focal Concern Theory

A final approach to the explanation of urban, gang delinquency came in 1958 from an anthropologist, Walter B. Miller. His theory was different from those above because he did not have intellectual ties with either the Chicago School or Mertonian strain theory. In fact, he went at the problem exactly as an anthropologist would—he decided to observe the way in which people live in lower-class urban areas. Miller's conclusions from these observations are at the heart of "focal concern" theory.

Contrary to views of lower-class values as being in opposition to middle-class values, Miller saw lower-class values as having developed from a long-term culture. The values were merely the result of cultural adaptation to living conditions in urban areas. Similar to culture conflict theory, Miller's theory stressed that lower-class values were legitimate in their own context. However, when lower-class youth came in contact with middle-class authorities, they could be defined as delinquent or criminal. Lower-class values, then, were simply in conflict with middle-class ones.

The lower-class areas Miller and his associates observed had households in which males were often absent. Therefore, Miller theorized that a male child had to escape the female-dominated household to find male role models. The gang filled this function and served as a place where young males could practice male roles and values. The essence of the lower-class value system, for males, can be characterized as emphasizing smartness, trouble, toughness, fate, autonomy, and excitement. All of these values contribute to delinquent behavior when viewed from the middle-class perspective. Thus, in following their own value systems and practicing the male role, young lower-class males will automatically come into conflict with larger society, and contact with law enforcement personnel will frequently result in a delinquent label.

Epilogue

Subculture theories lost popularity in the 1960s and 1970s. Reasons for this were: (1) different methods of determining who is delinquent, (2) the emergence of more radical versions of theory, and (3) the emergence of alternative conservative theories. With the "return" of gangs in the 1980s, however, interest in subculture theories appears to have revived, although that interest is no longer directly focused on the theories of the 1950s.

ENDNOTE

1   The term "strain" is used because these theories assume that problems in the way society is structured create a strain for certain groups, resulting in a push toward deviance. Thus, social disorganization creates social strain which creates deviance.

BIBLIOGRAPHY

Agnew, Robert (1992). "Foundation for a general strain theory of crime and delinquency," *Criminology* 30: 47-88.

Agnew, Robert (1989). "A longitudinal test of the revised strain theory," *Journal of Quantitative Criminology* 5: 373-87.

Agnew, Robert (1985). "A revised strain theory of delinquency," *Social Forces* 64: 151-67.

Bernard, Thomas J. (1987). "Testing structural strain theories," *Journal of Research in Crime and Delinquency* 24: 262-80.

Bordua, David J. (1962). "Some comments on theories of group delinquency," *Sociological Inquiry* 32: 245-60.

Bordua, David J. (1961). "Delinquent subcultures: Sociological interpretations of gang delinquency," *Annals of the American Academy of Political and Social Science* 338: 119-36.

Bordua, David J. (1960). *Sociological Theories and Their Implications for Juvenile Delinquency*. Facts and Facets, No. 2. Washington, DC: U.S. Government Printing Office.

Clinard, Marshall B. (1964). *Anomie and Deviant Behavior*. New York: Free Press.

Cloward, Richard A. (1959). "Illegitimate means, anomie, and deviant behavior," *American Sociological Review* 24: 164-76.

Cohen, Albert K. (1965). "The sociology of the deviant act: Anomie theory and beyond," *American Sociological Review* 30: 5-14.

Cohen, Albert K. (1958). "Research on delinquent subcultures," *Journal of Social Issues* 14: 20-37.

Cullen, Francis T. (1984). *Rethinking Crime and Deviance Theory: The Emergence of a Structuring Tradition*. Totowa, NJ: Rowman and Allanheld.

Dubin, Robert (1959). "Deviant behavior and social structure: Continuities in social theory," *American Sociological Review* 24: 147-64.

Durkheim, Emile (1897). *Suicide: A Study In Sociology*. New York: Free Press (reprinted and translated 1951).

Durkheim, Emile (1893). *The Division of Labor in Society*. New York: Free Press (reprinted and translated 1933).

Farnworth, Margaret and Michael Leiber (1989). "Strain theory revisited: Economic goals, educational means and delinquency," *American Sociological Review* 54: 263-74.

Harary, Frank (1966). "Merton revisited: A new classification for deviant behavior," *American Sociological Review* 31: 693-97.

Kitsuse, John I. and David C. Dietrick (1959). "Delinquent Boys: A critique," *American Sociological Review* 24: 208-15.

Kobrin, Solomon (1951). "The conflict of values in delinquency areas," *American Sociological Review* 16: 653-61.

Laub, John (1983). "Interview with Solomon Kobrin," in John Laub, *Criminology in the Making: An Oral History*. Boston: Northeastern University, 87-105.

Merton, Robert K. (1968). *Social Theory and Social Structure*, rev. and enlarged ed. New York: Free Press.

Merton, Robert K. (1964). "Anomie, anomia, and social interactions: Contexts of deviant behavior," in Marshall B. Clinard (ed.) *Anomie and Deviant Behavior*. New York: Free Press, 213-42.

Merton, Robert K. (1957). *Social Theory and Social Structure*, rev. ed. New York: Free Press.

Merton, Robert K. and M.F. Ashley-Montagu (1940). "Crime and the anthropologist," *American Anthropologist* 42: 384-408.

Messner, Steven F. and Richard Rosenfeld (1994). *Crime and the American Dream*. Belmont, CA: Wadsworth.

Schrag, Clarence C. (1962). "Delinquency and opportunity: Analysis of a theory," *Sociology and Social Research* 46: 167-75.

Robert King Merton (1910-   )

Merton was born in Philadelphia, Pennsylvania. He received an A.B. from Temple University in 1931 and an M.A. (1932) and Ph.D. in sociology in 1936 from Harvard University. Merton taught at Harvard University (1936-1939), Tulane University (1939-1941 and chair of the department 1940-1941), and Columbia University (1941-1979). He retired as University professor emeritus in 1979, continuing at Columbia as a special service professor for five more years.

Social Structure and Anomie*
Robert K. Merton

There persists a notable tendency in sociological theory to attribute the malfunctioning of social structure primarily to those of man's imperious biological drives which are not adequately restrained by social control. In this view, the social order is solely a device for "impulse management" and the "social processing" of tensions. These impulses which break through social control, be it noted, are held to be biologically derived. Nonconformity is assumed to be rooted in original nature.[1] Conformity is by implication the result of an utilitarian calculus or unreasoned conditioning. This point of view, whatever its other deficiencies, clearly begs one question. It provides no basis for determining the nonbiological conditions which induce deviations from prescribed patterns of conduct. In this paper, it will be suggested that certain phases of social structure generate the circumstances in which infringement of social codes constitutes a "normal" response.[2]

The conceptual scheme to be outlined is designed to provide a coherent, systematic approach to the study of sociocultural sources of deviate behavior. Our primary aim lies in discovering how some social structures *exert a definite pressure* upon certain persons in the society to engage in nonconformist rather than conformist conduct. The many ramifications of the scheme cannot all be discussed; the problems mentioned outnumber those explicitly treated.

Among the elements of social and cultural structure, two are important for our purposes. These are analytically separable although they merge imperceptibly in concrete situations. The first consists of cultur-

*Source: Robert K. Merton, 1938. "Social Structure and Anomie," *American Sociological Review* 3: 672-682. By permission of The American Sociological Association.

ally defined goals, purposes, and interests. It comprises a frame of aspirational reference. These goals are more or less integrated and involve varying degrees of prestige and sentiment. They constitute a basic, but not the exclusive, component of what Linton aptly has called "designs for group living." Some of these cultural aspirations are related to the original drives of man, but they are not determined by them. The second phase of the social structure defines, regulates, and controls the acceptable modes of achieving these goals. Every social group invariably couples its scale of desired ends with moral or institutional regulation of permissible and required procedures for attaining these ends. These regulatory norms and moral imperatives do not necessarily coincide with technical or efficiency norms. Many procedures which from the standpoint of *particular individuals* would be most efficient in securing desired values, e.g., illicit oil-stock schemes, theft, fraud, are ruled out of the institutional area of permitted conduct. The choice of expedients is limited by the institutional norms.

To say that these two elements, culture goals and institutional norms, operate jointly is not to say that the ranges of alternative behaviors and aims bear some constant relation to one another. The emphasis upon certain goals may vary independently of the degree of emphasis upon institutional means. There may develop a disproportionate, at times, a virtually exclusive, stress upon the value of specific goals, involving relatively slight concern with the institutionally appropriate modes of attaining these goals. The limiting case in this direction is reached when the range of alternative procedures is limited only by technical rather than institutional considerations. Any and all devices which promise attainment of the all important goal would be permitted in this hypothetical polar case.[3] This constitutes one type of cultural malintegration. A second polar type is found in groups where activities originally conceived as instrumental are transmuted into ends in themselves. The original purposes are forgotten and ritualistic adherence to institutionally prescribed conduct becomes virtually obsessive.[4] Stability is largely ensured while change is flouted. The range of alternative behaviors is severely limited. There develops a tradition-bound, sacred society characterized by neophobia. The occupational psychosis of the bureaucrat may be cited as a case in point. Finally, there are the intermediate types of groups where a balance between culture goals and institutional means is maintained. These are the significantly integrated and relatively stable, though changing, groups.

An effective equilibrium between the two phases of the social structure is maintained as long as satisfactions accrue to individuals who conform to both constraints, viz., satisfactions from the achievement of the goals and satisfactions emerging directly from the institutionally canalized modes of striving to attain these ends. Success, in such equilibrated cases, is twofold. Success is reckoned in terms of the product and in terms of the process, in terms of the outcome and in terms of activities.

Continuing satisfactions must derive from sheer participation in a competitive order as well as from eclipsing one's competitors if the order itself is to be sustained. The occasional sacrifices involved in institutionalized conduct must be compensated by socialized rewards. The distribution of statuses and roles through competition must be so organized that positive incentives for conformity to roles and adherence to status obligations are provided for *every position* within the distributive order. Aberrant conduct, therefore, may be viewed as a symptom of dissociation between culturally defined aspirations and socially structured means.

Of the types of groups which result from the independent variation of the two phases of the social structure, we shall be primarily concerned with the first, namely, that involving a disproportionate accent on goals. This statement must be recast in a proper perspective. In no group is there an absence of regulatory codes governing conduct, yet groups do vary in the degree to which these folkways, mores, and institutional controls are effectively integrated with the more diffuse goals which are part of the culture matrix. Emotional convictions may cluster about the complex of socially acclaimed ends, meanwhile shifting their support from the culturally defined implementation of these ends. As we shall see, certain aspects of the social structure may generate countermores and antisocial behavior precisely because of differential emphases on goals and regulations. In the extreme case, the latter may be so vitiated by the goal-emphasis that the range of behavior is limited only by considerations of technical expediency. The sole significant question then becomes, which available means is most efficient in netting the socially approved value?[5] The most technically feasible procedure, whether legitimate or not, is preferred to the institutionally prescribed conduct. As this process continues, the integration of the society becomes tenuous and anomie ensues.

Thus, in competitive athletics, when the aim of victory is shorn of its institutional trappings and success in contests becomes construed as "winning the game" rather than "winning through circumscribed modes of activity," a premium is implicitly set upon the use, of illegitimate but technically efficient means. The star of the opposing football team is surreptitiously slugged; the wrestler furtively incapacitates his opponent through ingenious but illicit techniques; university alumni covertly subsidize "students" whose talents are largely confined to the athletic field. The emphasis on the goal has so attenuated the satisfactions deriving from sheer participation in the competitive activity that these satisfactions are virtually confined to a successful outcome. Through the same process, tension generated by the desire to win in a poker game is relieved by successfully dealing oneself four aces, or, when the cult of success has become completely dominant, by sagaciously shuffling the cards in a game of solitaire. The faint twinge of uneasiness in the last instance and the surreptitious nature of public delicts indicate clearly that the institutional rules of the game are known to those who evade them, but that the emotional supports of these rules are largely vitiated by cultural exaggeration of the success-goal.[6] They are microcosmic images of the social macrocosm.

Of course, this process is not restricted to the realm of sport. The process whereby exaltation of the end generates a *literal demoralization,* i.e., a deinstitutionalization, of the means is one which characterizes many[7] groups in which the two phases of the social structure are not highly integrated. The extreme emphasis upon the accumulation of wealth as a symbol of success[8] in our own society militates against the completely effective control of institutionally regulated modes of acquiring a fortune.[9] Fraud, corruption, vice, crime, in short, the entire catalogue of proscribed behavior, becomes increasingly common when the emphasis on the culturally induced success-goal becomes divorced from a coordinated institutional emphasis. This observation is of crucial theoretical importance in examining the doctrine that antisocial behavior most frequently derives from biological drives breaking through the restraints imposed by society. The difference is one between a strictly utilitarian interpretation which conceives man's ends as random and an analysis which finds these ends deriving from the basic values of the culture.[10]

Our analysis can scarcely stop at this juncture. We must turn to other aspects of the social structure if we are to deal with the social genesis of the varying rates and types of deviate behavior characteristic of different societies. Thus far, we have sketched three ideal types of social orders constituted by distinctive patterns of relations between culture ends and means. Turning from these types of *culture patterning,* we find five logically possible, alternative modes of adjustment or adaptation by *individuals* within the culture-bearing society or group.[11] These are schematically presented in the following table, where (+) signifies "acceptance," (-) signifies "elimination" and (±) signifies "rejection and substitution of new goals and standards."

		Culture Goals	Institutionalized Means
I.	Conformity	+	+
II.	Innovation	+	-
III.	Ritualism	-	+
IV.	Retreatism	-	-
V.	Rebellion[12]	±	±

Our discussion of the relation between these alternative responses and other phases of the social structure must be prefaced by the observation that persons may shift from one alternative to other as they engage in different social activities. These categories refer to role adjustments in specific situations, not to personality in *toto*. To treat the development of this process in various spheres of conduct would introduce a complexity unmanageable within the confines of this paper. For this reason, we shall be concerned primarily with economic activity in the broad sense, "the production, exchange, distribution and consumption of goods and services" in our competitive society, wherein wealth has taken on a highly symbolic cast. Our task is to search out some of the factors which exert pressure upon individuals to engage in certain of these logically possible alternative responses. This choice, as we shall see, is far from random.

In every society, Adaptation I (conformity to both cultural goals and means) is the most common and widely diffused. Were this not so, the stability and continuity of the society could not be maintained. The mesh of expectancies which constitutes every social order is sustained by the modal behavior of its members falling within the first category. Conventional role behavior oriented toward the basic values of the group is the rule rather than the exception. It is this fact alone which permits us to speak of a human aggregate as comprising a group or society.

Conversely, Adaptation IV (rejection of goals and means) is the least common. Persons who "adjust" (or maladjust) in this fashion are, strictly speaking, in the society but not *of* it. Sociologically, these constitute the true "aliens." Not sharing the common frame of orientation, they can be included within the societal population merely in a fictional sense. In this category are *some* of the activities of psychotics, psychoneurotics, chronic autists, pariahs, outcasts, vagrants, vagabonds, tramps, chronic drunkards and drug addicts.[13] These have relinquished, in certain spheres of activity, the culturally defined goals, involving complete aim-inhibition in the polar case, and their adjustments are not in accord with institutional norms. This is not to say that in some cases the source of their behavioral adjustments is not in part the very social structure which they have in effect repudiated nor that their very existence within a social area does not constitute a problem for the socialized population.

This mode of "adjustment" occurs, as far as structural sources are concerned, when both the culture goals and institutionalized procedures have been assimilated thoroughly by the individual and imbued with affect and high positive value, but where those institutionalized procedures which promise a measure of successful attainment of the goals are not available to the individual. In such instances, there results a twofold mental conflict insofar as obligation for adopting institutional means conflicts with the pressure to resort to illegitimate means (which may attain the goal) and inasmuch as the individual is shut off from means which are both legitimate *and* effective. The competitive order is maintained, but the frustrated and handicapped individual who cannot cope with this order drops out. Defeatism, quietism and resignation are manifested in escape mechanisms which ultimately lead the individual to "escape" from the requirements of the society. It is an expedient which arises from continued failure to attain the goal by legitimate measures and from an inability to adopt the illegitimate route because of internalized prohibitions and institutionalized compulsives, *during which process the supreme value of the success-goal has as not yet been renounced*. The conflict is resolved by eliminating *both* precipitating elements, the goals and means. The escape is complete, the conflict is eliminated and the individual is asocialized.

Be it noted that where frustration derives from the inaccessibility of effective institutional means for attaining economic or any other type of highly valued "success," that Adaptations II, III and V (innovation, ritualism and rebellion) are also possible. The result will be determined by the particular personality, and thus, the *particular* cultural background, involved. Inadequate socialization will result in the innovation response whereby the conflict and frustration are eliminated by relinquishing the institutional means and retaining the success-aspiration; an extreme assimilation of institutional demands will lead to ritualism wherein the goal is dropped as beyond one's reach but conformity to the mores persists; and rebellion occurs when emancipation from the reigning standards, due to frustration or to marginalist perspectives, leads to the attempt to introduce a "new social order."

Our major concern is with the illegitimacy adjustment. This involves the use of conventionally proscribed but frequently effective means of attaining at least the simulacrum of culturally defined success—wealth, power, and the like. As we have seen, this adjustment occurs when the individual has assimilated the cultural emphasis on success without equally internalizing the morally prescribed norms governing means for its attainment. The question arises, Which phases of our social structure predispose toward this mode of adjustment? We may examine a concrete instance, effectively analyzed by Lohman,[14] which provides a clue to the answer. Lohman has shown that specialized areas of vice in the near north side of Chicago constitute a "normal" response to a situation where the cultural emphasis upon pecuniary success has been absorbed, but where there is little access to conventional and legitimate means for attaining such success. The conventional occupational opportunities of persons in this area are almost completely limited to manual labor. Given our cultural stigmatization of manual labor, and its correlate, the prestige of white collar work, it is clear that the result is a strain toward innovational practices. The limitation of opportunity to unskilled labor and the resultant low income cannot compete *in terms of conventional standards of achievement* with the high income from organized vice.

For our purposes, this situation involves two important features. First, such antisocial behavior is in a sense "called forth" by certain conventional values of the culture *and* by the class structure involving differential access to the approved opportunities for legitimate, prestige-bearing pursuit of the culture goals. The lack of high integration between the means-and-end elements of the cultural pattern and the particular class structure combine to favor a heightened frequency of antisocial conduct in such groups. The second consideration is of equal significance. Recourse to the first of the alternative responses, legitimate effort, is limited by the fact that actual advance toward desired success symbols through conventional channels is, despite our persisting open-class ideology,[15] relatively rare and difficult for those handicapped by little formal education and few economic resources. The dominant pressure of group standards of success is, therefore, on the gradual attenuation of legitimate, but by and large ineffective, strivings and the increasing use of illegitimate, but more or less effective, expedients of vice and crime. The cultural demands made on persons in this situation are incompatible. On the one hand, they are asked to orient their conduct toward the prospect of accumulating wealth and on the other, they are largely denied effective opportunities to do so institutionally. The consequences of such structural inconsistency are psychopathological personality, and/or antisocial conduct, and/or revolutionary activities. The equilibrium between culturally designated means and ends becomes highly unstable with the progressive emphasis on attaining the prestige-laden ends by any means whatsoever. Within this context, Capone represents the triumph of amoral intelligence over morally prescribed "failure," when the channels of vertical mobility are closed or narrowed[16] *in a society which places a high premium on economic affluence and social ascent for all its members.*[17]

This last qualification is of primary importance. It suggests that other phases of the social structure besides the extreme emphasis on pecuniary success, must be considered if we are to understand the social sources of antisocial behavior. A high frequency of deviate behavior is not generated simply by "lack of opportunity" or by this exaggerated pecuniary emphasis. A comparatively rigidified class structure, a feudalistic or caste order, may limit such opportunities far beyond the point which obtains in our society today. It is only when a system of cultural values extols, virtually above all else, certain *common* symbols of success *for the population at large* while its social structure rigorously restricts or completely eliminates access to approved modes of acquiring these symbols *for a considerable part of the same population,* that antisocial behavior ensues on a considerable scale. In other words, our egalitarian ideology denies by implication the existence of noncompeting groups and individuals in the pursuit of pecuniary success. The same body of success symbols is held to be desirable for all. These goals are held to *transcend class lines,* not to be bounded by them, yet the actual social organization is such that there exist class differentials in the accessibility of these *common* success symbols. Frustration and thwarted aspiration lead to the search for avenues of escape from a culturally induced intolerable situation; or unrelieved ambition may eventuate in illicit attempts to acquire the dominant values.[18] The American stress on pecuniary success and ambitiousness for all thus invites exaggerated anxieties, hostilities, neuroses, and antisocial behavior.

This theoretical analysis may go far toward explaining the varying correlations between crime and poverty.[19] Poverty is not an isolated variable. It is one in a complex of interdependent social and cultural variables. When viewed in such a context, it represents quite different states of affairs. Poverty as such, and consequent limitation of opportunity, are not sufficient to induce a conspicuously high rate of criminal behavior. Even the often mentioned "poverty in the midst of plenty" will not necessarily lead to this result. Only insofar as poverty and associated disadvantages in competition for the culture values approved for *all* members of the society is linked with the assimilation of a cultural emphasis on monetary accumulation as a symbol of success is antisocial conduct a "normal" outcome. Thus, poverty is less highly correlated with crime in southeastern Europe than in the United States. The possibilities of vertical mobility in these European areas would seem to be fewer than in this country, so that neither poverty *per se* nor its association with limited opportunity is sufficient to account for the varying correlations. It is only when the full configuration is considered, poverty, limited opportunity and a commonly shared system of success symbols, that we can explain the higher association between poverty and crime in our society than in others where rigidified class structure is coupled with *differential class symbols of achievement*. In societies such as our own, then, the pressure of prestige-bearing success tends to eliminate the effective social constraint over means employed to this end. "The-end-justifies-the-means" doctrine becomes a guiding tenet for action when the cultural structure unduly exalts the end and the social organization unduly limits possible recourse to approved means. Otherwise put, this notion and associated behavior reflect a lack of cultural coordination. In international relations, the effects of this lack of integration are notoriously apparent. An emphasis upon national power is not readily coordinated with an inept organization of legitimate, i.e., internationally defined and accepted, means for attaining this goal. The result is a tendency toward the abrogation of international law, treaties become scraps of paper, "undeclared warfare" serves as a technical evasion, the bombing of civilian populations is rationalized,[20] just as the same societal situation induces the same sway of illegitimacy among individuals.

The social order we have described necessarily produces this "strain toward dissolution." The pressure of such an order is upon outdoing one's competitors. The choice of means within the ambit of institutional control will persist as long as the sentiments supporting a competitive system, i.e., deriving from the possibility of outranking competitors and hence enjoying the favorable response of others, are distributed throughout the entire system of activities and are not confined merely to the final result. A stable social structure demands a balanced distribution of affect among its various segments. When there occurs a shift of emphasis from the satisfactions deriving from competition itself to almost exclusive concern with successful competition, the resultant stress leads to the breakdown of the regulatory structure.[21] With the resulting attenuation of the institutional imperatives, there occurs an approximation of the situation erroneously held by utilitarians to be typical of society generally wherein calculations of advantage and fear of punishment are the sole regulating agencies. In such situations, as Hobbes observed, force and fraud come to constitute the sole virtues in view of their relative efficiency in attaining goals,—which were for him, of course, not culturally derived.

It should be apparent that the foregoing discussion is not pitched on a moralistic plane. Whatever the sentiments of the writer or reader concerning the ethical desirability of coordinating the means-and-goals phases of the social structure, one must agree that lack of such coordination leads to anomie. Insofar as one of the most general functions of social organization is to provide a basis for calculability and regularity of behavior, it is increasingly limited in effectiveness as these elements of the structure become dissociated. At the extreme, predictability virtually disappears and what may be properly termed cultural chaos or anomie intervenes.

This statement, being brief, is also incomplete. It has not included an exhaustive treatment of the various structural elements which predispose toward one rather than another of the alternative responses open to individuals; it has neglected, but not denied the relevance of, the factors determining the specific incidence of these responses; it has not enumerated the various concrete responses which are constituted by combinations of specific values of the analytical variables; it has omitted, or included only by implication, any consideration of the social functions performed by illicit responses; it has not tested the full explanatory power of the analytical scheme by examining a large number of group variations in the frequency of deviate and conformist behavior; it has not adequately dealt with rebellious conduct which seeks to refashion the social framework radically; it has not examined the relevance of cultural conflict for an analysis of culture-goal and institutional-means malintegration. It is suggested that these and related problems may be profitably analyzed by this scheme.

ENDNOTES

1   E.g., Ernest Jones, *Social Aspects of Psychoanalysis*, 28, London, 1924. If the Freudian notion is a variety of the "original sin" dogma, then the interpretation advanced in this paper may be called the doctrine of "socially derived sin."

2   "Normal" in the sense of a culturally oriented, if not approved, response. This statement does not deny the relevance of biological and personality differences which may be significantly involved in the *incidence* of deviate conduct. Our focus of interest is the social and cultural matrix; hence we abstract from other factors. It is in this sense, I take it, that James S. Plant speaks of the "normal reaction of normal people to abnormal conditions." See his *Personality and the Cultural Pattern*, 248, New York, 1937.

3   Contemporary American culture has been said to tend in this direction. See Andre Siegfried, *America Comes of Age*, 26-37, New York, 1927. The alleged extreme (?) emphasis on the goals of monetary success and material prosperity leads to dominant concern with techno-

logical and social instruments designed to produce the desired result, inasmuch as institutional controls become of secondary importance. In such a situation, innovation flourishes as the *range of means* employed is broadened. In a sense, then, there occurs the paradoxical emergence of "materialists" from an "idealistic" orientation. C.f. Durkheim's analysis of the cultural conditions which predispose toward crime and innovation, both of which are aimed toward efficiency, not moral norms. Durkheim was one of the first to see that "contrairement aux idees courantes le criminel n'apparait plus comme un etre radicalement insociable, comme une sorte d'element parasitaire, de corps etranger et inassimilable, introduit au sein de la societe; c'est un agent regulier de la vie sociale." See *Les Regles de la Methode Sociologique*, 86-89, Paris, 1927.

4   Such ritualism may be associated with a mythology which rationalizes these actions so that they appear to retain their status as means, but the dominant pressure is in the direction of strict ritualistic conformity, irrespective of such rationalizations. In this sense, ritual has proceeded farthest when such rationalizations are not even called forth.

5   In this connection, one may see the relevance of Elton Mayo's paraphrase of the title of Tawney's well known book. "Actually the problem is *not that of the sickness of an acquisitive society; it is that of the acquisitiveness of a sick society." Human Problems of an Industrial Civilization*, 153, New York, 1933. Mayo deals with the process through which wealth comes to be a symbol of social achievement. He sees this as arising from a state of anomie. We are considering the unintegrated monetary-success goal as an element in producing anomie. A complete analysis would involve both phases of this system of interdependent variables.

6   It is unlikely that interiorized norms are completely eliminated. Whatever residuum persists will induce personality tensions and conflict. The process involves a certain degree of ambivalence. A manifest rejection of the institutional norms is coupled with some latent retention of their emotional correlates. "Guilt feelings," "sense of sin," "pangs of conscience" are obvious manifestations of this unrelieved tension; symbolic adherence to the nominally repudiated values or rationalizations constitute a more subtle variety of tensional release.

7   "Many," and not all, unintegrated groups, for the reason already mentioned. In groups where the primary emphasis shifts to institutional means, i.e., when the range of alternatives is very limited, the outcome is a type of ritualism rather than anomie.

8   Money has several peculiarities which render it particularly apt to become a symbol of prestige divorced from institutional controls. As Simmel emphasized, money is highly abstract and impersonal. However acquired, through fraud or institutionally, it can be used to purchase the same goods and services. The anonymity of metropolitan culture, in conjunction with this peculiarity of money, permits wealth, the sources which may be unknown to the community in which the plutocrat lives, to serve as a symbol of status.

9   The emphasis upon wealth as a success symbol is possibly reflected in the use of the term "fortune" to refer to a stock of accumulated wealth. This meaning becomes common in the late sixteenth century (Spenser and Shakespeare). A similar usage of the Latin *fortuna* comes into prominence during the first century B.C. Both these periods were marked by the rise to prestige and power of the "bourgeoisie."

10   See Kingsley Davis, "Mental Hygiene and the Class Structure," *Psychiatry,* 1928, I, esp. 62-63; Talcott Parsons, *The Structure of Social Action*, 59-60, New York, 1937.

11   This is a level intermediate between the two planes distinguished by Edward Sapir; namely culture patterns and personal habit systems. See his "Contribution of Psychiatry to an Understanding of Behavior in Society" *Amer. J. Sociol.,* 1937, 42:862-70.

12   This fifth alternative is on a plane clearly different from that of the others. It represents a *transitional* response which seeks to *institutionalize* new procedures oriented toward revamped cultural goals shared by the members of the society. It thus involves efforts to *change* the existing structure rather than to perform accommodative actions *within* this structure and introduces additional problems with which we are not at the moment concerned.

13   Obviously, this is an elliptical statement. These individuals may maintain some orientation to the values of their particular differentiated groupings within the larger society or, in part, of the conventional society itself. Insofar as they do so, their conduct cannot be classified in

the "passive rejection" category (IV). Nels Anderson's description of the behavior and attitudes of the bum, for example, can readily be recast in terms of our analytical scheme. See *The Hobo*, 93-98, *et passim*, Chicago, 1923.

14 Joseph D. Lohman, "The Participant Observer in Community Studies," *Amer. Sociol. Rev.*, 1937, 2:890-98.

15 The shifting historical role of this ideology is a profitable subject for exploration. The "office-boy-to-president" stereotype was once in approximate accord with the facts. Such vertical mobility was probably more common then than now, when the class structure is more rigid. (See the following note.) The ideology largely persists, however, possibly because it still performs a useful function for maintaining the *status quo*. For insofar as it is accepted by the "masses," it constitutes a useful sop for those who might rebel against the entire structure, were this consoling hope removed. This ideology now serves to lessen the probability of Adaptation V. In short, the role of this notion has changed from that of an approximately valid empirical theorem to that of an ideology, in Mannheim's sense.

16 There is a growing body of evidence, though none of it is clearly conclusive, to the effect that our class structure is becoming rigidified and that vertical mobility is declining. Taussig and Joslyn found that American business leaders are being *increasingly* recruited from the upper ranks of our society. The Lynds have also found a "diminished chance to get ahead" for the working classes in Middletown. Manifestly, these objective changes are not alone significant; the individual's subjective evaluation of the situation is a major determinant of the response. The extent to which this change in opportunity for social mobility has been recognized by the least advantaged classes is still conjectural, although the Lynds present some suggestive materials. The writer suggests that a case in point is the increasing frequency of cartoons which observe in a tragi-comic vein that "my old man says everybody can't be President. He says if ya can get three days a week steady on W.P.A. work ya ain't doin' so bad either." See F.W. Taussig and C.S. Joslyn, *American Business Leaders*, New York, 1932; R.S. and H.M. Lynd, *Middletown in Transition*, 67 ff., chap. 12, New York, 1937.

17 The role of the Negro in this respect is of considerable theoretical interest. Certain elements of the Negro population have assimilated the dominant caste's values of pecuniary success and social advancement, but they also recognize that social ascent is at present restricted to their own caste almost exclusively. The pressures upon the Negro which would otherwise derive from the structural inconsistencies we have noticed are hence not identical with those upon lower-class whites. See Kingsley Davis, *op. cit.*, 63; John Dollard, *Caste and Class In a Southern Town*, 66 ff., New Haven, 1936; Donald Young, *American Minority Peoples*, 581, New York, 1932.

18 The psychical coordinates of these processes have been partly established by the experimental evidence concerning *Anspruchsniveaus* and levels of performance. See Kurt Lewin, Vorsatz, Willie und Bedurfnis, Berlin, 1926; N.F. Hoppe, "Erfolg und Misserfolg," *Psychol. Forschung*, 1930, 14:1-63; Jerome D. Frank, "Individual Differences in Certain Aspects of the Level of Aspiration," *Amer. J. Psychol.*, 1935, 47: 119-28.

19 Standard criminology texts summarize the data in this field. Our scheme of analysis may serve to resolve some of the theoretical contradictions which P.A. Sorokin indicates. For example, "not everywhere nor always do the poor show a greater proportion of crime . . . many poorer countries have had less crime than the richer countries . . . The [economic] improvement in the second half of the nineteenth century, and the beginning of the twentieth, has not been followed by a decrease of crime." See his *Contemporary Sociological Theories*, 560-61, New York, 1928. The crucial point is, however, that poverty has varying social significance in different social structures, as we shall see. Hence, one would not expect a linear correlation between crime and poverty.

20 See M.W. Royse, *Aerial Bombardment and the International Regulation of War*, New York, 1928.

21 Since our primary concern is with the socio-cultural aspects of this problem, the psychological correlates have been only implicitly considered. See Karen Horney, The Neurotic Personality of Our Time, New York, 1937, for a psychological discussion of this process.

Albert Kircidel Cohen (1918-   )

Cohen was born in Boston, Massachusetts. He was educated at Harvard University (B.A. in sociology, 1939; Ph.D. in sociology, 1951) and Indiana University (M.A. in sociology, 1949). Cohen taught at Indiana University (sociology) from 1947-1965. In 1965, he moved to the sociology department at the University of Connecticut and is now retired as professor emeritus.

Delinquent Boys*
Albert K. Cohen

THE CONTENT OF THE DELINQUENT SUBCULTURE

THE COMMON EXPRESSION, "juvenile crime," has unfortunate and misleading connotations. It suggests that we have two kinds of criminals, young and old, but only one kind of crime. It suggests that crime has its meanings and its motives which are much the same for young and old; that the young differ from the old as the apprentice and the master differ at the same trade; that we distinguish the young from the old only because the young are less "set in their ways," less "confirmed" in the same criminal habits, more amenable to treatment and more deserving, because of their tender age, of special consideration.

The problem of the relationship between juvenile delinquency and adult crime has many facets. To what extent are the offenses of children and adults distributed among the same legal categories, "burglary," "larceny," "vehicletaking," and so forth? To what extent, even when the offenses are legally identical, do these acts have the same meaning for children and adults? To what extent are the careers of adult criminals continuations of careers of juvenile delinquency? We cannot solve these problems here, but we want to emphasize the danger of making facile and unproven assumptions. If we assume that "crime is crime," that child and adult criminals are practitioners of the same trade, and if our assumptions are false, then the road to error is wide and clear. Easily and unconsciously, we may impute a whole host of notions concerning the nature of crime and its causes, derived from our knowledge and fancies about adult crime, to a large realm of behavior to which these notions are irrelevant. It is better to make no such assumptions; it is better to look at juvenile delinquency with a fresh eye and try to explain what we see.

What we see when we look at the delinquent subculture (and we must not even assume that this describes *all juvenile crime*) is that it is *non-utilitarian, malicious,* and *negativistic.*

We usually assume that when people steal things, they steal because they want them. They may want them because they can eat them, wear them or otherwise use them; or because they can sell them; or even—if we are given to a psychoanalytic turn of mind—because on some deep symbolic level they substitute or stand for something unconsciously desired but forbidden. All of these explanations have this in common, that they assume that the stealing is a means to an end, namely, the possession of some object of value, and that it is, in this sense, rational and "utilitarian." However, the fact cannot be blinked—and this fact is of crucial importance in defining our problem—that much gang stealing has no such motivation at all. Even where the value of the object stolen is itself a motivating consideration, the stolen sweets are often sweeter than those acquired by more legitimate and prosaic means. In homelier language, stealing "for the hell of it" and apart from considerations of gain and profit is a valued activity to which attaches glory, prowess, and profound satisfaction. There is no accounting in rational and utilitarian terms for the effort expended and the danger run in stealing things which are often discarded, destroyed or casually given away. A group of boys enters a store where each takes a hat, a ball or a light bulb. They then move on to another store where these things are covertly exchanged for like articles. Then they move on to other stores to continue the game indefinitely. They steal a basket of peaches, desultorily munch on a few of them and leave the rest to spoil. They steal clothes they cannot wear and toys they will not use. Unquestionably, most delinquents are from the more "needy" and "underprivileged" classes, and unquestionably many things are stolen because they are intrinsically valued. However, a humane and compassionate regard for their economic disabilities should not blind us to the fact that stealing is not merely an alternative means to the acquisition of objects otherwise difficult of attainment.[1]

Can we then account for this stealing by simply describing it as another form of recreation, play or sport? Surely it is that, but why is this form of play so attractive to some and so unappealing to others? Mountain climbing, chess, pinball, number pools and bingo are also different kinds of recreation. Each of us, child or adult, can choose from a host of alternative means for satisfying our common "need" for recreation. But every choice expresses a preference, and every preference reflects something about the chooser or his circumstances that endows the object of his choice with some special quality or virtue. The choice is not self-explanatory nor is it arbitrary or random. Each form of recreation is distributed in a characteristic way among the age, sex and social class sectors of our population. The explanation of these distributions and of the way they change is often puzzling, sometimes fascinating and rarely platitudinous.

By the same logic, it is an imperfect answer to our problem to say: "Stealing is but another way of satisfying the universal desire for status." Nothing is more obvious from numberless case histories of subcultural delinquents that they steal to achieve recognition and to avoid isolation or opprobrium. This is an important insight and part of the foundation on which we shall build. But the question still haunts us: "Why is stealing a claim to status in one group and a degrading blot in another?"

If stealing itself is not motivated by rational, utilitarian considerations, still less are the manifold other activities which constitute the delinquent's repertoire. Throughout there is a kind of *malice* apparent, an enjoyment in the discomfiture of others, a delight in the defiance of taboos itself. Thrasher quotes one gang delinquent:

> We did all kinds of dirty tricks for fun. We'd see a sign, "Please keep the streets clean," but we'd tear it down and say, "We don't feel like keeping it clean." One day we put a can of glue in the engine of a man's car. We would always tear things down. That would make us laugh and feel good, to have so many jokes.[2]

The gang exhibits this gratuitous hostility toward nongang peers as well as adults. Apart from its more dramatic manifestations in the form of gang wars, there is keen delight in terrorizing "good" children, in driving them from playgrounds and gyms for which the gang itself may have little use, and in general in making themselves obnoxious to the virtuous. The same spirit is evident in playing hookey and in misbehavior in school. The teacher and her rules are not merely something onerous to be evaded. They are to be *flouted*. There is an element of active spite and malice, contempt and ridicule, challenge and defiance, exquisitely symbolized, in an incident described to the writer by Mr. Henry D. McKay, of defecating on the teacher's desk.[3]

All this suggests also the intention of our term "negativistic." The delinquent subculture is not only a set of rules, a design for living which is different from or indifferent to or even in conflict with the norms of the "respectable" adult society. It would appear at least plausible that it is defined by its "negative polarity" to those norms. That is, the delinquent subculture takes its norms from the larger culture but turns them upside down. The delinquent's conduct is right, by the standards of his subculture, precisely *because* it is wrong by the norms of the larger culture.[4] "Malicious" and "negativistic" are foreign to the delinquent's vocabulary but he will often assure us, sometimes ruefully, sometimes with a touch of glee or even pride, that he is "just plain mean."

In describing what might be called the "spirit" of the delinquent culture, we have suggested also its *versatility*. Of the "antisocial" activities of the delinquent gangs, stealing, of course, looms largest. Stealing itself can be, and for the gang usually is, a diversified occupation. It may steal milk bottles, candy, fruit, pencils, sports equipment and cars; it may steal from drunks, homes, stores, schools and filling stations. No gang runs the whole gamut but neither is it likely to "specialize" as do many adult criminal gangs and "solitary" delinquents. More to our point, however, is the fact that stealing tends to go hand-in-hand with "other property offenses," "malicious mischief," "vandalism," "trespass," and truancy. This quality of versatility and the fusion of versatility and malice are manifest in the following quotation:

> We would get some milk bottles in front of the grocery store and break them in somebody's hallway. Then we would break windows or get some garbage cans and throw them down someone's front stairs. After doing all this dirty work and running through alleys and yards, we'd go over to a grocery store. There, some of the boys would hide in a hallway while I would get a basket of grapes. When the man came after me, why the boys would jump out of their places and each grab a basket of grapes.[5]

Dozens of young offenders, after relating to the writer this delinquent episode and that, have summarized: "I guess we was just ornery." A generalized, diversified, protean "orneriness," not this or that specialized delinquent pursuit seems best to describe the vocation of the delinquent gang.[6]

Another characteristic of the subculture of the delinquent gang is short-run *hedonism*. There is little interest in long-run goals, in planning activities and budgeting time, or in activities involving knowledge and skills to be acquired only through practice, deliberation and study. The members of the gang typically congregate, with no specific activity in mind, at some street corner, candy store or other regular rendezvous. They "hang around," "roughhousing," "chewing the fat," and "waiting for something to turn up." They may respond impulsively to somebody's suggestion to play ball, go swimming, engage in some sort of mischief, or do something else that offers excitement. They do not take kindly to organized and supervised recreation, which subjects them to a regime of schedules and impersonal rules. They are impatient, impetuous and out for "fun," with little heed to the remoter gains and costs. It is to be noted that this short-run hedonism is not inherently delinquent and indeed it would be a serious error to think of the delinquent gang as dedicated solely to the cultivation of juvenile crime. Even in the most seriously delinquent gang only a small fraction of the "fun" is specifically and intrinsically delinquent. Furthermore, short-run hedonism is not characteristic of delinquent groups alone. On the contrary, it is common throughout the social class from which delinquents characteristically come. However, in the delinquent gang it reaches its finest flower. It is the fabric, as it were, of which delinquency is the most brilliant and spectacular thread.[7]

Another characteristic not peculiar to the delinquent gang but a conspicuous ingredient of its culture is an emphasis on *group autonomy*, or intolerance of restraint except from the informal pressures within the group itself. Relations with gang members tend to be intensely solidary and imperious. Relations with other groups tend to be indifferent, hostile or rebellious. Gang members are unusually resistant to the efforts of home, school and other agencies to regulate, not only their delinquent activities, but any activities carried on within the group, and to efforts to compete with the gang for the time and other resources of its members. It may be argued that the resistance of gang members to the authority of the home may not be a result of their membership in gangs but that membership in gangs, on the contrary, is a result of ineffective family supervision, the breakdown of parental authority and the hostility of the child toward the parents; in short, that the delinquent gang recruits members who have already achieved autonomy. Certainly a previous breakdown in family controls facilitates recruitment into delinquent gangs. But we are not speaking of the autonomy, the emancipation of *individuals*. It is not the individual delinquent but the gang that is autonomous. For many of our subcultural delinquents the claims of the home are very real and very compelling. The point is that the gang is a separate, distinct and often irresistible focus of attraction, loyalty and solidarity. The claims of the home versus the claims of the gang may present a real dilemma, and in such cases the breakdown of family controls is as much a casualty as a cause of gang membership.[8] . . .

HOW SUBCULTURAL SOLUTIONS ARISE

NOW WE confront a dilemma and a paradox. We have seen how difficult it is for the individual to cut loose from the culture models in his milieu, how his dependence upon his fellows compels him to seek conformity and to avoid innovation. But these models and precedents which we call the surrounding culture are ways in which other people think and other people act, and these other people are likewise constrained by models in *their* milieux. *These models themselves, however, continually change.* How is it possible for cultural innovations to emerge while each of the participants in the culture is so powerfully motivated to conform to what is already established? This is the central theoretical problem of this book.

The crucial condition for the emergence of new cultural forms is the existence, *in effective interaction with one another, of a number of actors with similar problems of adjustment.* These may be the entire membership of a group or only certain members, similarly circumstanced, within the group. Among the conceivable solutions to their problems may be one which is not yet embodied in action and which does not therefore exist as a cultural model. This solution, except for the fact that it does not already carry the social criteria of validity and promise the social rewards of consensus, might well answer more neatly to the problems of this group and appeal to its members more effectively than any of the solutions already institutionalized. For each participant, this solution would be adjustive and adequately motivated provided that he could anticipate a simultaneous and corresponding transformation in the frames of reference of his fellows. Each would welcome a sign from the others that a new departure in this direction would receive approval and support. But how does one *know* whether a gesture toward innovation will strike a responsive and sympathetic chord in others or whether it will elicit hostility, ridicule and punishment? *Potential* concurrence is always problematical and innovation or the impulse to innovate a stimulus for anxiety.

The paradox is resolved when the innovation is broached in such a manner as to elicit from others reactions suggesting their receptivity; and when, at the same time, the innovation occurs by increments so small, tentative and ambiguous as to permit the actor to retreat, if the signs be unfavorable, without having become identified with an unpopular position. Perhaps all social actions have, in addition to their instrumental, communicative and expressive functions, this quality of being *exploratory gestures.* For the actor with problems of adjustment which cannot be resolved within the frame of reference of the established culture, each response of the other to what the actor says and does is a clue to the directions in which change may proceed further in a way congenial to the other and to the direction in which change will lack social support. And if the probing gesture is motivated by tensions common to other participants it is likely to initiate a process of *mutual* exploration and *joint* elaboration of a new solution. My exploratory gesture functions as a cue to you; your exploratory gesture as a cue to me. By a casual, semi-serious, noncommittal or tangential remark I may stick my neck out just a little way, but I will quickly withdraw it unless you, by some sign of affirmation, stick *yours* out. I will permit myself to become progressively committed but only as others, by some visible sign, become likewise committed. The final product, to which we are jointly committed, is likely to be a compromise formation of all the participants to what we may call a cultural process, a formation perhaps unanticipated by any of them. Each actor may contribute something directly to the growing product, but he may also contribute indirectly by encouraging others to advance, inducing them to retreat, and suggesting new avenues to be explored. The product cannot be ascribed to any one of the participants; it is a real "emergent" on a group level.

We may think of this process as one of mutual conversion. The important thing to remember is that we do not first convert ourselves and then others. The acceptability of an idea to oneself depends upon its acceptability to others. Converting the other is part of the process of converting oneself. . .

. . . The emergence of these "group standards" of this shared frame of reference, is the emergence of a new subculture. It is cultural because each actor's participation in this system of norms is influenced by his perception of the same norms in other actors. It is *sub*cultural because the norms are shared only among those actors who stand somehow to profit from them and who find in one another a sympathetic moral climate within which these norms may come to fruition and persist. In this fashion culture is continually being created, re-created and modified wherever individuals sense in one another like needs, generated by like circumstances, not shared generally in the larger social system. Once established, such a subcultural system may persist, but not by sheer inertia. It may achieve a life which outlasts that of the individuals who participated in its creation, but only so long as it continues to serve the needs of those who succeed its creators.

SUBCULTURAL SOLUTIONS
TO STATUS PROBLEMS

ONE VARIANT of this cultural process interests us especially because it provides the model for our explanation of the delinquent subculture. Status problems are problems of achieving respect in the eyes of one's fellows. Our ability to achieve status depends upon the criteria of status applied by our fellows, that is, the standards or norms they go by in evaluating people. These criteria are an aspect of their cultural frames of reference. If we lack the characteristics or capacities which give status in terms of these criteria, we are beset by one of the most typical and yet distressing of human problems of adjustment. One solution is for individuals who share such problems to gravitate toward one another and jointly to establish new norms, new criteria of status which define as meritorious the characteristics they *do* posses, the kinds of conduct of which they *are* capable. It is clearly necessary for each participant, if the innovation is to solve his status problem, that these new criteria be shared with others, that the solution be a group and not a private solution. If he "goes it alone" he succeeds only in further estranging himself from his fellows. Such new status criteria would represent new subcultural values different from or even antithetical to those of the larger social system. . .

WHAT THE DELINQUENT SUBCULTURE HAS TO OFFER

THE DELINQUENT subculture, we suggest, is a way of dealing with the problems of adjustment we have described. These problems are chiefly status problems: certain children are denied status in the respectable society because they cannot meet the criteria of the respectable status system. The delinquent subculture deals with these problems by providing criteria of status which these children *can* meet. . . .

. . . What does the delinquent response have to offer? Let us be clear, first, about what this response is and how it differs from the stable corner-boy response. The hallmark of the delinquent subculture is the explicit and wholesale repudiation of middle-class standards and the adoption of their very antithesis. The *corner-boy culture is not specifically delinquent.* Where it leads to behavior which may be defined as delinquent, *e.g.,* truancy, it does so not because nonconformity to middle-class norms *defines* conformity to corner-boy norms but because conformity to middle-class norms *interferes with* conformity to corner-boy norms. The corner-boy plays truant because he does not like school, because he wishes to escape from a dull and unrewarding and perhaps humiliating situation. But truancy is not defined as intrinsically valuable and statusgiving. The member of the delinquent subculture plays truant because "good" middle-class (and working-class) children do not play truant. Corner-boy resistance to being herded and marshalled by middle-class figures is not the same as the delinquent's flouting and jeering of those middle-class figures and active ridicule of those who submit. The corner-boy's ethic of reciprocity, his quasi-communal attitude toward the property of in-group members, is shared by the delinquent. But this ethic of reciprocity does not sanction the deliberate and "malicious" violation of the property rights of persons outside the in-group. We have observed that the differences between the corner-boy and the college-boy or middle-class culture are profound but that in many ways they are profound differences in emphasis. We have remarked that the corner-boy culture does not so much repudiate the value of many middle-class achievements as it emphasizes certain other values which make such achievements improbable. In short, the corner-boy culture temporizes with middle-class morality; the full-fledged delinquent subculture does not.

It is precisely here, we suggest, in the refusal to temporize, that the appeal of the delinquent subculture lies. Let us recall that it is characteristically American, not specifically working-class or middle-class, to measure oneself against the widest possible status universe, to seek status against "all comers," to be "as good as" or "better than" anybody—anybody, that is, within one's own age and sex category. As long as the working-class corner-boy clings to a version, however attenuated and adulterated, of the middle-class culture, he must recognize his inferiority to working-class and middle-class college boys. The delinquent subculture, on the other hand, permits no ambiguity of the status of the delinquent relative to that of anybody else. In terms of the norms of the delinquent subculture, defined by its negative polarity to the respectable status system, the delinquent's very nonconformity to middle-class standards sets him above the most exemplary college boy.

Another important function of the delinquent subculture is the legitimation of aggression. We surmise that a certain amount of hostility is generated among working-class children against middle-class persons, with their airs of superiority, disdain or condescension and against middle-class norms, which are, in a sense, the cause of their status-frustration. To infer inclinations to aggression from the existence of frustration is hazardous; we know that aggression is not an inevitable and not the only consequence of frustration. So here too we must feel our way with caution. Ideally, we should like to see systematic research, probably employing "depth interview" and "projective" techniques, to get at the relationship between status position and aggressive dispositions toward the rules which determine status and toward persons variously distributed in the status hierarchy. Nevertheless, despite our imperfect knowledge of these things, we would be blind if we failed to recognize that bitterness, hostility and jealousy and all sorts of retributive fantasies are among the most common and typically human responses to public humiliation. However, for the child who temporizes with middle-class morality, overt aggression and even the conscious recognition of his own hostile impulses are inhibited, for he acknowledges the *legitimacy* of the rules in terms of which he is stigmatized. For the child who breaks clean with middle-class morality, on the other hand, there are no moral inhibitions on the free expression of aggression against the sources of his frustration. Moreover, the connection we suggest between status-frustration and the aggressiveness of the delinquent subculture seems to us more plausible than many frustration-aggression hypotheses because it involves no assumptions about obscure and dubious "displacement" of aggression against "substitute" targets. The target in this case is the manifest cause of the status problem.

It seems to us that the mechanism of "reaction-formation" should also play a part here. We have made much of the corner-boy's basic ambivalence, his uneasy acknowledgement, while he lives by the standards of his cornerboy culture, of the legitimacy of college-boy standards. May we assume that when the delinquent seeks to obtain unequivocal status by repudiating, once and for all, the norms of the college-boy culture, these norms really undergo total extinction? Or do they, perhaps, linger on, underground, as it were, repressed, unacknowledged but an everpresent threat to the adjustment which has been achieved at no small cost? There is much evidence from clinical psychology that moral norms, once effectively internalized, are not lightly thrust aside or extinguished. If a new moral order is involved which offers a more satisfactory solution to one's life problems, the old order usually continues to press for recognition, but if this recognition is granted, the applecart is upset. The symptom of this obscurely felt, ever-present threat is clinically known as "anxiety," and the literature of psychiatry is rich with devices for combatting this anxiety, this threat to a hard-won victory. One such device is reaction-formation. Its hallmark is an "exaggerated," "disproportionate," "abnormal" intensity of response, "inappropriate" to the stimulus which seems to elicit it. The unintelligibility of the response, the "overreaction," becomes intelligible when we see that it has the function of reassuring the actor against an inner threat to his defenses as well as the function of meeting an external situation on its own terms. Thus we have the mother who "compulsively" showers "inordinate" affection upon a child to reassure herself against her latent hostility and we have the male adolescent whose awkward and immoderate masculinity reflects a basic insecurity about his own sex role. In like manner, we would expect the delinquent boy who, after all, has been socialized in a society dominated by a middle-class morality and who can never quite escape the blandishments of middle-class society, to seek to maintain his safeguards against seduction. Reaction-formation, in his case, should take the form of an "irrational," "malicious," "unaccountable" hostility to the enemy within the gates as well as without: the norms of the respectable middle-class society.[9]

If our reasoning is correct, it should throw some light upon the peculiar quality of "property delinquency" in the delinquent subculture. We have already seen how the rewardingness of a college-boy and middle-class way of life depends, to a great extent, upon general respect for property rights. In an urban society, in particular, the possession and display of property are the most ready and public badges of reputable social class status and are, for that reason, extraordinarily ego-involved. That property actually is a reward for middle-class morality is in part only a plausible fiction, but in general there is certainly a relationship between the practice of that morality and the possession of property. The middle-classes have, then, a strong interest in scrupulous regard for property rights, not only because property is "intrinsically" valuable but because the full enjoyment of their status requires that status be readily recognizable and therefore that property adhere to those who earn it. The cavalier misappropriation or destruction of property, therefore, is not only a diversion or diminution of wealth; it is an attack on the middle-class where their egos are most vulnerable. Group stealing, institutionalized in the delinquent subculture, is not just a way of *getting* something. It is a means that is the antithesis of sober and diligent "labour in a calling." It expresses contempt for a way of life by making its opposite a criterion of status. Money and other valuables are not, as such, despised by the delinquent. For the delinquent and the non-delinquent alike, money is a most glamorous and efficient means to a variety of ends and one cannot have too much of it. But, in the delinquent subculture, the stolen dollar has an odor of sanctity that does not attach to the dollar saved or the dollar earned.

This delinquent system of values and way of life does its job of problem-solving most effectively when it is adopted as a group solution. We have stressed in our chapter on the general theory of subcultures that the efficacy of a given change in values as a solution and therefore the motivation to such a change depends heavily upon the availability of "reference groups" within which the "deviant values" are already institutionalized, or whose members would stand to profit from such a system of deviant values if each were assured of the support and concurrence of the others. So it is with delinquency. We do not suggest that joining in the creation or perpetuation of a delinquent subculture is the only road to delinquency. We do believe, however, that for most delinquents delinquency would not be available as a response were it not socially legitimized and given a kind of respectability, albeit by a restricted community of fellow-adventurers. In this respect, the adoption of delinquency is like the adoption of the practice of appearing at the office in open-collar and shirt sleeves. Is it much more comfortable, is it more sensible than the full regalia? Is it neat? Is it dignified? The arguments in the affirmative will appear much more forceful if the practice is already established in one's milieu or if one senses that others are prepared to go along if someone makes the first tentative gestures. Indeed, to many of those who sweat and chafe in ties and jackets, the possibility of an alternative may not even occur until they discover that it has been adopted by their colleagues.

This way of looking at delinquency suggests an answer to a certain paradox. Countless mothers have protested that their "Johnny" was a good boy until he fell in with a certain bunch. But the mothers of each of Johnny's companions hold the same view with respect to their own offspring. It is conceivable and even probable that some of these mothers are naive, that one or more of these youngsters are "rotten apples" who infected the others. We suggest, however, that all of the mothers may be right, that there is a certain chemistry in the group situation itself which engenders that which was not there before, that group interaction is a sort of catalyst which releases potentialities not otherwise visible. This is especially true when we are dealing with a problem of status-frustration. Status, by definition, is a grant of respect from others. A new system of norms, which measures status by criteria which one can meet, is of no value unless others are prepared to apply those criteria, and others are not likely to do so unless one is prepared to reciprocate.[10]

We have referred to a lingering ambivalence in the delinquent's own value system, an ambivalence which threatens the adjustment he has achieved and which is met through the mechanism of reaction-formation. The delinquent may have to contend with another ambivalence, in the area of his status sources. The delinquent subculture offers him status *as against* other children of whatever social level, but it offers him this status *in the eyes of* his fellow delinquents only. To the extent that there remains a desire for recognition from groups whose respect has been forfeited by commitment to a new subculture, his satisfaction in his solution is imperfect and adulterated. He can perfect his solution only by rejecting as status sources those who reject him. This too may require a certain measure of reaction- formation, going beyond indifference to active hostility and contempt for all those who do not share his subculture. He becomes all the more dependent upon his delinquent gang. Outside that gang his status position is now weaker than ever. The gang itself tends toward a kind of sectarian solidarity, because the benefits of membership can only be realized in active face-to-face relationships with group members.

ENDNOTES

1　　See H.M. Tiebout and M.E. Kirkpatrick, "Psychiatric Factors in Stealing," *American Journal of Orthopsychiatry*, II (April, 1932), 114-123, which discusses, in an exceptionally lucid manner, the distinction between motivating factors which center around the acquisition of the object and those which center around the commission of the act itself.

The non-utilitarian nature of juvenile delinquency has been noted by many students. ". . . while older offenders may have definitely crystallized beliefs about profitable returns from anti-social conduct, it is very clear that in childhood and in earlier youth delinquency is certainly not entered into as a paying proposition in any ordinary sense." William Healy and Augusta F. Bronner, *op. cit.*, p. 22. "The juvenile property offender's thefts at least at the start, are usually 'for fun' and not for gain." Paul Tappan, *Juvenile Delinquency* (New York: McGraw Hill Book Company, 1949), p. 143. "Stealing the leading predatory activity of the adolescent gang, is as much a result of the sport motive as of a desire for revenue." Frederic M. Thrasher, *The Gang* (Chicago: University of Chicago Press, 1936), p. 143. "In its early stages, delinquency is clearly a form of play." Henry D. McKay, "The Neighborhood and Child Conduct," *Annals of the American Academy of Political and Social Science*, CCLXI (January, 1949), 37. See also Barbara Bellow, Milton L. Blum, Kenneth B. Clark, et al., "Prejudice in Seaside," *Human Relations*, I (1947), 15-16 and Sophia M. Robison, Nathan Cohen and Murray Sachs, "An Unsolved Problem in Group Relations," *Journal of Educational Psychology*, XX (November, 1946), 154-162. The last cited paper is an excellent description of the non-utilitarian, malicious and negativistic quality of the delinquent subculture and is the clearest statement in the literature that a satisfactory theory of delinquency must make sense of these facts.

2　　Frederic M. Thrasher, *The Gang* (Chicago: University of Chicago Press, 1936), pp. 94-95.

3　　To justify the characterization of the delinquent subculture as "malicious" by multiplying citations from authorities would be empty pedantry. The malice is evident in any detailed description of juvenile gang life. We commend in particular, however, the cited works of Thrasher,

Shaw and McKay and Robinson *et al.* One aspect of this "gratuitous hostility" deserves special mention, however, for the benefit of those who see in the provision of facilities for "wholesome recreation" some magical therapeutic virtue. "On entering a playground or a gym the first activity of gang members is to disrupt and interrupt whatever activities are going on. Nongang members flee, and when the coast is clear the gang plays desultorily on the apparatus or carries on horseplay." Sophia Robison *et al., op. cit.,* p. 159. See, to the same effect, the excellent little book by Kenneth H. Rogers, *Street Gangs in Toronto* (Toronto: The Ryerson Press, 1945), pp. 18-19.

4   Shaw and McKay, in their *Social Factors in Juvenile Delinquency,* p. 241, come very close to making this point quite explicitly: "In fact the standards of these groups may represent a complete reversal of the standards and norms of conventional society. Types of conduct which result in personal degradation and dishonor in a conventional group, serve to enhance and elevate the personal prestige and status of a member of the delinquent group."

5   Clifford R. Shaw and Henry D. McKay, *Social Factors in Juvenile Delinquency,* Vol. II of National Commission on Law Observance and Enforcement, *Report on the Causes of Crime* (Washington: U.S. Government Printing Office, 1931), p. 18.

6   *Federal Probation,* XVIII (March, 1954), 3-16 contains an extremely valuable symposium on vandalism, which highlights all of the characteristics we have imputed to the delinquent subculture. In the belief that no generalization can convey the flavor and scope of this subculture as well as a simple but massive enumeration, we quote at length from Joseph E. Murphy's contribution, pp. 8-9:

> Studies of the complaints made by citizens and public officials reveal that hardly any property is safe from this form of aggression. Schools are often the object of attack by vandals. Windows are broken; records, books, desks, typewriters, supplies, and other equipment are stolen or destroyed. Public property of all types appears to offer peculiar allurement to children bent on destruction. Parks, playgrounds, highway signs, and markers are frequently defaced or destroyed. Trees, shrubs, flowers, benches, and other equipment suffer in like manner. Autoists are constantly reporting the slashing or releasing of air from tires, broken windows, stolen accessories. Golf clubs complain that benches, markers, flags, and even expensive and difficult-to- replace putting greens are defaced, broken or uprooted. Libraries report the theft and destruction of books and other equipment. Railroads complain of and demand protection from the destruction of freight car seals, theft of property, willful and deliberate throwing of stones at passenger car windows, tampering with rails and switches. Vacant houses are always the particular delight of children seeking outlets for destructive instincts; windows are broken, plumbing and hardware stolen, destroyed, or rendered unusable. Gasoline operators report pumps and other service equipment stolen, broken, or destroyed. Theater managers, frequently in the "better" neighborhoods, complain of the slashing of seats, willful damaging of toilet facilities, even the burning of rugs, carpets, etc.
>
> Recently the Newark *Evening News,* commenting editorially on the problem of vandalism in New York City housing projects, stated "housing authorities complain of the tearing out of steel banisters, incinerator openings, and mail boxes, damaging of elevators, defacing walls, smashing windows and light bulbs, stealing nozzles of fire hoses, destroying trees and benches on the project's grounds and occasionally plundering and setting fire to parked cars. Moreover, gangs have terrorized not only tenants but also the three hundred unarmed watchmen hired to protect the property."

This quotation places "stealing" in the context of a host of other manifestations of the protean "orneriness" of which we have spoken. The implication is strong that the fact than an object is "stolen" rather than destroyed or damaged is, from the standpoint of motivation, almost incidental. J.P. Shalloo, *ibid.,* pp. 6-7, states in a forceful way the problem which this creates for criminological theory: "Delinquency and crime are, and have been regarded as, purposeful behavior. But wanton and vicious destruction of property both public and private by teen-age hoodlums reveals no purpose, no rhyme, no reason . . . These are not the actions of thoughtless youth. These are actions based upon a calculated contempt for the rights of others . . ."

It is widely believed that vandalism, on the scale we know it today, is a relatively recent phenomenon. Douglas H. MacNeil, *ibid.*, p. 16, observes that, although vandalism is a form of delinquency which has been neglected by social scientists, there is little reason to believe that it has increased spectacularly, if at all, in recent years. Apparently it is and it has been for many years part and parcel, indeed the very spirit, of the delinquent subculture.

In connection with the versatility of the delinquent subculture, it should be noted that truancy is also institutionalized in the delinquent gang. In Lester E. Hewitt and Richard L. Jenkins, *op. cit.*, p. 94, habitual truancy as found to have a tetrachoric coefficient of correlation of .10 with the "unsocialized aggressive" syndrome, -.08 with the "over-inhibited behavior" syndrome and .75 with the "socialized delinquent" syndrome. These findings are of special interest because the latter syndrome corresponds closely to what we have called the delinquent subculture. For summaries of studies on the relationship between truancy and other forms of delinquency see Norman Fenton, *The Delinquent Boy and the Correctional School* (Claremont, California; Claremont Colleges Guidance Center, 1935), pp. 66-69 and William Kvaraceus, *Juvenile Delinquency and the School* (Yonkers-on-Hudson: World Book Company, 1945), pp. 144-146.

7   See the splendid report on "Working with a Street Gang" in Sylvan S. Furman (ed.), *Reaching the Unreached* (New York: New York City Youth Board, 1952), pp. 112-121. On this quality of short-run hedonism we quote, p. 13:

> One boy once told me, "Now, for example, you take an average day. What happens? We come down to the restaurant and we sit in the restaurant, and sit and sit. All right, say er. . . after a couple of hours in the restaurant, maybe we'll go to a poolroom, shoot a little pool, that's if somebody's got the money. O.K., a little pool, come back. By this time the restaurant is closed. We go in the candy store, sit around the candy store for a while, and that's it, that's all we do, man."

See also Barbara Bellow *et al.*, *op. cit.*, pp. 4-15, and Ruth Topping, *op. cit.*, p. 353.

8   The solidarity of the gang and the dependence of its members upon one another are especially well-described in Barbara Bellow *et al.*, *op. cit.*, p. 16 and Sophia Robison *et al.*, *op. cit.*, p. 158.

9   No single strand of our argument concerning the motivation of the delinquent subculture is entirely original. All have been at least adumbrated and some quite trenchantly formulated by others.

The idea that aggressive behavior, including crime and delinquency are often reactions to difficulties in achieving status in legitimate status systems has been remarked by many, although the systematic linkage between the particular status problems we have described and social class position has not been well developed in the literature. Caroline B. Zachry, for example, in *Emotion and Conduct in Adolescence* (New York: D. Appleton Century Company, 1940), pp. 187, 200-209, 245-246, has a thoughtful discussion of the ego-damage resulting from inability to compete effectively in school and of the function of aggressive behavior in maintaining self-esteem. Arthur L. Wood, in "Social Disorganization and Crime," *Encyclopedia of Criminology* (New York: Philosophical Library, 1949), pp. 466-471, states that the highest crime rates tend to occur in those minority culture groups "which have become acculturated to the majority-group patterns of behavior, but due to hostility toward them they have failed to succeed in competition for social status." Robert B. Zajonc, in "Aggressive Attitudes of the 'Stranger' as a Function of Conformity Pressures," *Human Relations*, V (1952), 205-216, has experimentally tested the general hypothesis, although not in connection with delinquency or crime, that a "need to conform" with a pattern of behavior coupled with inability to conform successfully generates hostile attitudes towards that pattern.

The general notion of negativism as an ego salving type of reaction-formation, which plays such an important part in the theory we have outlined, is common in the psychoanalytical literature. It has been brilliantly developed with specific reference to criminality in a paper by George Devereux, "Social Negativism and Criminal Psychopathology," *Journal of Criminal Psychopathology*, I (April, 1940), 322-338 and applied to other behavior problems in George Devereux and Malcolm E. Moos, "The Social Structure of Prisons, and the Organic Tensions," *Journal of Criminal Psychopathology*, IV (October, 1942), 306-324.

10   The distinguished criminologist, Sutherland, apparently had this in mind when he wrote: "It is
      not necessary that there be bad boys inducing good boys to commit offenses. It is generally a
      mutual stimulation, as a result of which each of the boys commits delinquencies which he
      would not commit alone." Edwin H. Sutherland, *Principles of Criminology* (New York: J.B.
      Lippincott Company, 1947), p. 145. Having made the point, however, Sutherland failed to
      develop its implications, and in his general theory of criminal behavior the function of the
      group or the gang is not collectively to *contrive* delinquency but merely to *transmit* the delin-
      quent tradition and to provide protection to the members of the group. Fritz Redl on the other
      hand, in "The Psychology of Gang Formation and the Treatment of Juvenile Delinquents,"
      The Psychoanalytic Study of the Child, Vol I, (New York: International Universities Press,
      1945), pp.367-377, has developed at considerable length the ways in which the group makes
      possible for its members behavior which would otherwise not be available to them.

Richard Andrew Cloward (1926-   )

Cloward was born in Rochester, New York. He was educated at the University of Rochester (B.A., 1949) and at Columbia University (M.A. in social work, 1950; Ph.D. in social work, 1958). He has taught at the School of Social Work at Columbia since 1954.

Lloyd Edgar Ohlin (1918-   )

Ohlin was born in Belmont, Massachusetts. He was educated at Brown University (A.B. in sociology, 1940), Indiana University (M.A. in sociology, 1942), and the University of Chicago (Ph.D. in sociology, 1954). He taught at Indiana University (sociology, 1941-1942) and Columbia University (sociology, 1956-1967). His last teaching position was at Harvard Univ. Law School where he was the Touroff-Glueck Professor of Criminal Justice. In addition, he served as a sociologist and actuary for the Illinois Pardon and Parole Board from 1947-1950, and as a research director at the University of Chicago from 1950-1956. He is now retired as professor emeritus at Harvard.

Delinquency and Opportunity*
Richard A. Cloward and Lloyd E. Ohlin

ILLEGITIMATE MEANS AND DELINQUENT SUBCULTURES[1]

IN THIS CHAPTER. . . we shall be dealing with the differentiation of delinquent subcultures. Although we have discussed the pressures that give rise to delinquency and the forces that result in collective attempts to meet these pressures, we have yet to consider the question of why delinquent subcultures develop distinctive content. In this chapter, we shall develop a general hypothesis that, we believe, helps to answer this question. . . . the specific applicability of this hypothesis to the criminal, conflict, and retreatist subcultures will be discussed in greater detail.

The Availability of Illegitimate Means

SOCIAL NORMS are two-sided. A prescription implies the existence of a prohibition, and *vice versa*. To advocate honesty is to demarcate and condemn a set of actions which are dishonest. In other words, norms that define legitimate practices also implicitly define illegitimate practices. One purpose of norms, in fact, is to delineate the boundary between legitimate and illegitimate practices. In setting this boundary, in segregating and classifying various types of behavior, they make us

---

*Source: Reprinted with the permission of The Free Press, a Division of Simon & Schuster from DELINQUENCY AND OPPORTUNITY: A Theory of Delinquent Gangs by Richard A. Cloward and Lloyd E. Ohlin. Copyright © 1960 by The Free Press; copyright renewed 1988 by Richard A. Cloward and Lloyd E. Ohlin. Excerpts from pp. 144-152, 161- 163, 165-166, 171-172, 177-178, 181, and 184.

aware not only of behavior that is regarded as right and proper but also of behavior that is said to be wrong and improper. Thus the criminal who engages in theft or fraud does not invent a new way of life; the possibility of employing alternative means is acknowledged, tacitly at least, by the norms of the culture.

This tendency for proscribed alternatives to be implicit in every prescription, and *vice versa,* although widely recognized, is nevertheless a reef upon which many a theory of delinquency has foundered. Much of the criminological literature assumes, for example, that one may explain a criminal act simply by accounting for the individual's readiness to employ illegal alternatives of which his culture, through its norms, has already made him generally aware. Such explanations are quite unsatisfactory, however, for they ignore a host of questions regarding the *relative availability* of illegal alternatives to various potential criminals. The aspiration to be a physician is hardly enough to explain the fact of becoming a physician; there is much that transpires between the aspiration and the achievement. This is no less true of the person who wants to be a successful criminal. Having decided that he "can't make it legitimately," he cannot simply choose among an array of illegitimate means, all equally available to him. As we have noted earlier, it is assumed in the theory of anomie that access to conventional means is differentially distributed, that some individuals, because of their social class, enjoy certain advantages that are denied to those elsewhere in the class structure. For example, there are variations in the degree to which members of various classes are fully exposed to and thus acquire the values, knowledge, and skills that facilitate upward mobility. It should not be startling, therefore, to suggest that there are socially structured variations in the availability of illegitimate means as well. In connection with delinquent subcultures, we shall be concerned principally with differentials in access to illegitimate means within the lower class.

Many sociologists have alluded to differentials in access to illegitimate means without explicitly incorporating this variable into a theory of deviant behavior. This is particularly true of scholars in the "Chicago tradition" of criminology. Two closely related theoretical perspectives emerged from this school. The theory of "cultural transmission," advanced by Clifford R. Shaw and Henry D. McKay, focuses on the development in some urban neighborhoods of a criminal tradition that persists from one generation to another despite constant changes in population.[2] In the theory of "differential association," Edwin H. Sutherland described the processes by which criminal values are taken over by the individual.[3] He asserted that criminal behavior is learned, and that it is learned in interaction with others who have already incorporated criminal values. Thus the first theory stresses the value systems of different areas; the second, the systems of social relationships that facilitate or impede the acquisition of these values.

Scholars in the Chicago tradition, who emphasized the processes involved in learning to be criminal, were actually pointing to differentials in the availability of illegal means—although they did not explicitly recognize this variable in their analysis. This can perhaps best by seen by examining Sutherland's classic work, *The Professional Thief*. "An inclination to steal," according to Sutherland, "is not a sufficient explanation of the genesis of the professional thief."[4] The "self-made" thief, lacking knowledge of the ways of securing immunity from prosecution and similar techniques of defense, "would quickly land in prison; . . . a person can be a professional thief only if he is recognized and received as such by other professional thieves." But recognition is not freely accorded: "Selection and tutelage are the two necessary elements in the process of acquiring recognition as a professional thief. . . . A person cannot acquire recognition as a professional thief until he has had tutelage in professional theft, *and tutelage is given only to a few persons selected from the total population*." For one thing, "the person must be appreciated by the professional thieves. He must be appraised as having an adequate equipment of wits, front, talking-ability, honesty, reliability, nerve and determination." Furthermore, the aspirant is judged by high standards of performance, for only "a very small percentage of those who start on this process ever reach the stage of professional thief. . . ." Thus motivation and pressures toward deviance do not fully account for deviant behavior any more than motivation and pressures toward conformity account for conforming behavior. The individual must have access to a learning environment and, once having been trained, must be allowed to perform his role. Roles, whether conforming or deviant in content, are not necessarily freely available; access to them depends upon a variety of factors, such as one's socioeconomic position, age, sex, ethnic affiliation, personality characteristics, and the like. The potential thief, like the potential physician, finds that access to his goal is governed by many criteria other than merit and motivation.

What we are asserting is that access to illegitimate roles is not freely available to all, as is commonly assumed. Only those neighborhoods in which crime flourishes as a stable, indigenous institution are fertile criminal learning environments for the young. Because these environments afford integration of different age-levels of offenders, selected young people are exposed to "differential association" through which tutelage is provided and criminal values and skills are acquired. To be prepared for the role may not, however, ensure that the individual will ever discharge it. One important limitation is that more youngsters are recruited into these patterns of differential associations than the adult criminal structure can possibly absorb. Since there is a surplus of contenders for these elite positions, criteria and mechanisms of selection must be evolved. Hence a certain proportion of those who aspire may not be permitted to engage in the behavior for which they have prepared themselves.

Thus we conclude that access to illegitimate roles, no less than access to legitimate roles, is limited by both social and psychological factors. We shall here be concerned primarily with socially structured differentials in illegitimate opportunities. Such differentials, we contend, have much to do with the type of delinquent subculture that develops.

Learning and Performance Structures

OUR USE of the term "opportunities," legitimate or illegitimate, implies access to both learning and performance structures. That is, the individual must have access to appropriate environments for the acquisition of the values and skills associated with the performance of a particular role, and he must be supported in the performance of the role once he has learned it.

Tannenbaum, several decades ago, vividly expressed the point that criminal role performance, no less than conventional role performance, presupposes a patterned set of relationships through which the requisite values and skills are transmitted by established practitioners to aspiring youth:

> It takes a long time to make a good criminal, many years of specialized training and much preparation. But training is something that is given to people. People learn in a community where the materials and the knowledge are to be had. A craft needs an atmosphere saturated with purpose and promise. The community provides the attitudes, the point of view, the philosophy of life, the example, the motive, the contacts, the friendships, the incentives. No child brings those into the world. He finds them here and available for use and elaboration. The community gives the criminal his materials and habits, just as it gives the doctor, the lawyer, the teacher, and the candlestick-maker theirs.[5]

Sutherland systematized this general point of view, asserting that opportunity consists, at least in part, of learning structures. Thus "criminal behavior is learned" and, furthermore, it is learned "in interaction with other persons in a process of communication." However, he conceded that the differential-association theory does not constitute a full explanation of criminal behavior. In a paper circulated in 1944, he noted that "criminal behavior is partially a function of opportunities to commit [i.e., to perform] specific classes of crime, such as embezzlement, bank burglary, or illicit heterosexual intercourse." Therefore, "while opportunity may be partially a function of association with criminal patterns and of the specialized techniques thus acquired, it is not determined entirely in that manner, and consequently differential association is not the sufficient cause of criminal behavior."[6]

To Sutherland, then, illegitimate opportunity included conditions favorable to the performance of a criminal role as well as conditions favorable to the learning of such a role (differential associations). These conditions, we suggest, depend upon certain features of the social structure of the community in which delinquency arises.

Differential Opportunity: A Hypothesis

WE BELIEVE that each individual occupies a position in both legitimate and illegitimate opportunity structures. This is a new way of defining the situation. The theory of anomie views the individual primarily in terms of the legitimate opportunity structure. It poses questions regarding differentials in access to legitimate routes to success-goals; at the same time it assumes either that illegitimate avenues to success-goals are freely available or that differentials in their availability are of little significance. This tendency may be seen in the following statement by Merton:

> Several researches have shown that specialized areas of vice and crime constitute a "normal" response to a situation where the cultural emphasis upon pecuniary success has been absorbed, but where there is little access to conventional and legitimate means for becoming successful. The occupational opportunities of people in these areas are largely confined to manual labor and the lesser white-collar jobs. Given the American stigmatization of manual labor *which has been found to hold rather uniformly for all social classes,* and the absence of realistic opportunities for advancement beyond this level, the result is a marked tendency toward deviant behavior. The status of unskilled labor and the consequent low income cannot readily compete *in terms of established standards of worth* with the promises of power and high income from organized vice, rackets and crime. . . . [Such a situation] leads toward the gradual attenuation of legitimate, but by and large ineffectual, strivings and the increasing use of illegitimate, but more or less effective, expedients.[7]

The cultural-transmission and differential-association tradition, on the other hand, assumes that access to illegitimate means is variable, but it does not recognize the significance of comparable differentials in access to legitimate means. Sutherland's "ninth proposition" in the theory of differential association states:

> *Though criminal behavior is an expression of general needs and values, it is not explained by those general needs and values since non-criminal behavior is an expression of the same needs and values.* Thieves generally steal in order to secure money, but likewise honest laborers work

in order to secure money. The attempts by many scholars to explain criminal behavior by general drives and values, such as the happiness principle, striving for social status, the money motive, or frustration, have been and must continue to be futile since they explain lawful behavior as completely as they explain criminal behavior.[8]

In this statement, Sutherland appears to assume that people have equal and free access to legitimate means regardless of their social position. At the very least, he does not treat access to legitimate means as variable. It is, of course, perfectly true that "striving for social status," "the money motive," and other socially approved drives do not fully account for either deviant or conforming behavior. But if goal-oriented behavior occurs under conditions in which there are socially structured obstacles to the satisfaction of these drives by legitimate means, the resulting pressures, we contend, might lead to deviance.

The concept of differential opportunity structures permits us to unite the theory of anomie, which recognizes the concept of differentials in access to legitimate means, and the "Chicago tradition," in which the concept of differentials in access to illegitimate means is implicit. We can now look at the individual, not simply in relation to one or the other system of means, but in relation to both legitimate and illegitimate systems. This approach permits us to ask, for example, how the relative availability of illegitimate opportunities affects the resolution of adjustment problems leading to deviant behavior. We believe that the way in which these problems are resolved may depend upon the kind of support for one or another type of illegitimate activity that is given at different points in the social structure. If, in a given social location, illegal or criminal means are not readily available, then we should not expect a criminal subculture to develop among adolescents. By the same logic, we should expect the manipulation of violence to become a primary avenue to higher status only in areas where the means of violence are not denied to the young. To give a third example, drug addiction and participation in subcultures organized around the consumption of drugs presuppose that persons can secure access to drugs and knowledge about how to use them. In some parts of the social structure, this would be very difficult; in others, very easy. In short, there are marked differences from one part of the social structure to another in the types of illegitimate adaptation that are available to persons in search of solutions to problems of adjustment arising from the restricted availability of legitimate means.[9] In this sense, then, we can think of individuals as being located in two opportunity structures—one legitimate, the other illegitimate. Given limited access to success-goals by legitimate means, the nature of the delinquent response that may result will vary according to the availability of various illegitimate means.[10] . . .

SUBCULTURAL DIFFERENTIATION

WE COME NOW to the question of the specific social conditions that make for the emergence of distinctive delinquent subcultures. Throughout this analysis, we shall make extensive use of the concepts of social organization developed in the preceding chapter: namely, integration of different age-levels of offenders, and integration of carriers of conventional and deviant values. Delinquent responses vary from one neighborhood to another, we believe, according to the articulation of these structures in the neighborhood. Our object here is to show more precisely how various forms of neighborhood integration affect the development of subcultural content.

The Criminal Subculture

THE CRIMINAL SUBCULTURE, like the conflict and retreatist adaptations, requires a specialized environment if it is to flourish. Among the environmental supports of a criminal style of life are integration of offenders at various age-levels and close integration of the carriers of conventional and illegitimate values.

Integration of Age-levels

Nowhere in the criminological literature is the concept of integration between different age-levels of offender made more explicit than in discussions of criminal learning. Most criminologists agree that criminal behavior presupposes patterned sets of relationships through which the requisite values and skills are communicated or transmitted from one age-level to another. What, then, are some of the specific components of systems organized for the socialization of potential criminals?

Criminal Role-Models—The lower class is not without its own distinctive and indigenous illegitimate success-models. Many accounts in the literature suggest that lower-class adults who have achieved success by illegitimate means not only are highly visible to young people in slum areas but often are willing to establish intimate relationships with these youth.

> Every boy has some ideal he looks up to and admires. His ideal may be Babe Ruth, Jack Dempsey, or Al Capone. When I was twelve, we moved into a neighborhood with a lot of gangsters. They were all swell dressers and had big cars and carried "gats." Us kids saw these swell guys and mingled with them in the cigar store on the corner. Jack

Gurney was the one in the mob that I had a fancy to. He used to take my sis out and that way I saw him often. He was in the stick-up rackets before he was in the beer rackets, and he was a swell dresser and had lots of dough. . . I liked to be near him and felt stuck up over the other guys because he came to my home to see my sis.[11]

Just as the middle-class youth, as a consequence of intimate relationships with, say, a banker or a businessman, may aspire to *become* a banker or a businessman, so the lower-class youth may be associated with and aspire to become a "policy king": " 'I want to be a big shot. . . Have all the guys look up to me. Have a couple of Lincolns, lots of broads, and all the coppers licking my shoes.' "[12] The crucial point here is that success-goals are not equally available to persons in different positions in the social structure. To the extent that social-class lines act as barriers to interaction between persons in different social strata, conventional success-models may not be salient for lower-class youth. The successful criminal, on the other hand, may be an intimate, personal figure in the fabric of the lower- class area. Hence one of the forces leading to rational, disciplined, crime-oriented delinquency may be the availability of criminal success-models. . . .

Integration of Values

Unless the carriers of criminal and conventional values are closely bound to one another, stable criminal roles cannot develop. The criminal, like the occupant of a conventional role, must establish relationships with other categories of persons, all of whom contribute in one way or another to the successful performance of criminal activity. As Tannenbaum says, "The development of the criminal career requires and finds in the immediate environment other supporting elements in addition to the active 'criminal gangs'; to develop the career requires the support of middlemen. These may be junk men, fences, lawyers, bondsmen, 'backers,' as they are called."[13] The intricate systems of relationship between these legitimate and illegitimate persons constitute the type of environment in which the juvenile criminal subculture can come into being.[14]

An excellent example of the way in which the content of a delinquent subculture is affected by its location in a particular milieu is afforded by the "fence," a dealer in stolen goods who is found in some but not all lower-class neighborhoods. Relationships between such middlemen and criminals are not confined to adult offenders; numerous accounts of lower-class life suggest not only that relationships form between fences and youngsters but also that the fence is a crucial element in the structure of illegitimate opportunity. He often caters to and encourages delinquent activities among the young. He may even exert controls leading the young to orient their stealing in the most lucrative and least risky directions. The same point may be made of junk dealers in some areas, racketeers who permit minors to run errands, and other occupants of illegitimate or semilegitimate roles.

As the apprentice criminal passes from one status to another in the illegitimate opportunity system, we should expect him to develop an ever-widening set of relationships with members of the semilegitimate and legitimate world. For example, a delinquent who is rising in the structure might begin to come into contact with mature criminals, law-enforcement officials, politicians, bail bondsmen, "fixers," and the like. As his activities become integrated with the activities of these persons, his knowledge of the illegitimate world is deepened, new skills are acquired, and the opportunity to engage in new types of illegitimate activity is enhanced. Unless he can form these relationships, the possibility of a stable, protected criminal style of life is effectively precluded.

The type of environment that encourages a criminal orientation among delinquents is, then, characterized by close integration of the carriers of conventional and illegitimate values. The *content* of the delinquent subculture is a more or less direct response to the local milieu in which it emerges. And it is the "integrated" neighborhood, we suggest, that produces the criminal type of delinquent subculture. . . .

. . . In summary, the criminal subculture is likely to arise in a neighborhood milieu characterized by close bonds between different age-levels of offender, and between criminal and conventional elements. As a consequence of these integrative relationships, a new opportunity structure emerges which provides alternative avenues to success-goals. Hence the pressures generated by restrictions on legitimate access to success-goals are drained off. Social controls over the conduct of the young are effectively exercised, limiting expressive behavior and constraining the discontented to adopt instrumental, if criminalistic, styles of life.

The Conflict Subculture

BECAUSE youngsters caught up in the conflict subculture often endanger their own lives and the lives of others and cause considerable property damage, the conflict form of delinquency is a source of great public concern. Its prevalence, therefore, is probably exaggerated. There is no evidence to suggest that the conflict subculture is more widespread than the other subcultures, but the nature of its activities makes it more visible and thus attracts public attention. As a consequence, many people erroneously equate "delinquency" and "conflict behavior." But whatever its prevalence, the conflict subculture is of both theoretical and social importance, and calls for explanation.

Earlier in this book, we questioned the common belief that slum areas, because they are slums, are necessarily disorganized. We pointed to forms of integration which give some slum areas unity and cohesion. Areas in which these integrative structures are found, we suggested, tend to be characterized by criminal rather than conflict or retreatist subcultures. But not all slums are integrated. Some lower-class urban neighborhoods lack unity and cohesiveness. Because the prerequisites for the emergence of stable systems of social relations are not present, a state of social disorganization prevails.

The many forces making for instability in the social organization of some slum areas include high rates of vertical and geographic mobility; massive housing projects in which "site tenants" are not accorded priority in occupancy, so that traditional residents are dispersed and "strangers" re-assembled; and changing land use, as in the case of residential areas that are encroached upon by the expansion of adjacent commercial or industrial areas. Forces of this kind keep a community off balance, for tentative efforts to develop social organization are quickly checked. Transiency and instability become the overriding features of social life.

Transiency and instability, in combination, produce powerful pressures for violent behavior among the young in these areas. First, an unorganized community cannot provide access to legitimate channels to success-goals, and thus discontent among the young with their life-chances is heightened. Secondly, access to stable criminal opportunity systems is also restricted, for disorganized neighborhoods do not develop integration of different age-levels of offender or integration of carriers of criminal and conventional values. The young, in short, are relatively deprived of both conventional and criminal opportunity. Finally, social controls are weak in such communities. These conditions, we believe, lead to the emergence of conflict subcultures. . . .

. . . In summary, severe limitations on both conventional and criminal opportunity intensify frustrations and position discontent. Discontent is heightened further under conditions in which social control is relaxed, for the area lacking integration between age- levels of offender and between carriers of conventional and criminal values cannot generate pressures to contain frustrations among the young. These are the circumstances, we suggest, in which adolescents turn to violence in search of status. Violence comes to be ascendant, in short, under conditions of relative detachment from all institutionalized systems of opportunity and social control.

The Retreatist Subculture

THE CONSUMPTION of drugs—one of the most serious forms of retreatist behavior—has become a severe problem among adolescents and young adults, particularly in lower-class urban areas. By and large, drug use in these areas has been attributed to rapid geographic mobility, inadequate social controls, and other manifestations of social disorganization. In this section, we shall suggest a hypothesis that may open up new avenues of inquiry in regard to the growing problem of drug use among the young.

Pressures leading to retreatist subcultures

Retreatism is often conceived as an isolated adaptation, characterized by a breakdown in relationships with other persons. Indeed, this is frequently true, as in the case of psychotics. The drug-user, however, must become affiliated with others, if only to secure access to a steady supply of drugs. Just as stable criminal activity cannot be explained by reference to motivation alone, neither can stable drug use be fully explained in this way. Opportunity to use drugs must also be present. But such opportunities are restricted. As Becker notes, the illegal distribution of drugs is limited to "sources which are not available to the ordinary person. In order for a person to begin marihuana use, he must begin participation in some group through which these sources of supply become available to him."[15] . . .

. . . If internalized prohibitions are not a necessary component of the process by which retreatism is generated, then how are we to account for such behavior? We have noted that there are differentials in access both to illegitimate and to legitimate means; not all of those who seek to attain success-goals by prohibited routes are permitted to proceed. There are probably many lower-class adolescents oriented toward success in the criminal world who fail; similarly, many who would like to acquire proficiency in the use of violence also fail. We might ask, therefore, what the response would be among those faced with failure in the use of both legitimate and illegitimate means. We suggest that persons who experience this "double failure" are likely to move into a retreatist pattern of behavior. That is, retreatist behavior may arise as a consequence of limitations on the use of illegitimate means, whether the limitations are internalized prohibitions or socially structured barriers. . . .

. . . Our hypothesis states that adolescents who are double failures are more vulnerable than others to retreatist behavior; it does not imply that all double failures will subsequently become retreatists. Some will respond to failure by adopting a law-abiding lower-class style of life—

the "corner boy" adaptation. It may be that those who become retreatists are incapable of revising their aspirations downward to correspond to reality. Some of those who shift to a corner-boy adaptation may not have held high aspirations initially. It has frequently been observed that some adolescents affiliate with delinquent groups simply for protection in gang-ridden areas; they are motivated not by frustration so much as by the "instinct of self-preservation." In a less hostile environment, they might simply have made a corner-boy adjustment in the first place. But for those who continue to exhibit high aspirations under conditions of double failure, retreatism is the expected result. . . .

ENDNOTES

1   Substantial portions of this chapter have been taken from R.A. Cloward, "Illegitimate Means, Anomie and Deviant Behavior," *American Sociological Review*, Vol. 24, No. 2 (April 1959), pp. 164-76. See also R.K. Merton, "Social Conformity, Deviation, and Opportunity Structures: A Comment on the Contributions of Dubin and Cloward," *idem.*, pp. 177-89.

2   See esp. C.R. Shaw, *The Jack-Roller* (Chicago: University of Chicago Press, 1930); Shaw, *The Natural History of a Delinquent Career* (Chicago: University of Chicago Press, 1931); Shaw et al., *Delinquency Areas* (Chicago: University of Chicago Press, 1940); and Shaw and H.D. McKay, *Juvenile Delinquency and Urban Areas* (Chicago: University of Chicago Press, 1942).

3   L.H. Sutherland, ed., *The Professional Thief* (Chicago: University of Chicago Press, 1937); and Sutherland, *Principles of Criminology*, 4th Ed. (Philadelphia: Lippincott, 1947).

4   All quotations on this page are from *The Professional Thief*, pp. 211-13. Emphasis added.

5   Frank Tannenbaum, "The Professional Criminal," *The Century*, Vol. 110 (May-Oct. 1925), p. 577.

6   See A.K. Cohen, Alfred Lindesmith, and Karl Schuessler, eds., *The Sutherland Papers* (Bloomington, Ind.: Indiana University Press, 1956), pp. 31-35.

7   R.K. Merton, *Social Theory and Social Structure*, Rev. and Enl. Ed. (Glencoe, Ill.: Free Press, 1957), pp. 145-46.

8   *Principles of Criminology, op. cit.*, pp. 7-8.

9   For an example of restrictions on access to illegitimate roles, note the impact of racial definitions in the following case: "I was greeted by two prisoners who were to be my cell buddies. Ernest was a first offender, charged with being a 'hold-up' man. Bill, the other buddy, was an old offender, going through the machinery of becoming a habitual criminal, in and out of jail.... The first thing they asked me was, 'What are you in for?' I said, 'Jack- rolling.' The hardened one (Bill) looked at me with a superior air and said, 'A hoodlum eh? An ordinary sneak thief. Not willing to leave jack-rolling to the niggers, eh? That's all they're good for. Kid, jack-rolling's not a white man's job.' I could see that he was disgusted with me, and I was too scared to say anything" (Shaw, *The Jack-Roller, op. cit.*, p. 101).

10 For a discussion of the way in which the availability of illegitimate means influences the adaptations of inmates to prison life, see R.A. Cloward, "Social Control in the Prison," *Theoretical Studies of The Social Organization of the Prison*, Bulletin No. 15 (New York: Social Science Research Council, March 1960), pp. 20-48.

11 C.R. Shaw, "Juvenile Delinquency—A Group Tradition," *Bulletin of the State University of Iowa*, No. 23, N. S. No. 700, 1933, p. 8.

12 *Ibid.*, p. 9.

13 Frank Tannenbaum, *Crime and the Community* (New York: Columbia University Press 1938), p. 60.

14 In this connection see R.A. Cloward, "Social Control in the Prison," *Theoretical Studies of the Social Organization of the Prison*, Bulletin No. 15 (New York: Social Science Research Council, March 1960), pp. 20-48, which illustrates similar forms of integration in a penal setting.

15 H.S. Becker, "Marihuana Use and Social Control," *Social Problems*, Vol. 3, No. 1 (July 1955), pp. 36-37.

Criminologist Profile

Walter Benson Miller (1920-   )

Miller was born in Philadelphia, Pennsylvania. He received an M.A. in 1950 from the University of Chicago in anthropology and a Ph.D. in 1954 from Harvard University in social relations. He has worked as a researcher in various projects including those on American Indians (1948-1953), public health (1953-1955), the Boston Delinquency Project (1955-1958, and as director from 1958-1965), urban studies (1956-1972), and the Youth Gang Survey (1974-1978). He has held positions at Boston University, Brandeis University, Harvard University, and the State University of New York at Albany. Since 1973, he has been a research fellow at the Center for Criminal Justice at the Harvard Law School.

Lower Class Culture as a Generating Milieu of Gang Delinquency*

Walter B. Miller

The etiology of delinquency has long been a controversial issue, and is particularly so at present. As new frames of reference for explaining human behavior have been added to traditional theories, some authors have adopted the practice of citing the major postulates of each school of thought as they pertain to delinquency, and going on to state that causality must be conceived in terms of the dynamic interaction of a complex combination of variables on many levels. The major sets of etiological factors currently adduced to explain delinquency are, in simplified terms, the physiological (delinquency results from organic pathology), the psychodynamic (delinquency is a "behavioral disorder" resulting primarily from emotional disturbance generated by a defective mother-child relationship), and the environmental (delinquency is the product of disruptive forces, "disorganization," in the actor's physical or social environment).

This paper selects one particular kind of "delinquency"[1]—law-violating acts committed by members of adolescent street corner groups in lower class communities—and attempts to show that the dominant component of motivation underlying these acts consists in a directed attempt by the actor to adhere to forms of behavior, and to achieve standards of value as they are defined within that community. It takes as a premise that the motivation of behavior in this situation can be approached most productively by attempting to understand the nature of cultural forces

*Source: Walter B. Miller, 1958. "Lower Class Culture as a Generating Milieu of Gang Delinquency," *Journal of Social Issues* Vol XIV, 3: 5-19.

impinging on the acting individual as they are perceived *by the actor himself*—although by no means only that segment of these forces of which the actor is consciously aware—rather than as they are perceived and evaluated from the reference position of another cultural system. In the case of "gang" delinquency, the cultural system which exerts the most direct influence on behavior is that of the lower class community itself—a long-established, distinctively patterned tradition with an integrity of its own—rather than a so-called "delinquent subculture" which has arisen through conflict with middle class culture and is oriented to the deliberate violation of middle class norms.

The bulk of the substantive data on which the following material is based was collected in connection with a service-research project in the control of gang delinquency. During the service aspect of the project, which lasted for three years, seven trained social workers maintained contact with twenty-one corner group units in a "slum" district of a large eastern city for periods of time ranging from ten to thirty months. Groups were Negro and white, male and female, and in early, middle, and late adolescence. Over eight thousand pages of direct observational data on behavior patterns of group members and other community residents were collected; almost daily contact was maintained for a total time period of about thirteen worker years. Data include workers' contact reports, participant observation reports by the writer—a cultural anthropologist—and direct tape recordings of group activities and discussions.[2]

Focal Concerns of Lower Class Culture

There is a substantial segment of present-day American society whose way of life, values, and characteristic patterns of behavior are the product of a distinctive cultural system which may be termed "lower class." Evidence indicates that this cultural system is becoming increasingly distinctive, and that the size of the group which shares this tradition is increasing.[3] The lower class way of life, in common with that of all distinctive cultural groups, is characterized by a set of focal concerns—areas or issues which command widespread and persistent attention and a high degree of emotional involvement. The specific concerns cited here, while by no means confined to the American lower classes, constitute a distinctive *patterning* of concerns which differs significantly, both in rank order and weighting from that of American middle class culture. The following chart presents a highly schematic and simplified listing of six of the major concerns of lower class culture. Each is conceived as a "dimension" within which a fairly wide and varied range of alternative behavior patterns may be followed by different individuals under different situations. They are listed roughly in order of the degree of *explicit* attention accorded each, and, in this sense represent a weighted ranking of concerns. The "perceived alternatives" represent polar positions which define certain parameters within each dimension. As will be explained in more detail, it is necessary in relating the influence of these "concerns" to the motivation of delinquent behavior to specify *which* of its aspects is oriented to, whether orientation is *overt* or *covert, positive* (conforming to or seeking the aspect), or *negative* (rejecting or seeking to avoid the aspect).

The concept "focal concern" is used here in preference to the concept "value" for several interrelated reasons: (1) It is more readily derivable from direct field observation. (2) It is descriptively neutral—permitting independent consideration of positive and negative valences as varying under different conditions, whereas "value" carries a built-in positive valence. (3) It makes possible more refined analysis of subcultural differences, since it reflects actual behavior, whereas "value" tends to wash out intracultural differences since it is colored by notions of the "official" ideal.

Trouble: Concern over "trouble" is a dominant feature of lower class culture. The concept has various shades of meaning; "trouble" in one of its aspects represents a situation or a kind of behavior which results in unwelcome or complicating involvement with official authorities or agencies of middle class society. "Getting into trouble" and "staying out of trouble" represent major issues for male and female, adults and children. For men, "trouble" frequently involves fighting or sexual adventures while drinking; for women, sexual involvement with disadvantageous consequences. Expressed desire to avoid behavior which violates moral or legal norms is often based less on an explicit commitment to "official" moral or legal standards than on a desire to avoid "getting into trouble," e.g., the complicating consequences of the action.

The dominant concern over "trouble" involves a distinction of critical importance for the lower class community—that between "law-abiding" and "non-law-abiding" behavior. There is a high degree of sensitivity as to where each person stands in relation to these two classes of activity. Whereas in the middle class community a major dimension for evaluating a person's status is "achievement" and its external symbols, in the lower class, personal status is very frequently gauged along the law-abiding/non-law-abiding dimension. A mother will evaluate the suitability of her daughter's boyfriend less on the basis of his achievement potential than on the basis of his innate "trouble" potential. This sensitive awareness of the opposition of "trouble-producing" and "non-trouble-producing" behavior represents both a major basis for deriving status distinctions, and an internalized conflict potential for the individual.

As in the case of other focal concerns, which of two perceived alternatives—"law-abiding" or "non-law-abiding"—is valued varies according to the individual and the circumstances; in many instances there is an overt commitment to the "law-abiding" alternative, but a covert commitment to the "non-law-abiding." In certain situations, "getting into trouble" is overtly recognized as prestige-conferring; for example, membership in certain adult and adolescent primary groupings ("gangs") is contingent on having demonstrated an explicit commitment to the law-violating alternative. It is most important to note that the choice between "law-abiding" and "non-law-abiding" behavior is still a choice *within* lower class culture; the distinction between the policeman and the criminal, the outlaw and the sheriff, involves primarily this one dimension; in other respects they have a high community of interests. Not infrequently brothers raised in an identical cultural milieu will become police and criminals respectively.

CHART 1
FOCAL CONCERNS OF LOWER CLASS CULTURE

Area	Perceived Alternatives (state, quality, condition)	
1. *Trouble:*	law-abiding behavior	law-violating behavior
2. *Toughness:*	physical prowess, skill; "masculinity"; fearlessness, bravery, daring	weakness, ineptitude; effeminacy; timidity, cowardice, caution
3. *Smartness:*	ability to outsmart, dupe, "con"; gaining money by "wits"; shrewdness, adroitness in repartee	gullibility, "con-ability"; gaining money by hard work; slowness, dull-wittedness, verbal maladroitness
4. *Excitement:*	thrill: risk, danger; change, activity	boredom: "deadness," safeness: sameness, passivity
5. *Fate:*	favored by fortune, being "lucky"	ill-omened, being "unlucky"
6. *Autonomy:*	freedom from external constraint; freedom from superordinate authority; independence	presence of external constraint presence of strong authority; dependency, being "cared for"

For a substantial segment of the lower class population "getting into trouble" is not in itself overtly defined as prestige-conferring, but is implicitly recognized as a means to other valued ends, e.g., the covertly valued desire to be "cared for" and subject to external constraint, or the overtly valued state of excitement or risk. Very frequently "getting into trouble" is multifunctional, and achieves several sets of valued ends.

Toughness: The concept of "toughness" in lower class culture represents a compound combination of qualities or states. Among its most important components are physical prowess, evidenced both by demonstrated possession of strength and endurance and athletic skill; "masculinity," symbolized by a distinctive complex of acts and avoidances (bodily tat[t]ooing; absence of sentimentality; non-concern with "art," "literature," conceptualization of women as conquest objects, etc.); and bravery in the face of physical threat. The model for the "tough guy"—hard, fearless, undemonstrative, skilled in physical combat—is represented by the movie gangster of the thirties, the "private eye," and the movie cowboy.

The genesis of the intense concern over "toughness" in lower class culture is probably related to the fact that a significant proportion of lower class males are reared in a predominantly female household, and lack a consistently present male figure with whom to identify and from whom to learn essential components of a "male" role. Since women serve as a primary object of identification during pre-adolescent years, the almost obsessive lower class concern with "masculinity" probably resembles a type of compulsive reaction-formation. A concern over homosexuality runs like a persistent thread through lower class culture. This is manifested by the institutionalized practice of baiting "queers," often accompanied by violent physical attacks, an expressed contempt for "softness" or frills, and the use of the local term for "homosexual" as a generalized pejorative epithet (e.g., higher class individuals or upwardly mobile peers are frequently characterized as "fags" or "queers"). The distinction between "overt" and "covert" orientation to aspects of an area of concern is especially important in regard to "toughness." A positive overt evaluation of behavior defined as "effeminate" would be out of the question for a lower class male; however, built into lower class culture is a range of devices which permit men to adopt behaviors and concerns which in other cultural milieux fall within the province of women, and at the same time to be defined as "tough" and manly. For example, lower class men can be professional short-order cooks in a diner and still be regarded as "tough." The highly intimate circumstances of the street corner gang involve the recurrent expression of strongly affectionate feelings towards other men. Such expressions, however, are disguised as their opposite, taking the form of ostensibly aggressive verbal and physical interaction (kidding, "ranking," roughhousing, etc.).

Smartness: "Smartness," as conceptualized in lower class culture, involves the capacity to outsmart, outfox, outwit, dupe, "take," "con" another or others, and the concomitant capacity to avoid being outwitted, "taken," or duped oneself. In its essence, smartness involves the capacity to achieve a valued entity—material goods, personal status—

through a maximum use of mental agility and a minimum use of physical effort. This capacity has an extremely long tradition in lower class culture, and is highly valued. Lower class culture can be characterized as "non-intellectual" only if intellectualism is defined specifically in terms of control over a particular body of formally learned knowledge involving "culture" (art, literature, "good" music, etc.), a generalized perspective on the past and present conditions of our own and other societies, and other areas of knowledge imparted by formal educational institutions. This particular type of mental attainment is, in general, overtly disvalued and frequently associated with effeminancy, "smartness" in the lower class sense, however, is highly valued.

The lower class child learns and practices the use of this skill in the street corner situation. Individuals continually practice duping and outwitting one another through recurrent card games and other forms of gambling, mutual exchanges of insults, and "testing" for mutual "conability." Those who demonstrate competence in this skill are accorded considerable prestige. Leadership roles in the corner group are frequently allocated according to demonstrated capacity in the two areas of "smartness" and "toughness"; the ideal leader combines both, but the "smart" leader is often accorded more prestige than the "tough" one—reflecting a general lower class respect for "brains" in the "smartness" sense.[4]

The model of the "smart" person is represented in popular media by the card shark, the professional gambler, the "con" artist, the promoter. A conceptual distinction is made between two kinds of people: "suckers," easy marks, "lushes," dupes, who work for their money and are legitimate targets of exploitation; and sharp operators, the "brainy" ones, who live by their wits and "getting" from the suckers by mental adroitness.

Involved in the syndrome of capacities related to "smartness" is a dominant emphasis in lower class culture on ingenious aggressive repartee. This skill, learned and practiced in the context of the corner group, ranges in form from the widely prevalent semi-ritualized teasing, kidding, razzing, "ranking," so characteristic of male peer group interaction, to the highly ritualized type of mutual insult interchange known as "the dirty dozens," "the dozens," "playing house," and other terms. This highly patterned cultural form is practiced on its most advanced level in adult male Negro society, but less polished variants are found throughout lower class culture—practiced, for example, by white children, male and female, as young as four or five. In essence, "doin' the dozens" involves two antagonists who vie with each other in the exchange of increasingly inflammatory insults, with incestuous and perverted sexual relations with the mother a dominant theme. In this form of insult interchange, as well as on other less ritualized occasions for joking, semi-serious, and serious mutual invective, a very high premium is placed on ingenuity, hair-trigger responsiveness, inventiveness, and the acute exercise of mental faculties.

Excitement: For many lower class individuals the rhythm of life fluctuates between periods of relatively routine or repetitive activity and sought situations of great emotional stimulation. Many of the most characteristic features of lower class life are related to the search for excitement or "thrill." Involved here are the highly prevalent use of alcohol by both sexes and the widespread use of gambling of all kinds—playing the numbers, betting on horse races, dice, cards. The quest for excitement finds what is perhaps its most vivid expression in the highly patterned practice of the recurrent "night on the town." This practice, designated by various terms in different areas ("honky-tonkin'"; "goin' out on the town"; "bar hoppin'"), involves a patterned set of activities in which alcohol, music, and sexual adventuring are major components. A group or individual sets out to "make the rounds" of various bars or night clubs. Drinking continues progressively throughout the evening. Men seek to "pick up" women, and women play the risky game of entertaining sexual advances. Fights between men involving women, gambling, and claims of physical prowess, in various combinations, are frequent consequences of a night of making the rounds. The explosive potential of this type of adventuring with sex and aggression, frequently leading to "trouble," is semi-explicitly sought by the individual. Since there is always a good likelihood that being out on the town will eventuate in fights, etc., the practice involves elements of sought risk and desired danger.

Counterbalancing the "flirting with danger" aspect of the "excitement" concern is the prevalence in lower class culture of other well established patterns of activity which involve long periods of relative inaction, or passivity. The term "hanging out" in lower class culture refers to extended periods of standing around, often with peer mates, doing what is defined as "nothing," "shooting the breeze," etc. A definite periodicity exists in the pattern of activity relating to the two aspects of the "excitement" dimension. For many lower class individuals the venture into the high-risk world of alcohol, sex, and fighting occurs regularly once a week, with interim periods devoted to accommodating to possible consequences of these periods, along with recurrent resolves not to become so involved again.

Fate: Related to the quest for excitement is the concern with fate, fortune, or luck. Here also a distinction is made between two states— being "lucky" or "in luck," and being unlucky or jinxed. Many lower class individuals feel that their lives are subject to a set of forces over which they have relatively little control. These are not directly equated with the supernatural forces of formally organized religion, but relate more to a concept of "destiny," or man as a pawn of magical powers. Not infrequently this often implicit world view is associated with a conception of the ultimate futility of directed effort towards a goal: if the cards are right, or the dice good to you, or if your lucky number comes up things will go your way; if luck is against you, it's not worth trying. The concept of performing semi-magical rituals so that one's "luck will change" is prevalent; one hopes that as a result he will move from the state of being "unlucky" to that of being "lucky." The element of fantasy plays an important part in this area. Related to and complementing the notion that "only suckers work" (Smartness) is the idea that once things start going your way, relatively independent of your own effort, all good things will come to you. Achieving great material rewards (big cars, big houses, a roll of cash to flash in a fancy nightclub), valued in lower class as well as in other parts of American culture, is a recurrent theme in lower class fantasy and folklore; the cocaine dreams of Willie the Weeper or Minnie the Moocher present the components of this fantasy in vivid detail.

The prevalence in the lower class community of many forms of gambling, mentioned in connection with the "excitement" dimension, is also relevant here. Through cards and pool which involve skill, and thus both "toughness" and "smartness"; or through race horse betting, involving "smartness"; or through playing the numbers, involving predominantly "luck," one may make a big killing with a minimum of directed and persistent effort within conventional occupational channels. Gambling in its many forms illustrates the fact that many of the persistent features of lower class culture are multifunctional—serving a range of desired ends at the same time. Describing some of the incentives behind gambling has involved mention of all of the focal concerns cited so far—Toughness, Smartness, and Excitement, in addition to Fate.

Autonomy: The extent and nature of control over the behavior of the individual—an important concern in most cultures—has a special significance and is distinctively patterned in lower class culture. The discrepancy between what is overtly valued and what is covertly sought is particularly striking in this area. On the overt level there is a strong and frequently expressed resentment of the idea of external controls, restrictions on behavior, and unjust or coercive authority. "No one's gonna push me around," or "I'm gonna tell him he can take the job and shove it. . . ." are commonly expressed sentiments. Similar explicit attitudes are maintained to systems of behavior-restricting rules, insofar as these are perceived as representing the injunctions, and bearing the sanctions of superordinate authority. In addition, in lower class culture a close conceptual connection is made between "authority" and "nurturance." To be restrictively or firmly controlled is to be cared for. Thus the overtly negative evaluation of superordinate authority frequently extends as well to nurturance, care, or protection. The desire for personal independence is often expressed in such terms as "I don't need *nobody* to take care of me. I can take care of myself!" Actual patterns of behavior, however, reveal a marked discrepancy between expressed sentiment and what is covertly valued. Many lower class people appear to seek out highly restrictive social environments wherein stringent external controls are maintained over their behavior. Such institutions as the armed forces, the mental hospital, the disciplinary school, the prison or correctional institution, provide environments which incorporate a strict and detailed set of rules defining and limiting behavior, and enforced by an authority system which controls and applies coercive sanctions for deviance from these rules. While under the jurisdiction of such systems, the lower class person generally expresses to his peers continual resentment of the coercive, unjust, and arbitrary exercise of authority. Having been released, or having escaped from these milieux, however, he will often act in such a way as to insure recommitment, or choose recommitment voluntarily after a temporary period of "freedom."

Lower class patients in mental hospitals will exercise considerable ingenuity to insure continued commitment while voicing the desire to get out; delinquent boys will frequently "run" from a correctional institution to activate efforts to return them; to be caught and returned means that one is cared for. Since "being controlled" is equated with "being cared for," attempts are frequently made to "test" the severity or strictness of superordinate authority to see if it remains firm. If intended or executed rebellion produces swift and firm punitive sanctions, the individual is reassured, at the same time that he is complaining bitterly at the injustice of being caught and punished. Some environmental milieux, having been tested in this fashion for the "firmness" of their coercive sanctions, are rejected, ostensibly for being too strict, actually for not being strict enough. This is frequently so in the case of "problematic" behavior by lower class youngsters in the public schools, which generally cannot command the coercive controls implicitly sought by the individual.

A similar discrepancy between what is overtly and covertly desired is found in the area of dependence-independence. The pose of tough rebellious independence often assumed by the lower class person frequently conceals powerful dependency cravings. These are manifested primarily by obliquely expressed resentment when "care" is not forthcoming rather than by expressed satisfaction when it is. The concern over autonomy dependency is related both to "trouble" and "fate." Insofar as the lower class individual feels that his behavior is controlled by forces which often propel him into "trouble" in the face of an explicit determination to avoid it, there is an implied appeal to "save me from myself." A solution appears to lie in arranging things so that his behavior will be coercively restricted by an externally imposed set of controls strong enough to forcibly restrain his inexplicable inclination to get in trouble.

The periodicity observed in connection with the "excitement" dimension is also relevant here; after involvement in trouble-producing behavior (assault, sexual adventure, a "drunk"), the individual will actively seek a locus of imposed control (his wife, prison, a restrictive job); after a given period of subjection to this control, resentment against it mounts, leading to a "break away" and a search for involvement in further "trouble."

Focal Concerns of the Lower Class Adolescent Street Corner Group

The one-sex peer group is a highly prevalent and significant structural form in the lower class community. There is a strong probability that the prevalence and stability of this type of unit is directly related to the prevalence of a stabilized type of lower class child-rearing unit the "female-based" household. This is a nuclear kin unit in which a male parent is either absent from the household, present only sporadically, or, when present, only minimally or inconsistently involved in the support and rearing of children. This unit usually consists of one or more females of child-bearing age and their offspring. The females are frequently related to one another by blood or marriage ties, and the unit often includes two or more generations of women, e.g., the mother and/or aunt of the principal child-bearing female.

The nature of social groupings in the lower class community may be clarified if we make the assumption that it is the *one-sex peer unit* rather than the two-parent family unit which represents the most significant relational unit for both sexes in lower class communities. Lower class society may be pictured as comprising a set of age-graded one-sex groups which constitute the major psychic focus and reference group for those over twelve or thirteen. Men and women of mating age leave these groups periodically to form temporary marital alliances, but these lack stability, and after varying periods of "trying out" the two-sex family arrangement, gravitate back to the more "comfortable" one-sex grouping, whose members exert strong pressure on the individual *not* to disrupt the group by adopting a two-sex household pattern of life.[5] Membership in a stable and solidary peer unit is vital to the lower class individual precisely to the extent to which a range of essential functions—psychological, educational, and others, are not provided by the "family" unit.

The adolescent street corner group represents the adolescent variant of this lower class structural form. What has been called the "delinquent gang" is one subtype of this form, defined on the basis of frequency of participation in law-violating activity; this subtype should not be considered a legitimate unit of study per se, but rather as one particular variant of the adolescent street corner group. The "hanging" peer group is a unit of particular importance for the adolescent male. In many cases it is the most stable and solidary primary group he has ever belonged to; for boys reared in female-based households the corner group provides the first real opportunity to learn essential aspects of the male role in the context of peers facing similar problems of sex-role identification.

The form and functions of the adolescent corner group operate as a selective mechanism in recruiting members. The activity patterns of the group require a high level of intra-group solidarity; individual members must possess a good capacity for subordinating individual desires to general group interests as well as the capacity for intimate and persisting interaction. Thus highly "disturbed" individuals, or those who cannot tolerate consistently imposed sanctions on "deviant" behavior cannot remain accepted members; the group itself will extrude those whose behavior exceeds limits defined as "normal." This selective process produces a type of group whose members possess to an unusually high degree both the *capacity* and *motivation* to conform to perceived cultural norms, so that the nature of the system of norms and values oriented to is a particularly influential component of motivation.

Focal concerns of the male adolescent corner group are those of the general cultural milieu in which it functions. As would be expected, the relative weighting and importance of these concerns pattern somewhat differently for adolescents than for adults. The nature of this patterning centers around two additional "concerns" of particular importance to this group—concern with "belonging," and with "status." These may be conceptualized as being on a higher level of abstraction than concerns previously cited, since "status" and "belonging" are achieved via cited concern areas of Toughness, etc.

Belonging: Since the corner group fulfills essential functions for the individual, being a member in good standing of the group is of vital importance for its members. A continuing concern over who is "in" and who is not involves the citation and detailed discussion of highly refined criteria for "in-group" membership. The phrase "he hangs with us" means "he is accepted as a member in good standing by current consensus"; conversely, "he don't hang with us" means he is not so accepted. One achieves "belonging" primarily by demonstrating knowledge of and a determination to adhere to the system of standards and valued qualities defined by the group. One maintains membership by acting in conformity with valued aspects of Toughness, Smartness, Autonomy, etc. In those instances where conforming to norms of this reference group at the same time violates norms of other reference groups (e.g., middle class adults, institutional "officials"), immediate reference group norms are much more compelling since violation risks invoking the group's most powerful sanction: exclusion.

Status: In common with most adolescents in American society, the lower class corner group manifests a dominant concern with "status." What differentiates this type of group from others, however, is the particular set of criteria and weighting thereof by which "status" is defined. In general, status is achieved and maintained by demonstrated possession of the valued qualities of lower class culture—Toughness, Smartness, expressed resistance to authority, daring, etc. It is important to stress once, more that the individual orients to these concerns *as they are defined within lower class society;* e.g., the status-conferring potential of "smartness" in the sense of scholastic achievement generally ranges from negligible to negative.

The concern with "status" is manifested in a variety of ways. Intragroup status is a continued concern, and is derived and tested constantly by means of a set of status-ranking activities; the intragroup "pecking order" is constantly at issue. One gains status within the group by demonstrated superiority in Toughness (physical prowess, bravery, skill in athletics and games such as pool and cards), Smartness (skill in repartee, capacity to "dupe" fellow group members), and the like. The term "ranking," used to refer to the pattern of intragroup aggressive repartee, indicates awareness of the fact that this is one device for establishing the intragroup status hierarchy.

The concern over status in the adolescent corner group involves in particular the component of "adultness," the intense desire to be seen as "grown up," and a corresponding aversion to "kid stuff." "Adult" status is defined less in terms of the assumption of "adult" responsibility than in terms of certain external symbols of adult status—a car, ready cash, and, in particular, a perceived "freedom" to drink, smoke, and gamble as one wishes and to come and go without external restrictions. The desire to be seen as "adult" is often a more significant component of much involvement in illegal drinking, gambling, and automobile driving than the explicit enjoyment of these acts as such.

The intensity of the corner group member's desire to be seen as "adult" is sufficiently great that he feels called upon to demonstrate qualities associated with adultness (Toughness, Smartness, Autonomy) to a much greater degree than a lower class adult. This means that he will seek out and utilize those avenues to these qualities which he perceives as available with greater intensity than an adult and less regard for their "legitimacy." In this sense the adolescent variant of lower class culture represents a maximization or an intensified manifestation of many of its most characteristic features.

Concern over status is also manifested in reference to other street corner groups. The term "rep" used in this regard is especially significant, and has broad connotations. In its most frequent and explicit connotation, "rep" refers to the "toughness" of the corner group as a whole relative to that of other groups; a "pecking order" also exists among the several corner groups in a given interactional area, and there is a common perception that the safety or security of the group and all its members depends on maintaining a solid "rep" for toughness vis-à-vis other groups. This motive is most frequently advanced as a reason for involvement in gang fights: "We *can't* chicken out on this fight; our rep would be shot!"; this implies that the group would be relegated to the bottom of the status ladder and become a helpless and recurrent target of external attack.

On the other hand, there is implicit in the concept of "rep" the recognition that "rep" has or may have a dual basis—corresponding to the two aspects of the "trouble" dimension. It is recognized that group as well as individual status can be based on both "law-abiding" and "law-violating" behavior. The situational resolution of the persisting conflict between the "law-abiding" and "law-violating" bases of status comprises a vital set of dynamics in determining whether a "delinquent" mode of behavior will be adopted by a group, under what circumstances, and how persistently. The determinants of this choice are evidently highly complex and fluid, and rest on a range of factors including the presence and perceptual immediacy of different community reference-group loci (e.g., professional criminals, police, clergy, teachers, settlement house workers), the personality structures and "needs" of group members, the presence in the community of social work, recreation, or educational programs which can facilitate utilization of the "law-abiding" basis of status, and so on.

What remains constant is the critical importance of "status" both for the members of the group as individuals and for the group as a whole insofar as members perceive their individual destinies as linked to the destiny of the group, and the fact that action geared to attain status is much more acutely oriented to the fact of status itself than to the legality or illegality, morality or immorality of the means used to achieve it.

Lower Class Culture and the
Motivation of Delinquent Behavior

The customary set of activities of the adolescent street corner group includes activities which are in violation of laws and ordinances of the legal code. Most of these center around assault and theft of various types (the gang fight; auto theft; assault on an individual; petty pilfering and shoplifting; "mugging"; pocketbook theft). Members of street corner gangs are well aware of the law-violating nature of these acts; they are not psychopaths, nor physically or mentally "defective"; in fact, since the corner group supports and enforces a rigorous set of standards which demand a high degree of fitness and personal competence, it tends to recruit from the most "able" members of the community.

Why, then, is the commission of crimes a customary feature of gang activity? The most general answer is that the commission of crimes by members of adolescent street corner groups is motivated primarily by the attempt to achieve ends, states, or conditions which are valued, and to avoid those that are disvalued within their most meaningful cultural milieu, through those culturally available avenues which appear as the most feasible means of attaining those ends.

The operation of these influences is well illustrated by the gang fight—a prevalent and characteristic type of corner group delinquency. This type of activity comprises a highly stylized and culturally patterned set of sequences. Although details vary under different circumstances, the following events are generally included. A member or several members of group A "trespass" on the claimed territory of group B. While there they commit an act or acts which group B defines as a violation of its rightful privileges, an affront to their honor, or a challenge to their "rep." Frequently this act involves advances to a girl associated with group B; it may occur at a dance or party; sometimes the mere act of "trespass" is seen as deliberate provocation. Members of group B then assault members of group A, if they are caught while still in B's territory. Assaulted members of group A return to their "home" territory and recount to members of their group details of the incident, stressing the insufficient nature of the provocation ("I just *looked* at her! Hardly even said anything!"), and the unfair circumstances of the assault ("About *twenty* guys jumped just the *two* of us!"). The highly colored account is acutely inflammatory; group A, perceiving its honor violated and its "rep" threatened, feels obligated to retaliate in force. Sessions of detailed planning now occur; allies are recruited if the size of group A and its potential allies appears to necessitate larger numbers; strategy is plotted, and messengers dispatched. Since the prospect of a gang fight is frightening to even the "toughest" group members, a constant rehearsal of the provocative incident or incidents and the essentially evil nature of the opponents accompanies the planning process to bolster possibly weakening motivation to fight. The excursion into "enemy" territory sometimes results in a full scale fight; more often group B cannot be found, or the police appear and stop the fight, "tipped off" by an anonymous informant. When this occurs, group members express disgust and disappointment; secretly there is much relief; their honor has been avenged without incurring injury; often the anonymous tipster is a member of one of the involved groups.

The basic elements of this type of delinquency are sufficiently stabilized and recurrent as to constitute an essentially ritualized pattern, resembling both in structure and expressed motives for action classic forms such as the European "duel," the American Indian tribal war, and the Celtic clan feud. Although the arousing and "acting out" of individual aggressive emotions are inevitably involved in the gang fight, neither its form nor motivational dynamics can be adequately handled within a predominantly personality-focused frame of reference.

It would be possible to develop in considerable detail the processes by which the commission of a range of illegal acts is either explicitly supported by, implicitly demanded by, or not materially inhibited by factors relating to the focal concerns of lower class culture. In place of such a development, the following three statements condense in general terms the operation of these processes:

1. *Following cultural practices which comprise essential elements of the total life pattern of lower class culture automatically violates certain legal norms.*

2. *In instances where alternate avenues to similar objectives are available, the non-law-abiding avenue frequently provides a relatively greater and more immediate return for a relatively smaller investment of energy.*

3. *The "demanded" response to certain situations recurrently engendered within lower class culture involves the commission of illegal acts.*

The primary thesis of this paper is that the dominant component of the motivation of "delinquent" behavior engaged in by members of lower class corner groups involves a positive effort to achieve states, conditions, or qualities valued within the actor's most significant cultural milieu. If "conformity to immediate reference group values" is the major component of motivation of "delinquent" behavior by gang members, why is such behavior frequently referred to as negativistic, malicious, or rebellious? Albert Cohen, for example, in *Delinquent Boys* (Glencoe: Free Press, 1955) describes behavior which violates school rules as comprising elements of "active spite and malice, contempt and ridicule, challenge and defiance." He ascribes to the gang "keen delight in terrorizing 'good' children, and in general making themselves obnoxious to the virtuous." A recent national conference on social work with "hard-to-reach" groups characterized lower class corner groups as "youth groups in conflict with the culture of their *(sic)* communities." Such characterizations are obviously the result of taking the middle class community and its institutions as an implicit point of reference.

A large body of systematically interrelated attitudes, practices, behaviors, and values characteristic of lower class culture are designed to support and maintain the basic features of the lower class way of life. In areas where these differ from features of middle class culture, action oriented to the achievement and maintenance of the lower class system may violate norms of middle class culture and be perceived as deliberately non-conforming or malicious by an observer strongly cathected to middle class norms. This does not mean, however, that violation of the middle class norm is the dominant component of motivation; it is a by-product of action primarily oriented to the lower class system. The standards of lower class culture cannot be seen merely as a reverse function of middle class culture—as middle class standards "turned upside down"; lower class culture is a distinctive tradition many centuries old with an integrity of its own.

From the viewpoint of the acting individual, functioning within a field of well-structured cultural forces, the relative impact of "conforming" and "rejective" elements in the motivation of gang delinquency is weighted preponderantly on the conforming side. Rejective or rebellious elements are inevitably involved, but their influence during the actual commission of delinquent acts is relatively small compared to the influence of pressures to achieve what is valued by the actor's most immediate reference groups. Expressed awareness by the actor of the element of rebellion often represents only that aspect of motivation of which he is explicitly conscious; the deepest and most compelling components of motivation—adherence to highly meaningful group standards of Toughness, Smartness, Excitement, etc.—are often unconsciously patterned. No cultural pattern as well-established as the practice of illegal acts by members of lower class corner groups could persist if buttressed primarily by negative, hostile, or rejective motives; its principal motivational support, as in the case of any persisting cultural tradition, derives from a positive effort to achieve what is valued within that tradition, and to conform to its explicit and implicit norms.

ENDNOTES

1   The complex issues involved in deriving a definition of "delinquency" cannot be discussed here. The term "delinquent" is used in this paper to characterize behavior or acts committed by individuals within specified age limits which if known to official authorities could result in legal action. The concept of a "delinquent" individual has little or no utility in the approach used here; rather, specified types of *acts* which may be committed rarely or frequently by few or many individuals are characterized as "delinquent."

2   A three-year research project is being financed under National Institutes of Health Grant M-1414, and administered through the Boston University School of Social Work. The primary research effort has subjected all collected material to a uniform data-coding process. All information bearing on some seventy areas of behavior (behavior in reference to school, police, theft, assault, sex, collective athletics, etc.) is extracted from the records, recorded on coded data cards, and filed under relevant categories. Analysis of these data aims to ascertain the actual nature of customary behavior in these areas, and the extent to which the social work effort was able to effect behavioral changes.

3   Between 40 and 60 percent of all Americans are directly influenced by lower class culture, with about 15 percent, or twenty-five million, comprising the "hard core" lower class group defined primarily by its use of the "female-based" household as the basic form of child-rearing unit and of the "serial monogamy" mating pattern as the primary form of marriage. The term "lower class culture" as used here refers most specifically to the way of life of the "hard core" group; systematic research in this area would probably reveal at least four to six major subtypes of lower class culture, for some of which the "concerns" presented here would be differently weighted, especially for those subtypes in which "law-abiding" behavior has a high overt valuation. It is impossible within the compass of this short paper to make the finer intra-cultural distinctions which a more accurate presentation would require.

4   The "brains-brawn" set of capacities are often paired in lower class folklore or accounts of lower class life, e.g., "Brer Fox" and "Brer Bear" in the Uncle Remus stories, or George and Lennie in "Of Mice and Men."

5   Further data on the female-based household unit (estimated as comprising about 15 percent of all American "families") and the role of one-sex groupings in lower class culture are contained in Walter B. Miller, Implications of Urban Lower Class Culture for Social Work. *Social Service Review*, 1959, 33, No. 3.

Essay/Discussion Questions for Section III

Note to the student: If you are able to provide thorough responses to all of the following questions, you have mastered excellent comprehension of the classic readings presented in this section.

1. What do anomie and most subculture theories have in common? (From the section introduction.)

2. What is anomie? What is the difference between Durkheim's conception of anomie and Merton's conception? (From the section introduction.)

3. What are the major differences between the three subculture theories of Cohen, Cloward and Ohlin, and Miller? (From the section introduction.)

4. Explain the concepts of "goals" and "means." How do these concepts interact to generate deviance in a society? (From the Merton reading.)

5. Describe the five deviant modes of adaptation. How is it possible that conformity can be a deviant mode? (From the Merton reading.)

6. According to Cohen, how does the delinquent subculture arise? Once it is developed, how does it contribute to delinquency? (From the Cohen reading.)

7. What are the three forms of gang subcultures and in what types of neighborhoods might you expect to find them? (From the Cloward & Ohlin reading.)

8. Miller's theory of delinquency is substantially different from Cohen's and Cloward and Ohlin's versions. How is his theory different? (From the Miller reading.)

Section IV
LABELING THEORY

Introduction

Following the strain theories, criminologists began to ask new questions and express new concerns about the way the crime picture was being painted. At least part of this new direction came from the events of the day, some of which were the civil rights movement, protests, and a questioning of inequality. Symbolic interactionism, which had not been used directly as a theory of crime or delinquency, reappeared as the foundation of the dominant theory of the 1960s: labeling theory. Declaring there was another side to the deviance equation, some Chicago School students began questioning what they saw as an overemphasis on the criminal and delinquent and his or her characteristics.

Proceeding from the basic assumptions of symbolic interactionism, these theorists maintained that criminal behavior was not innate but was a product of the social environment. By that, they did not mean that behavior was *caused* by the social environment, but rather that it was *defined* by the social environment. Symbolic interactionism teaches that the process of communicating (i.e., symbolizing) defines both self and others' perceptions of events and actions. In other words, communicated symbols affect the way we see ourselves, each other, and the world.

Because of the 1950s emphasis on criminals and delinquents, those trained in symbolic interactionism asked about the neglected side of the deviance coin: the reaction of others to deviance and the product of that reaction. Since labeling theorists were concerned with the attribution of deviance, they were not interested with how an original deviant act occurred or what caused it. This does not mean that they ignored behavior but simply that they were not as concerned about it and instead focused on the social reaction side of deviance. Coupled with the initial questions about an absence of studying the reaction to deviance, labeling theorists developed a perspective that emphasized the impor-

181

tance of society's role in defining a person as a criminal or delinquent. In fact, the new perspective was alternatively known as the *societal reaction school*.

This new direction to theorizing was supported by a new methodology, a new way of determining who engaged in delinquent acts. In 1958, James F. Short, Jr. and F. Ivan Nye published an article detailing the findings of their *self-report* study of delinquency. This study used a questionnaire and interview technique that literally asked juveniles what sort of illegal acts they had committed. Because previous theories were based on official statistics,[1] everyone knew that the groups most involved in crime and delinquency were the lower class and minorities. The new self-report data cast doubt upon the validity of those findings. It seemed that juveniles of all classes and race/ethnicity reported delinquent activity. While the lower-classes and most minorities reported delinquent acts that were a little more serious and a little more frequent than the other groups, the differences were not as large as the official statistics indicated. Some criminologists then proceeded to ask how this difference could be explained.

The first approach to the problem was to ask what the official statistics really measured. Aaron Cicourel and John Kitsuse answered that, rather than being a measure of criminal and delinquent activity, official statistics were really measures of the activity of processing agencies. That is, the Uniform Crime Reports were better viewed as an indicator of the way in which the police took information about crime and the way in which they reported it—the process by which the police account for their activities. If official statistics indicated that lower-class and minority youths were more likely to be arrested and processed, those differences were a product of arrest decisions made by the police and processing decisions made by the juvenile and criminal justice systems. Further, some observed, if police spend large amounts of time watching lower-class youths (as opposed to watching middle-class youths), they will routinely arrest more of them.

Second, some noted that in other areas, such as the sociology of occupations, theorists took for granted that one should not only examine the worker, but the employer as well, to understand behavior. Where, they asked, was the equivalent of an "employer" of crime? The answer, of course, was the criminal justice system itself.

Societal Reaction

Howard Becker was one of the first writers in this new perspective and his 1963 book, *Outsiders: Studies in the Sociology of Deviance* exemplifies the approach of labeling theory. He noted that deviance is not a quality of the person but is dependent on the reaction of others. An individual may, for instance, commit a deviant act but unless that act is noticed and acted upon by others, the person is not considered a deviant. Conversely, even though an individual has not committed a deviant act, if people think that person committed an act, he or she is labeled a deviant. For all intents, then, *deviance is a quality attached by an outside reaction*. This means that deviance is "caused" by the reaction to it.

Becker also paid attention to statuses that are assigned to individuals. All statuses, he claimed, were not equal; some were much more important and powerful than others. The most powerful of these he called *master status*. For instance, a person may be a spouse, parent, and gardener, yet if that person is also a physician, the master status is "doctor." No matter what, most people will react to the person simply because of the "doctor" label. An important factor in master statuses is that they tend to be stereotyped. Therefore, the "doctor" label carries with it a host of other qualities and traits that people will assume a physician to possess. Obviously, master statuses tend to dominate all other statuses. Another master status is gender. If the physician is a female, most would claim that her gender would be reacted to first.

"Criminal," "delinquent," and "ex-con" are other master statuses, but negative ones. With all the qualities and traits associated with them, it might become difficult for persons so labeled to get a job and have normal relationships with people. As a result, labeling theorists talk about the *restricted life opportunities* available to those who are negatively labeled. If those life opportunities are restricted enough, the only avenue to surviving may be a life of crime. This process of the way people react to labels and the effect on the person labeled was termed *criminogenesis*, or the later creation of crime from the initial labeling of a person as a criminal. In addition, once persons are labeled as a criminal or delinquent, the justice system pays much more attention to them, thus increasing the chances of their rearrest.

Secondary Deviance

Edwin Lemert, in a 1951 book titled *Social Pathology: A Systematic Approach to the Theory of Sociopathic Behavior*, asked questions about the effect of labels on the person labeled. Coining the term *secondary deviance*, Lemert noted that the effect of social reactions on an individual varied according to a person's self-concept. If a person has a self-concept of himself or herself as a non-criminal, then the labeling of that person as a criminal has little personal effect. However, when the self-concept is weak, the labeling process may induce the person to accept the label as an important part of the self. Similarly, the repeated labeling of a person might result in a changed self-concept in even the most resistant individual.

Lemert paints the changing self-concept process as happening in a sequence of deviance, labeling and stigmatizing, further deviance, further labeling and stigmatizing, resentment on the part of the individual, formal action by the community, and movement toward the deviant role by the individual. Once the self-concept has changed to match the deviant label, Lemert argued that all behaviors associated with the deviant role become possible for the person. At the point the individual accepts the new self-concept and the associated deviant role, secondary deviance becomes possible. From this perspective, labeling causes even more deviance by forcing individuals into adopting conceptions of themselves as deviants and then engaging in deviant behaviors associated with the new conception of self.

Epilogue

Labeling is still part of criminology today, although not as a full theoretical perspective. Most of today's criminologists simply take a labeling effect for granted. The theory had an effect on the processing of individuals, especially in the juvenile justice system. The entire juvenile diversion movement was a solution to the problems of officially labeling juveniles as delinquent. Even within the adult system, programs such as release-on-recognizance can be partially attributed to the influence of labeling theorists. As the 1960s progressed, several of the labeling proponents embraced the new conflict perspective and much of the labeling message carried on under that banner. However, newer perspectives that use labeling in deterrence (Paternoster & Iovanni, 1989) and in integrated theories (Braithwaite, 1989) have been proposed. The latter version has received the most acclaim. In it, John Braithwaite borrows labeling concepts to construct a theory of "shaming," and uses disintegrative and integrative shaming to explain how behavior might be negatively or positively affected by public reactions.

ENDNOTE

[1]   Official statistics are data collected and reported by government agencies based on their processing of criminal justice information, such as police counts of crime and arrests known as the Uniform Crime Reports. The basis of using official statistics for criminological data in the United States stems from the Chicago School ecological studies.

BIBLIOGRAPHY

Akers, Ronald L. (1968). "Problems in the sociology of deviance," *Social Forces* 46: 455-65.

Becker, Howard S. (1973). "Labeling theory reconsidered," in Sheldon Messinger et al. (eds.) *The Aldine Crime and Justice Annual—1973*. Chicago: Aldine.

Braithwaite, John (1989). *Crime, Shame, and Reintegration*. Cambridge, UK: Cambridge University Press.

Debro, Julius (1970). "Dialogue with Howard S. Becker," *Issues in Criminology* 5: 159-79.

Erikson, Kai T. (1962). "Notes on the sociology of deviance," *Social Problems* 9: 307-14.

Garfinkel, Harold (1956). "Conditions of successful degradation ceremonies," *American Journal of Sociology* 61: 420-24.

Goffman, Erving (1963). *Stigma: Notes on the Management of Spoiled Identity*. Englewood Cliffs, NJ: Prentice-Hall.

Goffman, Erving (1959). "The moral career of the mental patient," *Psychiatry: Journal for the Study of Interpersonal Processes* 22: 123-35.

Gove, Walter R. (ed.) (1975). *The Labeling of Deviance: Evaluating a Perspective*. New York: Halsted.

Hughes, Everett C. (1945). "Dilemmas and contradictions of status," *American Journal of Sociology* 50: 353-59.

Kitsuse, John (1962). "Societal reaction to deviance: Problems of theory and method," *Social Problems* 9: 247-56.

Kitsuse, John and Aaron V. Cicourel (1963). "A note on the use of official statistics," *Social Problems* 11: 131-39.

Lemert, Edwin M. (1967). *Human Deviance, Social Problems and Social Control*. Englewood Cliffs, NJ: Prentice-Hall.

Lofland, John (1969). *Deviance and Identity*. Englewood Cliffs, NJ: Prentice-Hall.

Matza, David (1969). *Becoming Deviant*. New York: Prentice-Hall.

Orcutt, James A. (1973). "Societal reaction and the response to deviation in small groups," *Social Forces* 52: 259-67.

Paternoster, Raymond and Lee Iovanni (1989). "The labeling perspective and delinquency: An elaboration of the theory and assessment of the evidence," *Justice Quarterly* 6: 359-94.

Schur, Edwin M. (1971). *Labeling Deviant Behavior: Its Sociological Implications*. New York: Harper and Row.

Schwartz, Richard D. and Jerome H. Skolnick (1962). "Two studies of legal stigma," *Social Problems* 10: 133-38.

Short, James F., Jr. and F. Ivan Nye (1958). "Extent of unrecorded juvenile delinquency: Tentative conclusions," *Journal of Criminal Law, Criminology, and Police Science* 49: 296-302.

Simmons, J.L. (1969). *Deviants*. Berkeley, CA: Glendessary Press.

Tannenbaum, Frank (1938). *Crime and the Community*. New York: Columbia University Press.

Wellford, Charles F. (1975). "Labelling theory and criminology: An assessment," *Social Problems* 22: 332-45.

Wilkins, Leslie T. (1965). *Social Deviance: Social Policy, Action, and Research*. Englewood Cliffs, NJ: Prentice-Hall.

Howard Saul Becker (1928-   )

Becker was born in Chicago, Illinois. He was educated at the University of Chicago in sociology (A.B., 1946; M.A., 1949; Ph.D., 1951). He also studied photography at the San Francisco Art Institute. Becker taught sociology at the University of Chicago (1952-1953), Stanford University (1962-1965), Northwestern University (1965-1991), and is now at the University of Washington as a professor of sociology and music (1991-   ). In addition, he was a community studies research sociologist from 1955-1962.

Outsiders*
Howard S. Becker

OUTSIDERS

All social groups make rules and attempt, at some times and under some circumstances, to enforce them. Social rules define situations and the kinds of behavior appropriate to them, specifying some actions as "right" and forbidding others as "wrong." When a rule is enforced, the person who is supposed to have broken it may be seen as a special kind of person, one who cannot be trusted to live by the rules agreed on by the group. He is regarded as an *outsider.*

But the person who is thus labeled an outsider may have a different view of the matter. He may not accept the rule by which he is being judged and may not regard those who judge him as either competent or legitimately entitled to do so. Hence, a second meaning of the term emerges: the rulebreaker may feel his judges are *outsiders.*

In what follows, I will try to clarify the situation and process pointed to by this double-barrelled term: the situations of rule-breaking and rule-enforcement and the processes by which some people come to break rules and others to enforce them.

Some preliminary distinctions are in order. Rules may be of a great many kinds. They may be formally enacted into law, and in this case the police power of the state may be used in enforcing them. In other cases, they represent informal agreements, newly arrived at or encrusted with the sanction of age and tradition; rules of this kind are enforced by informal sanctions of various kinds.

Similarly, whether a rule has the force of law or tradition or is simply the result of consensus, it may be the task of some specialized body, such as the police or the committee on ethics of a professional association, to enforce it; enforcement, on the other hand, may be everyone's job or, at least, the job of everyone in the group to which the rule is meant to apply.

Many rules are not enforced and are not, in any except the most formal sense, the kind of rules with which I am concerned. Blue laws, which remain on the statute books though they have not been enforced for a hundred years, are examples. (It is important to remember, however, that an unenforced law may be reactivated for various reasons and regain all its original force, as recently occurred with respect to the laws governing the opening of commercial establishments on Sunday in Missouri.) Informal rules may similarly die from lack of enforcement. I shall mainly be concerned with what we can call the actual operating rules of groups, those kept alive through attempts at enforcement.

Finally, just how far "outside" one is, in either of the senses I have mentioned, varies from case to case. We think of the person who commits a traffic violation or gets a little too drunk at a party as being, after all, not very different from the rest of us and treat his infraction tolerantly. We regard the thief as less like us and punish him severely. Crimes such as murder, rape, or treason lead us to view the violator as a true outsider.

In the same way, some rule-breakers do not think they have been unjustly judged. The traffic violator usually subscribes to the very rules he has broken. Alcoholics are often ambivalent, sometimes feeling that those who judge them do not understand them and at other times agreeing that compulsive drinking is a bad thing. At the extreme, some deviants (homosexuals and drug addicts are good examples) develop full-blown ideologies explaining why they are right and why those who disapprove of and punish them are wrong.

Definitions of Deviance

The outsider—the deviant from group rules—has been the subject of much speculation, theorizing, and scientific study. What laymen want to know about deviants is: why do they do it? How can we account for their rule-breaking? What is there about them that leads them to do forbidden things? Scientific research has tried to find answers to these questions. In doing so it has accepted the common-sense premise that there is something inherently deviant (qualitatively distinct) about acts that break (or seem to break) social rules. It has also accepted the common-sense assumption that the deviant act occurs because some characteristic of the person who commits it makes it necessary or inevitable that he should. Scientists do not ordinarily question the label "deviant" when it is applied to particular acts or people but rather take it as given. In so doing, they accept the values of the group making the judgment.

It is easily observable that different groups judge different things to be deviant. This should alert us to the possibility that the person making the judgment of deviance, the process by which that judgment is arrived at, and the situation in which it is made may all be intimately involved in the phenomenon of deviance. To the degree that the common-sense view of deviance and the scientific theories that begin with its premises assume that acts that break rules are inherently deviant and thus take for granted the situations and processes of judgment, they may leave out an important variable. If scientists ignore the variable character of the process of judgment, they may by that omission limit the kinds of theories that can be developed and the kind of understanding that can be achieved.[1]

Our first problem, then, is to construct a definition of deviance. Before doing this, let us consider some of the definitions scientists now use, seeing what is left out if we take them as a point of departure for the study of outsiders.

The simplest view of deviance is essentially statistical, defining as deviant anything that varies too widely from the average. When a statistician analyzes the results of an agricultural experiment, he describes the stalk of corn that is exceptionally tall and the stalk that is exceptionally short as deviations from the mean or average. Similarly, one can describe anything that differs from what is most common as a deviation. In this view, to be left-handed or redheaded is deviant, because most people are right-handed and brunette.

So stated, the statistical view seems simple-minded, even trivial. Yet it simplifies the problem by doing away with many questions of value that ordinarily arise in discussions of the nature of deviance. In assessing any particular case, all one need do is calculate the distance of the behavior involved from the average. But it is too simple a solution. Hunting with such a definition, we return with a mixed bag—people who are excessively fat or thin, murderers, redheads, homosexuals, and traffic violators. The mixture contains some ordinarily thought of as deviants and others who have broken no rule at all. The statistical definition of deviance, in short, is too far removed from the concern with rule-breaking which prompts scientific study of outsiders.

A less simple but much more common view of deviance identifies it as something essentially pathological, revealing the presence of a "disease." This view rests, obviously, on a medical analogy. The human organism, when it is working efficiently and experiencing no discomfort, is said to be "healthy." When it does not work efficiently, a disease is present. The organ or function that has become deranged is said to be pathological. Of course, there is little disagreement about what constitutes a healthy state of the organism. But there is much less agreement when one uses the notion of pathology analogically, to describe kinds of behavior that are regarded as deviant, because people do not agree on what constitutes healthy behavior. It is difficult to find a definition that will satisfy even such a select and limited group as psychiatrists; it is impossible to find one that people generally accept as they accept criteria of health for the organism.[2]

Sometimes people mean the analogy more strictly, because they think of deviance as the product of mental disease. The behavior of a homosexual or drug addict is regarded as the symptom of a mental disease just as the diabetic's difficulty in getting bruises to heal is regarded as a symptom of his disease. But mental disease resembles physical disease only in metaphor:

> Starting with such things as syphilis, tuberculosis, typhoid fever, and carcinomas and fractures, we have created the class "illness." At first, this class was composed of only a few items, all of which shared the common feature of reference to a state of disordered structure or function of the human body as a physiochemical machine. As time went on, additional items were added to this class. They were not added, however, because they were newly discovered bodily disorders. The physician's attention had been deflected from this criterion and had become focused instead on disability and suffering as new criteria for selection. Thus, at first slowly, such things as hysteria, hypochondriasis, obsessive-compulsive neurosis, and depression were added to the category of illness. Then, with increasing zeal, physicians and especially psychiatrists began to call "illness" (that is, of course, "mental illness") anything and everything in which they could detect any sign of malfunctioning, based on no matter what norm. Hence, agoraphobia is illness because one should not be afraid of open spaces. Homosexuality is illness because heterosexuality is the social norm. Divorce is illness because it signals failure of marriage. Crime, art, undesired political leadership, participation in social affairs, or withdrawal from such participation—all these and many more have been said to be signs of mental illness.[3]

The medical metaphor limits what we can see much as the statistical view does. It accepts the lay judgment of something as deviant and, by use of analogy, locates its source within the individual, thus preventing us from seeing the judgment itself as a crucial part of the phenomenon.

Some sociologists also use a model of deviance based essentially on the medical notions of health and disease. They look at a society, or some part of a society, and ask whether there are any processes going on in it that tend to reduce its stability, thus lessening its chance of survival. They label such processes deviant or identify them as symptoms of social disorganization. They discriminate between those features of society which promote stability (and thus are "functional") and those which disrupt stability (and thus are "dysfunctional"). Such a view has the great virtue of pointing to areas of possible trouble in a society of which people may not be aware.[4]

But it is harder in practice than it appears to be in theory to specify what is functional and what dysfunctional for a society or social group. The question of what the purpose or goal (function) of a group is and, consequently, what things will help or hinder the achievement of that purpose, is very often a political question. Factions within the group disagree and maneuver to have their own definition of the group's function accepted. The function of the group or organization, then, is decided in political conflict, not given in the nature of the organization. If this is true, then it is likewise true that the questions of what rules are to be enforced, what behavior regarded as deviant, and which people labeled as outsiders must also be regarded as political.[5] The functional view of deviance, by ignoring the political aspect of the phenomenon, limits our understanding.

Another sociological view is more relativistic. It identifies deviance as the failure to obey group rules. Once we have described the rules a group enforces on its members, we can say with some precision whether or not a person has violated them and is thus, on this view, deviant.

This view is closest to my own, but it fails to give sufficient weight to the ambiguities that arise in deciding which rules are to be taken as the yardstick against which behavior is measured and judged deviant. A society has many groups, each with its own set of rules and people belong to many groups simultaneously. A person may break the rules of one group by the very act of abiding by the rules of another group. Is he, then, deviant? Proponents of this definition may object that while ambiguity may arise with respect to the rules peculiar to one or another group in society, there are some rules that are very generally agreed to by everyone, in which case the difficulty does not arise. This, of course, is a question of fact, to be settled by empirical research. I doubt there are many such areas of consensus and think it wiser to use a definition that allows us to deal with both ambiguous and unambiguous situations.

Deviance and the Responses of Others

The sociological view I have just discussed defines deviance as the infraction of some agreed-upon rule. It then goes on to ask who breaks rules, and to search for the factors in their personalities and life situations that might account for the infractions. This assumes that those who have broken a rule constitute a homogeneous category, because they have committed the same deviant act.

Such an assumption seems to me to ignore the central fact about deviance: it is created by society. I do not mean this in the way it is ordinarily understood, in which the causes of deviance are located in the social situation of the deviant or in "social factors" which prompt his action. I mean, rather, that *social groups create deviance by making the rules whose infraction constitutes deviance,* and by applying those rules to particular people and labeling them as outsiders. From this point of view, deviance is *not* a quality of the act the person commits, but rather a consequence of the application by others of rules and sanctions to an "offender." The deviant is one to whom that label has successfully been applied; deviant behavior is behavior that people so label.[6]

Since deviance is, among other things, a consequence of the responses of others to a person's act, students of deviance cannot assume that they are dealing with a homogeneous category when they study people who have been labeled deviant. That is, they cannot assume that these people have actually committed a deviant act or broken some rule, because the process of labeling may not be infallible; some people may be labeled deviant who in fact have not broken a rule. Furthermore, they cannot assume that the category of those labeled deviant will contain all those who actually have broken a rule, for many offenders may escape apprehension and thus fail to be included in the population of "deviants" they study. Insofar as the category lacks homogeneity and fails to include all the cases that belong in it, one cannot reasonably expect to find common factors of personality or life situation that will account for the supposed deviance.

What, then, do people who have been labeled deviant have in common? At the least, they share the label and the experience of being labeled as outsiders. I will begin my analysis with this basic similarity and view deviance as the product of a transaction that takes place between some social group and one who is viewed by that group as a rule-breaker. I will be less concerned with the personal and social characteristics of deviants than with the process by which they come to be thought of as outsiders and their reactions to that judgment. . . .

. . . Whether an act is deviant, then, depends on how other people react to it. . . . The point is that the response of other people has to be regarded as problematic. Just because one has committed an infraction of a rule does not mean that others will respond as though this had happened. (Conversely, just because one has not violated a rule does not mean that he may not be treated, in some circumstances, as though he had.)

The degree to which other people will respond to a given act as deviant varies greatly. Several kinds of variation seem worth noting. First of all, there is variation over time. A person believed to have committed a given "deviant" act may at one time be responded to much more leniently than he would be at some other time. The occurrence of "drives" against various kinds of deviance illustrates this clearly. At various times, enforcement officials may decide to make an all-out attack on some particular kind of deviance, such as gambling, drug addiction, or homosexuality. It is obviously much more dangerous to engage in one of these activities when a drive is on than at any other time. (In a very interesting study of crime news in Colorado newspapers, Davis found that the amount of crime reported in Colorado newspapers showed very little association with actual changes in the amount of crime taking place in Colorado. And, further, that peoples' estimate of how much increase there had been in crime in Colorado was associated with the increase in the amount of crime news but not with any increase in the amount of crime.)[7]

The degree to which an act will be treated as deviant depends also on who commits the act and who feels he has been harmed by it. Rules tend to be applied more to some persons than others. Studies of juvenile delinquency make the point clearly. Boys from middle-class areas do not get as far in the legal process when they are apprehended as do boys from slum areas. The middle-class boy is less likely, when picked up by the police, to be taken to the station; less likely when taken to the station to be booked; and it is extremely unlikely that he will be convicted and sentenced.[8] This variation occurs even though the original infraction of the rule is the same in the two cases. Similarly, the law is differentially applied to Negroes and whites. It is well-known that a black man believed to have attacked a white woman is much more likely to be punished than a white man who commits the same offense; it is only slightly less well known that a black man who murders another black man is much less likely to be punished than a white man who commits murder.[9] This, of course, is one of the main points of Sutherland's analysis of white-collar crime: crimes committed by corporations are almost always prosecuted as civil cases, but the same crime committed by an individual is ordinarily treated as a criminal offense.[10]

Some rules are enforced only when they result in certain consequences. The unmarried mother furnishes a clear example. Vincent[11] points out that illicit sexual relations seldom result in severe punishment or social censure for the offenders. If, however, a girl becomes pregnant as a result of such activities, the reaction of others is likely to be severe. (The illicit pregnancy is also an interesting example of the differential enforcement of rules on different categories of people. Vincent notes that unmarried fathers escape the severe censure visited on the mother.)

Why repeat these commonplace observations? Because, taken together, they support the proposition that deviance is not a simple quality, present in some kinds of behavior and absent in others. Rather, it is the product of a process which involves responses of other people to the behavior. The same behavior may be an infraction of the rules at one time and not at another; may be an infraction when committed by one person, but not when committed by another; some rules are broken with impunity, others are not. In short, whether a given act is deviant depends in part on the nature of the act (that is, whether it violates some rule) and in part on what other people do about it.

Some people may object that this is merely a terminological quibble, that one can, after all, define terms any way he wants to and that if some people want to speak of rule-breaking behavior as deviant without reference to the reactions of others they are free to do so. This, of course, is true. Yet it might be worthwhile to refer to such behavior as *rule-breaking behavior* and reserve the term *deviant* for those labeled as deviant by some segment of society. I do not insist that this usage be followed. But it should be clear that insofar as a scientist uses "deviant" to refer to any rule-breaking behavior and takes as his subject of study only those who have been *labeled* deviant, he will be hampered by the disparities between the two categories.

If we take as the object of our attention behavior which comes to be labeled as deviant, we must recognize that we cannot know whether a given act will be categorized as deviant until the response of others has occurred. Deviance is not a quality that lies in behavior itself, but in the interaction between the person who commits an act and those who respond to it.

Whose Rules?

I have been using the term "outsiders" to refer to those people who are judged by others to be deviant and thus to stand outside the circle of "normal" members of the group. But the term contains a second meaning, whose analysis leads to another important set of sociological problems: "outsiders," from the point of view of the person who is labeled deviant, may be the people who make the rules he had been found guilty of breaking.

Social rules are the creation of specific social groups. Modern societies are not simple organizations in which everyone agrees on what the rules are and how they are to be applied in specific situations. They are, instead, highly differentiated along social class lines, ethnic lines, occupational lines, and cultural lines. These groups need not and, in fact, often do not share the same rules. The problems they face in dealing with their environment, the history and traditions they carry with them, all lead to the evolution of different sets of rules. Insofar as the rules of various groups conflict and contradict one another, there will be disagreement about the kind of behavior that is proper in any given situation.

Italian immigrants who went on making wine for themselves and their friends during Prohibition were acting properly by Italian immigrant standards, but were breaking the law of their new country (as, of course, were many of their Old American neighbors). Medical patients who shop around for a doctor may, from the perspective of their own group, be doing what is necessary to protect their health by making sure they get what seems to them the best possible doctor; but, from the perspective of the physician, what they do is wrong because it breaks down the trust the patient ought to put in his physician. The lower-class delinquent who fights for his "turf" is only doing what he considers necessary and right, but teachers, social workers, and police see it differently.

While it may be argued that many or most rules are generally agreed to by all members of a society, empirical research on a given rule generally reveals variation in people's attitudes. Formal rules, enforced by some specially constituted group, may differ from those actually thought appropriate by most people.[12] Factions in a group may disagree on what I have called actual operating rules. Most important for the study of behavior ordinarily labeled deviant, the perspectives of the people who engage in the behavior are likely to be quite different from those of the people who condemn it. In this latter situation, a person may feel that he is being judged according to rules he has had no hand in making and does not accept, rules forced on him by outsiders.

To what extent and under what circumstances do people attempt to force their rules on others who do not subscribe to them? Let us distinguish two cases. In the first, only those who are actually members of the group have any interest in making and enforcing certain rules. If an orthodox Jew disobeys the laws of kashruth, only other orthodox Jews will regard this as a transgression; Christians or nonorthodox Jews will not consider this deviance and would have no interest in interfering. In the second case, members of a group consider it important to their welfare that members of certain other groups obey certain rules. Thus, people consider it extremely important that those who practice the healing arts abide by certain rules; this is the reason the state licenses physicians, nurses, and others, and forbids anyone who is not licensed to engage in healing activities.

To the extent that a group tries to impose its rules on other groups in the society, we are presented with a second question: Who can, in fact, force others to accept their rules and what are the causes of their success? This is, of course, a question of political and economic power. Later we will consider the political and economic process through which rules are created and enforced. Here it is enough to note that people are in fact always *forcing* their rules on others, applying them more or less against the will and without the consent of those others. By and large, for example, rules are made for young people by their elders. Though the youth of this country exert a powerful influence culturally—the mass media of communication are tailored to their interests, for instance—many important kinds of rules are made for our youth by adults. Rules regarding school attendance and sex behavior are not drawn up with regard to the problems of adolescence. Rather, adolescents find themselves surrounded by rules about these matters which have been made by older and more settled people. It is considered legitimate to do this, for youngsters are considered neither wise enough nor responsible enough to make proper rules for themselves.

In the same way, it is true in many respects that men make the rules for women in our society (though in America this is changing rapidly). Negroes find themselves subject to rules made for them by whites. The foreign-born and those otherwise ethnically peculiar often have their rules made for them by the Protestant Anglo-Saxon minority. The middle class makes rules the lower class must obey—in the schools, the courts, and elsewhere.

Differences in the ability to make rules and apply them to other people are essentially power differentials (either legal or extralegal). Those groups whose social position gives them weapons and power are best able to enforce their rules. Distinctions of age, sex, ethnicity, and class are all related to differences in power, which accounts for differences in the degree to which groups so distinguished can make rules for others.

In addition to recognizing that deviance is created by the responses of people to particular kinds of behavior, by the labeling of that behavior as deviant, we must also keep in mind that the rules created and maintained by such labeling are not universally agreed to. Instead, they are the object of conflict and disagreement, part of the political process of society.

ENDNOTES

1   Cf. Donald R. Cressey, "Criminological Research and the Definition of Crimes," *American Journal of Sociology*, LVI (May, 1951), 546-551.

2   See the discussion in C. Wright Mills, "The Professional Ideology of Social Pathologists," *American Journal of Sociology*, XLIX (September, 1942), 165-180.

3   Thomas Szasz, *The Myth of Mental Illness* (New York: Paul B. Hoeber, Inc., 1961), pp. 44-45; see also Erving Goffman, "The Medical Model and Mental Hospitalization," in *Asylums: Essays on the Social Situation of Mental Patients and Other Inmates* (Garden City: Anchor Books, 1961), pp. 321-386.

4   See Robert K. Merton, "Social Problems and Sociological Theory," in Robert K. Merton and Robert A. Nisbet, editors, *Contemporary Social Problems* (New York: Harcourt, Brace and World, Inc., 1961), pp. 697-737; and Talcott Parsons, *The Social System* (New York: The Free Press of Glencoe, 1951), pp. 249-325.

5   Howard Brotz similarly identifies the question of what phenomena are "functional" or "dysfunctional" as a political one in "Functionalism and Dynamic Analysis." *European Journal of Sociology*, II (1961), 170-179.

6   The most important earlier statements of this view can be found in Frank Tannenbaum, *Crime and the Community* (New York: McGraw-Hill Book Co., Inc., 1951), and E.M. Lemert, *Social Pathology* (New York: McGraw-Hill Book Co., Inc., 1951). A recent article stating a position very similar to mine is John Kitsuse, "Societal Reaction to Deviance: Problems of Theory and Method," *Social Problems*, 9 (Winter, 1962), 247-256.

7   F. James Davis, "Crime News in Colorado Newspapers," *American Journal of Sociology,* LVII (January, 1952), 325-330.

8   See Albert K. Cohen and James F. Short, Jr., "Juvenile Delinquency," in Merton and Nisbet, *Op. Cit.,* p. 87.

9   See Harold Garfinkel, "Research Notes on Inter-and Intra-Racial Homicides," *Social Forces,* 27 (May, 1949), 369-381.

10   Edwin H. Sutherland, "White Collar Criminality," *American Sociological Review,* V (February, 1940), 1-12.

11   Clark Vincent, *Unmarried Mothers* (New York: The Free Press of Glencoe, 1961), pp. 3-5.

12   Arnold M. Rose and Arthur E. Prell, "Does the Punishment Fit the Crime?—A Study in Social Valuation," *American Journal of Sociology* LXl (November, 1955), 247-259.

Edwin McCarty Lemert (1912-1996)

Lemert was born in Norwood, Ohio. He was educated at Miami University (Ohio), receiving an A.B. in 1934, and at The Ohio State University in sociology and anthropology with a Ph.D. in 1939. Lemert taught at Kent State University (social science, 1939-1941), Western Michigan University (sociology, 1941-1944), University of California, Los Angeles (sociology, 1944-1953), and founded and taught in the University of California, Davis sociology department (1953-1996).

Secondary Deviance*
Edwin M. Lemert

There has been an embarrassingly large number of theories, often without any relationship to a general theory, advanced to account for various specific pathologies in human behavior. For certain types of pathology, such as alcoholism, crime, or stuttering, there are almost as many theories as there are writers on these subjects. This has been occasioned in no small way by the preoccupation with the origins of pathological behavior and by the fallacy of confusing *original* causes with *effective* causes. All such theories have elements of truth, and the divergent viewpoints they contain can be reconciled with the general theory here if it is granted that original causes or antecedents of deviant behaviors are many and diversified. This holds especially for the psychological processes leading to similar pathological behavior, but it also holds for the situational concomitants of the initial aberrant conduct. A person may come to use alcohol excessively not only for a wide variety of subjective reasons but also because of diversified situational influences, such as the death of a loved one, business failure, or participating in some sort of organized group activity that is conducive to heavy drinking of liquor. Whatever the original reasons for violating the norms of the community, they are important only for certain research purposes, such as assessing the extent of the "social problem" at a given time or determining the requirements for a rational program of social control. From a narrower sociological viewpoint the deviations are not significant until they are organized subjectively and transformed into active roles and become the social criteria for assigning status. The deviant individuals

---

*Source: Edwin M. Lemert, 1951. *Social Pathology: A Systematic Approach to the Theory of Sociopathic Behavior.* New York: McGraw-Hill, pp. 70-71, 75-78. By permission of the publisher.

must react symbolically to their own behavior aberrations and fix them in their sociopsychological patterns. The deviations remain primary deviations or symptomatic and situational as long as they are rationalized or otherwise dealt with as functions of a socially acceptable role. Under such conditions normal and pathological behaviors remain strange and somewhat tensional bedfellows in the same person. Undeniably a vast amount of such segmental and partially integrated pathological behavior exists in our society and has impressed many writers in the field of social pathology.

Just how far and for how long a person may go on dissociating his sociopathic tendencies so that they are merely troublesome adjuncts of normally conceived roles is not known. Perhaps it depends upon the number of alternative definitions of the same overt behavior that he can develop; perhaps certain physiological factors (limits) are also involved. However, if the deviant acts are repetitive and have a high visibility, and if there is a severe societal reaction, which, through a process of identification is incorporated as part of the "me" of the individual, the probability is greatly increased that the integration of existing roles will be disrupted and that reorganization based upon a new role or roles will occur. (The "me" in this context is simply the subjective aspect of the societal reaction.) Reorganization may be the adoption of another normal role in which the tendencies previously defined as "pathological" are given a more acceptable social expression. The other general possibility is the assumption of a deviant role, if such exists; or, more rarely, the person may organize an aberrant sect or group in which he creates a special role of his own. *When a person begins to employ his deviant behavior or a role based upon it as a means of defense, attack, or adjustment to the overt and covert problems created by the consequent societal reaction to him, his deviation is secondary.* Objective evidences of this change will be found in the symbolic appurtenances of the new role, in clothes, speech, posture, and mannerisms, which in some cases heighten social visibility, and which in some cases serve as symbolic cues to professionalization.

Role Conceptions of the Individual Must Be Reinforced by Reactions of Others

It is seldom that one deviant act will provoke a sufficiently strong societal reaction to bring about secondary deviation, unless in the process of introjection the individual imputes or projects meanings into the social situation which are not present. In this case anticipatory fears are involved. For example, in a culture where a child is taught sharp distinctions between "good" women and "bad" women, a single act of questionable morality might conceivably have a profound meaning for the girl so indulging. However, in the absence of reactions by the person's family, neighbors, or the larger community, reinforcing the tentative "bad-girl" self-definition, it is questionable whether a transition to secondary deviation would take place. It is also doubtful whether a temporary exposure to a severe punitive reaction by the community will lead a person to identify himself with a pathological role, unless, as we have said, the experience is highly traumatic. Most frequently there is a progressive reciprocal relationship between the deviation of the individual and the societal reaction, with a compounding of the societal reaction out of the minute accretions in the deviant behavior, until a point is reached where ingrouping and outgrouping between society and the deviant is manifest.[1] At this point a stigmatizing of the deviant occurs in the form of name calling, labeling, or stereotyping.

The sequence of interaction leading to secondary deviation is roughly as follows: (1) primary deviation; (2) social penalties; (3) further primary deviation; (4) stronger penalties and rejections; (5) further deviation, perhaps with hostilities and resentment beginning to focus upon those doing the penalizing; (6) crisis reached in the tolerance quotient, expressed in formal action by the community stigmatizing of the deviant; (7) strengthening of the deviant conduct as a reaction to the stigmatizing and penalties; (8) ultimate acceptance of deviant social status and efforts at adjustment on the basis of the associated role.

As an illustration of this sequence the behavior of an errant schoolboy can be cited. For one reason or another, let us say excessive energy, the schoolboy engages in a classroom prank, and he is penalized for it by the teacher. Later, due to clumsiness, he creates another disturbance and again he is reprimanded. Then, as sometimes happens, the boy is blamed for something he did not do. When the teacher uses the tag "bad boy" or "mischief maker" or other invidious terms, hostility and resentment are excited in the boy, and he may feel that he is blocked in playing the role expected of him. Thereafter, there may be a strong temptation to assume his role in the class as defined by the teacher, particularly when he discovers that there are rewards as well as penalties deriving from such a role. There is, of course, no implication here that such boys go on to become delinquents or criminals, for the mischief-maker role may later become integrated with or retrospectively rationalized as part of a role more acceptable to school authorities.[2] If such a boy continues this unacceptable role and becomes delinquent, the process must be accounted for in the light of the general theory of this volume. There must be a spreading corroboration of a sociopathic self-conception and societal reinforcement at each step in the process.

The most significant personality changes are manifest when societal definitions and their subjective counterpart become generalized. When this happens, the range of major role choices becomes narrowed to one general class.[3] This was very obvious in the case of a young girl who was the daughter of a paroled convict and who was attending a small midwestern college. She continually argued with herself and with the author, in whom she had confided, that in reality she belonged on the "other side of the railroad tracks" and that her life could be enormously simplified by acquiescing in this verdict and living accordingly. While in her case there was a tendency to dramatize her conflicts, nevertheless there was enough societal reinforcement of her self-conception by the treatment she received in her relationship with her father and on dates with college boys to lend it a painful reality. Once these boys took her home to the shoddy dwelling in a slum area where she lived with her father, who was often in a drunken condition, they abruptly stopped seeing her again or else became sexually presumptive.

The Symbolic Consequences of Control

Among the unanticipated consequences of therapy, treatment, or administrative manipulations, none are more important than those which are symbolic in nature. More and more we are coming to realize that the actual symbolic impact of a control or therapeutic experience often is a far cry from what has been intended. The way in which a social worker, a psychiatrist, or a judge conceives of his own role and the meaning of the administrative or clinical situation for the deviant may or may not coincide with the average or modal perception of the latter. If we are to understand in a worthwhile way the reactions of deviants brought under societal control we must get at the effective rather than the formal or intended symbols in control situations. They are not the whole of the symbolic environment in which deviation develops, but they make up a very significant part of it. Frequently they are instrumental in giving unintended but critical meanings to deviant conduct. Court hearings, home investigations by social workers, arrests, clinical visits, segregation within the school system and other formal dispositions of deviants under the aegis of public welfare or public protection in many instances are cause for dramatic redefinitions of the self and role of deviants which may or may not be desired.

ENDNOTES

1   Mead, G., "The Psychology of Punitive Justice." *American Journal of Sociology*, 23, (March, 1918), pp. 577-602.

2   Evidence for fixed or inevitable sequences from predelinquency to crime is absent. Sutherland, E.H., *Principles of Criminology*, 1939, 4th ed., p. 202.

3   Sutherland seems to say something of this sort in connection with the development of criminal behavior. *Ibid.*, p. 86.

Essay/Discussion Questions for Section IV

Note to the student: If you are able to provide thorough responses to all of the following questions, you have mastered excellent comprehension of the classic readings presented in this section.

1. What is symbolic interactionism and how did this affect labeling? (From the section introduction.)

2. Labeling theory used different evidence than anomie or ecological theories. What was this evidence and how did it help to create labeling? (From the section introduction.)

3. How can labeling affect people? Are there positive labels as well as negative ones? If so, give an example of each. (From the section introduction.)

4. Becker's use of the term "outsider" is significant. How so? (From the Becker reading.)

5. Does a deviant behavior have to occur for a person to be labeled as a "deviant"? Why or why not? (From the Becker reading.)

6. What is the difference between primary and secondary deviance? (From the Lemert reading.)

7. How does secondary deviance occur? What does this concept add to labeling theory? (From the Lemert reading.)

Section V
CONFLICT THEORIES

Introduction

Conflict theories are, in one sense, an extension of labeling theories. After examining the characteristics of those most likely to be labeled, some theorists concluded that the laws themselves focused on the powerless. Beginning in the mid-to-late 1960s and continuing through today, several writers contributed to analyses of the creation and application of law. Issues included the definition of crime, discrimination in the criminal justice system, and the ideological content of law. Those same issues remain current.

There are so many different approaches that the only point one can be sure conflict theories share is *an assumption that conflict is the natural state of human society*. According to this assumption, the values of any society are established through conflict rather than through consensus. This means that groups in society are always competing against each other in an attempt to get their interests represented in major social values and institutions. These contests serve to define *power* in society, and those whose interests are most closely allied with law are among the most powerful.

There are two major thrusts to conflict theories: one following a more radical direction and the other a more conservative track. These two thrusts are not too easily distinguished but, in general, one focuses on society itself as the basis for conflict and the other on power conflicts as part of society. The former—radical versions—are quite divergent. They are represented by Marxist, anarchist, economic determinist, value-diversity, and postmodern/constitutive theories (to name just a few general perspectives). Most commonly associated with Marxist and economic determinist positions, radical theories usually assume a sort of class war or at least a powerful elite intent on getting its own way.

Crime, Ideology, and Reality

Richard Quinney's name is synonymous with conflict theory. For a generation of graduate students in criminology, Quinney symbolized the radical critique of capitalist society. His preliminary work in the conflict approach began in 1964 with an article questioning the definitions used to create the category of crime. By 1970, he had written a quintessential work on crime (*The Social Reality of Crime*) incorporating conflict themes with those from existing theories. The essence of that work is that reality is ideologically-constructed. That is, power groups are able to define reality to their advantage. Thus, rather than being something inherently "evil," crime is a social construction benefitting those in power.

Quinney's six propositions in the social reality of crime convey a picture of a "real world" based on images. His perspective begins with the point that crime is defined politically by those authorized to make and enforce law. Second, he notes that definitions of crime are largely based on the interests of those who have the power to shape public policy. Third, crime definitions are applied to individuals and groups whose interests conflict with those in power. When conflict is greater, behaviors are more likely to be defined as crime and more likely to be responded to. Fourth, behavior is a product of the segment of society to which one belongs. Thus, those from segments of society with less power are more likely to act in ways defined as criminal and more likely to be reacted to than those from more powerful segments of society. Fifth, our various forms of communication create images of crime and criminals that support political definitions and interests. Just as important, those same communication forms portray images of non-criminality. Finally, all these points come together to construct an integrated version of a society that creates a social reality of crime through defining, reacting to, and portraying images of various patterns of behavior as criminal and non-criminal.

After this work, Quinney proceeded to incorporate Marxist concepts into his approach and wrote two major critiques of the capitalist order, *Critique of the Legal Order* (1974) and *Class, State and Crime* (1977). By the 1980s, he had begun to incorporate elements of eastern religion into his work and turned to metaphysical interests. At the end of the 1980s, Quinney had incorporated all of these interests into a new approach he called "peacemaking criminology." His work today is predicated on peacemaking concepts that view existing crime prevention practices as producing conflict in society, and he is working to bring about a non-coercive, re-integrative response to crime.

Radical Conflict Theory

The reading by Steven Spitzer ("Toward a Marxian Theory of Deviance") was chosen as a representative of the radical approach because he did an excellent job of capturing the essence of class-based theories. Spitzer argued that when the *mode of production* and the superstructure of society are threatened, individuals are defined as problem populations. He saw two general conditions as a cause of problems for capitalist states: (1) *surplus labor* and (2) the *contradictions inherent in state institutions* (e.g., the creation of educated people). These conditions produce individuals who require management.

From this problem population, two discrete groupings are identified according to the type of threat they represent and the social control mechanisms necessary to manage them. The two groups are *social junk* and *social dynamite*. Social junk are those who do not actively support the capitalist social order, but who also are relatively quiet. Examples are the elderly, mentally retarded, and the homeless. They are a burden on a capitalist economy, but are generally harmless. As long as they remain quiet, or there is no public concern, the management of this population is largely done by containment and regulation. Members of the social junk population are often the main clientele of welfare and therapeutic agencies. When social junk gets out of hand, larger expenditures of resources are required.

The second group, social dynamite, is a different issue altogether. These are active individuals in society who can directly threaten the capitalist social order, particularly the economic relations in the mode of production. Clear examples of social dynamite are rebels, activists, protestors, and the idle young. These populations are usually managed with the legal system; thus, they are defined as criminals and juvenile delinquents and targeted by specific control measures. These two groups are not always mutually exclusive. The capitalist state gets concerned when social situations change and some categories of social junk become social dynamite.

Conservative/Pluralist Conflict Theory

Conservative, or pluralist, conflict theories assume that there are groups contesting with each other for control over particular issues, situations, or events. The size and number of the groups vary. *Resources*, though, are the most critical component of this perspective. The ability to control and use resources reflects a group's ability to gain and maintain control over its interests and affect decision-making processes.

Resources include such ingredients as political power, law, money, and bargaining power. When a group vies for control of an issue, these resources are employed. Often, several groups will unite on an issue and pool their resources; this unity is usually temporary and will dissolve as soon as the issue is decided. Thus, *power* can be short- or long-lived. The degree of power may also vary according to the particular issue. Some groups have more power than others by virtue of the class position of their members. In these cases, the resources are long-term, the degree of power is considerable, and the interests are wide-ranging. The interests of the most powerful members of society are often tied directly to the structure of the society itself. In any event, *law* is a resource that, when available, adds immensely to the power of a group. If law can be invoked, then the machinery of government (the legal system) can be brought into the conflict on the side of the group. One possibility is that those on the other side of the issue can be defined as criminals.

The reading by Austin Turk is a version of this brand of conflict theory and is from a book titled *Political Criminality*. In the book, Turk explored the nature of the South African political system and its implications for law-making and relationships of authorities and subjects. The theoretical framework he employed dates to earlier works in 1969 and in the 1970s. The central concern of this excerpt is the creation and maintenance of social order by a group attempting to control a society.

Turk discussed the various problems of gaining and maintaining power over other groups in society and determined there are always *authority-subject relationships* in a society. Those who can control authority put themselves in a position of dominance over the other groups in a society, who become subjects. Authority-subject relationships are, then, a fact of life in any society. The problem is the form in which those relationships exist. Turk answered this by exploring several forms of *control*, two of which we will focus on here.

The first form of control of subjects is *physical coercion*. Such control is very costly in both labor and resources. In addition, when subjects are made to conform with physical coercion, the fact of control itself is quite evident, making control that much more difficult. In general, the more visible authorities are, the greater are the problems of control. More effective and less costly forms of control are necessary.

The second form of control resolves the problems of visibility, cost, and effectiveness and is much more subtle in its presence. Turk posited that this form of control is represented by *legal images* and *living time*. Once a society is dominated by a group, the use of law becomes critical. If the group can write its interests into law, even physical coercion changes from an occupying force to "policing." In time, subjects will police themselves in the interest of maintaining law—in short, the law becomes theirs. One form of law, procedural, is crucial because it dictates how people will be processed and how the law will be applied. Both of these components can be set up to benefit the powerful.

Living time represents the most subtle form of control. After an extended period of control, most of the generation of subjects who knew "how it was before" become extinct. This leaves behind a group of subjects who have known only the present society. The newer subjects have no basis for comparison and are less likely to question the social order. Thus, the society, and its rules, become theirs also. The authority-subject relationship becomes permanent and requires a low expenditure of resources.

Epilogue

Conflict theories are now an accepted part of criminological theory. In fact, many of today's newer theories have accepted and incorporated conflict propositions, although rarely from the radical versions. Some of the older theories have even been adjusted to incorporate conflict ideas as well. Since the late 1970s, however, the increasingly conservative mood of the country has led to most criminologists ignoring the more radical conflict formulations. In the face of this, there has been a re-examination of radical conflict theory and some writers have called for a more practical approach often referred to as "left realism." Some former radical conflict theorists have even moved to a non-Marxist position referred to as postmodernist theory. This new approach is, in reality, a wide variety of different theoretical efforts ranging from language-based (semiotics) to chaos-theory-based. Regardless of the version, conflict theory has a long heritage and, in one form or another, will remain with criminology.

BIBLIOGRAPHY

Bohm, Robert M. (1982). "Radical criminology: An explication," *Criminology* 19: 565-89.

Bonger, William A. (1916). *Criminality and Economic Conditions*. Trans. H.P. Horton. Boston: Little, Brown.

Chambliss, William B. (1975). "Toward a political economy of crime," *Theory and Society* 2: 152-53.

Chambliss, William B. and Robert B. Seidman (1982). *Law, Order and Power*, 2nd ed. Reading, MA: Addison-Wesley.

Coser, Lewis (1956). *The Functions of Social Conflict*. New York: Macmillan.

Dahrendorf, Ralf (1959). *Class and Class Conflict in an Industrial Society*. London: Routledge & Kegan Paul.

Dahrendorf, Ralf (1958). "Out of utopia: Toward a reconstruction of sociological analysis," *American Journal of Sociology*, 67: 115-27.

Dekeseredy, Walter S. and Martin D. Schwartz (1991). "British and U.S. left realism: A critical comparison," *International Journal of Offender Therapy and Comparative Criminology* 35: 248-62.

Ferrell, Jeff (1993). *Crimes of Style: Urban Graffiti and the Politics of Criminality.* New York: Garland.

Gordon, David M. (1973). "Capitalism, class and crime in America," *Crime and Delinquency* 19: 163-86.

Greenberg, David F. (1981). *Crime and Capitalism.* Palo Alto, CA: Mayfield.

Lynch, Michael J. and Byron W. Groves (1989). *A Primer in Radical Criminology,* 2nd ed. New York: Harrow and Heston.

McShane, Marilyn D. (1987). "Immigration processing and the alien inmate: Constructing a conflict perspective," *Journal of Crime and Justice* 10:171-94.

Michalowski, Raymond J. (1983). "Crime control in the 1980s: A progressive agenda," *Crime and Social Justice* 19: 13-23.

Michalowski, Raymond J. and Edward W. Bohlander (1976). "Repression and criminal justice in capitalist America," *Sociological Inquiry* 46: 95-106.

Milovanovic, Dragan (ed.) (1997a). *Chaos, Criminology, and Social Justice: The New Orderly (Dis)Order.* Westport, CT: Praeger.

Milovanovic, Dragan (1997b). *Postmodern Criminology.* New York: Garland.

Milovanovic, Dragan (1996). "Postmodern criminology: Mapping the terrain," *Justice Quarterly* 13: 567-610.

National Commission on the Causes and Prevention of Violence (1969). *The Politics of Protest: Task Force Report on Violent Aspects of Protest and Confrontation.* New York: Simon and Schuster.

Pepinsky, Harold E. and Paul Jesilow (1985). *Myths that Cause Crime,* 2nd ed., annotated. Cabin John, MD: Seven Locks Press.

Platt, Tony (1985). "Criminology in the 1980s: Progressive alternatives to law and order," *Crime and Social Justice* 21-22: 191-99.

Platt, Tony (1974). "Prospects for a radical criminology in the United States," *Crime and Social Justice* 1: 2-6.

Quinney, Richard (1977). *Class, State and Crime: On the Theory and Practice of Criminal Justice.* New York: McKay.

Quinney, Richard (1974). *Critique of the Legal Order.* Boston: Little, Brown.

Quinney, Richard (1970). *The Social Reality of Crime.* Boston: Little, Brown.

Quinney, Richard (1965). "Is criminal behaviour deviant behaviour?" *British Journal of Criminology* 5: 132-42.

Schwendinger, Herman and Julia Schwendinger (1970). "Defenders of order or guardians of human rights?" *Issues in Criminology* 7: 72-81.

Sykes, Gresham M. (1974). "Critical criminology," *Journal of Criminal Law and Criminology* 65: 206-13.

Taylor, Ian, Paul Walton, and Jock Young (1973). *The New Criminology: For a Social Theory of Deviance*. London: Routledge & Kegan Paul.

Tifft, Larry L. (1979). "The coming redefinitions of crime: An anarchist perspective," *Social Problems* 26: 392-402.

Turk, Austin T. (1976). "Law as a weapon in social conflict," *Social Problems* 23: 276-91.

Turk, Austin T. (1969). *Criminality and Legal Order*. Chicago: Rand McNally.

Turk, Austin T. (1966). "Conflict and criminality," *American Sociological Review* 31: 338-52.

Turk, Austin T. (1964). "Prospects for theories of criminal behavior," *Journal of Criminal Law, Criminology, and Police Science* 55: 454-61.

Vold, George B. (1958). *Theoretical Criminology*. New York: Oxford University Press.

Vold, George B. and Thomas J. Bernard (1986). *Theoretical Criminology*, 3rd ed. New York: Oxford University Press.

Williams, Frank P., III (1998). *Imagining Criminology: An Alternative Paradigm*. New York: Garland.

Williams, Frank P., III (1997). "Constructing criminological sandpiles: New domain assumptions from physics," *Social Pathology* 2: 218-29.

Williams, Frank P., III (1980). "Conflict theory and differential processing: An analysis of the research literature," in J.A. Inciardi (ed.) *Radical Criminology: The Coming Crises*. Beverly Hills: Sage, 213-32.

Young, Jock (1992). "Ten points of realism," in R. Matthews and J. Young (eds.) *Rethinking Criminology: The Realist Debate*. Newbury Park, CA: Sage, 24-68.

Young, T.R. (1991). "Chaos and crime: Non-linear and fractal forms of crime," *Critical Criminologist* 3(2): 3-4, 10-11.

Richard Earl Quinney (1934-   )

Quinney was born in Elkhorn, Wisconsin. He was educated at Carroll College (B.S., 1956), Northwestern University (M.S., 1957), and the University of Wisconsin (Ph.D. in sociology, 1962). Quinney has taught at St. Lawrence University (New York) from 1960-1962, University of Kentucky from 1962-1965, New York University from 1965-1972, Brooklyn College and Graduate Center of the City University of New York from 1974-1975, Brown University from 1975-1978, Boston College from 1978-1979, and University of Wisconsin in 1980. He has been in the sociology department of Northern Illinois University since 1983.

The Social Reality of Crime*
Richard Quinney

ASSUMPTIONS: MAN AND SOCIETY IN A THEORY OF CRIME

In studying any social phenomenon we must hold to some general perspective. Two of those used by sociologists, and by most social analysts for that matter, are the *static* and the *dynamic* interpretations of society. Either is equally plausible, though most sociologists take the static viewpoint.[1] This emphasis has relegated forces and events, such as deviance and crime, which do not appear to be conducive to stability and consensus, to the pathologies of society.

My theory of crime, however, is based on the dynamic perspective. The theory is based on these assumptions about man and society: (1) process, (2) conflict, (3) power, and (4) social action.

Process. The dynamic aspect of social relations may be referred to as "social process." Though in analyzing society we use static descriptions, that is, we define the structure and function of social relations, we must be aware that social phenomena fluctuate continually.[2]

We apply this assumption to all social phenomena that have duration and undergo change, that is, all those which interest the sociologist. A social process is a continuous series of actions, taking place in time, and leading to a special kind of result: "a system of social change taking place within a defined situation and exhibiting a particular order of change through the operation of forces present from the first within the situation."[3] Any particular phenomenon, in turn, is viewed

---

*Source: Richard Quinney, 1970. *The Social Reality of Crime*. Boston: Little, Brown, and Company, pp. 8-23. By permission of the author.

as contributing to the dynamics of the total process. As in the "modern systems approach," social phenomena are seen as generating out of an interrelated whole.[4] The methodological implication of the process assumption is that any social phenomenon may be viewed as part of a complex network of events, structures, and underlying processes.

Conflict. In any society conflicts between persons, social units, or cultural elements are inevitable, the normal consequences of social life. Conflict is especially prevalent in societies with diverse value systems and normative groups. Experience teaches that we cannot expect to find consensus on all or most values and norms in such societies.

Two models of society contrast sharply: one is regarded as "conflict" and the other, "consensus." With the consensus model we describe social structure as a functionally integrated system held together in equilibrium. In the conflict model, on the other hand, we find that societies and social organizations are shaped by diversity, coercion, and change. The differences between these contending but complementary conceptions of society have been best characterized by Dahrendorf.[5] According to his study, we assume in postulating the consensus (or integrative) model of society that: (1) society is a relatively persistent, stable structure, (2) it is well integrated, (3) every element has a function—it helps maintain the system, and (4) a functioning social structure is based on a consensus on values. For the conflict (or coercion) model of society, on the other hand, we assume that: (1) at every point society is subject to change, (2) it displays at every point dissensus and conflict, (3) every element contributes to change, and (4) it is based on the coercion of some of its members by others. In other words, society is held together by force and constraint and is characterized by ubiquitous conflicts that result in continuous change: "values are ruling rather than common, enforced rather than accepted, at any given point of time."[6]

Although in society as a whole conflict may be general, according to the conflict model, it is still likely that we will find stability and consensus on values among subunits in the society. Groups with their own cultural elements are found in most societies, leading to social differentiation with conflict between the social units; nonetheless integration and stability may appear within specific social groups: "Although the total larger society may be diverse internally and may form only a loosely integrated system, within each subculture there may be high integration of institutions and close conformity of individuals to the patterns sanctioned by their own group."[7]

Conflict need not necessarily disrupt society. Some sociologists have been interested in the *functions* of social conflict, "that is to say, with those consequences of social conflict which make for an increase rather than a decrease in the adaptation or adjustment of particular social relationships or groups."[8] It seems that conflict can promote cooperation, establish group boundaries, and unite social factions.

Furthermore, it may lead to new patterns that may in the long run be beneficial to the whole society or to parts of it.[9] Any doubts about its functional possibilities have been dispelled by Dahrendorf: "I would suggest . . . that all that is creativity, innovation, and development in the life of the individual, his group, and his society is due, to no small extent, to the operation of conflicts between group and group, individual and individual, emotion and emotion within one individual. This fundamental fact alone seems to me to justify the value judgment that conflict is essentially "good" and "desirable.""[10] Conflict is not always the disruptive agent in a society; at certain times it may be meaningful to see it as a cohesive force.

Power. The conflict conception of society leads us to assume that coherence is assured in any social unit by coercion and constraint. In other words, *power* is the basic characteristic of social organization. "This means that in every social organization some positions are entrusted with a right to exercise control over other positions in order to ensure effective coercion; it means, in other words, that there is a differential distribution of power and authority."[11] Thus, conflict and power are inextricably linked in the conception of society presented here. The differential distribution of power produces conflict between competing groups, and conflict, in turn, is rooted in the competition for power. Wherever men live together conflict and a struggle for power will be found.

Power, then, is the ability of persons and groups to determine the conduct of other persons and groups.[12] It is utilized not for its own sake, but is the vehicle for the enforcement of scarce values in society, whether the values are material, moral, or otherwise. The use of power affects the distribution of values and values affect the distribution of power. The "authoritative allocation of values" is essential to any society.[13] In any society, institutional means are used to officially establish and enforce sets of values for the entire population.

Power and the allocation of values are basic in forming *public policy*. Groups with special *interests* become so well organized that they are able to influence the policies that are to affect all persons. These interest groups exert their influence at every level and branch of government in order to have their own values and interests represented in the policy decisions.[14] Any interest group's ability to influence public policy depends on the group's position in the political power structure. Furthermore, access to the formation of public policy is unequally distributed because of the structural arrangements of the political state. "Access is one of the advantages unequally distributed by such arrangements; that is, in consequence of the structural peculiarities of our government some groups have better and more varied opportunities to influence key points of decision than do others."[15] Groups that have the power to gain access to the decision-making process also inevitably control the lives of others.

A major assumption in my conception of society, therefore, is the importance of interest groups in shaping public policy. Public policy is formed so as to represent the interests and values of groups that are in positions of power. Rather than accept the pluralistic conception of the political process, which assumes that all groups make themselves heard in policy decision-making, I am relying upon a conception that assumes an unequal distribution of power in formulating and administering public policy.[16]

Social Action. An assumption of man that is consistent with the conflict-power conception of society asserts that man's actions are purposive and meaningful, that man engages in voluntary behavior. This *humanistic* conception of man contrasts with the oversocialized conception of man. Man is, after all, capable of considering alternative actions, of breaking from the established social order.[17] Once he gains an awareness of self, by being a member of society, he is able to choose his actions. The extent to which he does conform depends in large measure upon his own self-control.[18] Nonconformity may also be part of the process of finding self-identity. It is thus *against* something that the self can emerge.[19]

By conceiving of man as able to reason and choose courses of action, we may see him as changing and becoming, rather than merely being.[20] The kind of culture that man develops shapes his ability to be creative. Through his culture he may develop the capacity to have greater freedom of action.[21] Not only is he shaped by his physical, social, and cultural experiences, he is able to select what he is to experience and develop. The belief in realizing unutilized human potential is growing and should be incorporated in a contemporary conception of human behavior.[22]

The social action frame of reference that serves as the basis of the humanistic conception of man is drawn from the work of such writers as Weber, Znaniecki, MacIver, Nadel, Parsons, and Becker.[23] It was originally suggested by Max Weber: "Action is social in so far as, by virtue of the subjective meaning attached to it by the acting individual (or individuals), it takes account of the behavior of others and is thereby oriented in its own course."[24] Hence, human behavior is intentional, has meaning for the actors, is goal-oriented, and takes place with an awareness of the consequences of behavior.

Because man emerges in social action, a *social reality* is created. That is, man in interaction with others constructs a meaningful world of everyday life.

> It is the world of cultural objects and social institutions into which we are all born, within which we have to find our bearings, and with which we have to come to terms. From the outset, we, the actors on the social scene, experience the world we live in as a world both of

nature and of culture, not as a private but as an intersubjective one, that is, as a world common to all of us, either actually given or potentially accessible to everyone; and this involves intercommunication and language.[25]

Social reality consists of both the social meanings and the products of the subjective world of persons. Man, accordingly, constructs activities and patterns of actions as he attaches meaning to his everyday existence.[26] Social reality is thus both a *conceptual reality* and a *phenomenal reality*. Having constructed social reality, man finds a world of meanings and events that is real to him as a conscious social being.

THEORY: THE SOCIAL REALITY OF CRIME

The theory contains six propositions and a number of statements within the propositions. With the first proposition I define crime. The next four are the explanatory units. In the final proposition the other five are collected to form a composite describing the social reality of crime. The propositions and their integration into a theory of crime reflect the assumptions about explanation and about man and society outlined above.[27]

PROPOSITION 1 (DEFINITION OF CRIME): *Crime is a definition of human conduct that is created by authorized agents in a politically organized society.*

This is the essential starting point in the theory—a definition of crime—which itself is based on the concept of definition. Crime is a *definition* of behavior that is conferred on some persons by others. Agents of the law (legislators, police, prosecutors, and judges), representing segments of a politically organized society, are responsible for formulating and administering criminal law. Persons and behaviors, therefore, become criminal because of the *formulation* and *application* of criminal definitions. Thus, *crime is created.*

By viewing crime as a definition, we are able to avoid the commonly used "clinical perspective," which leads one to concentrate on the quality of the act and to assume that criminal behavior is an individual pathology.[28] Crime is not inherent in behavior, but is a judgment made by some about the actions and characteristics of others.[29] This proposition allows us to focus on the formulation and administration of the criminal law as it touches upon the behaviors that become defined as criminal. Crime is seen as a result of a process which culminates in the defining of persons and behaviors as criminal. It follows, then, that *the greater the number of criminal definitions formulated and applied, the greater the amount of crime.*

PROPOSITION 2 (FORMULATION OF CRIMINAL DEFINITIONS):
Criminal definitions describe behaviors that conflict with the interests of the segments of society that have the power to shape public policy.

Criminal definitions are formulated according to the interests of those *segments* (types of social groupings) of society which have the *power* to translate their interests into *public policy*. The interests—based on desires, values and norms—which are ultimately incorporated into the criminal law are those which are treasured by the dominant interest groups in the society.[30] In other words, those who have the ability to have their interests represented in public policy regulate the formulation of criminal definitions.

That criminal definitions are formulated is one of the most obvious manifestations of conflict in society. By formulating criminal law (including legislative statutes, administrative rulings, and judicial decisions), some segments of society protect and perpetuate their own interests. Criminal definitions exist, therefore, because some segments of society are in conflict with others.[31] By formulating criminal definitions these segments are able to control the behavior of persons in other segments. It follows that *the greater the conflict in interests between the segments of a society, the greater the probability that the power segments will formulate criminal definitions.*

The interests of the power segments of society are reflected not only in the content of criminal definitions and the kinds of penal sanctions attached to them, but also in the *legal policies* stipulating how those who come to be defined as "criminal" are to be handled. Hence, procedural rules are created for enforcing and administering the criminal law. Policies are also established on programs for treating and punishing the criminally defined and for controlling and preventing crime. In the initial criminal definitions or the subsequent procedures, and in correctional and penal programs or policies of crime control and prevention, the segments of society that have power and interests to protect are instrumental in regulating the behavior of those who have conflicting interests and less power.[32] Finally, law changes with modifications in the interest structure. When the interests that underlie a criminal law are no longer relevant to groups in power, the law will be reinterpreted or altered to incorporate the dominant interests. Hence, *the probability that criminal definitions will be formulated is increased by such factors as (1) changing social conditions, (2) emerging interests, (3) increasing demands that political, economic, and religious interests be protected, and (4) changing conceptions of the public interest.* The social history of law reflects changes in the interest structure of society.

PROPOSITION 3 (APPLICATION OF CRIMINAL DEFINITIONS):

Criminal definitions are applied by the segments of society that have the power to shape the enforcement and administration of criminal law.

The powerful interests intervene in all stages in which criminal definitions are created. Since interests cannot be effectively protected by merely formulating criminal law, enforcement and administration of the law are required. The interests of the powerful, therefore, operate in applying criminal definitions. Consequently, crime is "political behavior and the criminal becomes in fact a member of a 'minority group' without sufficient public support to dominate the control of the police power of the state."[33] Those whose interests conflict with the interests represented in the law must either change their behavior or possibly find it defined as "criminal."

The probability that criminal definitions will be applied varies according to the extent to which the behaviors of the powerless conflict with the interests of the power segments. Law enforcement efforts and judicial activity are likely to be increased when the interests of the powerful are threatened by the opposition's behavior. Fluctuations and variations in the application of criminal definitions reflect shifts in the relations of the various segments in the power structure of society.

Obviously, the criminal law is not applied directly by the powerful segments. They delegate enforcement and administration of the law to authorized *legal agents*, who, neverthelesss, represent their interests. In fact, the security in office of legal agents depends on their ability to represent the society's dominant interests.

Because the interest groups responsible for creating criminal definitions are physically separated from the groups to which the authority to enforce and administer law is delegated, local conditions affect the manner in which criminal definitions are applied.[34] In particular, communities vary in the law enforcement and administration of justice they expect. Application is also affected by the visibility of acts in a community and by its norms about reporting possible offenses. Especially important are the occupational organization and ideology of the legal agents.[35] Thus, *the probability that criminal definitions will be applied is influenced by such community and organizational factors as (1) community expectations of law enforcement and administration, (2) the visibility and public reporting of offenses, and (3) the occupational organization, ideology, and actions of the legal agents to whom the authority to enforce and administer criminal law is delegated.* Such factors determine how the dominant interests of society are implemented in the application of criminal definitions.

The probability that criminal definitions will be applied in specific situations depends on the actions of the legal agents. In the final analysis, a criminal definition is applied according to an evaluation by someone charged with the authority to enforce and administer the law. In the course of "criminalization," a criminal label may be affixed to a person because of real or fancied attributes: "Indeed, a person is evaluated, either favorably or unfavorably, not because he does something, or even because he is something, but because others react to their perceptions of him as offensive or inoffensive."[36] Evaluation by the definers is affected by the way in which the suspect handles the situation, but ultimately their evaluations and subsequent decisions determine the criminality of human acts. Hence, *the more legal agents evaluate behaviors and persons as worthy of criminal definition, the greater the probability that criminal definitions will be applied.*

PROPOSITION 4 (DEVELOPMENT OF BEHAVIOR PATTERNS IN RELATION TO CRIMINAL DEFINITIONS): *Behavior patterns are structured in segmentally organized society in relation to criminal definitions and within this context persons engage in actions that have relative probabilities of being defined as criminal.*

Although behavior varies, all behaviors are similar in that they represent the *behavior patterns* of segments of society. Therefore, all persons—whether they create criminal definitions or are the objects of criminal definitions—act according to *normative systems* learned in relative social and cultural settings.[37] Since it is not the quality of the behavior but the action taken against the behavior that makes it criminal, that which is defined as criminal in any society is relative to the behavior patterns of the segments of society that formulate and apply criminal definitions. Consequently, *persons in the segments of society whose behavior patterns are not represented in formulating and applying criminal definitions are more likely to act in ways that will be defined as criminal than those in the segments that formulate and apply criminal definitions.*

Once behavior patterns are established with some regularity within the respective segments of society, individuals are provided with a framework for developing *personal action patterns*. These patterns continually develop for each person as he moves from one experience to another. It is the development of these patterns that gives his behavior its own substance in relation to criminal definitions.

Man constructs his own patterns of action in participating with others. It follows, then, that *the probability that a person will develop action patterns that have a high potential of being defined as criminal depends on the relative substance of (1) structured opportunities, (2) learning experiences, (3) interpersonal associations and identifications, and (4) self-conceptions.* Throughout his experiences, each person creates a conception of himself as a social being. Thus prepared, he behaves according to the anticipated consequences of his actions.[38]

During experiences shared by the criminal definers and the criminally defined, personal action patterns develop among the criminally defined because they are so defined. After such persons have had continued experience in being criminally defined, they learn to manipulate the application of criminal definitions.[39]

Furthermore, those who have been defined as criminal begin to conceive of themselves as criminal; as they adjust to the definitions imposed upon them, they learn to play the role of the criminal.[40] Because of others' reactions, therefore, persons may develop personal action patterns that increase the likelihood of their being defined as criminal in the future. That is, *increased experience with criminal definitions increases the probability of developing actions that may be subsequently defined as criminal.*

Thus, both the criminal definers and the criminally defined are involved in reciprocal action patterns. The patterns of both the definers and the defined are shaped by their common, continued, and related experiences. The fate of each is bound to that of the other.

PROPOSITION 5 (CONSTRUCTION OF CRIMINAL CONCEPTIONS): *Conceptions of crime are constructed and diffused in the segments of society by various means of communication.*

The "real world" is a social construction: man with the help of others creates the world in which he lives. Social reality is thus the world a group of people create and believe in as their own. This reality is constructed according to the kind of "knowledge" they develop, the ideas they are exposed to, the manner in which they select information to fit the world they are shaping and the manner in which they interpret these conceptions.[41] Man behaves in reference to the *social meanings* he attaches to his experiences.

Among the constructions that develop in a society are those which determine what man regards as crime. Wherever we find the concept of crime, there we will find conceptions about the relevance of crime, the offender's characteristics, and the relation of crime to the social order.[42] These conceptions are constructed by communication. In fact, *the construction of criminal conceptions depends on the portrayal of crime in all personal and mass communications.* By such means, criminal conceptions are constructed and diffused in the segments of a society. The most critical conceptions are those held by the power segments of society. These are the conceptions that are certain of becoming incorporated into the social reality of crime. In general then, the more the power segments are concerned about crime, the greater the probability that criminal definitions will be created and that behavior patterns will develop in opposition to criminal definitions. The formulation and application of criminal definitions and the development of behavior patterns related to criminal definitions are thus joined in full circle by the construction of criminal conceptions.

PROPOSITION 6 (THE SOCIAL REALITY OF CRIME): *The social reality of crime is constructed by the formulation and application of criminal definitions, the development of behavior patterns related to criminal definitions, and the construction of criminal conceptions.*

These five propositions can be collected into a composite. The theory, accordingly, describes and explains phenomena that increase the probability of crime in society, resulting in the social reality of crime.

Since the first proposition is a definition and the sixth is a composite, the body of the theory consists of the four middle propositions. These form a model, as diagrammed in Figure 1.1, which relates the propositions into a theoretical system. Each proposition is related to the others forming a theoretical system of developmental propositions interacting with one another. The phenomena denoted in the propositions and their relationships culminate in what is regarded as the amount and character of crime in a society at any given time, that is, in the social reality of crime.

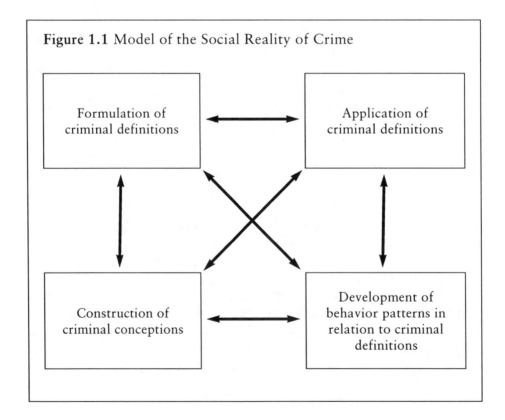

Figure 1.1 Model of the Social Reality of Crime

ENDNOTES

1 See Robert A. Nisbet, *The Sociological Tradition* (New York: Basic Books, 1966); Reinhard Bendix and Bennett Berger, "Images of Society and Problems of Concept Formation in Sociology," in Gross, *Symposium on Sociological Theory*, pp. 92-118.

2 Howard Becker, *Systematic Sociology on the Basis of the Beziehungslehre and Gebildelehre of Leopold von Wiess* (New York: John Wiley & Sons, 1932).

3 Robert MacIver, *Social Causation* (New York: Ginn, 1942), p. 130.

4 Walter Buckley, "A Methodological Note," in Thomas J. Scheff, *Being Mentally Ill* (Chicago: Aldine, 1966), pp. 201-205.

5 Ralf Dahrendorf, *Class and Class Conflict in Industrial Society* (Stanford: Stanford University Press, 1959), pp. 161-162.

6 Ralf Dahrendorf, "Out of Utopia: Toward a Reorientation in Sociological Analysis," *American Journal of Sociology*, 67 (September, 1958), p. 127.

7 Robin M. Williams, Jr., *American Society*, 2nd ed. (New York: Alfred A. Knopf, 1960), p. 375.

8 Lewis A. Coser, *The Functions of Social Conflict* (New York: The Free Press, 1956), p. 8.

9 Lewis A. Coser, "Social Conflict and the Theory of Social Change," *British Journal of Sociology*, 8 (September, 1957), pp. 197-207.

10 Dahrendorf, *Class and Class Conflict in Industrial Society*, p. 208. The importance of conflict in society is also discussed in, among other works, George Simmel, *Conflict*, trans. Kurt H. Wolff (New York: The Free Press, 1955); Irving Louis Horowitz, "Consensus, Conflict and Cooperation: A Sociological Inventory," *Social Forces*, 41 (December, 1962), pp. 177-188; Raymond W. Mack, "The Components of Social Conflict," *Social Problems*, 12 (Spring, 1965), pp. 388-397.

11 Dahrendorf, *Class and Class Conflict in Industrial Society*, p. 165.

12 Max Weber, *From Max Weber: Essays in Sociology*, trans. H. H. Gerth and C. Wright Mills (New York: Oxford University Press, 1946); Hans Gerth and C. Wright Mills, *Character and Social Structure* (New York: Harcourt, Brace, 1953), especially pp. 192-273; C. Wright Mills, *The Power Elite* (New York: Oxford University Press, 1956); George Simmel, *The Sociology of George Simmel*, trans. Kurt H. Wolff (New York: The Free Press, 1950), pp. 181-186; Robert Bierstedt, "An Analysis of Social Power," *American Sociological Review*, 15 (December, 1950), pp. 730-738.

13 David Easton, *The Political System* (New York: Alfred A. Knopf, 1953), p. 137. Similar ideas are found in Harold D. Lasswell, *Politics: Who Gets What, When, How* (New York: McGraw-Hill, 1936); Harold D. Lasswell and Abraham Kaplan, *Power and Society* (New Haven: Yale University Press, 1950.

14 Among the vast amount of literature on interest groups, see Donald C. Blaisdell, *American Democracy Under Pressure* (New York: Ronald Press, 1957); V. O. Key, Jr., *Politics, Parties, and Pressure Groups* (New York: Thomas Y. Crowell, 1959); Earl Latham, *Group Basis of Politics* (Ithaca, N.Y.: Cornell University Press, 1952); David Truman, *The Governmental Process* (New York: Alfred A. Knopf, 1951); Henry W. Ehrmann (ed.), *Interest Groups on Four Continents* (Pittsburgh: University of Pittsburgh Press, 1958); Henry A. Turner, "How Pressure Groups Operate," *Annals of the American Academy Political and Social Science*, 319 (September, 1958), pp. 63-72; Richard W. Gable, "Interest Groups as Policy Shapers,"

Annals of the American Academy Political and Social Science, 319 (September, 1958), pp. 84-93; Murray S. Stedman, "Pressure Group and the American Tradition," *Annals of the American Academy Political and Social Science,* 319 (September, 1958), pp. 123-219. For documentation on the influence of specific interest groups, see Robert Engler, *The Politics of Oil* (New York: MacMillan, 1961); Oliver Garceau, *The Political Life of the American Medical Association* (Cambridge: Harvard University Press, 1941); Charles M. Hardin, *The Politics of Agriculture: Soil Conservation and the Struggle for Power in Rural America* (New York: The Free Press of Glencoe, 1962); Grant McConnell, *Private Power and American Democracy* (New York: Alfred A. Knopf, 1966); Harry A. Millis and Royal E. Montgomery, *Organized Labor* (New York: McGraw Hill, 1945); Warner Schilling, Paul Y. Hammond, and Glenn H. Snyder, *Strategy, Politics and Defense* (New York: Columbia University Press, 1962); William R. Willoughby, *The St. Lawrence Waterway: A Study in Politics and Diplomacy* (Madison: University of Wisconsin Press, 1961).

15   Truman, *The Governmental Process,* p. 322.

16   Evaluations of the pluralistic and power approaches are found in Peter Bachrach and Morton S. Baratz, "Two Faces of Power," *American Political Science Review,* 61 (December, 1962), pp. 947-952; Thomas I. Cook, "The Political System: The Stubborn Search for a Science of Politics," *Journal of Philosophy,* 51 (February, 1954), pp. 128-137; Charles S. Hyneman, *The Study of Politics* (Urbana: University of Illinois Press, 1959); William C. Mitchell, "Politics as the Allocation of Values: A Critique," *Ethics,* 71 (January, 1961), pp. 79-89; Talcott Parsons, "The Distribution of Power in American Society," *World Politics,* 10 (October, 1957), pp. 123-143; Charles Perrow, "The Sociological Perspective and Political Pluralism," *Social Research,* 31 (Winter, 1964), pp. 411-422.

17   For essentially this aspect of man see Peter Berger, *Invitation to Sociology: A Humanistic Perspective* (New York: Doubleday, 1963), chap. 6; Max Mark, "What Image of Man for Political Science?" *Western Political Quarterly,* 15 (December, 1962), pp. 593-604; Dennis Wrong, "The Oversocialized Conception of Man in Modern Sociology," *American Sociological Review,* 26 (April, 1961), pp. 183-193.

18   Tamotsu Shibutani, *Society and Personality: An Internactionist Approach to Social Psychology* (Englewood Cliffs, N. J.: Prentice Hall, 1961), especially pp. 60, 91-94, 276-278. Also see S. F. Nadel, "Social Control and Self-Regulation," *Social Forces,* 31 (March, 1953), pp. 265-273.

19   Erving Goffman, *Asylums* (New York: Doubleday, 1961), pp. 318-320.

20   Richard A. Schermerhorn, "Man the Unfinished," *Sociological Quarterly,* 4 (Winter, 1963), pp. 5-17; Gordon W. Allport, *Becoming: Basic Considerations for a Psychology of Personality* (New Haven: Yale University Press, 1955).

21   Herbert J. Muller, *The Uses of the Past* (New York: Oxford University Press, 1952), especially pp. 40-42.

22   Julian Huxley, *New Bottles for New Wines* (New York: Harper, 1957).

23   Florian Znaniecki, *Social Actions* (New York: Farrar and Rinehart, 1936); MacIver, *Social Causation;* S. F. Nadel, *Foundations of Social Anthropology* (New York: The Free Press, 1951); Talcott Parsons, *The Structure of Social Action* (New York: The Free Press, 1949); Howard Becker, *Through Values to Social Interpretation* (Durham: Duke University Press, 1950).

24   Max Weber, *The Theory of Social and Economic Organization,* trans. A. M. Henderson and Talcott Parsons (New York: The Free Press), p. 88.

25 Alfred Schutz, *The Problem of Social Reality: Collected Papers I* (The Hague: Martinus Nijhoff, 1962), p. 53.

26 See Peter L. Berger and Thomas Luckmann, *The Social Construction of Reality* (Garden City, N.Y.: Doubleday, 1966).

27 For earlier background material, see Richard Quinney, "A Conception of Man and Society for Criminology," *Sociological Quarterly,* 6 (Spring, 1965), pp. 119-127; Quinney, "Crime in Political Perspective," *American Behavioral Scientist,* 8 (December, 1964), pp. 19-22; Quinney, "Is Criminal Behavior Deviant Behavior?" *British Journal of Criminology,* 5 (April, 1965), pp. 132-142.

28 See Jane R. Mercer, "Social System Perspective and Clinical Perspective: Frames of Reference for Understanding Career Patterns of Persons Labelled as Mentally Retarded," *Social Problems,* 13 (Summer, 1966), pp. 18-34.

29 This perspective in the study of social deviance has been developed in Becker, *Outsiders*; Kai T. Erikson, "Notes on the Sociology of Deviance," *Social Problems,* 9 (Spring, 1962), pp. 307-314; John I. Kitsuse, "Societal Reactions to Deviant Behavior: Problems of Theory and Method," *Social Problems,* 9 (Winter, 1962), pp. 247-256. Also see Ronald L. Akers, "Problems in the Sociology of Deviance: Social Definitions and Behavior," *Social Forces,* 46 (June, 1968), pp. 455-465; David J. Bordua, "Recent Trends: Deviant Behavior and Social Control," *Annals of the American Academy of Political and Social Science,* 369 (January, 1967), pp. 149-163; Jack P. Gibbs, "Conceptions of Deviant Behavior: The Old and the New," *Pacific Sociological Review,* 9 (Spring, 1966), pp. 9-14; Clarence R. Jeffery, "The Structure of American Criminological Thinking," *Journal of Criminal Law, Criminology and Police Science,* 46 (January-February, 1956), pp. 658-672; Austin T. Turk, "Prospects for Theories of Criminal Behavior," *Journal of Criminal Law, Criminology and Police Science,* 55 (December, 1964), pp. 454-461.

30 See Richard C. Fuller, "Morals and the Criminal Law," *Journal of Criminal Law, Criminology and Police Science,* 32 (March-April, 1942), pp. 624-630; Thorsten Sellin, *Culture Conflict and Crime* (New York: Social Science Research Council, 1938), pp. 21-25; Clarence R. Jeffery, "Crime, Law and Social Structure," *Journal of Criminal Law, Criminology and Police Science,* 47 (November-December, 1956), pp. 423-435; John J. Honigmann, "Value Conflict and Legislation," *Social Problems,* 7 (Summer, 1959), pp. 34-40; George Rusche and Otto Kirchheimer, *Punishment and Social Structure* (New York: Columbia University Press, 1939); Roscoe Pound, *An Introduction to the Philosophy of Law* (New Haven: Yale University Press, 1922).

31 I am obviously indebted to the conflict formulation of George B. Vold, *Theoretical Criminology* (New York: Oxford University Press, 1958), especially pp. 203-242. A recent conflict approach to crime is found in Austin T. Turk, "Conflict and Criminality," *American Sociological Review,* 31 (June, 1966), pp. 338-352.

32 Considerable support for this proposition is found in the following studies: William J. Chambliss, "A Sociological Analysis of the Law of Vagrancy," *Social Problems,* 12 (Summer, 1964), pp. 66-77; Kai T. Erikson, *Wayward Puritans* (New York: John Wiley, 1966); Jerome Hall, *Theft, Law and Society,* 2nd ed. (Indianapolis: Bobbs-Merrill, 1952); Clarence R. Jeffery, "The Development of Crime in Early England," *Journal of Criminal Law, Criminology and Police Science,* 47 (March-April, 1957), pp. 647-666; Alfred R. Lindesmith, *The Addict and the Law* (Bloomington: Indiana University Press, 1965); Rusche and Kirchheimer, *Punishment and Social Structure;* Andrew Sinclair, *Era of Excess: A Social History of the Prohibition Movement* (New York: Harper & Row, 1964); Edwin H. Sutherland, "The Sexual Psychopath Law," *Journal of Criminal Law, Criminology and Police Science,* 40 (January-February, 1950), pp. 543-554.

33   Vold, *Theoretical Criminology*, p. 202. Also see Irving Louis Horowitz and Martin Liebowitz, "Social Deviance and Political Marginality: Toward a Redefinition of the Relation Between Sociology and Politics," *Social Problems*, 15 (Winter, 1968), pp. 280-296.

34   See Michael Banton, *The Policeman and the Community* (London: Tavistock, 1964); Egon Bittner, "The Police on Skid-Row: A Study of Peace Keeping," *American Sociological Review*, 32 (October, 1967), pp. 699-715; John P. Clark, "Isolation of the Police: A Comparison of the British and American Situations," *Journal of Criminal Law, Criminology and Police Science*, 56 (September , 1965), pp. 307-319; Nathan Goldman, *The Differential Selection of Juvenile Offenders for Court Appearance* (New York National Council on Crime and Delinquency, 1963); James Q. Wilson, *Varieties of Police Behavior* (Cambridge: Harvard University Press, 1968).

35   Abraham S. Blumberg, *Criminal Justice* (Chicago: Quadrangle Books, 1967); David J. Bordua and Albert J. Reiss, Jr., "Command, Control and Charisma: Reflections on Police Bureaucracy," *American Journal of Sociology*, 72 (July, 1966), pp. 68-76; Aaron V. Cicourel, *The Social Organization of Juvenile Justice* (New York: John Wiley, 1968); Arthur Niederhoffer, *Behind the Shield: The Police in Urban Society* (Garden City, N.Y.: Doubleday, 1967); Jerome H. Skolnick, *Justice Without Trial: Law Enforcement in Democratic Society* (New York: John Wiley, 1966); Arthur L. Stinchcombe, "Institutions of Privacy in the Determination of Police Administrative Practice," *American Journal of Sociology*, 69 (September, 1963), pp. 150-160; David Sudnow, "Normal Crimes: Sociological Features of the Penal Code in a Public Defender Office," *Social Problems*, 12 (Winter, 1965), pp. 255-276; William A. Westley, "Violence and the Police," *American Journal of Sociology*, 59 (July, 1953), pp. 34-41; Arthur Lewis Wood, *Criminal Lawyer* (New Haven: College & University Press, 1967).

36   Turk, "Conflict and Criminality," p. 340. For research on the evaluation of suspects by policemen, see Irving Piliavin and Scott Briar, "Police Encounters with Juveniles," *American Journal of Sociology*, 70 (September, 1964), pp. 206-214.

37   Assumed within the theory of the social reality of crime is Sutherland's theory of differential association. See Edwin H. Sutherland, *Principles of Criminology*, 4th ed. (Philadelphia: J.B. Lippincott, 1947). An analysis of the differential association theory is found in Melvin L. De Fleur and Richard Quinney, "A Reformulation of Sutherland's Differential Association Theory and a Strategy for Empirical Verification," *Journal of Research in Crime and Delinquency*, 3 (January, 1966), pp. 1-22.

38   On the operant nature of criminally defined behavior, see Robert L. Burgess and Ronald L. Akers, "A Differential Association-Reinforcement Theory of Criminal Behavior," *Social Problems*, 14 (Fall, 1966), pp. 128-147; C. R. Jeffery, "Criminal Behavior and Learning Theory," *Journal of Criminal Law, Criminology, and Police Science*, 56 (September, 1965), pp. 294-300.

39   A discussion of the part the person plays in manipulating the deviant defining situation is found in Judith Lorber, "Deviance as Performance: The Case of Illness, "*Social Problems*, 14 (Winter, 1967), pp. 302-310.

40   Edwin M. Lemert, *Human Deviance, Social Problems, and Social Control* (Englewood Cliffs, N.J.: Prentice Hall, 1964), pp. 40-64; Edwin M. Lemert, *Social Pathology* (New York: McGraw-Hill, 1951), pp. 3-98. A related and earlier discussion is in Frank Tannenbaum, *Crime and the Community* (New York: Columbia University Press, 1938), pp. 3-81.

41   See Berger and Luckmann, *The Social Construction of Reality*. Relevant research on the diffusion of information is discussed in Everett M. Rogers, *Diffusion of Innovations* (New York: The Free Press of Glencoe, 1962).

42 Research on public conceptions of crime is only beginning. See Alexander L. Clark and Jack P. Gibbs, "Social Control: A Reformulation," *Social Problems,* 12 (Spring, 1965), pp. 398-415; Thomas E. Dow, Jr., "The Role of Identification in Conditioning Public Attitude Toward the Offender," *Journal of Criminal Law, Criminology and Police Science,* 58 (March, 1967), pp. 75-79; William P. Lentz, "Social Status and Attitudes Toward Delinquency Control," *Journal of Research in Crime and Delinquency,* 3 (July, 1966), pp. 147-154; Jennie McIntyre, "Public Attitudes Toward Crime and Law Enforcement," *Annals of the American Academy of Political and Social Science,* 374 (November, 1967), pp. 34-46; Anastassios D. Mylonas and Walter C. Reckless, "Prisoners' Attitudes Toward Law and Legal Institutions," *Journal of Criminal Law, Criminology and Police Science,* 54 (December, 1963), pp. 479-484; Elizabeth A. Rooney and Don C. Gibbons, "Social Reactions to 'Crimes Without Victims,'" *Social Problems,* 13 (Spring, 1966), pp. 400-410.

Criminologist Profile

Steven Spitzer (1944-   )

Steven Spitzer was born in Philadelphia, Pennsylvania. He received a B.A. in sociology at the University of Maryland, an M.A. in criminology from the University of Maryland, and a Ph.D. in sociology from Indiana University. Spitzer taught at the University of Pennsylvania (sociology, 1971-1977), the University of Northern Iowa (sociology, 1977-1980), and since 1980 has been a professor in the sociology department at Suffolk University (Boston).

Toward a Marxian Theory of Deviance*
Steven Spitzer

The Production of Deviance in Capitalist Society

The concept of deviance production offers a starting point for the analysis of both deviance and control. But for such a construct to serve as a critical tool it must be grounded in a historical and structural investigation of society. For Marx, the crucial unit of analysis is the mode of production that dominates a given historical period. If we are to have a Marxian theory of deviance, therefore, deviance production must be understood in relationship to specific forms of socioeconomic organization. In our society, productive activity is organized capitalistically and it is ultimately defined by "the process that transforms on the one hand, the social means of subsistence and of production into capital, on the other hand the immediate producers into wage labourers" (Marx, 1967:714).

There are two features of the capitalist mode of production important for purposes of this discussion. First, as a mode of production it forms the foundation or infrastructure of our society. This means that the starting point of our analysis must be an understanding of the economic organization of capitalist societies and the impact of that organization on all aspects of social life. But the capitalist mode of production is an important starting point in another sense. It contains contradictions which reflect the internal tendencies of capitalism. These contradictions are important because they explain the changing character of the capitalist system and the nature of its impact on social, political and

---

*Source: Steven Spitzer, "Toward a Marxian Theory of Deviance." © 1975 by the Society for the Study of Social Problems. Reprinted from *Social Problems*, Vol. 22, No. 5, June 1975, pp. 641-651 by permission.

intellectual activity. The formulation of a Marxist perspective on deviance requires the interpretation of the process through which the contradictions of capitalism are expressed. In particular, the theory must illustrate the relationship between specific contradictions, the problems of capitalist development and the production of a deviant class.

The superstructure of society emerges from and reflects the ongoing development of economic forces (the infrastructure). In class societies this superstructure preserves the hegemony of the ruling class through a system of class controls. These controls, which are institutionalized in the family, church, private associations, media, schools and the state, provide a mechanism for coping with the contradictions and achieving the aims of capitalist development.

Among the most important functions served by the superstructure in capitalist societies is the regulation and management of problem populations. Because deviance processing is only one of the methods available for social control, these groups supply raw material for deviance production, but are by no means synonymous with deviant populations. Problem populations tend to share a number of social characteristics, but most important among these is the fact that their behavior, personal qualities and/or position threaten the *social relations of production* in capitalist societies. In other words, populations become generally eligible for management as deviant when they disturb, hinder or call into question any of the following:

1. capitalist modes of appropriating the product of human labor (e.g., when the poor "steal" from the rich)

2. the social conditions under which capitalist production takes place (e.g., those who refuse or are unable to perform wage labor)

3. patterns of distribution and consumption in capitalist society (e.g., those who use drugs for escape and transcendence rather than sociability and adjustment)

4. the process of socialization for productive and non-productive roles (e.g., youth who refuse to be schooled or those who deny the validity of "family life")[1]

5. the ideology which supports the functioning of capitalist society (e.g., proponents of alternative forms of social organization)

Although problem populations are defined in terms of the threat and costs that they present to the social relations of production in capitalist societies, these populations are far from isomorphic with a revolutionary class. It is certainly true that some members of the problem population may, under specific circumstances, possess revolutionary potential. But this potential can only be realized if the problematic group is located in a position of functional indispensability within the capitalist system.

Historically, capitalist societies have been quite successful in transforming those who are problematic and indispensable (the protorevolutionary class) into groups who are either problematic and dispensable (candidates for deviance processing), or indispensable but not problematic (supporters of the capitalist order). On the other hand, simply because a group is manageable does not mean that it ceases to be a problem for the capitalist class. Even though dispensable problem populations cannot overturn the capitalist system, they can represent a significant impediment to its maintenance and growth. It is in this sense that they become eligible for management as deviants.

Problem populations are created in two ways—either directly through the expression of fundamental contradictions in the capitalist mode of production or indirectly through disturbances in the system of class rule. An example of the first process is found in Marx's analysis of the "relative surplus-population."

Writing on the "General Law of Capitalist Accumulation" Marx explains how increased social redundance is inherent in the development of the capitalist mode of production:

> With the extension of the scale of production, and the mass of the labourers set in motion, with the greater breadth and fullness of all sources of wealth, there is also an extension of the scale on which greater attraction of labourers by capital is accompanied by their greater repulsion . . . The labouring population therefore produces, along with the accumulation of capital produced by it, the means by which itself is made relatively superfluous, . . . and it does this to an always increasing extent (Marx, 1967:631).

In its most limited sense the production of a relative surplus-population involves the creation of a class which is economically redundant. But insofar as the conditions of economic existence determine social existence, this process helps explain the emergence of groups who become both threatening and vulnerable at the same time. The marginal status of those populations reduces their stake in the maintenance of the system while their powerlessness and dispensability renders them increasingly susceptible to the mechanisms of official control.

The paradox surrounding the production of the relative surplus-population is that this population is both useful and menacing to the accumulation of capital. Marx describes how the relative surplus-population "forms a disposable industrial army, that belongs to capital quite as absolutely as if the latter had bred it at its own cost," and how this army, "creates, for the changing, needs of the self-expansion of capital, a mass of human material always ready for exploitation" (Marx, 1967:632).

On the other hand, it is apparent that an excessive increase in what Marx called the "lowest sediment" of the relative surplus-population might seriously impair the growth of capital. The social expenses and threat to social harmony created by a large and economically stagnant surplus-population could jeopardize the preconditions for accumulation by undermining the ideology of equality so essential to the legitimation of production relations in bourgeois democracies, diverting revenues away from capital investment toward control and support operations, and providing a basis for political organization of the dispossessed.[2] To the extent that the relative surplus-population confronts the capitalist class as a threat to the social relations of production it reflects an important contradiction in modern capitalist societies: a surplus-population is a necessary product of and condition for the accumulation of wealth on a capitalist basis, but it also creates a form of social expense which must be neutralized or controlled if production relations and conditions for increased accumulation are to remain unimpaired.

Problem populations are also generated through contradictions which develop in the system of class rule. The institutions which make up the superstructure of capitalist society originate and are maintained to guarantee the interests of the capitalist class. Yet these institutions necessarily reproduce, rather than resolve, the contradictions of the capitalist order. In a dialectical fashion, arrangements which arise in order to buttress capitalism are transformed into their opposite—structures for the cultivation of internal threats. An instructive example of this process is found in the emergence and transformation of educational institutions in the United States.

The introduction of mass education in the United States can be traced to the developing needs of corporate capitalism (cf. Karier, 1973; Cohen and Lazerson, 1972; Bowles and Gintis, 1972; Spring, 1972). Compulsory education provided a means of training, testing and sorting, and assimilating wage-laborers, as well as withholding certain populations from the labor market. The system was also intended to preserve the values of bourgeois society and operate as an "inexpensive form of police" (Spring, 1973:31). However, as Gintis (1973) and Bowles (1973) have suggested, the internal contradictions of schooling can lead to effects opposite of those intended. For the poor, early schooling can make explicit the oppressiveness and alienating character of capitalist institutions, while higher education can instill critical abilities which lead students to "bite the hand that feeds them." In both cases educational institutions create troublesome populations (i.e., drop outs and student radicals) and contribute to the very problems they were designed to solve.

After understanding how and why specific groups become generally bothersome in capitalist society, it is necessary to investigate the conditions under which these groups are transformed into proper objects for social control. In other words, we must ask what distinguishes the generally problematic from the specifically deviant. The rate at which problem populations are converted into deviants will reflect the relationship between these populations and the control system. This rate is likely to be influenced by the:

1. *Extensiveness and Intensity of State Controls.* Deviance processing (as opposed to other control measures) is more likely to occur when problem management is monopolized by the state. As state controls are applied more generally the proportion of official deviants will increase.

2. *Size and Level of Threat Presented by the Problem Population.* The larger and more threatening the problem population, the greater the likelihood that this population will have to be controlled through deviance processing rather than other methods. As the threat created by these populations exceeds the capacities of informal restraints, their management requires a broadening of the reaction system and an increasing centralization and coordination of control activities.

3. *Level of Organization of the Problem Population.* When and if problem populations are able to organize and develop limited amounts of political power, deviance processing becomes increasingly less effective as a tool for social control. The attribution of deviant status is most likely to occur when a group is relatively impotent and atomized.

4. *Effectiveness of Control Structures Organized through Civil Society.* The greater the effectiveness of the organs of civil society (i.e., the family, church, media, schools, sports) in solving the problems of class control, the less the likelihood that deviance processing (a more explicitly political process) will be employed.

5. *Availability and Effectiveness of Alternative Types of Official Processing.* In some cases the state will be able effectively to incorporate certain segments of the problem population into specially created "pro-social" roles. In the modern era, for example, conscription and public works projects (Piven and Cloward, 1971) helped neutralize the problems posed by troublesome populations without creating new or expanding old deviant categories.

6. *Availability and Effectiveness of Parallel Control Structures.* In many instances the state can transfer its costs of deviance production by supporting or at least tolerating the activities of independent control networks which operate in its interests. For example, when the state is denied or is reluctant to assert a monopoly over the use of force it is frequently willing to encourage vigilante organizations and private police in the suppression of problem popula-

tions. Similarly, the state is often benefitted by the policies and practices of organized crime, insofar as these activities help pacify, contain and enforce order among potentially disruptive groups (Schelling, 1967).

7. *Utility of Problem Populations.* While problem populations are defined in terms of their threat and costs to capitalist relations of production, they are not threatening in every respect. They can be supportive economically (as part of a surplus labor pool or dual labor market), politically (as evidence of the need for state intervention) and ideologically (as scapegoats for rising discontent). In other words, under certain conditions capitalist societies derive benefits from maintaining a number of visible and uncontrolled "troublemakers" in their midst. Such populations are distinguished by the fact that while they remain generally bothersome, the costs that they inflict are most immediately absorbed by other members of the problem population. Policies evolve, not so much to eliminate or actively suppress these groups, but to deflect their threat away from targets which are sacred to the capitalist class. Victimization is permitted and even encouraged, as long as the victims are members of an expendable class.

Two more or less discrete groupings are established through the operations of official control. These groups are a product of different operating assumptions and administrative orientations toward the deviant population. On the one hand, there is *social junk* which, from the point of view of the dominant class, is a costly yet relatively harmless burden to society. The discreditability of social junk resides in the failure, inability or refusal of this group to participate in the roles supportive of capitalist society. Social junk is most likely to come to official attention when informal resources have been exhausted or when the magnitude of the problem becomes significant enough to create a basis for "public concern." Since the threat presented by social junk is passive, growing out of its inability to compete and its withdrawal from the prevailing social order, controls are usually designed to regulate and contain rather than eliminate and suppress the problem. Clear-cut examples of social junk in modern capitalist societies might include the officially administered aged, handicapped, mentally ill and mentally retarded.

In contrast to social junk, there is a category that can be roughly described as *social dynamite.* The essential quality of deviance managed as social dynamite is its potential actively to call into question established relationships, especially relations of production and domination. Generally, therefore, social dynamite tends to be more youthful, alienated and politically volatile than social junk. The control of social dynamite is usually premised on an assumption that the problem is acute in nature, requiring a rapid and focused expenditure of control resources. This is in contrast to the handling of social junk frequently based on a belief that the problem is chronic and best controlled through broad reactive, rather than intensive and selective measures. Correspondingly, social dynamite is normally processed through the legal system with its capacity for active intervention, while social junk is frequently (but not always)[3] administered by the agencies and agents of the therapeutic and welfare state.

Many varieties of deviant populations are alternatively or simultaneously dealt with as either social junk and/or social dynamite. The welfare poor, homosexuals, alcoholics and "problem children" are among the categories reflecting the equivocal nature of the control process and its dependence on the political, economic and ideological priorities of deviance production. The changing nature of these priorities and their implications for the future may be best understood by examining some of the tendencies of modern capitalist systems.

Monopoly Capital and Deviance Production

Marx viewed capitalism as a system constantly transforming itself. He explained these changes in terms of certain tendencies and contradictions immanent within the capitalist mode of production. One of the most important processes identified by Marx was the tendency for the organic composition of capital to rise. Simply stated, capitalism requires increased productivity to survive, and increased productivity is only made possible by raising the ratio of machines (dead labor) to men (living labor). This tendency is self-reinforcing since, "the further machine production advances, the higher becomes the organic composition of capital needed for an entrepreneur to secure the average profit." (Mandel, 1968:163). This phenomenon helps us explain the course of capitalist development over the last century and the rise of monopoly capital (Baran and Sweezy, 1966).

For the purposes of this analysis there are at least two important consequences of this process. First, the growth of constant capital (machines and raw material) in the production process leads to an expansion in the overall size of the relative surplus-population. The reasons for this are obvious. The increasingly technological character of production removes more and more laborers from productive activity for longer periods of time. Thus, modern capitalist societies have been required progressively to reduce the number of productive years in a worker's life, defining both young and old as economically superfluous. Especially affected are the unskilled who become more and more expendable as capital expands.

In addition to affecting the general size of the relative surplus-population, the rise of the organic composition of capital leads to an increase in the relative stagnancy of that population. In Marx's original analysis he distinguished between forms of superfluous population that were floating and stagnant. The floating population consists of workers who are "sometimes repelled, sometimes attracted again in greater masses, the number of those employed increasing on the whole, although in a constantly decreasing proportion to the scale of production" (1967:641). From the point of view of capitalist accumulation the floating population offers the greatest economic flexibility and the fewest problems of social control because they are most effectively tied to capital by the "natural laws of production." Unfortunately (for the capitalists at least), these groups come to comprise a smaller and smaller proportion of the relative surplus-population. The increasing specialization of productive activity raises the cost of reproducing labor and heightens the demand for highly skilled and "internally controlled" forms of wage labor (Gorz, 1970). The process through which unskilled workers are alternatively absorbed and expelled from the labor force is thereby impaired, and the relative surplus-population comes to be made up of increasing numbers of persons who are more or less permanently redundant. The boundaries between the "useful" and the "useless" are more clearly delineated, while standards for social disqualification are more liberally defined.

With the growth of monopoly capital, therefore, the relative surplus-population begins to take on the character of a population which is more and more absolute. At the same time, the market becomes a less reliable means of disciplining these populations and the "invisible hand" is more frequently replaced by the "visible fist." The implications for deviance production are twofold: (1) problem populations become gradually more problematic—both in terms of their size and their insensitivity to economic controls, and (2) the resources of the state need to be applied in greater proportion to protect capitalist relations of production and insure the accumulation of capital.

State Capitalism and New Forms of Control

The major problems faced by monopoly capitalism are surplus population and surplus production. Attempts to solve these problems have led to the creation of the welfare/warfare state (Baran and Sweezy, 1966; Marcuse, 1964; O'Connor, 1973; Gross, 1970). The warfare state attacks the problem of overconsumption by providing "wasteful" consumption and protection for the expansion of foreign markets. The welfare state helps absorb and deflect social expenses engendered by a redundant domestic population. Accordingly, the economic development of capitalist societies has come to depend increasingly on the support of the state.

The emergence of state capitalism and the growing interpenetration of the political and economic spheres have had a number of implications for the organization and administration of class rule. The most important effect of these trends is that control functions are increasingly transferred from the organs of civil society to the organs of political society (the state). As the maintenance of social harmony becomes more difficult and the contradictions of civil society intensify, the state is forced to take a more direct and extensive role in the management of problem populations. This is especially true to the extent that the primary socializing institutions in capitalist societies (e.g., the family and the church) can no longer be counted on to produce obedient and "productive" citizens.

Growing state intervention, especially intervention in the process of socialization, is likely to produce an emphasis on general-preventive (integrative), rather than selective-reactive (segregative) controls. Instead of waiting for troublemakers to surface and managing them through segregative techniques, the state is likely to focus more and more on generally applied incentives and assimilative controls. This shift is consistent with the growth of state capitalism because, on the one hand, it provides mechanisms and policies to nip disruptive influences "in the bud," and, on the other, it paves the way toward a more rational exploitation of human capital. Regarding the latter point, it is clear that effective social engineering depends more on social investment and anticipatory planning than coercive control, and societies may more profitably manage populations by viewing them as human capital, than as human waste. An investment orientation has long been popular in state socialist societies (Rimlinger, 1961, 1966), and its value, not surprisingly, has been increasingly acknowledged by many capitalist states.[4]

In addition to the advantages of integrative controls, segregative measures are likely to fall into disfavor for a more immediate reason— they are relatively costly to formulate and apply. Because of its fiscal problems the state must search for means of economizing control operations without jeopardizing capitalist expansion. Segregative handling, especially institutionalization, has been useful in manipulating and providing a receptacle for social junk and social dynamite. Nonetheless, the per capita cost of this type of management is typically quite high. Because of its continuing reliance on segregative controls the state is faced with a growing crisis—the overproduction of deviance. The magnitude of the problem and the inherent weaknesses of available approaches tend to limit the alternatives, but among those which are likely to be favored in the future are:

1. *Normalization.* Perhaps the most expedient response to the overproduction of deviance is the normalization of populations traditionally managed as deviant. Normalization occurs when deviance processing is reduced in scope without supplying specific alterna-

tives, and certain segments of the problem population are "swept under the rug." To be successful this strategy requires the creation of invisible deviants who can be easily absorbed into society and disappear from view

A current example of this approach is found in the decarceration movement which has reduced the number of inmates in prisons (BOP, 1972) and mental hospitals (NIMH, 1970) over the last fifteen years. By curtailing commitments and increasing turnover rates the state is able to limit the scale and increase the efficiency of institutionalization. If, however, direct release is likely to focus too much attention on the shortcomings of the state, a number of intermediate solutions can be adopted. These include subsidies for private control arrangements (e.g., foster homes, nursing homes) and decentralized control facilities (e.g., community treatment centers, halfway houses). In both cases, the fiscal burden of the state is reduced while the dangers of complete normalization are avoided.

2. *Conversion.* To a certain extent the expenses generated by problem and deviant populations can be offset by encouraging their direct participation in the process of control. Potential troublemakers can be recruited as policemen, social workers and attendants, while confirmed deviants can be "rehabilitated" by becoming counselors, psychiatric aides and parole officers. In other words, if a large number of the controlled can be converted into a first line of defense, threats to the system of class rule can be transformed into resources for its support.[5]

3. *Containment.* One means of responding to threatening populations without individualized manipulation is through a policy of containment or compartmentalization. This policy involves the geographic segregation of large populations and the use of formal and informal sanctions to circumscribe the challenges that they present. Instead of classifying and handling problem populations in terms of the specific expenses that they create, these groups are loosely administered as a homogeneous class who can be ignored or managed passively as long as they remain in their place.

Strategies of containment have always flourished where social segregation exists, but they have become especially favored in modern capitalist societies. One reason for this is their compatibility with patterns of residential segregation, ghettoization, and internal colonialism (Blauner, 1969).

4. *Support of Criminal Enterprise.* Another way the overproduction of deviance may be eased is by granting greater power and influence to organized crime. Although predatory criminal enterprise is assumed to stand in opposition to the goals of the state and the capitalist class, it performs valuable and unique functions in the service of class rule (McIntosh, 1973). By creating a parallel structure, organized crime provides a means of support for groups who might otherwise become a burden on the state. The activities of

organized crime are also important in the pacification of problem populations. Organized crime provides goods and services which ease the hardships and deflect the energies of the underclass. In this role the "crime industry" performs a cooling-out function and offers a control resource which might otherwise not exist. Moreover, insofar as criminal enterprise attempts to reduce uncertainty and risk in its operations, it aids the state in the maintenance of public order. This is particularly true to the extent that the rationalization of criminal activity reduces the collateral costs (i.e., violence) associated with predatory crime (Schelling, 1967).

ENDNOTES

1   To the extent that a group (e.g., homosexuals) blatantly and systematically challenges the validity of the bourgeois family it is likely to become part of the problem population. The family is essential to capitalist society as a unit for consumption, socialization and the reproduction of the socially necessary labor force (cf. Frankford and Snitow, 1972; Secombe, 1973; Zaretsky, 1973).

2   O'Connor (1973) discusses this problem in terms of the crisis faced by the capitalist state in maintaining conditions for profitable accumulation and social harmony.

3   It has been estimated, for instance, that 1/3 of all arrests in America are for the offense of public drunkenness. Most of these apparently involve "sick" and destitute "skid row alcoholics" (Morris and Hawkins, 1969).

4   Despite the general tendencies of state capitalism, its internal ideological contradictions may actually frustrate the adoption of an investment approach. For example, in discussing social welfare policy Rimlinger (1966:571) concludes that "in a country like the United States, which has a strong individualistic heritage, the idea is still alive that any kind of social protection has adverse productivity effects. A country like the Soviet Union, with a centrally planned economy and a collectivist ideology, is likely to make an earlier and more deliberate use of health and welfare programs for purposes of influencing productivity and developing manpower."

5   In his analysis of the lumpenproletariat Marx (1964) clearly recognized how the underclass could be manipulated as a "bribed tool of reactionary intrigue."

REFERENCES

Baran, Paul and Paul M. Sweezy (1966). *Monopoly Capital*. New York: Monthly Review Press.

Blauner, Robert (1969). "Internal colonialism and ghetto revolt." *Social Problems* 16 (Spring): 393-408.

Bowles, Samuel (1973). "Contradictions in United States higher education." Pp. 165-199 in James H. Weaver (ed.), *Modern Political Economy: Radical Versus Orthodox Approaches*. Boston: Allyn and Bacon.

Bowles, Samuel and Herbert Gintis (1972). "I.Q. in the U.S. class structure." *Social Policy* 3 (November/December): 65- 96.

Bureau of Prisons (1972). *National Prisoner Statistics. Prisoners in State and Federal Institutions for Adult Felons.* Washington, D.C.: Bureau of Prisons.

Cohen, David K. and Marvin Lazerson (1972). "Education and the corporate order." *Socialist Revolution* (March/April): 48-72.

Foucault, Michel (1965). *Madness and Civilization.* New York: Random House.

Frankford, Evelyn and Ann Snitow (1972). "The trap of domesticity: notes on the family." *Socialist Revolution* (July/August): 83-94.

Gintis, Herbert (1973). "Alienation and power." Pp. 431-465 in James H. Weaver (ed.), *Modern Political Economy: Radical Versus Orthodox Approaches.* Boston: Allyn and Bacon.

Gorz, Andre (1970). "Capitalist relations of production and the socially necessary labor force." Pp. 155-171 in Arthur Lothstein (ed.), *All We Are Saying . . .* New York: G.P. Putnam.

Gross, Bertram M. (1970). "Friendly fascism: a model for America." *Social Policy* (November/December): 44-52.

Helmer, John and Thomas Vietorisz (1973). "Drug use, the labor market and class conflict." Paper presented at Annual Meeting of the American Sociological Association.

Karier, Clarence J. (1973). "Business values and the educational state." Pp. 6-29 in Clarence J. Karier, Paul Violas, and Joel Spring (eds.), *Roots of Crisis: American Education in the Twentieth Century.* Chicago: Rand McNally.

Mandel, Ernest (1968). *Marxist Economic Theory* (Volume I). New York: Monthly Review Press.

Marcuse, Herbert (1964). *One-Dimensional Man.* Boston: Beacon Press.

Marx, Karl (1964). *Class Struggles in France 1848-1850.* New York: International Publishers.

Marx, Karl (1967). *Capital* (Volume I). New York: International Publishers.

McIntosh, Mary (1973). "The growth of racketeering." *Economy and Society* (February): 35-69.

Morris, Norval and Gordon Hawkins (1969). *The Honest Politician's Guide to Crime Control.* Chicago: University of Chicago Press.

Musto, David F. (1973). *The American Disease: Origins of Narcotic Control.* New Haven: Yale University Press.

National Institute of Mental Health (1970). *Trends in Resident Patients—State and County Mental Hospitals 1950-1968.* Biometry Branch, Office of Program Planning and Evaluation. Rockville, Maryland: National Institute of Mental Health.

O'Connor, James (1973). *The Fiscal Crisis of the State.* New York: St. Martin's Press.

Piven, Frances and Richard A. Cloward (1971). *Regulating the Poor: The Functions of Public Welfare.* New York: Random House.

Rimlinger, Gaston V. (1961). "Social security, incentives, and controls in the U.S. and U.S.S.R." *Comparative Studies in Society and History* 4 (November): 104-124.

Rimlinger, Gaston V. (1966). "Welfare policy and economic development: a comparative historical perspective." *Journal of Economic History* (December): 556-571.

Schelling, Thomas (1967). "Economics and criminal enterprise." *Public Interest* (Spring): 61-78.

Secombe, Wally (1973). "The housewife and her labour under capitalism." *New Left Review* (January- February): 3-24.

Spring, Joel (1972). *Education and the Rise of the Corporate State.* Boston: Beacon Press.

Spring, Joel (1973). "Education as a form of social control." Pp. 30-39 in Clarence J. Karier, Paul Violas and Joel Spring (eds.), *Roots of Crisis: American Education in the Twentieth Century.* Chicago: Rand McNally.

Turk, Austin T. (1969). *Criminality and Legal Order.* Chicago: Rand McNally and Company.

Zaretsky, Eli (1973). "Capitalism, the family and personal life: parts 1 & 2." *Socialist Revolution* (January-April/May-June): 69-126, 19-70.

Austin Theodore Turk (1934-   )

Turk was born in Gainesville, Georgia. He was educated at the University of Georgia (B.A. in sociology, 1956), the University of Kentucky (M.A. in sociology, 1959), and earned his Ph.D. in sociology at the University of Wisconsin in 1962. He taught at the University of Wisconsin (sociology) from 1961-1962, Indiana University (sociology) from 1962-1974, the University of Toronto (sociology) from 1974-1988, and the University of California, Riverside (sociology) from 1988 to the present. He was chair of the latter department from 1989 to 1994.

Political Criminality*
Austin T. Turk

> Conflict cannot be excluded from social life. . . . "Peace" is nothing
> more than a change in the form of the conflict or in the antagonists or
> in the objects of the conflict, or finally in the chances of selection.
>
> Max Weber (1949:27)

Both reactionaries and revolutionaries have dreamed of a human society in which everyone is profoundly concerned with the happiness and welfare of everyone else. No one coerces or exploits anyone else, and all know freedom, love, and the joy of life. Relationships are freely created and totally open. There are no real conflicts; whatever misunderstandings may arise are soon resolved by mutual enlightenment. Goodness, truth, and beauty are the same for everyone because they are commonly understood and appreciated. Life is unclouded by any basis for distrusting, fearing, or hurting any other person.

That is the dream. Without it there is little hope for anything more than the "nasty, brutish, and short" life of Hobbes's bleak vision of the "war of every man against every man." Lacking the dream of a perfect society, people settle for whatever particular constellation of miseries they find themselves in by becoming merely competitors, sycophants, or parasites. For those who cannot endure the idea that social Darwinism is all life can offer, there are the consolations of magic, other-worldly religious fatalism—and madness.

Social reality is, of course, neither the utopian dream nor the bleak vision, but a fascinating composite of both—of "dreams" and "realities," "dreamers" and "realists." The great majority of people both dream and try to get along as best they can. For the most part, we dream a little and settle a lot. Neither our selfishness and ruthlessness nor our altruism and compassion are total and consistent. In practice, we may hope vaguely for a better world for everyone, while behaving so as to make sure that we and ours will survive and prosper regardless of what may happen to others. Somewhere beyond the Hobbesian war and despair, but short of the dream society, lies real social life—where the tension between the war and the dream is expressed in that fundamental dimension of human relatedness which is the process of political organization.

The Process of Political Organization

The political organization of social life results from and is characterized by conflicts (often more implicit than explicit) among different individuals or groups of people trying to improve and ensure their life chances—that is, the likelihood that *they*, at least, will have the means and opportunities to realize their respective visions of the good life. Although conflicts between individuals sometimes play a significant part in instigating or aggravating wider conflicts, inter*personal* conflicts as such appear to be essentially irrelevant for understanding the systemic nature of inter-*group* conflicts (Rapoport, 1974:133-173). Therefore, for present purposes we may safely limit our attention to conflicts among people grouped together in some degree, whether by circumstances, their own inclinations and preferences, or the labeling behavior of other people.

Such groupings (anything from couples, families, tribes, or communities to churches, corporations, social classes, or nations) may arise from any perceived or imputed difference among human beings; and the conflicts among and within them may vary greatly in the extent to which they are directly and overtly linked to the material life chances of the people involved. Clearly the most consequential groupings are those defined by differences in the material resources available to members, and most directly involved in implicit and explicit conflicts over the terms of allocation. The fewer material resources available, the less chance of obtaining and enjoying life's goods, whatever they may be. Except, perhaps, for mystics genuinely indifferent to personal and intellectual survival, even persons whose primary concerns are nonmaterial—religious salvation, esthetic expression, scientific comprehension, or whatever—need material resources to sustain and further their enterprises. Every human effort and experience costs something, requires some expenditure of energy. This implies that any given distribution or projected redistribution of resources can be expected to facilitate certain enterprises, impede some, and preclude others.

For instance, the capitalist world system (Wallerstein, 1976; Gunder Frank, 1967) promotes the growth of multinational corporate power above all other concerns—including the development of Third World national and regional economies and, especially to the point, alternatives to Western world views and lifestyles. As financial strategies, changing production technologies, and/or shifting markets dictate the channeling of resources away from some areas and enterprises to others, the life chances of the people involved improve or deteriorate in nonmaterial as well as material terms. While it has long been understood that rapid and, especially, uneven economic development is incompatible with many traditional beliefs and ways of life (Spicer, 1952; Mead, 1955; Lerner, 1958; Finkle and Gable, 1966), it is even clearer—from the histories of colonized and exploited peoples everywhere—that impoverishment corrodes and ultimately destroys the faiths, moralities, sensibilities, and knowledge by and for which people live.

Individuals may, of course, be unaware of participating in conflictual intergroup relationships, may value intangible goods far more than material resources, and/or may be unconcerned about the implications of their activities for the distributing of life chances. Sufficiently insulated from contradicting and threatening experiences, they may never realize that in a finite world of distinctions between "them" and "us," simply to be alive is to be involved in intergroup struggles over the means and terms of collective existence. Mergers and alliances are forever changing the alignments, and overwhelmingly supportive and trusting relationships are possible—at least among individuals. Nevertheless, material resources are not infinite, and there are human limits to empathy and commitment (though we seldom love enough to reach them). Recognition of these constraints leads to the sociological postulate that any social relationship has a conflictual, or "competitive," dimension (Simmel, 1955:15; Collins, 1975:60, 89), and the theory that the most fundamental empirical sources and implications of the conflict lie in the distribution and redistribution of material life chances (Marx and Engels, 1962: 362-364, 368-369; Weber, 1968:38-40; Dahrendorf, 1979).

While any social relationship is by definition organized in some sense or other, to organize it *politically* is to construct and enforce explicit or implicit rules for making and implementing decisions about how the relationship is to be lived. The relative political power of a party in a social relationship is, then, definable as the degree to which that party is able to control the procedures for deciding what is to be done. From a couple deciding whether or not to marry to a nation deciding whether or not to go to war, the party whose arguments, promises, threats, or other manipulative actions disproportionately influence the eventual decision may be said to have demonstrated the greater political power.

Having power in a social relationship means having some relative control over the resources available to persons in that relationship. *Using* power means demonstrating that control by altering the range of relative attractiveness of behavioral options open to others in the relationship. Though the measurement of power continues to be a horrendous problem for social scientists, for analytical purposes five forms or dimensions of power may be distinguished in terms of five kinds of resource control:

(1) control of the means of direct physical violence, or *war* or *police* power;

(2) control of the production, allocation, and/or use of material resources, or *economic* power;

(3) control of decision-making processes, or *political* power;

(4) control of definitions of and access to knowledge, beliefs, and values, or *ideological* power; and

(5) control of human attention and living time, or *diversionary* power (Turk, 1976).

Depending on the nature of the relationship, people do not necessarily know or care how much power they have, and may be unaware of using any power in relating to one another. Either intimacy or distance may preclude awareness or concern. People in love are wise not to dwell on the fact that they have and use tremendous power—especially diversionary and ideological—to shape and sustain their relationship. At the other extreme, social class relationships and legal authority are most secure when few people know or concern themselves with the mechanisms by which power is allocated and mobilized in the absence of direct interaction and open confrontation (Baldus, 1975).

The concept of political organization differs from the more general one of social organization in that it focuses attention upon the manipulative devices by which people try to forestall or resolve conflicts with "them" on terms favorable to "us"—including all devices from the most subtle and gentle to the most obvious and cruel, and all forms of dominance and control from the most democratic to the most autocratic. Clearly, the process of political organization can be observed in any social relationship, any grouping from a friendship to an industry to a league of nations. However, insofar as a superordinate position within a territory is achieved by some grouping or alliance of groupings, it appears (as Machiavelli so well understood) that both the achievement and the maintenance of such a position depend upon the effective use of the full range of manipulative techniques, culminating in the formal control mechanisms of the polity, or state, with their main locus in the authorization (prototypically in the criminal law) and organization (prototypically in the police and army) of the means of violence.

The Political Organization of Societies

A fully elaborated conflict analysis of a given society would identify many isomorphisms between the processes by which the polity and the less inclusive or overriding social groupings in it are created, sustained, and changed or destroyed. A full analysis would also trace the functional or contradictory relationships between the polity and subpolity levels of political organization. Moreover, a complete analysis would extend to the geopolitical and other features of the social and natural environments in which the society is embedded, and by which the theoretical or legal autonomy of the polity is made empirically relative. The objective in this small volume is far more modest: to provide a general introductory analysis of what is viewed as the key to understanding the process of political organization at the societal or polity level, that is, the relationship between political criminality and political policing.

To begin, whatever else is or might be true of politically organized societies, or polities, the historical reality is that they are hierarchical. The emergent distribution of power among the various groupings involved in the process of organization is unequal. At least in relative terms, some are winners and some are losers. Moreover, as Jesus, Marx, and many other social analysts have observed, the initially advantaged are better able than the initially disadvantaged to improve and ensure their life chances by extending their control of resources—usually at the expense of the disadvantaged. "For to him who has will more be given; and from him who has not, even what he has will be taken away" (Mark 4:24 RSV). That is, emergent power differences tend to become established ones, a process implying the stabilization and probable widening of initial differences in life chances—that is, the creation of a stratification system.

As the structuring of power becomes increasingly explicit, a new and basic differentiation in terms of unequal power appears that between *authorities* and *subjects*. Authorities are those who make and try to implement decisions affecting the polity as a whole; subjects are those who are affected by, but do not themselves make, such strategic decisions (Turk, 1969:32-33; Dahrendorf, 1959:290-295).

To be sure, the analytical distinction between authorities and subjects requires much care in its use, minimally because of (1) the divisions of labor and power, and the differences of perception and interest, among different kinds and levels of officials; (2) the frequent discrepancies between public, formal, official, or apparent power and private, informal, unofficial, and real power; (3) the variable power of subjects, especially as variations in their power are related to variations in specific issues and concerns; and (4) the complexities of determining the nature and effects of (especially "meaningful") political participation (see Miliband, 1969:131-159). For example, the extent to which the ordinary police—as opposed to the Gestapo—of Nazi Germany were "authorities" in regard to the making and implementation of the "final solution" is clearly an empirical question, the answer to which varies from place to place and time to time (Peterson, 1969:125-148, 268; see also Delarue, 1964:27-166). Nonetheless, the essential point stands: that decisions affecting the life chances of all members of a polity are made by some, not all, members.

The transforming of power into authority is a process that is always problematic and never finished, and is therefore reversible. Elsewhere, in discussing the nature of legal order, I have characterized the process in "ideal type" terms as historical movement toward realization of the following conditions: military dominance, established jurisdiction, institutionalized policing, demographic continuity, and ideological hegemony (Turk, 1972a:173-175).

The most elementary form of the struggle for survival and control is resolved by the military ascendance of one party, including coalitions, over all others in the arena. At this level of conflict the arena is always territorial, whatever other features it may have. Who shall occupy the land, who has sole or prior claim to its resources—these are the questions answered by the demonstration of military superiority. Once achieved, military dominance is used to eliminate, as far as possible, the remaining military potential of the conquered. Monopoly of the means of collective violence on any militarily significant scale removes the possibility of reversing the military decision.

It was not merely indifference to the everyday lives of everyday people that led historians for so long to write almost as though waging and surviving warfare were the main things that went on in former societies, and as if the most important figures were always those who led people into and out of wars. Nor was it simply a taste for "blood and iron" that led thinkers from Polybius and Ibn Khaldun to Gumplowicz, Ratzenhofer, and Oppenheimer to emphasize military conquest in their evolutionary theories of the *polis* and state (for a brief review of these theories, see Becker and Barnes, 1952:702-730). Excepting perhaps a few extremely tiny and isolated tribes in Borneo and elsewhere, the people of every known society have had to meet the threat of intergroup violence to their collective survival. Andreski (1968) has provided impressive comparative and historical evidence for the thesis that societies failing to develop adequate institutions for controlling and mobilizing the means of violence will probably succumb to internal war, conquest, or both.

No society, however, has managed to eliminate completely the possibility of violent challenge. Apart from the continuing dangers of conventional wars and nuclear threats, collective violence repeatedly erupts not only where regimes are militarily weak and politically unstable (such as India and throughout eastcentral Africa), but also in nations (such as the

United States and China) characterized by the most awesome concentrations of military and political power the world has yet seen. Even so tightly monitored and regimented a polity as the Soviet Union has a long history of sometimes violent Ukrainian, Georgian, Moslem, and other ethnic-nationalist resistance to Russification and Politburo directives (Thaden, 1971:356, 470-472, 506-510, 572-573; Massell, 1968).

To the extent that stability in military terms is in fact established in an area, it at least becomes possible to define the arena within which the political organization of social life can occur. This is the point at which the idea of "jurisdiction" begins to acquire social reality as a constraint upon human mobility and interaction.

ESTABLISHED JURISDICTION

Establishing jurisdiction is a matter of successfully asserting the territorial and social boundaries of the polity. Egress and ingress are controlled; neither insiders nor outsiders can operate with impunity within the area marked off by the claims and definitions of the locally dominant. Their normative expectations and demands become unavoidable contingencies—"the law"—for anyone inhabiting or entering the area. Having the power, incipient or established authorities can claim the right to control, or at least monitor, social life within "their" land, and to present themselves as the embodiment (or, somewhat less pretentiously, as the leadership) of the people who live there.

The ability of authorities to create and maintain political boundaries depends, before all else, upon acceptance of those boundaries by external and militarily significant parties, most notably the authorities of contiguous polities. In its crudest expression, the drawing of boundaries is a function of the logistical limits of military conquest. The determinant is who can keep the strongest force operative at the greatest distance from the centers of supply and administration. Given an equivalent level of military technology, improvements in transportation and communications facilities favor bigger over smaller polities (Andreski, 1968:79), with a corresponding weakening of the jurisdictional claims of the authorities of smaller polities. Bigness alone, however, is not sufficient. More important is the efficiency of military organization, largely determined by the degree to which military dominance has been achieved within the polity. Success both in defending and in expanding polity boundaries has been associated with the creation of an army subservient only to the authorities, an overwhelming force of their own "and not the armed force of aristocratic or feudal retainers" (Eisenstadt, 1969:130).

Though hardly superseded, the military factor in defining jurisdictional boundaries has been augmented over centuries of interpolity contacts by the development of international law. Authorities have found it

usually and increasingly more advantageous to deal with (or try to sub-
vert) one another than to engage in open violations of the only generally
accepted "preemptory norm" of international law (overriding even
treaties): the basic rule against aggression (Akehurst, 1970:60-61).
Economic interdependence, mutual fear, recurring common problems
(such as controlling access to coastal waters and to air space, dealing
with fugitives and exiles, validating claims to newly discovered territo-
ries and resources), and the advantages of predictability over uncertainty
have strongly encouraged authorities to conform to the rules of international relations. As long as the long-term advantages of conformity are
believed to outweigh the short-term advantages of deviance, international law and custom constitute an ideological resource of enormous
significance in defining and confirming jurisdiction.

Because jurisdictional boundaries are functions of both the social
realities of military power and the cultural realities of international law,
they shift with changes in the balance of power. The total relative power
of a polity is a complex blend of the various kinds of resources which
authorities control and can mobilize. Military and economic resources
are the most obvious and empirically the most decisive, but to some
extent military and economic power may be offset by political realities
created under international law. Thus, the authorities of such a powerful
nation as the United States may eventually find it more expedient to recognize Cuban jurisdictional boundaries than to try another Bay of Pigs
invasion. Even then, the invasion was unsuccessful mainly because the
rule against aggression at least kept the Americans from sending in regular forces to help the "Cuban exiles seeking to regain their homeland"—
who were, of course, trained and equipped by the CIA.

Military and economic inequalities inevitably produce some discrepancies between the officially recognized and the actual limits of effective
control defining a polity. To handle problems arising from such discrepancies, the concept of "spheres of influence" has frequently been
invoked as a justification for actions otherwise prohibited by the rules of
international relations. The notion is simply that the authorities of a for-
midable polity consider their interests best served by forbidding other
authorities to "interfere" in the affairs of the affected area, while claim-
ing that right for themselves. A classic example is the Monroe Doctrine,
under which American governments have frequently intervened more
(for example, in the Nicaraguan, Dominican, and numerous other inva-
sions) and less (in the overthrow of Allende's elected government in
Chile) directly in Latin America. Another instance is the Soviet Union's
use of the concept to excuse the bloody 1968 invasion of
Czechoslovakia. That a self-proclaimed "sphere of influence" is a legally
and logically poor justification is almost beside the point: its value lies
only in signalling that a more or less demonstrable *factual* condition
must be accepted if war is to be avoided. In the absence of any justifica-

tion at all, other authorities could not as readily estimate the potential threat such aggressions pose to their own interests. Boundaries may be established by "tacit bargaining" (Schelling, 1960:53-80), but the more explicitly settled they are, the freer authorities will be to develop an effective structure of internal control.

INSTITUTIONALIZED POLICING

As military dominance and jurisdiction are achieved, authorities consolidate their position by instituting a system in which internal control is accomplished by the process of policing instead of the more costly and less efficient one of military occupation. *Occupation* is characterized by maximal social distance between controllers and controlled ("no fraternization"), primary reliance upon the threat and use of deadly violence by large units trained for war, only a rudimentary monitoring of the social life of the subject population, and minimal concern with justifying domination to the dominated. In contrast, *policing* is characterized by minimal social distance, primary reliance upon techniques of "coercive persuasion" employed by individuals or small units trained to minimize the use of violence, extensive and intensive monitoring, and a major concern with legitimation. Occupation confirms power; policing transforms power into authority.

In its earliest development, policing is scarcely more than the not always successful use of military force to quell particularly troublesome instances of collective resistance to impositions such as enslavement, conscription, and taxation. As recently as two centuries ago in England, policing the smugglers of Sussex amounted for many years to little more than sporadic ineffectual forays by military detachments sent to assist the beleaguered customs officials (Winslow, in Hay et al., 1975:119-166). Sometimes the expeditions ended in tragedy, but frequently they ended in comedy—the soldiers bought off or drunk under the table by the smugglers, or else abandoning the tax battles after exchanging a few token shots to earn their shillings.

Even after police forces are differentiated from the military, authorities may view them only as more finely calibrated and flexible instruments of controlled violence. "It has been a recent development which has seen the police as an appendage of the law rather than as an extension of the violence potential of the state" (Manning, 1977:40). Not until Sir Robert Peel finally persuaded Parliament in 1829 to authorize creation of the London Metropolitan Police was the idea firmly established that the objective of policing is not to terrorize people, but to tranquilize them. Thereafter, and notably during the halcyon days of British imperial grandeur in the late nineteenth century and early twentieth century, the London police became the nearest approximation to the ideal force—policing instead of occupying the land, and encouraging the populace to identify with the polity and to accept the decisions of their rulers as wise and just. Instead of just a coercive military, economic, and political order, the ideal polity comes to be also a *legal* order—that is, one sustained regularly by the pressure of ideological consensus instead of the threat of violence.

Ensuring that a police force does in fact police rather than attempt to occupy an area is a constant problem for authorities, who may themselves have no clear understanding of the nature and aims of policing. Even Peel seems to have had no ideologically consistent conception beyond a conviction, shared by many, that something had to be done about the abysmal quality of policing in the major governmental and commercial center that London had become (Manning, 1977:74-81). His genius was that he saw with remarkable clarity what it would take to have efficient policing, and was politically and administratively skilled enough to sell and implement his ideas with considerable success. Peel's key insight was that the less explicit the threat of violence and the more explicit the concern for public safety, the more effective policing is likely to be.

The trick is to keep the threat credible without tarnishing the image of an organization whose official *raison d'être* is "to serve and protect" (motto of the Toronto police). To this end, authorities must be able to count upon the police to distinguish among "situations where coercion is needed, situations where police action is unnecessary (given limits upon the resources which can be invested in policing), and situations where coercion is self-defeating in that the net result of the police effort is to increase, rather than decrease, the need for coercion" (Turk, 1972a:174).

Policing is inherently a difficult process to keep under administrative control, because to do their job police officers routinely have to be widely dispersed, alone or in very small groups, and given considerable discretion in judging when to threaten or use what degree of violence (Bordua and Reiss, 1966; Bittner, 1970:3647). Occupationally constrained to "take charge" (assert their authority) and "handle situations" with efficiency and dispatch, police officers are subject to the temptation to rely excessively upon their privileged access to the means of violence. Peel's solution was to recruit patient, imposing men who were strongly encouraged to rely upon courteous though firm admonition and example unless grievously provoked, and who then were to subdue the recalcitrant subject with as little injury as possible. To further induce them to accept this policy, the "bobbies" were armed only with stout clubs—which helped to reassure the populace and encourage offenders themselves to forgo deadly violence in contending with the police.

The limits of authorities' control within a polity are marked by their ability through institutionalized policing to define, detect, and punish criminality—including both preexisting (such as murder, rape, theft) and specially invented (treason, poaching, tax evasion) types of social deviance which are thereby made "official business." Effective control is demonstrated to the extent that there is little to detect and punish. Policing is the mechanism by which authorities, whether or not they realize it, establish the framework and gain the time needed for the development and operation of even more subtle and powerful modes of political socialization.

DEMOGRAPHIC CONTINUITY

An often neglected factor in analyzing the formation and character-istics of polities is that of sheer durability. Durability is, of course, a *consequence* of the process of political organization; the point here is that it is also a *condition* necessary for the process to occur. It may take years, perhaps centuries, for military dominance to be achieved, jurisdictional boundaries to be established, and the transition from occupation to policing to be made to any significant degree. For those years or cen-turies to be available, the population of a polity must survive as a demo-graphic entity. *The* people must continue even if *some* people do not, falling as military, policing, or economic casualties.

Demographic continuity is a function of population size and compo-sition, as well as the size and technologically available natural resources of the jurisdictional area. Given at least an agrarian economic base, the larger the population, the longer the polity is likely to survive (compare Lenski, 1966:195). Large populations can more readily sustain casual-ties, and especially are more likely than smaller ones to have function-ally equivalent replacements available. If, for example, skilled craftsmen such as toolmakers, medical practitioners, or military leaders are lost in a particular disaster, a large population will probably have "reserves" who happened to be elsewhere. In addition, the larger the population, the greater the rate at which equivalents and potential replacements are produced and—mainly because of administrative needs and economic exigencies—dispersed.

Finally, the greater social differentiation that tends to characterize large populations provides more alternative organizational pathways through which innovations and adaptations can be generated to repair or correct for breakdowns in the social structure. Larger units generally have many more kinds of emergency services and back-up systems, which can be mobilized as needed. "Repairing" is exemplified in the provision of alternative organizations able both to handle specialized tasks beyond the expertise of local officials and people and to relieve them of the "great overload of decision and administrative work" (Barton, 1970:284). "Correcting for" may take the form of deciding (perhaps by applying the principle of triage) which stricken communities, beleaguered frontier posts, or the like will be helped and which abandoned to their fate.

Population composition refers here to the age and sex distribution characterizing a population. A younger population is obviously more vigorous and hardy than an older one. Not of least importance, it can sustain a higher "military participation ratio" (Andreski, 1968:33); that is, a greater proportion of the population can be mobilized for military purposes. This is made possible not only by the greater ability of younger persons to withstand the physical and, perhaps, mental stresses of warfare, but also by—all else equal—the greater productivity of younger workers. Thus, the military participation ratio is closely linked to the dependency ratio—the ratio of productive people to those dependent upon them. The sex composition of a population is important not only because men tend to be stronger for work and warfare, but also because the higher the proportion of younger women, the greater the capacity of the population to reproduce itself at a rate exceeding the survival minimum—that is, to produce (from the perspective of grand strategists) workers, soldiers, and breeders faster than they are lost.

The extent of a polity's jurisdiction (not strictly conterminous with its officially designated territory, the reader will recall) is correlated with the extent of natural resources available within it. Larger areas are more likely than smaller ones to contain everything from sufficient water and arable land to essential mineral deposits. A polity whose jurisdictional boundaries are too truncated is unlikely to last as long as one with wide boundaries. Exceptions such as Switzerland and the small principalities of Europe are more apparent than real, existing mainly thanks to "accidents" of nature, of military technology and objectives in crucial eras, and of geopolitics. Therefore, unless their boundaries are erased by conquest or more or less superseded by political compromises with economic and/or military realities, small polities can be expected to war over territory, as in Africa now, and to be eventually forced to merge or be swallowed up as conquests, satellites, or economic dependencies by larger states. The various outcomes are illustrated in the incorporation of Latvia and Estonia into the Soviet Union, the formation of the European Economic Community, and the imposition of *Pax Romana* and the later *Pax Britannica* over sizable parts of the earth. In a novel reversal of the usual process of erasing or superseding previously meaningful boundaries, the Republic of South Africa has recently been "divested" of a fairly large territory granted formal independence in late 1976 as the Transkei Republic—the boundaries of which are effectively superseded at the outset (Carter et al., 1967; SAIRR, 1977:228-246).

The primary significance of demographic continuity is that the longer the polity endures, the more likely are military dominance, jurisdictional boundaries, and policing to constitute a controlled learning environment in which the inescapable reality of "the power structure" itself is the prime lesson to be learned. In particular, after two or more generations presumably no one is left who directly experienced the early struggles to decide the terms on which the process of political organization would begin.

> Later generations grow up with the limits and under the conditions set by the outcome of their ancestors' struggle to answer the power question. They start learning their places, acquiring identities, statuses, roles, from birth in a system whose main features are already set by the terms of the power settlement. The very idea that things were different and could be different becomes more and more just an idea, having no grounding in the actual experience of living people. It becomes, because of the increasing detachment of such ideas from the experiences of real people in real life, more and more difficult even for people to think about their situation in terms other than those set by a culture part of whose bedrock is the explanation and justification of the power structure [Turk, 1972a:174].

IDEOLOGICAL HEGEMONY

At its ultimate reach, the process of political organization culminates in control over feelings and thoughts as well as actions. Not only are there no challenges to the structure of authority, it does not even occur to people that there is anything to question. Authorities and subjects, respectively, act out their interdependence in terms of social norms of dominance and of deference (Turk, 1969:40-50), buttressed by a cultural consensus that the polity is a manifestation of nature's order. In the minds of the people, social life as it *is* becomes social life as it *ought* to be.

Such a model of the universal embracing of structured inequality has never been fully realized; but it has often been approximated to an extent reassuring to those who crave social order above all else, and chilling for those who value human freedom. Following Tocqueville, Bendix (1964:41-42) has described the patrimonial-feudal authority structure of medieval Europe as one in which, to an enormous degree, "aristocratic masters and their servants feel strongly identified with each other . . . think of each other as an inferior or superior extension of themselves." Though "selfish willfulness on one side and manipulating subservience on the other" were an obvious part of the reality, even such "abuses and aberrations" were still within the terms of a "finished rhetoric of manners and motives . . . which for centuries was based on the structure of medieval political life."

What came afterward has not been all that different, if one emphasizes general historical parallels rather than specific historical shifts. Since the end of the ancien régime in the eighteenth century, the "false

consciousness" of urban and rural proletariats has frustrated revolutionaries everywhere. Complementing proletarian diffidence, even the most
ruthless capitalists have easily come to believe in their superiority
(demonstrated, of course, by their power) as sufficient justification for
running everybody's business for their own ever-growing power and
profit. Detailed examples of the process by which capitalists may eventually metamorphose into aristocrats are found in Collier and Horowitz
(1976) on "the Rockefellers," Newman (1975) on "the Canadian establishment," and Sampson's (1971) "new anatomy" of British elitism.

A similar parallel appears in a kind of "revolutionary" inversion of
the capitalist hegemony. From the perspective of those trying to save the
world for the capitalist version of democracy, the "enslaved peoples"
behind various Iron and Bamboo Curtains have been frustratingly unre-
sponsive to exhortations from "the Free World," and Third World peoples have obtusely persisted in their resistance to enlightenment about
the benefits of neocolonial life. In turn complementing such *un*proletarian "false consciousness," triumphant revolutionaries and their succes-
sors—notably in the Soviet Union and China—have taken their
ascendancy to be the mark of their superior understanding of "what is
to be done" to move lesser mortals along the road to collectivized per-
fection. Thus, "Communist Parties direct and check up on all the work
of the organs of state power and administration, correct any shortcomings in their activity and help state organs to mobilize the working people for the active fulfillment of the tasks of socialist construction"
(Chkhikvadze, 1969:85).

Political socialization is far more than deliberate indoctrination. In
Sigel's (1965:4) words, it is a learning process which begins very early and
is most influenced by the same agents or forces which influence all social
behavior: first and foremost, the family; then socially relevant groups or
institutions, such as school, church, and social class; and finally—last but
not least—society at large and the political culture it fosters. . . . Much of
this learning is incidental to other experiences; . . . it is acquired in a subtle, nondeliberate way, often in a context which seems totally void of
political stimuli yet is often rife with political consequences.

Whatever teaches people that order is always better than disorder,
that consensus is always preferable to conflict, that governance is the
prerogative of some and obedience the duty of others, that authority
goes with power, helps to deaden concern about inequalities in the distribution of life chances, and about the institutions that maintain those
inequalities. As many dissident intellectuals have learned, "radical
answers cannot be given to students without radical questions"
(Michalowski, 1977:70).

Authorities are not, of course, indifferent to the possibility of
increasing by propaganda and censorship the effectiveness of political
socialization. In Chapter 4, information control as a major function of

political policing is examined in some detail. For now, we may simply observe that *totalitarianism*—defined as state control over all sectors of social life—is not an attribute of only some polities, but is instead a variable feature of all polities. Pro-Marxist university professors are certainly more likely to be found in the North American and Western European democracies than are anti-Marxist ones in the Eastern European, Soviet, and Chinese socialist states. Nonetheless, the freedoms of speech, association, and petition continue (as will be seen in subsequent chapters) to be only partially and fitfully available where they are most loudly proclaimed. In practice, "national security" turns all such freedoms into contingent privileges rather than inalienable rights.

Irrespective of the particular blend of inadvertent and deliberate political socialization through which it is attained, a high degree of ideological hegemony is the strongest support upon which political authority can rest. The stronger the consensual base, the more resources can be diverted from internal control to deal with natural and social environmental problems. Ideological power thus amplifies other forms of power in a kind of feedback process: as military, economic, and political power facilitate the creation of ideological resources, so does ideological power increase the available amounts and facilitate the mobilization of more tangible resources. Bonded together by the conviction that authority is "of, by, and for the people," a politically organized population can perform prodigious feats—whether of construction or destruction. Without that bond, authorities may have great difficulty in even mobilizing the polity against a despised and dreaded invader (for example, the terrible experience of the Soviet people under Stalin's dictatorship when the German army attacked in 1941).

To summarize, given that an initial *power* structure has resulted from struggles to maximize life chances, it becomes an *authority* structure (a "legal" order) to the degree that the people involved begin assuming the inevitability of the unequal distribution of resources, and therefore of life chances. Whether they believe in, much less agree on, the justice of their inegalitarian relationship is quite a different matter. In the real world, as distinct from the realm of legal and political philosophies, "legitimation" has meant acceptance of "the given order," regardless of why it is accepted.

Legitimation and Political Crime

The concept of *legitimation* has traditionally been taken to mean not only that people accept the power structure in which they live, but also that it is *right* for them to do so. Grounded in some variant of natural law theory, "ideologies of agreement" (Shklar, 1964: 88-110) have been developed to explain why people should defer to authority *qua* authority even when particular figures or acts are disapproved. The key notion is that, now or ultimately, the interests of authorities and subjects are identical. Given that common ideological premise, specific justifications for accepting the power structure as an authority structure may vary greatly in emphasis and complexity. Following Weber's (1968:212-216) familiar analysis, the major kinds of justification, or "types of legitimate domination," may be distinguished according to whether the justifications rest primarily upon *charismatic, rational,* or *traditional* grounds.

Charismatic legitimacy rests upon the belief that authority figures have unique sources of insight and power, derived either from their innate extrahumanness or from their having control of the symbols of office, such as a golden stool or an oval office. Legends of royalty everywhere emphasize the tests and signs by which "royalness" is "found" in a perhaps improbable individual (such as a young shepherd or a kidnapped princeling), or else "acquired" by a surpassing feat (such as drawing a magic sword from a rock or killing the current ruler). Modern equivalents of the royal legends tend to stress the unique "genius for leadership" of authority figures and/or "the charisma of the office." To such varied notables as Churchill, Gandhi, and Lenin is imputed an awesome personal capacity to determine collective destinies, to know what people should do and to get them to do it. Supporting personal charisma (or, in the case of less imposing figures, substituting for it) is the belief that insight and ability somehow adhere in a position or structure of authority—either by human design (the genius then perhaps being imputed to "the founding fathers") or supernatural intervention (such as the doctrine of Papal infallibility). A related idea is that even relatively mediocre individuals may be inspired or constrained by role expectations so that they rise to appropriate levels of performance ("some men have greatness thrust upon them").

Rational legitimacy is conferred by the belief that authority is structured and exercised according to accepted factual premises and logical principles. It is assumed that authorities act upon the basis of adequate objective knowledge rationally applied to particular situations. A reinforcing assumption is that authorities have greater knowledge and powers of reason than do subjects. Insofar as scientific and technical expertise are harnessed to the purposes of authorities, and most people are left ill-educated and ill-informed, the assumption may be empirically confirmed. Probably nothing promotes rational legitimacy more than the mystique of "the law"—that institutional complex of formulas, agencies, and procedures which serve, among other functions, to impress upon the uninitiated the feeling that extraordinary intellect and arcane knowledge are required to exercise political authority—at least at the higher levels.

Traditional legitimacy is founded in the belief that contemporary authorities are maintaining the ways found, through the experiences of preceding generations, to be the best. The closer the adherence to established norms, the better off everyone presumably will be. Security is equated with stability. However miserable the conditions of social life, people cling to their conviction that political changes can only bring worse. If no institutional solution to the problem of succession—of replacing deceased, retired, or failed incumbents—has been developed, then people may be genuinely terrified by the news that "the King is dead," until the continuity of political order is assured by the proclamation of "long live the King." Where authority depends much upon traditional legitimacy, innovations must be construed as applications or extensions of custom to particular cases. Thus, successful authorities tend to be those most adept at substantively camouflaging new ideas and practices in the familiar forms of old ones (and at seeing to it that unduly restrictive old ways are conveniently forgotten).

All three types of justifications may be found blended in varying proportions to constitute the ideological reflection of the structure of power. People may, for instance, accept and approve a bicameral legislature because of (1) the personal and/or office charisma of some legislators, (2) conviction that bicameralism is a technically superior organizational principle facilitating rational decision-making, and (3) belief that the two-class division of legislators is a precious legacy of ancestral enlightenment. In any case, the specifics of ideological consensus are far less significant than the fact of its accomplishment. The crucial element in legitimacy is that power is transformed into authority insofar as people learn to live with it—that is, either to exercise it if they have it or to defer to it if they do not have it (even if they defer only for tactical reasons stemming from fear or opportunism). For them, both the more and the less powerful, to accept and believe in the power distribution without question or even reflection would constitute the ultimate outcome of the learning process by which the structural reality of power generates the cultural reality of authority.

Apart from the question of whether people view their power relationships as inevitable and/or just, it has often been theorized that no social relationship is likely to persist unless the parties involved are getting at least something out of it. It has, for instance, been argued that social interaction is possible only where there is some basis in mutual gratification (Parsons, 1951:5-7, 9, 11-13). Such a proposition would seem to underlie the popular view that increasing misery must sooner or later result in a revolutionary explosion, as the mutuality of gratification drops below some critical minimum. Perhaps rather surprisingly, the Marxian expectation that exploitation and immiseration of the proletariat will (given certain facilitating conditions) generate class consciousness and class struggle apparently rests upon a similar line of reasoning. Against such reasoning, however, it seems more realistic to assume that large masses of people, and especially peasants, simply accept the social system under which they live without concern about any balance of benefits and pains, certainly without the least thought of whether a better one might be possible, unless and until something happens to threaten and destroy their daily routine. Hence it is quite possible for them to accept a society of whose working they are no more than victims [Moore, 1967:204].

While it does seem that exploitative relationships can indeed be maintained almost indefinitely, there is probably a limit to how much a dominant class can appropriate the fruits of their subjects' labor without "something happening to threaten and destroy the daily routine" of peasant or proletarian life. The more severe the exploitation, the more likely it is that acceptance of their lot by the exploited will depend more upon their being periodically and inescapably subjected to violent and ideological coercive persuasion than upon any dull lack of awareness and concern.

In any case, even though the degree of exploitation, as well as the degree of authority and the difference in power, may vary greatly among polities (with corresponding variation in the extent to which they rest directly and routinely upon coercion rather than consensus), all contemporary polities, at least, are characterized by the use of formal control mechanisms to promote acceptance of and identification with the structures and personages of authority, and to suppress at least the most insistent of those who resist. Challenges to authority are expected, do occur, and are met by the more or less routine mobilization of the agencies of control.

As long as people subject to a polity's jurisdiction believe—correctly or erroneously—that their life chances are reasonably improved, tolerably maintained, or at least largely unaffected by the actions of the polity's authorities, challenges to authority will most probably be limited to "conventional crimes" that is, officially prohibited deviations from such norms as those dealing with nonpolitical personal and property violence, sexual expression, responsible or "normal" role behavior, and the misappropriation or misuse of property (Turk, 1969: 80-90). When, however, all or some subjects believe—correctly or erroneously— that their life chances are excessively threatened or reduced by the actions (or inactions) of the authorities, they may challenge the authorities more directly and fundamentally by spontaneous or calculated, organized or unorganized dissent, evasion, disobedience, or violence. Such direct challenges to authority will at some point—depending upon the seriousness of the challenge as perceived and interpreted by the authorities—become intolerable enough to them to be either openly or "operationally" defined as *political crimes*.

Where the definition of challenges as political crimes is relatively open, the authorities will invoke laws expressly prohibiting various forms of resistance. Less openly, the definitional process may involve the invocation of laws, but is characterized by more or less covert police operations rather than formally legal procedures. In either case, identifying events and persons as politically criminal is (as will become evident in subsequent discussions) a complex process in which the congruence of perceptual and objective realities is highly problematic—as are the consequences of the process for the polity.

Some analysts, such as Sagarin (1973) and Quinney (1975:147-161), have argued strongly for including illegal acts of political repression in the concept of political criminality and, therefore, for defining the instigators and perpetrators of such acts as another category of political criminal. However, no matter how heinous such acts may be, calling them political crimes confuses political criminality with political policing or with conventional politics, and therefore obscures the structured relationship between authorities and subjects. There is also the considerable danger that an empirical criterion (what the authorities do) will be abandoned for a nonempirical one (our application of our own interpretations of law).

Even though authorities may indeed act illegally and authoritative personages may be criminalized by others, the crucial question is whether these events have any direct significance for the basic struggle over authority itself. Where they do, we are looking at political resistance and policing. Where they do not, the concepts of "conventional politics" and "factionalism" seem to be more appropriate. The ambiguities we encounter are a function of the complex structures of authority that characterize modern polities.

Summary

Neither the dream of earthly paradise nor the apparition of earthly hell adequately characterizes social reality. Instead, in real social life there is a constant tension between utopianism and realism. That tension is expressed in the process of political organization, set in motion and sustained by conflicts among people trying to secure their chances of living the good life as they understand it. Whether they realize it or not, people are inevitably involved in intergroup struggles over who shall have what resources in a finite world.

Given ultimately limited material resources and the human impossibility of loving everyone equally, distinctions between "them" and "us" become the bases for collective decisions on whose claims are to have priority. Such decisions are not easily reached, nor are they ever final. The process by which social differences are made criteria for social stratification is that of political organization—the ongoing creation through conflict of explicit or implicit rules for allocating resources, and therefore for deciding who shall have greater and who lesser chances in life.

Political organization inevitably favors the parties with the greater initial power, who predictably will try to use their advantage to consolidate their disproportionate control of the available resources. Because there is never total certainty that security has been achieved, there is a very strong (possibly inexorable in intergroup relations) tendency for the aim of consolidation to become the practice of increase—toward absolute, rather than relative, control of violence, economic, political, ideological, and diversionary resources. Of course, people may neither know nor care about the power aspect of a particular relationship; and both very intimate and very distant relationships are most secure when relative power is of no concern.

The key to understanding the process of political organization at the societal level is to analyze the relationship between political criminality and political policing. A polity is characterized by the emerging hierarchical differentiation of authorities and subjects. Intrinsic to that differentiation is the transformation of power into authority, a problematic and reversible movement toward the establishment of military dominance, jurisdictional boundaries, institutionalized policing, demographic continuity, and ideological hegemony. To the degree that people learn to live with one another in terms of the complementary social norms of dominance and of deference, and to believe the charismatic, rational, and/or traditional justifications legitimating their unequal life chances, the power structure that is the polity is also an authority structure. Insofar as the complete and final authority structure is not and cannot be realized, political policing is relied upon to define and control intolerable resistance to political socialization. Political criminality becomes understandable as a socially defined reality, produced by conflict between people who claim to be authorities and people who resist or may resist being their subjects.

REFERENCES

Akehurst, Michael (1970). *A Modern Introduction to International Law*. New York: Atherton.

Andreski, Stanislav (1968). *Military Organization and Society*. Berkeley: University of California Press.

Baldus, Bernd (1975). "The study of power: Suggestions for an alternative." *Canadian Journal of Sociology* 1(2):179-201.

Barton, Allen H. (1970). *Communities in Disaster*. New York: Anchor.

Becker, Howard P. and Harry Elmer Barnes (1952). *Social Thought from Lore to Science* (Volume 1). Washington, DC: Harren.

Bendix, Reinhard (1964). *Nation-Building and Citizenship: Studies of Our Changing Social Order*. New York: John Wiley.

Bittner, Egon (1970). *The Functions of the Police in Modern Society*. Washington, DC: Government Printing Office.

Bordua, David J. and Albert J. Reiss, Jr. (1966). "Command, control, and charisma: Reflections on police bureaucracy." *American Journal of Sociology* 72 (July): 68-76.

Carter, Gwendolen M., Thomas Karis and Newell M. Stultz (1967). *South Africa's Transkei: The Politics of Domestic Colonialism*. London: Heinemann.

Chkhikvadze, V.M. [ed.] (1969). *The Soviet State and Law*. Moscow: Progress Publishers.

Collier, Peter and David Horowitz (1976). *The Rockefellers: An American Dynasty*. New York: New American Library.

Collins, Randall (1975). *Conflict Sociology: Toward an Explanatory Science*. New York: Academic.

Dahrendorf, Ralf (1979). *Life Chances: Approaches to Social and Political Theory*. Chicago: University of Chicago Press.

_____ (1959). *Class and Class Conflict in Industrial Society*. Stanford, CA: Stanford University Press.

Delarue, Jacques (1964). *The Gestapo: A History of Horror*. New York: Dell.

Eisenstadt, S.N. (1969). *The Political Systems of Empires*. New York: Macmillan. (Original 1963 edition with new preface.)

Finkle, Jason L. and Richard W. Gable [eds.] (1966). *Political Development and Social Change*. New York: John Wiley.

Gunder Frank, Andre (1967). "Sociology of development and underdevelopment of sociology." *Catalyst* (Summer): 1-54 (in Warner Modular Publications reprint).

Lenski, Gerhard E. (1966). *Power and Privilege: A Theory of Social Stratification*. New York: McGraw-Hill.

Lerner, Daniel (1958). *The Passing of Traditional Society*. New York: Macmillan.

Manning, Peter K. (1977). *Police Work: The Social Organization of Policing*. Cambridge: MIT Press.

Marx, Karl and Frederick Engels (1962). *Selected Works* (Volume 1). Moscow: Foreign Language Publishing House.

Massell, Gregory J. (1968). "Law as an instrument of revolutionary change in a traditional milieu: The case of Soviet Central Asia." *Law and Society Review* 2 (February): 179-228.

Mead, Margaret [ed.] (1955). *Cultural Patterns and Technical Change*. New York: New American Library.

Michalowski, Ray (1977). "A gentle pedagogy: Teaching critical criminology in the South." *Crime and Social Justice* 7 (Spring-Summer): 69-73.

Miliband, Ralph (1969). *The State in Capitalist Society*. London: Quartet.

Moore, Barrington, Jr. (1967). *Social Origins of Dictatorship and Democracy: Lord and Peasant in the Making of the Modern World.* Boston: Beacon.

Newman, Peter C. (1975). *The Canadian Establishment* (Volume 1). Toronto: McClelland and Stewart-Bantam.

Parsons, Talcott (1951). *The Social System.* New York: Macmillan.

Peterson, Edward N. (1969). *The Limits of Hitler's Power.* Princeton, NJ: Princeton University Press.

Quinney, Richard (1975). *Criminology: Analysis and Critique of Crime in America.* Boston: Little, Brown.

Rapoport, Anatol (1974). *Conflict in Man-Made Environment.* Markham, Ontario: Penguin.

Sagarin, Edward (1973). "Introduction," in reprint of Louis Proal, *Political Crime* (first published in 1895). Montclair, NJ: Patterson Smith.

Sampson, Anthony (1974). *The Sovereign State of ITT.* Greenwich, CT: Fawcett.

Schelling, Thomas C. (1960). *The Strategy of Conflict.* Cambridge, MA: Harvard University Press.

Shklar, Judith N. (1964). *Legalism.* Cambridge, MA: Harvard University Press.

Sigel, Roberta (1965). "Assumptions about the learning of political values." *Annals of the American Academy of Political and Social Science* 361 (September): 1-9.

Simmel, Georg (1955). *Conflict.* New York: Macmillan.

South African Institute of Race Relations [SAIRR] (1977). *A Survey of Race Relations in South Africa, 1976.* Johannesburg: Author.

Spicer, Edward H. [ed.] (1952). *Human Problems in Technological Change.* New York: Russell Sage.

Thaden, Edward C. (1971). *Russia Since 1801.* New York: John Wiley.

Turk, Austin T. (1976). "Law as a weapon in social conflict." *Social Problems* 23 (February): 276-291.

———— (1972a). "The limits of coercive legalism in conflict regulation: South Africa," pp. 171-198 in Ernest Q. Campbell (ed.) *Racial Tensions and National Identity.* Nashville, TN: Vanderbilt University Press.

———— (1969). *Criminality and Legal Order.* Skokie, IL: Rand McNally.

Wallerstein, Immanuel (1976). *The Modern World-System: Capitalist Agriculture and the Origins of the European World-Economy in the Sixteenth Century.* New York: Academic.

Weber, Max (1968). *Economy and Society.* New York: Bedminster.

Winslow, Cal (1975). "Sussex smugglers," pp. 119-166 in Douglas Hay et al., *Albion's Fatal Tree: Crime and Society in Eighteenth-Century England.* New York: Pantheon.

Essay/Discussion Questions for Section V

Note to the student: If you are able to provide thorough responses to all of the following questions, you have mastered excellent comprehension of the classic readings presented in this section.

1. What are the major differences between consensus theories and conflict theories? (From the section introduction.)

2. What is the difference between conservative (pluralist) conflict theories and radical conflict theories? (From the section introduction.)

3. Across all of the readings in this section, what can you point to as elements that are common in conflict theories? (From the section introduction.)

4. What does Quinney mean by the "social reality of crime"? (From the Quinney reading.)

5. Quinney discusses the effect of the media on conceptions of crime. What role do the media play in crime definition and production? (From the Quinney reading.)

6. Explain how the "mode" of production affects the definition of and reaction to crime. (From the Spitzer reading.)

7. Why are the various populations (surplus laborers, social junk, and social dynamite) discussed by Spitzer important for crime and crime control? (From the Spitzer reading.)

8. Turk discusses the different forms of political control. What are they and why do you think there is more than one form of control? (From the Turk reading.)

9. What is "ideological hegemony" and what form of control does it exemplify? (From the Turk reading.)

Section VI
SOCIAL CONTROL THEORIES

Introduction

One of the most popular theoretical approaches of the 1970s and 1980s was social control theory. The general perspective is older than that period, dating back to at least Durkheim's writings in the 1890s. As strain and differential association theories grew old, and as labeling and conflict theories became more radical, many criminologists were looking for a sound sociological approach with a conservative bent. Social control theories seem to have filled that gap.

There are many social control theories, but all have in common an assumption that deviance really does not need to be explained. Conformity is the real problem for these theories and, in one way or another, they ask the question *"Why do people conform?"* The general answer to this is that people are somehow socialized into the major values and lifeways of society. Deviance occurs when socialization somehow breaks down. This theoretical framework requires the existence of a single, dominant value system, often called the *"moral order."*

Techniques of Neutralization

The first reading in this section is from Gresham Sykes and David Matza's 1957 article on "Techniques of Neutralization." The article was originally written as a response to Cohen's contention that lower-class delinquents cast off middle-class values and create their own set of delinquent values in opposition. Sykes and Matza contended that it was not necessary for lower-class delinquents to have different values and cited research showing that delinquents still had values similar to middle-class ones. Thus, they argued, delinquents were tied to the dominant culture, not to some anti-culture. There are ways in which delinquents can subscribe to middle-class values, temporarily overcome them, and commit delinquent acts.

267

This method of temporarily overcoming values was called *techniques of neutralization*. The use of these neutralizations enabled youths to suspend temporarily their commitment to societal values and freed them to commit a delinquent act. Sykes and Matza believed that neutralizations were available to virtually everyone, not just lower-class youth, and were part of the culture. In fact, Donald Cressey had used a similar concept in his discussion of embezzlement and argued that the rationalizations necessary to commit white-collar crime were simply part of the business culture.

There were five types of neutralizations used by delinquents: *denial or responsibility, denial of injury, denial of the victim, condemnation of the condemners*, and *appeal to higher loyalties*. In each case, they represented a way in which a youth could become "detached" from the dominant value system and justify the commission of a delinquent act. Matza later contributed a major elaboration on the perspective with his book *Delinquency and Drift*.

Containment Theory

At about the same time that Sykes and Matza were writing, Walter Reckless produced a social control perspective for explaining delinquency known as containment theory. He elaborated on the theory for several years and had several collaborators, the most well-known of whom was Simon Dinitz. The reading in this section is from a 1961 article in which Reckless summarized the theory and argued for its validity and usefulness. The theory contained two major components: external and internal containment. Each containment factor exerted control over a youth and prevented him or her from committing delinquent acts.

External containment involved such factors as a proper family life, institutional reinforcement (schools, church, clubs) for behaving well, and a good moral setting. In fact, the components of external containment were similar to the traditional sociological variables found in other criminological theories. If the theory rested primarily on these concepts, there would have been little new information in it.

Internal containment was the twist in Reckless's theory. Its components included ego strength, proper moral values, and a good sense of the self. Inner containment was largely psychological, involving the results of socialization on a child. Reckless most often called this the *self-concept* and maintained that it was the critical factor in delinquency. A good self-concept was probably sufficient to keep a youth from delinquency, no matter what the external environment was like. A bad self-concept was likely to result in delinquency, with the external environment providing pushes or pulls toward delinquency or conformity.

Hirschi's Social Control Theory

With other work in between, the most popular statement of social control theory during the 1970s and 1980s came from Travis Hirschi in his 1969 book *Causes of Delinquency*. Perhaps making the most thorough statement of social control theory, Hirschi elaborated on the components that caused youths to attach themselves to the dominant value system, or the *bond to the moral order*.

As with other social control theorists, Hirschi felt that delinquency would emerge if youths were not controlled in some fashion. He found four elements of the bond that created conformity. These were: attachment, commitment, involvement, and belief.

Attachment was the most important of the elements. It represented the effect of close ties with parents and friends, or even to institutions such as schools or clubs. The stronger these attachments, the less likely delinquency is to occur. *Commitment* was an investment in conventional things. A person with high levels of commitment might be someone with many years of education, a business owner, or even a good reputation in the community. For a youth, it could be a reputation in school or a spot on the varsity football team.

Involvement represented the time and energy spent in conventional activities. Highly involved youths have little time left for other activities, including delinquency. Finally, *belief* was a respect for society's values and the feeling of an obligation to obey them. Those who were well-socialized and who exhibited a high degree of allegiance to middle-class values and lifestyles would be unlikely to commit delinquent acts.

Hirschi realized that almost everyone had some bond to society, so the critical ingredient was not the total absence of the elements. The most important consideration was the degree to which the four elements needed to be weakened before deviance could take place. A weakening of any of the elements might make deviance possible. However, combinations of weakened elements remained to be examined.

Hirschi's more recent work has introduced another social control theory (Gottfredson & Hirschi, 1989, 1990) referred to as either the "general theory of crime" or as "self-control" theory. The new theory ties underlying propensities (crime-proneness) to early childhood socialization and the conditions under which these translate into crime. The most important ingredient in the approach is inadequate child-rearing practices (poor childhood socialization), which serve to create traits and propensities conducive to criminality. That is, improper socialization at an early age produces a lack of self-control to overcome the urge toward deviance. Notably, in this version of control theory, Hirschi and Gottfredson have eliminated discussion of the four elements of the bond.

Epilogue

Social control theory remains popular today. In fact, most of the theoretical research of the past decade has focused on Hirschi's theory. Criminologists have examined the various elements of the bond, and in some cases have proposed a blending of social control theory with other theories [e.g., Conger (1976), with social learning; Elliott, Huizinga & Ageton (1985), with social learning and anomie]. Because they incorporate most of the "gut-level" feelings people have about the causes of crime (poor family life, not enough religion, lack of education, idleness), social control theories should remain popular for some time to come.

BIBLIOGRAPHY

Briar, Scott and Irving Piliavin (1965). "Delinquency, situational inducements, and commitment to conformity," *Social Problems* 13: 33-45.

Conger, Rand (1976). "Social control and social learning models of delinquent behavior: A synthesis," *Criminology* 17: 17-40.

Durkheim, Emile (1895). *The Rules of the Sociological Method.* Trans. Sarah A. Solovay and John H. Mueller. New York: Free Press (reprinted 1965).

Elliott, Delbert S., David Huizinga, and Suzanne S. Ageton (1985). *Explaining Delinquency and Drug Use.* Beverly Hills: Sage.

Gottfredson, Michael and Travis Hirschi (1990). *A General Theory of Crime.* Stanford, CA: Stanford University Press.

Gottfredson, Michael and Travis Hirschi (1989). "A propensity-event theory of crime." in William S. Laufer and Freda Adler (eds.) *Advances in Criminological Theory*, vol. 1. New Brunswick, NJ: Transaction, 57-67.

Hirschi, Travis (1969). *Causes of Delinquency.* Berkeley: University of California Press.

Hirschi, Travis and Michael Gottfredson (1989). "The significance of white-collar crime for a general theory of crime," *Criminology* 27: 359-71.

Matza, David (1964). *Delinquency and Drift.* New York: John Wiley.

Nye, F. Ivan (1958). *Family Relationships and Delinquent Behavior.* New York: John Wiley.

Reckless, Walter C. (1955). *The Crime Problem.* New York: Appleton-Century-Crofts.

Reckless, Walter C. and Simon Dinitz (1967). "Pioneering with self-concept as a vulnerability factor in delinquency," *Journal of Criminal Law, Criminology, and Police Science* 58: 515-23.

Reckless, Walter C., Simon Dinitz, and Ellen Murray (1956). "Self-concept as an insulator against delinquency," *American Sociological Review* 21: 744-56.

Reiss, Albert J., Jr. (1951). "Delinquency as the failure of personal and social controls," *American Sociological Review* 16: 196-207.

Short, James F., Jr. and Fred L. Strodtbeck (1965). *Group Process and Gang Delinquency*. Chicago: University of Chicago Press.

Sykes, Gresham M. and David Matza (1957). "Techniques of neutralization: A theory of delinquency," *American Sociological Review* 22: 664-70.

Toby, Jackson (1957). "Social disorganization and stake in conformity: Complimentary factors in the predatory behavior of hoodlums," *Journal of Criminal Law, Criminology, and Police Science* 48: 12-17.

Criminologist Profiles

Gresham M'Cready Sykes (1922-   )

Sykes was born in Plainfield, New Jersey. He received an A.B. in sociology from Princeton University in 1950 and a Ph.D. in sociology from Northwestern University in 1953. Sykes taught at Princeton University (sociology) from 1952-1958, Northwestern University (sociology) from 1958-1960, Dartmouth College (sociology) from 1960-1963 (chair of the department from 1961-1963), University of Denver (sociology) from 1965-1972, University of Houston (sociology) in 1973 (and chair of the department), and University of Virginia from 1974-1988 (chair of the department from 1978-1981). He also served (1963-1964) as executive officer of the American Sociological Association. Sykes retired as professor emeritus in 1988.

David Matza (1930-   )

Matza was born in New York, New York. He was educated at the City College of New York, receiving a B.A. in social science in 1953. His graduate education took place at Princeton University, with an M.A. (1955) and a Ph.D. (1959) in sociology and economics. Matza taught in the sociology department of Temple University from 1957-1959, earned a post-doctorate with the University of Chicago Law School in law and society during 1959-1960, and taught in the sociology department of the University of California, Berkeley from 1960-1992, retiring as professor emeritus. Matza received the Society for the Study of Social Problems' first C. Wright Mills award in 1964 for his book *Delinquency and Drift*.

Techniques of Neutralization*
Gresham M. Sykes and David Matza

In attempting to uncover the roots of juvenile delinquency, the social scientist has long since ceased to search for devils in the mind or stigma of the body. It is now largely agreed that delinquent behavior, like most social behavior, is learned and that it is learned in the process of social interaction.

The classic statement of this position is found in Sutherland's theory of differential association, which asserts that criminal or delinquent behavior involves the learning of (a) techniques of committing crimes and (b) motives, drives, rationalizations, and attitudes favorable to the violation of law.[1] Unfortunately, the specific content of what is learned—as opposed to the process by which it is learned—has received relatively little attention in either theory or research. Perhaps the single strongest school of thought on the nature of this content has centered on the idea of a delinquent subculture. The basic characteristic of the delinquent subculture, it is argued, is a system of values that represents an inversion of the values held by respectable, law-abiding society. The world of the delinquent is the world of the law-abiding turned upside down and its norms constitute a countervailing force directed against the conforming social order. Cohen[2] sees the process of developing a delinquent subculture as a matter of building, maintaining, and reinforcing a code for behavior which exists by opposition, which stands in point by point contradiction to dominant values, particularly those of the middle class. Cohen's portrayal of delinquency is executed with a good deal of sophistication, and he carefully avoids overly simple explanations such as those based on the principle of "follow the leader" or easy generalizations about "emotional disturbances." Furthermore, he does not accept the delinquent subculture as something

*Source: Gresham M. Sykes and David Matza, 1957. "Techniques of Neutralization: A Theory of Delinquency," *American Sociological Review* 22 (December): 664-670. By permission of the publisher.

given, but instead systematically examines the function of delinquent values as a viable solution to the lower-class, male child's problems in the area of social status. Yet in spite of its virtues, this image of juvenile delinquency as a form of behavior based on competing or countervailing values and norms appears to suffer from a number of serious defects. It is the nature of these defects and a possible alternative or modified explanation for a large portion of juvenile delinquency with which this paper is concerned.

The difficulties in viewing delinquent behavior as springing from a set of deviant values and norms—as arising, that is to say, from a situation in which the delinquent defines his delinquency as "right"—are both empirical and theoretical. In the first place, if there existed in fact a delinquent subculture such that the delinquent viewed his illegal behavior as morally correct, we could reasonably suppose that he would exhibit no feelings of guilt or shame at detection or confinement. Instead, the major reaction would tend in the direction of indignation or a sense of martyrdom.[3] It is true that some delinquents do react in the latter fashion, although the sense of martyrdom often seems to be based on the fact that others "get away with it" and indignation appears to be directed against the chance events or lack of skill that led to apprehension. More important, however, is the fact that there is a good deal of evidence suggesting that many delinquents *do* experience a sense of guilt or shame, and its outward expression is not to be dismissed as a purely manipulative gesture to appease those in authority. Much of this evidence is, to be sure, of a clinical nature or in the form of impressionistic judgments of those who must deal firsthand with the youthful offender. Assigning a weight to such evidence calls for caution, but it cannot be ignored if we are to avoid the gross stereotype of the juvenile delinquent as a hardened gangster in miniature. In the second place, observers have noted that the juvenile delinquent frequently accords admiration and respect to law-abiding persons. The "really honest" person is often revered, and if the delinquent is sometimes overly keen to detect hypocrisy in those who conform, unquestioned probity is likely to win his approval. A fierce attachment to a humble, pious mother or a forgiving, upright priest (the former, according to many observers, is often encountered in both juvenile delinquents and adult criminals) might be dismissed as rank sentimentality, but at least it is clear that the delinquent does not necessarily regard those who abide by the legal rules as immoral. In a similar vein, it can be noted that the juvenile delinquent may exhibit great resentment if illegal behavior is imputed to "significant others" in his immediate social environment or to heroes in the world of sport and entertainment. In other words, if the delinquent does hold to a set of values and norms that stand in complete opposition to those of respectable society, his norm-holding is of a peculiar sort. While supposedly thoroughly committed to the deviant system of the delinquent subculture, he would appear to recognize the moral validity of the dominant normative system in many instances.[4]

In the third place, there is much evidence that juvenile delinquents often draw a sharp line between those who can be victimized and those who cannot. Certain social groups are not to be viewed as "fair game" in the performance of supposedly approved delinquent acts while others warrant a variety of attacks. In general, the potentiality for victimization would seem to be a function of the social distance between the juvenile delinquent and others and thus we find implicit maxims in the world of the delinquent such as "don't steal from friends" or "don't commit vandalism against a church of your own faith."[5] This is all rather obvious, but the implications have not received sufficient attention. The fact that supposedly valued behavior tends to be directed against disvalued social groups hints that the "wrongfulness" of such delinquent behavior is more widely recognized by delinquents than the literature has indicated. When the pool of victims is limited by considerations of kinship, friendship, ethnic group, social class, age, sex, etc., we have reason to suspect that the virtue of delinquency is far from unquestioned.

In the fourth place, it is doubtful if many juvenile delinquents are totally immune from the demands for conformity made by the dominant social order. There is a strong likelihood that the family of the delinquent will agree with respectable society that delinquency is wrong, even though the family may be engaged in a variety of illegal activities. That is, the parental posture conducive to delinquency is not apt to be a positive prodding. Whatever may be the influence of parental example, what might be called the "Fagin" pattern of socialization into delinquency is probably rare. Furthermore, as Redl has indicated, the idea that certain neighborhoods are completely delinquent, offering the child a model for delinquent behavior without reservations, is simply not supported by the data.[6]

The fact that a child is punished by parents, school officials, and agencies of the legal system for his delinquency may, as a number of observers have cynically noted, suggest to the child that he should be more careful not to get caught. There is an equal or greater probability, however, that the child will internalize the demands for conformity. This is not to say that demands for conformity cannot be counteracted. In fact, as we shall see shortly, an understanding of how internal and external demands for conformity are neutralized may be crucial for understanding delinquent behavior. But it is to say that a complete denial of the validity of demands for conformity and the substitution of a new normative system is improbable, in light of the child's or adolescent's dependency on adults and encirclement by adults inherent in his status in the social structure. No matter how deeply enmeshed in patterns of delinquency he may be and no matter how much this involvement may outweigh his associations with the law-abiding, he cannot escape the condemnation of his deviance. Somehow the demands for conformity must be met and answered; they cannot be ignored as part of an alien system of values and norms.

In short, the theoretical viewpoint that sees juvenile delinquency as a form of behavior based on the values and norms of a deviant subculture in precisely the same way as law-abiding behavior is based on the values and norms of the larger society is open to serious doubt. The fact that the world of the delinquent is embedded in the larger world of those who conform cannot be overlooked nor can the delinquent be equated with an adult thoroughly socialized into an alternative way of life. Instead, the juvenile delinquent would appear to be at least partially committed to the dominant social order in that he frequently exhibits guilt or shame when he violates its proscriptions, accords approval to certain conforming figures, and distinguishes between appropriate and inappropriate targets for his deviance. It is to an explanation for the apparently paradoxical fact of his delinquency that we now turn.

As Morris Cohen once said, one of the most fascinating problems about human behavior is why men violate the laws in which they believe. This is the problem that confronts us when we attempt to explain why delinquency occurs despite a greater or lesser commitment to the usages of conformity. A basic clue is offered by the fact that social rules or norms calling for valued behavior seldom if ever take the form of categorical imperatives. Rather, values or norms appear as *qualified* guides for action, limited in their applicability in terms of time, place, persons, and social circumstances. The moral injunction against killing, for example, does not apply to the enemy during combat in time of war, although a captured enemy comes once again under the prohibition. Similarly, the taking and distributing of scarce goods in a time of acute social need is felt by many to be right, although under other circumstances private property is held inviolable. The normative system of a society, then, is marked by what Williams has termed *flexibility;* it does not consist of a body of rules held to be binding under all conditions.[7]

This flexibility is, in fact, an integral part of the criminal law in that measures for "defenses to crimes" are provided in pleas such as nonage, necessity, insanity, drunkenness, compulsion, self-defense, and so on. The individual can avoid moral culpability for his criminal action—and thus avoid the negative sanctions of society—if he can prove that criminal intent was lacking. It is *our argument that much delinquency is based on what is essentially an unrecognized extension of defenses to crimes, in the form of justifications for deviance that are seen as valid by the delinquent but not by the legal system or society at large.*

These justifications are commonly described as rationalizations. They are viewed as following deviant behavior and as protecting the individual from self-blame and the blame of others after the act. But there is also reason to believe that they precede deviant behavior and make deviant behavior possible. It is this possibility that Sutherland mentioned only in passing and that other writers have failed to exploit from the viewpoint of sociological theory. Disapproval flowing from internalized norms and conforming others in the social environment is neutralized, turned back, or deflected in advance. Social controls that serve to check or inhibit deviant motivational patterns are rendered inoperative, and the individual is freed to engage in delinquency without serious damage to his self image. In this sense, the delinquent both has his cake and eats it too, for he remains committed to the dominant normative system and yet so qualifies its imperatives that violations are "acceptable" if not "right." Thus the delinquent represents not a radical opposition to law-abiding society but something more like an apologetic failure, often more sinned against than sinning in his own eyes. We call these justifications of deviant behavior techniques of neutralization; and we believe these techniques make up a crucial component of Sutherland's "definitions favorable to the violation of law." It is by learning these techniques that the juvenile becomes delinquent, rather than by learning moral imperatives, values or attitudes standing in direct contradiction to those of the dominant society. In analyzing these techniques, we have found it convenient to divide them into five major types.

The Denial of Responsibility. Insofar as the delinquent can define himself as lacking responsibility for his deviant actions, the disapproval of self or others is sharply reduced in effectiveness as a restraining influence. As Justice Holmes has said, even a dog distinguishes between being stumbled over and being kicked, and modern society is no less careful to draw a line between injuries that are unintentional, i.e., where responsibility is lacking, and those that are intentional. As a technique of neutralization, however, the denial of responsibility extends much further than the claim that deviant acts are an "accident" or some similar negation of personal accountability. It may also be asserted that delinquent acts are due to forces outside of the individual and beyond his control such as unloving parents, bad companions, or a slum neighborhood. In effect, the delinquent approaches a "billiard ball" conception of himself in which he sees himself as helplessly propelled into new situations. From a psychodynamic viewpoint, this orientation toward one's own actions may represent a profound alienation from self, but it is important to stress the fact that interpretations of responsibility are cultural constructs and not merely idiosyncratic beliefs. The similarity between this mode of justifying illegal behavior assumed by the delinquent and the implications of a "sociological" frame of reference or a "humane" jurisprudence is readily apparent.[8] It is not the validity of this orientation that concerns us here, but its function of deflecting blame attached to violations of social norms and its relative independence of a particular personality structure.[9] By learning to view himself as more acted upon than acting, the delinquent prepares the way for deviance from the dominant normative system without the necessity of a frontal assault on the norms themselves.

The Denial of Injury. A second major technique of neutralization centers on the injury or harm involved in the delinquent act. The criminal law has long made a distinction between crimes which are *mala in se* and *mala prohibita*—that is between acts that are wrong in themselves and acts that are illegal but not immoral—and the delinquent can make the same kind of distinction in evaluating the wrongfulness of his behavior. For the delinquent, however, wrongfulness may turn on the question of whether or not anyone has clearly been hurt by his deviance, and this matter is open to a variety of interpretations. Vandalism, for example, may be defined by the delinquent simply as "mischief"—after all, it may be claimed, the persons whose property has been destroyed can well afford it. Similarly, auto theft may be viewed as "borrowing," and gang fighting may be seen as a private quarrel, an agreed upon duel between two willing parties, and thus of no concern to the community at large. We are not suggesting that this technique of neutralization, labelled the denial of injury, involves an explicit dialectic, rather, we are arguing that the delinquent frequently, and in a hazy fashion, feels that his behavior does not really cause any great harm despite the fact that it runs counter to law. Just as the link between the individual and his acts may be broken by the denial of responsibility, so may the link between acts and their consequences by broken by the denial of injury. Since society sometimes agrees with the delinquent, e.g., in matters such as truancy, "pranks," and so on, it merely reaffirms the idea that the delinquent's neutralization of social controls by means of qualifying the norms is an extension of common practice rather than a gesture of complete opposition.

The Denial of the Victim. Even if the delinquent accepts the responsibility for his deviant actions and is willing to admit that his deviant actions involve an injury or hurt, the moral indignation of self and others may be neutralized by an insistence that the injury is not wrong in light of the circumstances. The injury, it may be claimed, is not really an injury; rather, it is a form of rightful retaliation or punishment. By a subtle alchemy the delinquent moves himself into the position of an avenger and the victim is transformed into a wrong-doer. Assaults on homosexuals or suspected homosexuals, attacks on members of minority groups who are said to have gotten "out of place," vandalism as revenge on an unfair teacher or school official, thefts from a "crooked" store owner—all may be hurts inflicted on a transgressor, in the eyes of the delinquent. As Orwell has pointed out, the type of criminal admired by the general public has probably changed over the course of years and Raffles no longer serves as a hero;[10] but Robin Hood, and his latter day derivatives such as the tough detective seeking justice outside the law, still capture the popular imagination, and the delinquent may view his acts as part of a similar role.

To deny the existence of the victim, then, by transforming him into a person deserving injury is an extreme form of a phenomenon we have mentioned before, namely, the delinquent's recognition of appropriate and inappropriate targets for his delinquent acts. In addition, however, the existence of the victim may be denied for the delinquent, in a somewhat different sense, by the circumstances of the delinquent act itself.

Insofar as the victim is physically absent, unknown, or a vague abstraction (as is often the case in delinquent acts committed against property), the awareness of the victim's existence is weakened. Internalized norms and anticipations of the reactions of others must somehow be activated, if they are to serve as guides for behavior; and it is possible that a diminished awareness of the victim plays an important part in determining whether or not this process is set in motion.

The Condemnation of the Condemners. A fourth technique of neutralization would appear to involve a condemnation of the condemners or, as McCorkle and Korn have phrased it, a rejection of the rejectors.[11] The delinquent shifts the focus of attention from his own deviant acts to the motives and behavior of those who disapprove of his violations. His condemners, he may claim, are hypocrites, deviants in disguise, or impelled by personal spite. This orientation toward the conforming world may be of particular importance when it hardens into a bitter cynicism directed against those assigned the task of enforcing or expressing the norms of the dominant society. Police, it may be said, are corrupt, stupid, and brutal. Teachers always show favoritism and parents always "take it out" on their children. By a slight extension, the rewards of conformity—such as material success—become a matter of pull or luck, thus decreasing still further the stature of those who stand on the side of the law-abiding. The validity of this jaundiced viewpoint is not so important as its function in turning back or deflecting the negative sanctions attached to violations of the norms. The delinquent, in effect, has changed the subject of the conversation in the dialogue between his own deviant impulses and the reactions of others and by attacking others, the wrongfulness of his own behavior is more easily repressed or lost to view.

The Appeal to Higher Loyalties. Fifth, and last, internal and external social controls may be neutralized by sacrificing the demands of the larger society for the demands of the smaller social groups to which the delinquent belongs such as the sibling pair, the gang, or the friendship clique. It is important to note that the delinquent does not necessarily repudiate the imperatives of the dominant normative system, despite his failure to follow them. Rather, the delinquent may see himself as caught up in a dilemma that must be resolved, unfortunately, at the cost of violating the law. One aspect of this situation has been studied by Stouffer and Toby in their research on the conflict between particularistic and universalistic demands, between the claims of friendship and general social obligations, and their results suggest that "it is possible to classify people according to a predisposition to select one or the other horn of a dilemma in role conflict."[12] For our purposes, however, the most important point is that deviation from certain norms may occur not because the norms are rejected but because other norms, held to be more pressing or involving a higher loyalty, are accorded precedence. Indeed, it is the fact that both sets of norms are believed in that gives meaning to our concepts of dilemma and role conflict.

The conflict between the claims of friendship and the claims of law, or a similar dilemma, has of course long been recognized by the social scientist (and the novelist) as a common human problem. If the juvenile delinquent frequently resolves his dilemma by insisting that he must "always help a buddy" or "never squeal on a friend," even when it throws him into serious difficulties with the dominant social order, his choice remains familiar to the supposedly law-abiding. The delinquent is unusual, perhaps, in the extent to which he is able to see the fact that he acts in behalf of the smaller social groups to which he belongs as a justification for violations of society's norms, but it is a matter of degree rather than of kind.

"I didn't mean it." "I didn't really hurt anybody." "They had it coming to them." "Everybody's picking on me." "I didn't do it for myself." These slogans or their variants, we hypothesize, prepare the juvenile for delinquent acts. These "definitions of the situation" represent tangential or glancing blows at the dominant normative system rather than the creation of an opposing ideology; and they are extensions of patterns of thought prevalent in society rather than something created *de novo*.

Techniques of neutralization may not be powerful enough to fully shield the individual from the force of his own internalized values and the reactions of conforming others, for as we have pointed out, juvenile delinquents often appear to suffer from feelings of guilt and shame when called into account for their deviant behavior. And some delinquents may be so isolated from the world of conformity that techniques of neutralization need not be called into play. Nonetheless, we would argue that techniques of neutralization are critical in lessening the effectiveness of social controls and that they lie behind a large share of delinquent behavior. Empirical research in this area is scattered and fragmentary at the present time, but the work of Redl,[13] Cressey,[14] and others has supplied a body of significant data that has done much to clarify the theoretical issues and enlarge the fund of supporting evidence. Two lines of investigation seem to be critical at this stage. First, there is need for more knowledge concerning the differential distribution of techniques of neutralization, as operative patterns of thought, by age, sex, social class, ethnic group, etc. On *a priori* grounds it might be assumed that these justifications for deviance will be more readily seized by segments of society for whom a discrepancy between common social ideals and social practice is most apparent. It is also possible however, that the habit of "bending" the dominant normative system—if not "breaking" it—cuts across our cruder social categories and is to be traced primarily to patterns of social interaction within the familial circle. Second, there is need for a greater understanding of the internal structure of techniques of neutralization, as a system of beliefs and attitudes, and its relationship to various types of delinquent behavior. Certain techniques of neutralization would appear to be better adapted to particular deviant acts than to others, as we have suggested, for example, in the case of offenses against property and the denial of the victim. But the issue remains far from clear and stands in need of more information.

In any case, techniques of neutralization appear to offer a promising line of research in enlarging and systematizing the theoretical grasp of juvenile delinquency. As more information is uncovered concerning techniques of neutralization, their origins, and their consequences, both juvenile delinquency in particular, and deviation from normative systems in general may be illuminated.

ENDNOTES

1   E.H. Sutherland, *Principles of Criminology*, revised by D.R. Cressey, Chicago: Lippincott, 1955, pp. 77-80.

2   Albert K. Cohen, *Delinquent Boys*, Glencoe, Ill.: The Free Press, 1955.

3   This form of reaction among the adherents of a deviant subculture who fully believe in the "rightfulness" of their behavior and who are captured and punished by the agencies of the dominant social order can be illustrated, perhaps, by groups such as Jehovah's Witnesses, early Christian sects, nationalist movements in colonial areas, and conscientious objectors during World Wars I and II.

4   As Weber has pointed out, a thief may recognize the legitimacy of legal rules without accepting their moral validity. Cf. Max Weber, *The Theory of Social and Economic Organization* (translated by A.M. Henderson and Talcott Parsons), New York: Oxford University Press, 1947, p. 125. We are arguing here, however, that the juvenile delinquent frequently recognizes both the legitimacy of the dominant social order and its moral "rightness."

5   Thrasher's account of the "Itschkies"—a juvenile gang composed of Jewish boys—and the immunity from "rolling" enjoyed by Jewish drunkards is a good illustration. Cf. F. Thrasher, *The Gang*, Chicago: The University of Chicago Press, 1947, p. 315.

6   Cf. Solomon Kobrin, "The Conflict of Values in Delinquency Areas," *American Sociological Review*, 16 (October, 1951), pp. 653-661.

7   Cf. Robin Williams, Jr., *American Society*, New York: Knopf, 1951, p. 28.

8   A number of observers have wryly noted that many delinquents seem to show a surprising awareness of sociological and psychological explanations for their behavior and are quick to point out the causal role of their poor environment.

9   It is possible, of course, that certain personality structures can accept some techniques of neutralization more readily than others, but this question remains largely unexplored.

10 George Orwell, *Dickens, Dali, and Others*, New York: Reynal, 1946.

11 Lloyd W. McCorkle and Richard Korn, "Resocialization Within Walls," *The Annals of the American Academy of Political and Social Science*, 293, (May, 1954), pp. 88-98.

12 See Samuel A. Stouffer and Jackson Toby, "Role Conflict and Personality," in *Toward a General Theory of Action*, edited by Talcott Parsons and Edward A. Shils, Cambridge: Harvard University Press, 1951, p. 494.

13 See Fritz Redl and David Wineman, *Children Who Hate*, Glencoe: The Free Press, 1956.

14 See D.R. Cressey, *Other People's Money*, Glencoe: The Free Press, 1953.

Walter Cade Reckless (1899-1988)

Reckless was born in Philadelphia, Pennsylvania. He attended the University of Chicago, receiving a Ph.B. in 1921 and a Ph.D. in sociology in 1925. Reckless taught at Vanderbilt University (sociology) from 1924-1940 and The Ohio State University from 1940-1969, retiring in the latter year. He was also a visiting professor at Florida State University's School of Criminology from 1969 to 1972.

A New Theory
of Delinquency and Crime*
Walter C. Reckless

CONTAINMENT THEORY is an explanation of conforming behavior as well as deviancy.[1] It has two reinforcing aspects: an inner control system and an outer control system. Are there elements within the self and within the person's immediate world that enable him to hold the line against deviancy or to hue to the line of social expectations? The assumption is that strong inner and reinforcing outer containment constitutes an insulation against normative deviancy (not constitutional or psychological deviancy), that is, violation of the sociolegal conduct norms.

A Middle Range Theory

Containment theory does not explain the entire spectrum of delinquency and crime. It does not explain crime or delinquency which emerges from strong inner pushes, such as compulsions, anxieties, phobias, hallucinations, personality disorders (including inadequate, unstable, antisocial personalities, etc.), from organic impairments such as brain damage and epilepsy, or from neurotic mechanisms (exhibitionists, peepers, fire setters, compulsive shoplifters). All told these cases are minimal. And containment theory does not explain criminal or delinquent

*Source: Walter C. Reckless, 1961. "A New Theory of Delinquency and Crime," *Federal Probation* 25, 4:42-46. Excerpts from pp. 42 and 44-46. By permission of the publisher.

activity which is a part of "normal" and "expected" roles and activities in families and communities, such as the criminal tribes of India, Gypsy vocations and trades (very similar to the former), begging families, and certain phases of delinquency subculture and organized crime. Between these two extremes in the spectrum of crime and delinquency is a very large middle range of norm violation, perhaps as big as two-thirds to three-quarters of officially reported cases as well as the unreported cases of delinquency and crime. Containment theory seeks to explain this large middle range of offenders. According to its place on the spectrum of delinquency and crime, one might say that it occupies the middle position. . . .

Ingredients of Inner and Outer Containment

. . . containment theory seeks to ferret out more specifically the inner and outer controls over normative behavior. It is attempting to get closer on the target of delinquency and crime by getting at the components which regulate conduct.

Inner containment consists mainly of self components, such as self-control, good self-concept, ego strength, well-developed superego, high frustration tolerance, high resistance to diversions, high sense of responsibility, goal orientation, ability to find substitute satisfactions, tension reducing rationalizations, and so on. These are the inner regulators.

Outer containment represents the structural buffer in the person's immediate social world which is able to hold him within bounds. It consists of such items as a presentation of a consistent moral front to the person, institutional reinforcement of his norms, goals, and expectations, the existence of a reasonable set of social expectations, effective supervision and discipline (social controls), provision for reasonable scope of activity (including limits and responsibilities) as well as for alternatives and safety-valves, opportunity for acceptance, identity, and belongingness. Such structural ingredients help the family and other supportive groups contain the individual.

Research will have to ferret out the one or two elements in inner and outer containment which are the basic regulators of normative behavior. Undoubtedly in the lists cited above there are items which, if present, determine the existence of other items and cause most of the regulation of conduct. Likewise, research must indicate the way in which the inner and outer regulatory systems operate conjointly. How much self-strength must be present in a fluid world with very little external buffer? How much weakness in self components is an effective external buffer able to manage? . . .

. . . Containment theory points to the regulation of normative behavior, through resistance to deviancy as well as through direction toward legitimate social expectations. It may very well be that most of the regulation is in terms of a defense or buffer against deflection. At any rate, it appears as if inner and outer containment occupies a central or core position in between the pressures and pulls of the external environment and the inner drives or pushes. Environmental pressures may be looked upon as conditions associated with poverty or deprivation, conflict and discord, external restraint, minority group status, limited access to success in an opportunity structure. The pulls of the environment represent the distractions, attractions, temptations, patterns of deviancy, advertising, propaganda, carriers of delinquent and criminal patterns (including pushers), delinquency subculture, and so forth. The ordinary pushes are the drives, motives, frustrations, restlessness, disappointments, rebellion, hostility, feelings of inferiority, and so forth. One notices at once that Bonger as well as Cloward fall into pressure theory, while Tarde, Sutherland, and Glaser fall into pull theory.

In a vertical order, the pressures and pulls of the environment are at the top or the side of containing structure, while the pushes are below the inner containment. If the individual has a weak outer containment, the pressures and pulls will then have to be handled by the inner control system. If the outer buffer of the individual is relatively strong and effective, the individual's inner defense does not have to play such a critical role. Likewise, if the person's inner controls are not equal to the ordinary pushes, an effective outer defense may help hold him within bounds. If the inner defenses are of good working order, the outer structure does not have to come to the rescue of the person. Mention has already been made of the fact that there are some extraordinary pushes, such as compulsions, which cannot be contained. The inner and outer control system is usually not equal to the task of containing the abnormal pushes. They are uncontainable, by ordinary controls.

Seven Tests of Validity

1. Containment theory is proposed as the theory of best fit for the large middle range of cases of delinquency and crime. It fits the middle range cases better than any other theory.

2. It explains crimes against the person as well as the crimes against property, that is the mine run of murder, assault, and rape, as well as theft, robbery, and burglary.

3. It represents a formulation which psychiatrists, psychologists, and sociologists, as well as practitioners, can use equally well. All of these experts look for dimensions of inner and outer strength and can specify these strengths in their terms. Differential association and/or pressure of the environment leave most psychiatrists and psychologists cold and an emphasis on push theory leaves the sociologists for the most part cold. But all of the experts can rally around inner and outer weakness and strengths.

4. Inner and outer containment can be discovered in individual case studies. Weaknesses and strengths are observable. Containment theory is one of the few theories in which the microcosm (the individual case history) mirrors the ingredients of the macrocosm (the general formulation).

5. Containment theory is a valid operational theory for treatment of offenders: for restructuring the milieu of a person or beefing up his self. The most knowledgeable probation workers, parole workers, and institutional staff are already focusing to some extent on helping the juvenile or adult offender build up ego strength, develop new goals, internalize new models of behavior. They are also working on social ties, anchors, supportive relationships, limits, and alternative opportunities in helping to refashion a new containing world for the person.

6. Containment theory is also an effective operational theory for prevention. Children with poor containment can be spotted early. Programs to help insulate vulnerable children against delinquency must operate on internalization of stronger self components and the strengthening of containing structure around the child.

7. Internal and external containment can be assessed and approximated. Its strengths and weaknesses can be specified for research. There is good promise that such assessments can be measured in a standard way.

Finally, it is probable that the theory which will best supplement containment theory in the future will be "damage theory," according to which a light to dark spectrum of damage produces maladjustment and deviancy. The problem here is to find measures to isolate the less serious and less obvious damage cases and to estimate how far into the middle range of delinquency and crime the lighter impairments go.

ENDNOTE

1   For the complete statement on Containment Theory, see Walter C. Reckless, *The Crime Problem,* 3rd Ed. New York: Appleton-Century-Crofts, 1961, pp. 335-359.

Criminologist Profile

Travis Hirschi (1935-   )

Hirschi was born in Rockville, Utah. He was educated at the University of Utah (B.S., 1957, and M.S., 1958) and the University of California, Berkeley (Ph.D. in sociology, 1968). Hirschi taught at the University of Washington (sociology, 1967-1971), University of California, Davis (sociology, 1971-1977), and the State University of New York at Albany (sociology, 1977-1981). He moved to the University of Arizona department of sociology in 1981, retiring in 1997 as professor emeritus.

A Control Theory of Delinquency[*]
Travis Hirschi

The more weakened the groups to which [the individual] belongs, the less he depends on them, the more he consequently depends only on himself and recognizes no other rules of conduct than what are founded on his private interests.[1]

Control theories assume that delinquent acts result when an individual's bond to society is weak or broken. Since these theories embrace two highly complex concepts, the *bond* of the individual to *society,* it is not surprising that they have at one time or another formed the basis of explanations of most forms of aberrant or unusual behavior. It is also not surprising that control theories have described the elements of the bond to society in many ways, and that they have focused on a variety of units as the point of control.

I begin with a classification and description of the elements of the bond to conventional society. I try to show how each of these elements is related to delinquent behavior and how they are related to each other. I then turn to the question of specifying the unit to which the person is presumably more or less tied, and to the question of the adequacy of the motivational force built into the explanation of delinquent behavior.

*Source: Travis Hirschi, 1969. *Causes of Delinquency,* pp. 16-34. By permission of the author.

Elements of the Bond

Attachment

In explaining conforming behavior, sociologists justly emphasize sensitivity to the opinion of others.[2] Unfortunately, as suggested in the preceding chapter, they tend to suggest that man is sensitive to the opinion of others and thus exclude sensitivity from their explanations of deviant behavior. In explaining deviant behavior, psychologists, in contrast, emphasize insensitivity to the opinion of others.[3] Unfortunately, they too tend to ignore variation, and, in addition, they tend to tie sensitivity inextricably to other variables, to make it part of a syndrome or "type," and thus seriously to reduce its value as an explanatory concept. The psychopath is characterized only in part by "deficient attachment to or affection for others, a failure to respond to the ordinary motivations founded in respect or regard for one's fellows";[4] he is also characterized by such things as "excessive aggressiveness," lack of superego control," and "an infantile level of response."[5] Unfortunately, too, the behavior that psychopathy is used to explain often becomes part of the *definition* of psychopathy. As a result, in Barbara Wootton's words: "[The psychopath] is . . . par excellence, and without shame or qualification, the model of the circular process by which mental abnormality is inferred from anti-social behavior while anti-social behavior is explained by mental abnormality."[6]

The problems of diagnosis, tautology, and name-calling are voided if the dimensions of psychopathy are treated as causally and therefore problematically interrelated, rather than as logically and therefore necessarily bound to each other. In fact, it can be argued that all of the characteristics attributed to the psychopath follow from, are effects of, his lack of attachment to others. To say that to lack attachment to others is to be free from moral restraints is to use lack of attachment to explain the guiltlessness of the psychopath, the fact that he apparently has no conscience or superego. In this view, lack of attachment to others is not merely a symptom of psychopathy, it *is* psychopathy; lack of conscience is just another way of saying the same thing; and the violation of norms is (or may be) a consequence.

For that matter, given that man is an animal, "impulsivity" and "aggressiveness" can also be seen as natural consequences of freedom from moral restraints. However, since the view of man as endowed with natural propensities and capacities like other animals is peculiarly unpalatable to sociologists, we need not fall back on such a view to explain the amoral man's aggressiveness.[7] The process of becoming alienated from others often involves or is based on active interpersonal conflict. Such conflict could easily supply a reservoir of *socially derived* hostility sufficient to account for the aggressiveness of those whose attachments to others have been weakened.

Durkheim said it many years ago: "We are moral beings to the extent that we are social beings."[8] This may be interpreted to mean that we are moral beings to the extent that we have "internalized the norms" of society. But what does it mean to say that a person has internalized the norms of society? The norms of society are by definition shared by the members of society. To violate a norm is, therefore, to act contrary to the wishes and expectations of other people. If a person does not care about the wishes and expectations of other people—that is, if he is insensitive to the opinion of others—then he is to that extent not bound by the norms. He is free to deviate.

The essence of internalization of norms, conscience, or superego thus lies in the attachment of the individual to others.[9] This view has several advantages over the concept of internalization. For one, explanations of deviant behavior based on attachment do not beg the question, since the extent to which a person is attached to others can be measured independently of his deviant behavior. Furthermore, change or variation in behavior is explainable in a way that it is not when notions of internalization or superego are used. For example, the divorced man is more likely after divorce to commit a number of deviant acts, such as suicide or forgery. If we explain these acts by reference to the superego (or internal control), we are forced to say that the man "lost his conscience" when he got a divorce; and, of course, if he remarries, we have to conclude that he gets his conscience back.

This dimension of the bond to conventional society is encountered in most social control-oriented research and theory. F. Ivan Nye's "internal control" and "indirect control" refer to the same element, although we avoid the problem of explaining changes over time by locating the "conscience" in the bond to others rather than making it part of the personality.[10] Attachment to others is just one aspect of Albert J. Reiss's "personal controls"; we avoid his problems of tautological empirical observations by making the relationship between attachment and delinquency problematic rather than definitional.[11] Finally, Scott Briar and Irving Piliavin's "commitment" or "stake in conformity" subsumes attachment, as their discussion illustrates, although the terms they use are more closely associated with the next element to be discussed.[12]

Commitment

"Of all passions, that which inclineth men least to break the laws, is fear. Nay, excepting some generous natures, it is the only thing, when there is the appearance of profit or pleasure by breaking the laws, that makes men keep them."[13] Few would deny that men on occasion obey the rules simply from fear of the consequences. This rational component in conformity we label commitment. What does it mean to say that a person is committed to conformity? In Howard S. Becker's formulation it means the following:

> First, the individual is in a position in which his decision with regard to some particular line of action has consequences for other interests and activities not necessarily [directly] related to it. Second, he has placed himself in that position by his own prior actions. A third element is present though so obvious as not to be apparent: the committed person must be aware [of these other interests] and must recognize that his decision in this case will have ramifications beyond it.[14]

The idea, then, is that the person invests time, energy, himself, in a certain line of activity—say, getting an education, building up a business, acquiring a reputation for virtue. When or whenever he considers deviant behavior, he must consider the costs of this deviant behavior, the risk he runs of losing the investment he has made in conventional behavior.

If attachment to others is the sociological counterpart of the superego or conscience, commitment is the counterpart of the ego or common sense. To the person committed to conventional lines of action, risking one to ten years in prison for a ten-dollar holdup is stupidity, because to the committed person the costs and risks obviously exceed ten dollars in value. (To the psychoanalyst, such an act exhibits failure to be governed by the "reality-principle." In the sociological control theory, it can be and is generally assumed that the decision to commit a criminal act may well be rationally determined—that the actor's decision was not irrational given the risks and costs he faces. Of course, as Becker points out, if the actor is capable of in some sense calculating the costs of a line of action, he is also capable of calculational errors: ignorance and error return, in the control theory, as possible explanations of deviant behavior.

The concept of commitment assumes that the organization of society is such that the interests of most persons would be endangered if they were to engage in criminal acts. Most people, simply by the process of living in an organized society, acquire goods reputations, prospects that they do not want to risk losing. These accumulations are society's insurance that they will abide by the rules. Many hypotheses about the antecedents of delinquent behavior are based on this premise. For example, Arthur L. Stinchcombe's hypothesis that "high school rebellion . . . occurs when future status is not clearly related to present performance"[15] suggests that one is committed to conformity not only by what one has but also by what one hopes to obtain. Thus "ambition" and/or "aspiration" play an important role in producing conformity. The person becomes committed to a conventional line of action, and he is therefore committed to conformity.

Most lines of action in a society are of course conventional. The clearest examples are educational and occupational careers. Actions thought to jeopardize one's chances in these areas are presumably avoided. Interestingly enough, even nonconventional commitments may operate to produce conventional conformity. We are told, at least, that boys aspiring to careers in the rackets or professional thievery are judged by their "honesty" and "reliability"—traits traditionally in demand among seekers of office boys.[16]

Involvement

Many persons undoubtedly owe a life of virtue to a lack of opportunity to do otherwise. Time and energy are inherently limited: "Not that I would not, if I could, be both handsome and fat and well dressed, and a great athlete, and make a million a year, be a wit, a bon vivant, and a lady killer, as well as a philosopher, a philanthropist, a statesman, warrior, and African explorer, as well as a 'tone-poet' and saint. But the thing is simply impossible."[17] The things that William James here says he would like to be or do are all, I suppose, within the realm of conventionality, but if he were to include illicit actions he would still have to eliminate some of them as simply impossible.

Involvement or engrossment in conventional activities is thus often part of a control theory. The assumption, widely shared, is that a person may be simply too busy doing conventional things to find time to engage in deviant behavior. The person involved in conventional activities is tied to appointments, deadlines, working hours, plans, and the like, so the opportunity to commit deviant acts rarely arises. To the extent that he is engrossed in conventional activities, he cannot even think about deviant acts, let alone act out his inclinations.[18]

This line of reasoning is responsible for the stress placed on recreational facilities in many programs to reduce delinquency, for much of the concern with the high school dropout, and for the idea that boys should be drafted into the Army to keep them out of trouble. So obvious and persuasive is the idea that involvement in conventional activities is a major deterrent to delinquency that it was accepted even by Sutherland: "In the general area of juvenile delinquency it is probable that the most significant difference between juveniles who engage in delinquency and those who do not is that the latter are provided abundant opportunities of a conventional type for satisfying their recreational interests, while the former lack those opportunities or facilities."[19]

The view that "idle hands are the devil's workshop" has received more sophisticated treatment in recent sociological writings on delinquency. David Matza and Gresham M. Sykes, for example, suggest that delinquents have the values of a leisure class, the same values ascribed by Veblen to *the* leisure class: a search for kicks, disdain of work, a desire for the big score, and acceptance of aggressive toughness as proof of masculinity.[20] Matza and Sykes explain delinquency by reference to this system of values, but they note that adolescents at all class levels are "to some extent" members of a leisure class, that they "move in a limbo between earlier parental domination and future integration with the social structure through the bonds of work and marriage."[21] In the end, then, the leisure of the adolescent produces a set of values, which, in turn, leads to delinquency.

Belief

Unlike the cultural deviance theory, the control theory assumes the existence of a common value system within the society or group whose norms are being violated. If the deviant is committed to a value system different from that of conventional society, there is, within the context of the theory, nothing to explain. The question is, "Why does a man violate the rules in which he believes?" It is not, "Why do men differ in their beliefs about what constitutes good and desirable conduct?" The person is assumed to have been socialized (perhaps imperfectly) into the group whose rules he is violating; deviance is not a question of one group imposing its rules on the members of another group. In other words, we not only assume the deviant has believed the rules, we assume he believes the rules even as he violates them.

How can a person believe it is wrong to steal at the same time he is stealing? In the strain theory, this is not a difficult problem. (In fact, as suggested in the previous chapter, the strain theory was devised specifically to deal with this question.) The motivation to deviance adduced by the strain theorist is so strong that we can well understand the deviant act even assuming the deviator believes strongly that it is wrong.[22] However, given the control theory's assumptions about motivation, if both the deviant and the nondeviant believe the deviant act is wrong, how do we account for the fact that one commits it and the other does not?

Control theories have taken two approaches to this problem. In one approach, beliefs are treated as mere words that mean little or nothing if the other forms of control are missing. "Semantic dementia," the dissociation between rational faculties and emotional control which is said to be characteristic of the psychopath, illustrates this way of handling the problem.[23] In short, beliefs, at least insofar as they are expressed in words, drop out of the picture; since they do not differentiate between deviants and nondeviants, they are in the same class as "language" or any other characteristic common to all members of the group. Since they represent no real obstacle to the commission of delinquent acts, nothing needs be said about how they are handled by those committing such acts. The control theories that do not mention beliefs (or values), and many do not, may be assumed to take this approach to the problem.

The second approach argues that the deviant rationalizes his behavior so that he can at once violate the rule and maintain his belief in it. Donald R. Cressey has advanced this argument with respect to embezzlement,[24] and Sykes and Matza have advanced it with respect to delinquency.[25] In both Cressey's and Sykes and Matza's treatments, these rationalizations (Cressey calls them "verbalizations," Sykes and Matza term them "techniques of neutralization") occur prior to the commission of the deviant act. If the neutralization is successful, the person is free to commit the act(s) in question. Both in Cressey and in Sykes and Matza, the strain that prompts the effort at neutralization also provides the motive force that results in the subsequent deviant act. Their theories are thus, in this sense, strain theories. Neutralization is difficult to handle within the context of a theory that adheres closely to control theory assumptions, because in the control theory there is no special motivational force to account for the neutralization. This difficulty is especially noticeable in Matza's later treatment of this topic, where the motivational component, the "will to delinquency" appears *after* the moral vacuum has been created by the techniques of neutralization.[26] The question thus becomes: Why neutralize?

In attempting to solve a strain theory problem with control theory tools, the control theorist is thus led into a trap. He cannot answer the crucial question. The concept of neutralization assumes the existence of moral obstacles to the commission of deviant acts. In order plausibly to account for a deviant act, it is necessary to generate motivation to deviance that is at least equivalent in force to the resistance provided by these moral obstacles. However, if the moral obstacles are removed, neutralization and special motivation are no longer required. We therefore follow the implicit logic of control theory and remove these moral obstacles by hypothesis. Many persons do not have an attitude of respect toward the rules of society; many persons feel no moral obligation to conform regardless of personal advantage. Insofar as the values and beliefs of these persons are consistent with their feelings, and there should be a tendency toward consistency, neutralization is unnecessary; it has already occurred.

Does this merely push the question back a step and at the same time produce conflict with the assumption of a common value system? I think not. In the first place, we do not assume, as does Cressey, that neutralization occurs in order to make a specific criminal act possible.[27] We do not assume, as do Sykes and Matza, that neutralization occurs to make many delinquent acts possible. We do not assume, in other words, that the person constructs a system of rationalizations in order to justify commission of acts he wants to commit. We assume, in contrast, that the beliefs that free a man to commit deviant acts are unmotivated in the sense that he does not construct or adopt them in order to facilitate the attainment of illicit ends. In the second place, we do not assume, as does Matza, that "delinquents concur in the conventional assessment of delinquency."[28] We assume, in contrast, that there is variation in the extent to which people believe they should obey the rules of society, and, furthermore, that the less a person believes he should obey the rules, the more likely he is to violate them.[29]

In chronological order, then, a person's beliefs in the moral validity of norms are, for no teleological reason, weakened. The probability that he will commit delinquent acts is therefore increased. When and if he commits a delinquent act, we may justifiably use the weakness of his beliefs in explaining it, but no special motivation is required to explain either the weakness of his beliefs or, perhaps, his delinquent act.

The keystone of this argument is of course the assumption that there is variation in belief in the moral validity of social rules. This assumption is amenable to direct empirical test and can thus survive at least until its first confrontation with data. For the present, we must return to the idea of a common value system with which this section was begun.

The idea of a common (or, perhaps better, a single) value system is consistent with the fact, or presumption, of variation in the strength of moral beliefs. We have not suggested that delinquency is based on beliefs counter to conventional morality; we have not suggested that delinquents do not believe delinquent acts are wrong. They may well believe these acts are wrong, but the meaning and efficacy of such beliefs are contingent upon other beliefs and, indeed, on the strength of other ties to the conventional order.[30]

Relations Among the Elements

In general, the more closely a person is tied to conventional society in any of these ways, the more closely he is likely to be tied in the other ways. The person who is attached to conventional people is, for example, more likely to be involved in conventional activities and to accept conventional notions of desirable conduct. Of the six possible combinations of elements, three seem particularly important and will therefore be discussed in some detail.

Attachment and Commitment

It is frequently suggested that attachment and commitment (as the terms are used here) tend to vary inversely. Thus, according to delinquency research, one of the lower-class adolescent's "problems" is that he is unable to sever ties to parents and peers, ties that prevent him from devoting sufficient time and energy to educational and occupational aspirations. His attachments are thus seen as getting in the way of conventional commitments.[31] According to stratification research, the lower-class boy who breaks free from these attachments is more likely to be upwardly mobile.[32] Both research traditions thus suggest that those bound to conformity for instrumental reasons are less likely to be bound to conformity by emotional ties to conventional others. If the unattached compensate for lack of attachment by commitment to achievement, and if the uncommitted make up for their lack of commitment by becoming more attached to persons, we could conclude that neither attachment nor commitment will be related to delinquency.

Actually, despite the evidence apparently to the contrary, I think it safe to assume that attachment to conventional others and commitment to achievement tend to vary together. The common finding that middle-class boys are likely to choose instrumental values over those of family and friendship while the reverse is true of lower-class boys cannot, I think, be properly interpreted as meaning that middle-class boys are less attached than lower-class boys to their parents and peers. The zero-sum methodological model that produces such findings is highly likely to be misleading.[33] Also, although many of the characteristics of the upwardly mobile alluded to by Seymour M. Lipset and Reinhard Bendix could be accounted for as consequences rather than causes of mobility, a methodological critique of these studies is not necessary to conclude that we may expect to find a positive relation between attachment and commitment in the data to be presented here. The present study and the one study Lipset and Bendix cite as disagreeing with their general conclusion that the upwardly mobile come from homes in which interpersonal relations were unsatisfactory are both based on high school samples.[34] As Lipset and Bendix note, such studies necessarily focus on aspirations rather than actual mobility. For the present, it seems, we must choose between studies based on hopes for the occupational future and those based on construction or reconstruction of the familial past. Interestingly enough, the former are at least as likely to be valid as the latter.

Commitment and Involvement

Delinquent acts are events. They occur at specific points in space and time. For a delinquent act to occur, it is necessary, as is true of all events, for a series of causal chains to converge at a given moment in time. Events are difficult to predict, and specification of some of the conditions necessary for them to occur often leaves a large residue of indeterminacy. For example, to say that a boy is free of bonds to conventional society is not to say that he will necessarily commit delinquent acts; he may and he may not. All we can say with certainty is that he is *more likely* to commit delinquent acts than the boy strongly tied to conventional society. It is tempting to make a virtue of this defect and espouse "probabilistic theory," since it, and it alone, is consistent with "the facts."[35] Nevertheless, this temptation should be resisted. The primary virtue of control theory is not that it relies on conditions that make delinquency possible while other theories rely on conditions that make delinquency necessary. On the contrary, with respect to their logical framework, these theories are superior to control theory, and, if they were as adequate empirically as control theory, we should not hesitate to advocate their adoption in preference to control theory.

But they are not as adequate, and we must therefore seek to reduce the indeterminacy within control theory. One area of possible development is with respect to the link between elements of the bond affecting the probability that one will yield to temptation and those affecting the probability that one will be exposed to temptation.

The most obvious link in this connection is between educational and occupational aspirations (commitment) and involvement in conventional activities. We can attempt to show how commitment limits one's opportunities to commit delinquent acts and thus get away from the assumption implicit in many control theories that such opportunities are simply randomly distributed through the population in question.

Attachment and Belief

That there is a more or less straightforward connection between attachment to others and belief in the moral validity of rules appears evident. The link we accept here and which we shall attempt to document is described by Jean Piaget:

> It is not the obligatory character of the rule laid down by an individual that makes us respect this individual, it is the respect we feel for the individual that makes us regard as obligatory the rule he lays down. The appearance of the sense of duty in a child thus admits of the simplest explanation, namely that he receives commands from older children (in play) and from adults (in life), and that he respects older children and parents.[36]

In short, "respect is the source of law."[37] Insofar as the child respects (loves and fears) his parents, and adults in general, he will accept their rules. Conversely, insofar as this respect is undermined, the rules will tend to lose their obligatory character. It is assumed that belief in the obligatory character of rules will to some extent maintain its efficacy in producing conformity even if the respect which brought it into being no longer exists. It is also assumed that attachment may produce conformity even in the face of beliefs favorable to nonconformity. In short, these two sources of moral behavior, although highly and complexly related, are assumed to have an independent effect that justifies their separation.

The Bond to What?

Control theorists sometimes suggest that attachment to any object outside one's self, whether it be the home town, the starry heavens, or the family dog, promotes moral behavior.[38] Although it seems obvious that some objects are more important than others and that the important objects must be identified if the elements of the bond are to produce the consequences suggested by the theory, *a priori* rankings of the objects of attachment have proved peculiarly unsatisfactory. Durkheim, for example, concludes that the three groups to whom attachment is most important in producing morality are the family, the nation, and humanity. He further concludes that, of these, the nation is most important.[39] All of which, given much contemporary thinking on the virtues of patriotism,[40] illustrates rather well the difficulty posed by such questions as: Which is more important in the control of delinquency, the father or the mother, the family or the school?

Although delinquency theory in general has taken a stand on many questions about the relative importance of institutions (for example, that the school is more important than the family), control theory has remained decidedly eclectic, partly because each element of the bond directs attention to different institutions. For these reasons, I shall treat specification of the units of attachment as a problem in the empirical interpretation of control theory, and not attempt at this point to say which should be more or less important.

Where Is the Motivation?

The most disconcerting question the control theorist faces goes something like this: "Yes, but *why* do they do it?" In the good old days, the control theorist could simply strip away the "veneer of civilization" and expose man's "animal impulses" for all to see. These impulses appeared to him (and apparently to his audience) to provide a plausible account of the motivation to crime and delinquency. His argument was not that delinquents and criminals alone are animals, but that we are all animals, and thus all naturally capable of committing criminal acts. It took no great study to reveal that children, chickens, and dogs occasionally assault and steal from their fellow creatures; that children, chickens, and dogs also behave for relatively long periods in a perfectly moral manner. Of course the acts of chickens and dogs are not "assault" or "theft," and such behavior is not "moral"; it is simply the behavior of a chicken or a dog. The chicken stealing corn from his neighbor knows nothing of the moral law; he does not *want* to violate rules; he wants merely to eat corn. The dog maliciously destroying a pillow or feloniously assaulting another dog is the moral equal of the chicken. No motivation to deviance is required to explain his acts. So, too, no special motivation to crime within the human animal was required to explain his criminal acts.

Times changed. It was no longer fashionable (within sociology, at least) to refer to animal impulses. The control theorist needed more and more to deemphasize the motivational component of his theory. He might refer in the beginning to "universal human needs," or some such, but the driving force behind crime and delinquency was rarely alluded to. At the same time, his explanations of crime and delinquency increasingly left the reader uneasy. What, the reader asked, is the control theorist assuming? Albert K. Cohen and James F. Short answer the question this way:

> . . . it is important to point out one important limitation of both types of theory. They [culture conflict and social disorganization theories] are both *control* theories in the sense that they explain delinquency in terms of the *absence* of effective controls. They appear, therefore, to imply a model of motivation that assumes that the impulse to delinquency is an inherent characteristic of young people and does not itself need to be explained; it is something that erupts when the lid—i.e., internalized cultural restraints or external authority—is off.[41]

There are several possible and I think reasonable reactions to this criticism. One reaction is simply to acknowledge the assumption, to grant that one is assuming what control theorists have always assumed about the motivation to crime—that it is constant across persons (at least within the system in question): "There is no reason to assume that only those who finally commit a deviant act usually have the impulse to do so. It is much more likely that most people experience deviant impulses frequently. At least in fantasy, people are much more deviant than they appear."[42] There is certainly nothing wrong with *making* such an assumption. We are free to assume anything we wish to assume; the truth of our theory is presumably subject to empirical test.[43]

A second reaction, involving perhaps something of a quibble, is to defend the logic of control theory and to deny the alleged assumption. We can say the fact that control theory suggests the absence of something causes delinquency is not a proper criticism, since negative relations have as much claim to scientific acceptability as do positive relations.[44] We can also say that the present theory does not impute an inherent impulse to delinquency to anyone.[45] That, on the contrary, it denies the necessity of such an imputation: "The desires, and other passions of man, are in themselves no sin. No more are the actions, that proceed from those passions, till they know a law that forbids them."[46]

A third reaction is to accept the criticism as valid, to grant that a complete explanation of delinquency would provide the necessary impetus, and proceed to construct an explanation of motivation consistent with control theory. Briar and Piliavin provide situational motivation: "We assume these acts are prompted by short-term situationally induced desires experienced by all boys to obtain valued goods, to portray courage in the presence of, or be loyal to peers, to strike out at someone who is disliked, or simply to 'get kicks.'"[47] Matza, too, agrees that delinquency cannot be explained simply by removal of controls:

> Delinquency is only epiphenomenally action. . . . [It] is essentially infraction. It is rule-breaking behavior performed by juveniles aware that they are violating the law and of the nature of their deed, and made permissible by the neutralization of infractious [!] elements. Thus, Cohen and Short are fundamentally right when they insist that social control theory is incomplete unless it provides an impetus by which the potential for delinquency may be realized.[48]

The impetus Matza provides is a "feeling of desperation," brought on by the "mood of fatalism," "the experience of seeing one's self as effect" rather than cause. In a situation in which manliness is stressed, being pushed around leads to the mood of fatalism which in turn produces a sense of desperation. In order to relieve his desperation, in order to cast off the mood of fatalism, the boy "makes things happen"—he commits delinquent acts.[49]

There are several additional accounts of "why they do it" that are to my mind persuasive and at the same time generally compatible with control theory.[50] But while all of these accounts may be compatible with control theory, they are by no means deducible from it. Furthermore, they rarely impute built-in, unusual motivation to the delinquent: he is attempting to satisfy the same desires, he is reacting to the same pressures as other boys (as is clear, for example, in the previous quotation from Briar and Piliavin). In other words, if included, these accounts of motivation would serve the same function in the theory that "animal impulses" traditionally served: they might add to its persuasiveness and plausibility, but they would add little else, since they do not differentiate delinquents from nondelinquents. In the end, then, control theory remains what it has always been: a theory in which deviation is not problematic. The question "Why do they do it?" is simply not the question the theory is designed to answer. The question is, "Why don't we do it?" There is much evidence that we would if we dared.

ENDNOTES

1   Emile Durkheim, *Suicide*, trans. John A. Spaulding and George Simpson (New York: The Free Press, 1951), p. 209.

2   Books have been written on the increasing importance of interpersonal sensitivity in modern life. According to this view, controls from within have become less important than controls

from without in producing conformity. Whether or not this observation is true as a description of historical trends, it is true that interpersonal sensitivity has become more important in explaining conformity. Although logically it should also have become more important in explaining nonconformity, the opposite has been the case, once again showing that Cohen's observation that "an explanation of conformity should be an explanation of deviance" cannot be translated as "an explanation of conformity has to be an explanation of deviance." For the view that interpersonal sensitivity currently plays a greater role than formerly in producing conformity, see William J. Goode, "Norm Commitment and Conformity to Role-Status Obligations," *American Journal of Sociology,* LXVI (1960), 246-258. And of course, also see David Riesman, Nathan Glazer, and Reuel Denney, *The Lonely Crowd* (Garden City, New York: Doubleday, 1950), especially Part 1.

3   The literature on psychopathy is voluminous. See William McCord and Joan McCord, *The Psychopath* (Princeton: D. Van Nostrand, 1964).

4   John M. Martin and Joseph P. Fitzpatrick, *Delinquent Behavior* (New York: Random House, 1964), p. 130.

5   *Ibid.* For additional properties of the psychopath, see McCord and McCord, *The Psychopath,* pp. 1-22.

6   Barbara Wootton, *Social Science and Social Pathology* (New York: Macmillan, 1959), p. 250.

7   "The logical untenability [of the position that there are forces in man 'resistant to socialization'] was ably demonstrated by Parsons over 30 years ago, and it is widely recognized that the position is empirically unsound because it assumes [!] some universal biological drive system distinctly separate from socialization and social context—a basic and intransigent human nature" (Judith Blake and Kingsley Davis, "Norms, Values, and Sanctions," *Handbook of Modern Sociology,* ed. Robert E.L. Faris [Chicago: Rand McNally, 1964], p. 471).

8   Emile Durkheim, *Moral Education,* trans. Everett K. Wilson and Herman Schnurer (New York: The Free Press, 1961), p. 64.

9   Although attachment alone does not exhaust the meaning of internalization, attachments and beliefs combined would appear to leave only a small residue of "internal control" not susceptible in principle to direct measurement.

10   F. Ivan Nye, *Family Relationships and Delinquent Behavior* (New York: Wiley, 1958), pp. 5-7.

11   Albert J. Reiss, Jr., "Delinquency as the Failure of Personal and Social Controls," *American Sociological Review,* XVI (1951), 96-207. For example, "Our observations show . . . that delinquent recidivists are less often persons with mature ego ideals or nondelinquent social roles" (p. 204).

12   Scott Briar and Irving Piliavin, "Delinquency, Situational Inducements and Commitment to Conformity," *Social Problems,* XIII (1965), 41-42. The concept "stake in conformity" was introduced by Jackson Toby in his "Social Disorganization and Stake in Conformity: Complementary Factors in the Predatory Behavior of Hoodlums," *Journal of Criminal Law, Criminology and Police Science,* XLVIII (1957), 12-17. See also his "Hoodlum or Business Man: An American Dilemma," *The Jews,* ed. Marshall Sklare (New York: The Free Press, 1958), pp. 542-550. Throughout the text, I occasionally use "stake in conformity" in speaking in general of the strength of the bond to conventional society. So used, the concept is somewhat broader than is true for either Toby or Briar and Piliavin, where the concept is roughly equivalent to what is here called "commitment."

13   Thomas Hobbes, *Leviathan* (Oxford: Basil Blackwell, 1957), p. 195.

14   Howard S. Becker, "Notes on the Concept of Commitment," *American Journal of Sociology,* LXVI (1960), 35-36.

15   Arthur L. Stinchcombe, *Rebellion in a High School* (Chicago: Quadrangle, 1964), p. 5.

16   Richard A. Cloward and Lloyd E. Ohlin, *Delinquency and Opportunity* (New York: The Free Press, 1960), p. 147, quoting Edwin H. Sutherland, ed., *The Professional Thief* (Chicago: University of Chicago Press, 1937), pp. 211-213.

17 William James, *Psychology* (Cleveland: World Publishing Co., 1948), p. 186.

18 Few activities appear to be so engrossing that they rule out contemplation of alternative lines of behavior, at least if estimates of the amount of time men spend plotting sexual deviations have any validity.

19 *The Sutherland Papers,* ed. Albert K. Cohen et al. (Bloomington: Indiana University Press, 1956), p. 37.

20 David Matza and Gresham M. Sykes, "Juvenile Delinquency and Subterranean Values," *American Sociological Review,* XXVI (1961), 712-719.

21 *Ibid.,* p. 718.

22 The starving man stealing the loaf of bread is the image evoked by most strain theories. In this image, the starving man's belief in the wrongness of this act is clearly not something that must be explained away. It can be assumed to be present without causing embarrassment to the explanation.

23 McCord and McCord, *The Psychopath,* pp. 12-15.

24 Donald R. Cressey, *Other People's Money* (New York: The Free Press, 1953).

25 Gresham M. Sykes and David Matza, "Techniques of Neutralization: A Theory of Delinquency," *American Sociological Review,* XXII (1957), 664-670.

26 David Matza, *Delinquency and Drift* (New York: Wiley, 1964), pp. 181-191.

27 In asserting that Cressey's assumption is invalid with respect to delinquency, I do not wish to suggest that it is invalid for the question of embezzlement, where the problem faced by the deviator is fairly specific and he can reasonably be assumed to be an upstanding citizen. (Although even here the fact that the embezzler's nonshareable financial problem often results from some sort of hanky-panky suggests that "verbalizations" may be less necessary than might otherwise be assumed.)

28 *Delinquency and Drift,* p. 43.

29 This assumption is not, I think, contradicted by the evidence presented by Matza against the existence of a delinquent subculture. In comparing the attitudes and actions of delinquents with the picture painted by delinquent subculture theorists, Matza emphasizes—and perhaps exaggerates—the extent to which delinquents are tied to the conventional order. In implicitly comparing delinquents with a supermoral man, I emphasize—and perhaps exaggerate—the extent to which they are not tied to the conventional order.

30 The position taken here is therefore somewhere between the "semantic dementia" and the "neutralization" positions. Assuming variation, the delinquent is, at the extremes, freer than the neutralization argument assumes. Although the possibility of wide discrepancy between what the delinquent professes and what he practices still exists, it is presumably much rarer than is suggested by studies of articulate "psychopaths."

31 The idea that the middle-class boy is less closely tied than the lower-class boy to his peers has been widely adopted in the literature on delinquency. The middle-class boy's "cold and rational" relations with his peers are in sharp contrast with the "spontaneous and warm" relations of the lower-class boy. See, for example, Albert K. Cohen, *Delinquent Boys* (New York: The Free Press, 1955), pp. 102-109.

32 The evidence in favor of this proposition is summarized in Seymour M. Lipset and Reinhard Bendix, *Social Mobility in Industrial Society* (Berkeley: University of California Press, 1959), especially pp. 249-259. For example: "These [business leaders] show strong traits of independence, they are characterized by an inability to form intimate relations and are consequently often socially isolated men" (p. 251).

33 Relations between measures of attachment and commitment are examined in Chapter VIII.

34 *Social Mobility,* p. 253.

35   Briar and Piliavin, "Situational Involvements," p. 45.

36   Jean Piaget, *The Moral Judgment of the Child,* trans. Marjorie Gabain (New York: The Free Press, n.d.), p. 101.

37   *Ibid.,* p. 379.

38   Durkheim, *Moral Education,* p. 83.

39   *Ibid.,* pp. 73-79.

40   In the end, Durkheim distinguishes between a patriotism that leads to concern for domestic problems and one that emphasizes foreign relations (especially that variety which puts "national sentiment in conflict with commitments of mankind").

41   See their "Juvenile Delinquency," in *Contemporary Social Problems,* ed. Robert K. Merton and Robert A. Nisbet (New York: Harcourt, Brace and World, 1961), p. 106.

42   Howard S. Becker, *Outsiders* (New York: The Free Press, 1963), p. 26. See also Kate Friedlander, *The Psycho-Analytic Approach to Juvenile Delinquency* (New York: International Universities Press, 1947), p.7.

43   Cf. Albert K. Cohen, *Deviance and Control* (Englewood Cliffs, N.J.: Prentice-Hall, 1966), pp. 59-62.

44   I have frequently heard the statement "it's an absence of something explanation" used as an apparently damning criticism of a sociological theory. While the origins of this view are unknown to me, the fact that such a statement appears to have some claim to plausibility suggests one of the sources of uneasiness in the face of a control theory.

45   The popular "it's-an-id-argument" dismissal of explanations of deviant behavior assumes that the founding fathers of sociology somehow proved that the blood of man is neither warm nor red, but spiritual. The intellectual trap springs shut on the counterassumption that innate aggressive-destructive impulses course through the veins, as it should. The solution is not to accept both views, but to accept neither.

46   Thomas Hobbes, *Leviathan,* p. 83. Given the history of the sociological response to Hobbes, it is instructive to compare Hobbes' picture of the motivation behind the deviant act with that painted by Talcott Parsons. According to Parsons, the motive to deviate is a psychological trait or need that *the deviant* carries with him at all times. This need is itself deviant: it *cannot be satisfied by conformity.* Social controls enter merely as reality factors that determine the form and manner in which this need will be satisfied. If one path to deviant behavior is blocked, the deviant will continue searching until he finds a path that is open. Perhaps because this need arises from interpersonal conflict, and is thus socially derived, the image it presents of the deviant as fundamentally immoral, as doing evil because it is evil, has been largely ignored by those objecting to the control theorist's tendency to fall back on natural propensities as a source of the energy that results in the activities society defines as wrong. See Talcott Parsons, *The Social System* (New York: The Free Press, 1951), Chapter 7.

47   Briar and Piliavin, "Situational Inducements," p. 36.

48   *Delinquency and Drift,* p. 182.

49   Matza warns us that we cannot take the fatalistic mood out of context and hope to find important differences between delinquents and other boys: "That the subcultural delinquent is not significantly different from other boys is precisely the point" (*Ibid.,* p. 89).

50   For example: Carl Werthman, "The Function of Social Definitions in the Development of Delinquent Careers," *Juvenile Delinquency and Youth Crime,* Report of the President's Commission on Law Enforcement and Administration of Justice (Washington: USGP0, 1967), pp. 155-170; Jackson Toby, "Affluence and Adolescent Crime," *Ibid.,* pp. 132-144; James F. Short, Jr., and Fred L. Strodtbeck, *Group Process and Gang Delinquency* (Chicago: University of Chicago Press, 1965), pp. 248-264.

Essay/Discussion Questions for Section VI

Note to the student: If you are able to provide thorough responses to all of the following questions, you have mastered excellent comprehension of the classic readings presented in this section.

1. What makes social control theories different from other types of theories? (From the section introduction.)

2. Looking at the three selections in this section, what do you think are the common elements? (From the section introduction.)

3. Sykes and Matza talk about "techniques of neutralization" in discussing delinquents. What are "neutralizations"? (From the Sykes & Matza reading.)

4. Are neutralizations available to delinquents only, or are they more conventionally available? (From the Sykes & Matza reading.)

5. Compare Reckless's inner and outer containment. Which do you think is most important in determining delinquency? (From the Reckless reading.)

6. Hirschi's social control theory is based on the bond to society. What is this "bond" and why is it needed? (From the Hirschi reading.)

7. Describe Hirschi's four elements of the bond. Is any one of them more important than the others? Can they be combined, and if so, what does that mean? (From the Hirschi reading.)

Section VII
CONTEMPORARY PERSPECTIVES

Introduction

There are several new varieties of criminological theory. Perhaps two of the most important new directions are rationalist theories and feminist (or gender) theories. This section includes two readings, each of which represents a pioneering work in their perspective.

Routine Activities

We read it in the newspapers every day. A woman mugged at an automated teller machine (ATM) at 11 p.m., a young man assaulted outside a bar at closing, a fight erupting between gang members in a park late at night. These events do not surprise us because they fit into notions we have about where and when crime is most likely to occur and to whom it may happen. These notions also underlie the theory of routine activities, the perspective presented in a 1979 article by Lawrence Cohen and Marcus Felson.

Routine activities theorists like Cohen and Felson build on early works of ecological criminology (Guerry & Quetelet in the early 1800s; the Chicago School in the early part of the twentieth century). Thus, there is an emphasis on official crime rates and police and victimization reports. A second major influence on this theory is the theme of social disorganization as found in the work of Shaw and McKay. Their emphasis was on the features of neighborhoods, rather than on the different groups of people who came and went from them over the years. In this context, crime was believed to be tied to the characteristics of the environment and events in time and space. Varying rates of crime are seen as a function of changes in the *number of potential victims and targets*, the *number of possible offenders,* and *the absence of guardians* to protect against the occurrence of crime.

The attraction of routine activities theory is its potential to predict increases or decreases in crime. Any event that changes the number of victims/targets, offenders, or guardians constitutes an influence on the crime rate. Police strikes, women returning to work, rises in unemployment, and families away on vacation all produce opportunities for crime to occur.

The rational part of the theory involves the potential calculation, on the part of the offender, of the chance of successfully committing crime in a particular area. If guardians can be increased, or targets decreased, potential offenders should decide that risks are not worth the effort (or seek criminal opportunities elsewhere). While the exact nature of criminal rationality is not yet known, there is growing evidence that most offenders do calculate their potential risks and profits.

Other theories have been developed along the lines of routine activities theory. At virtually the same time Cohen and Felson were developing their theory, another group of criminologists (Hindelang, Gottfredson & Garofalo, 1978) were creating a similar approach that they called "lifestyle" theory. In this case, lifestyles were tantamount to routine activities. Other theories, trading on the rationalist component, become quite popular during the 1980s, especially among those in government circles. One of those was proposed by Derek Cornish and Ronald Clarke (1986), who used rational concepts to describe the decision to commit a crime as a product of expected effort, anticipated rewards, and assumed costs. If effort and costs are high while rewards are relatively low, there would be no crime. Deterrence theories also made a comeback during the period. Most contemporary theorists perceive a rational component to behavior, albeit a small one, which is sometimes termed "soft determinism." Finally, the main message of routine activities theory—that one's lifestyle and common activities results in differential chances of victimization—is taken as a truism today.

Gender and Criminological Theories

Over the years, it has become obvious that most major criminological theories have been focused on males. This has been supported with the contention that, because males commit 80 percent of the reported crime, the theories *ought* to focus on males as the most efficient approach to explaining *most* crime. Feminists, and others, have challenged this position. It makes sense, they say, to consider gender issues as one of the most important factors in criminological explanations, *simply because so little crime is committed by females*. In short, gender is the best predictor of crime and delinquency. We need to establish why, and leaving females out of criminological theory is tantamount to ignoring the most critical variable.

Dorie Klein published a classic article in 1973 on the failure of criminological theory to adequately consider female criminality. That article is included here as an example of the beginnings of critical, feminist analyses. Klein examined and took to task almost every attempt to characterize female criminality. Universally, it seemed that theorists had considered females to be relatively simple creatures and had made little attempt to deal with female criminality on any level other than a superficial one. Ironically, even after Klein's article, some theorists who were using the women's liberation as a reason for presuming an increase in female criminal activity were saying that women commit more crime when they become more like men.

Today's versions of gender-based theory have improved substantially since Klein wrote her article. The theories are now sophisticated, complex, and deeply tied to differential socialization arguments. Feminist theorists have now developed a typology of specialized perspectives (liberal, radical, Marxist, and socialist feminism) that have been applied to crime. In addition, the overlapping effects of class, race, and gender are becoming a staple of feminist analysis. Whether mainstream criminology makes use of these contributions remains to be seen, but clearly we now have a much greater appreciation of the complexity of the issues involved in crime and delinquency than we did 20 years ago.

BIBLIOGRAPHY

Adler, Freda (1981). *The Incidence of Female Criminality in the Contemporary World*. New York: New York University Press.

Adler, Freda (1975). *Sisters in Crime*. New York: McGraw-Hill.

Black, Donald (1983). "Crime as social control," *American Sociological Review* 48: 34-45.

Braithwaite, John (1989). *Crime, Shame, and Reintegration*. Cambridge: Cambridge University Press.

Bursik, Robert J., Jr. (1988). "Social disorganization and theories of crime and delinquency," *Criminology* 26: 519-45.

Cornish, Derek B. and Ronald V. Clarke (1986). *The Reasoning Criminal*. New York: Springer Verlag.

Cullen, Francis T. (1984). *Rethinking Crime and Deviance Theory: The Emergence of a Structuring Tradition*. Totowa, NJ: Rowman and Allanheld.

Daly, Kathleen and Meda Chesney-Lind (1988). "Feminism and criminology." *Justice Quarterly* 5: 497-538.

Danner, Mona (1989). "Socialist feminism: A brief introduction," *Critical Criminologist* 1: 1-2.

Elliott, Delbert, David Huizinga and Suzanne Ageton (1985). *Explaining Delinquency and Drug Use*. Beverly Hills: Sage.

Eysenck, Hans J. and I. Gudjonnson (1989). *The Causes and Cures of Criminality*. New York: Plenum Press.

Gottfredson, Michael and Travis Hirschi (1989). "A propensity-event theory of crime," in William S. Laufer and Freda Adler (eds.) *Advances in Criminological Theory*, Vol. 1. New Brunswick, NJ: Transaction, 57-67.

Hagan, John (1989a). *Structural Criminology*. New Brunswick, NJ: Rutgers University Press.

Hagan, John (1989b). "Micro- and macro-structures of delinquency causation and a power-control theory of gender and delinquency," in Steven F. Messner, Marvin D. Krohn, and Alan A. Liska (eds.) *Theoretical Integration in the Study of Deviance and Crime: Problems and Prospects*. Albany: State University of New York Press, 213-27.

Hagan, John, A.R. Gillis, and John Simpson (1985). "The class structure of gender and delinquency: Toward a power-control theory of common delinquent behavior," *American Journal of Sociology* 90: 1151-78.

Hindelang, Michael J., Michael Gottfredson, and James Garofalo (1978). *Victims of Personal Crime: An Empirical Foundation for a Theory of Personal Victimization*. Cambridge, MA: Ballinger.

Jeffery, Clarence R. (1989). "An interdisciplinary theory of criminal behavior," in William S. Laufer and Freda Adler (eds.) *Advances in Criminological Theory*, Vol. 1. New Brunswick, NJ: Transaction, 69-87.

Katz, Jack (1988). *Seductions of Crime: Moral and Sensual Attractions in Doing Evil*. New York: Basic Books.

Luckenbill, David and B. Doyle (1989). "Structural position and violence: Developing a cultural explanation," *Criminology* 27(3): 419-33.

Messerschmidt, James (1997). *Crime as Structured Action: Gender, Race, Class, and Crime in the Making*. Thousand Oaks, CA: Sage.

Messerschmidt, James (1986). *Capitalism, Patriarchy and Crime: Toward a Socialist Feminist Criminology*. Totowa, NJ: Rowman & Littlefield Publishers, Inc.

Minor, William (1977). "A deterrence-control theory of crime," in *Theory in Criminology: Contemporary Views*. Beverly Hills: Sage.

Nagin, Daniel S. and Raymond Paternoster (1991). "Preventive effects of the perceived risk of arrest: Testing an expanded conception of deterrence," *Criminology* 29: 561-85.

Paternoster, Raymond (1989). "Decisions to participate in and desist from four types of common delinquency: Deterrence and the rational choice perspective," *Law and Society Review* 23: 7-40.

Paternoster, Raymond and L. Iovanni (1989). "The labeling perspective and delinquency: An elaboration of the theory and assessment of the evidence," *Justice Quarterly*, 6(3): 359-94.

Pepinsky, Harold E. and Paul Jesilow (1985). *Myths That Cause Crime*, 2nd ed., annotated. Cabin John, MD: Seven Locks Press.

Radosh, Polly F. (1990). "Women and crime in the United States: A Marxian explanation," *Sociological Spectrum*, 10: 105-31.

Rafter, Nicole H. and Elena M. Natalizia (1982). "Marxist feminism: Implications for criminal justice," in Barbara Price and Natalie Sokoloff (eds.) *The Criminal Justice System and Women*. New York: Clark Boardman, 465-84.

Richie-Mann, Coramae (1984). *Female Crime and Delinquency*. University: University of Alabama Press.

Schwendinger, Herman and Julia S. Schwendinger (1985). *Adolescent Subcultures and Delinquency*. New York: Praeger.

Simon, Rita J. (1975). *The Contemporary Woman and Crime*. Washington, DC: U.S. Government Printing Office.

Simpson, Sally (1989). "Feminist theory, crime and justice," *Criminology* 27(4): 605-25.

Smart, Carol (1979). "The new female criminality: Reality or myth?" *British Journal of Criminology* 19: 50-59.

Smart, Carol (1976). *Women, Crime and Criminology: A Feminist Critique*. London: Routledge & Kegan Paul.

Walters, Glenn D. and Thomas W. White (1989). "The thinking criminal: A cognitive model of lifestyle criminality," *Criminal Justice Research Bulletin* 4(4): 1-10.

Williams, Frank P., III and Marilyn D. McShane (1990). "Problems of crime and delinquency: Diversity of perspectives," in Joseph Gittler (ed.) *The Annual Review Conflict Knowledge and Conflict Resolution*, Vol. 2. New York: Garland.

Wilson, James Q. and Richard Herrnstein (1985). *Crime and Human Nature*. New York: Simon and Schuster.

Criminologist Profiles

Lawrence Edward Cohen (1945-   )

Cohen was born in Los Angeles, California. He was educated at the University of California, Berkeley (B.A., 1969), California State University (M.A., 1971), and the University of Washington (Ph.D. in sociology, 1974). In addition, he did post-doctorate study at the State University of New York at Albany from 1973-1974. Cohen worked as a research associate at the SUNY, Albany School of Criminal Justice from 1973-1976. He taught at the University of Illinois (sociology, 1976-1980), the University of Texas at Austin (sociology, 1980-1985), Indiana University (sociology, 1985-1988), and is presently in the sociology department at the University of California, Davis.

Marcus K. Felson (1949-   )

Marcus K. Felson was born in Cincinnati, Ohio. He received a B.A. (1969) in sociology from the University of Chicago and an M.A. (1971) and Ph.D. (1973) in sociology from the University of Michigan. He has taught in the sociology department of the University of Illinois (1972-1984), the sociology department of the University of Southern California (1984-1994), and since 1994 has been a professor in the criminal justice department of Rutgers University.

A Routine Activity Approach*
Lawrence E. Cohen and Marcus Felson**

INTRODUCTION

In its summary report the National Commission on the Causes and Prevention of Violence (1969: xxxvii) presents an important sociological paradox:

> Why, we must ask, have urban violent crime rates increased substantially during the past decade when the conditions that are supposed to cause violent crime have not worsened—have, indeed, generally improved?

> The Bureau of the Census, in its latest report on trends in social and economic conditions in metropolitan areas, states that most "indicators of wellbeing point toward progress in the cities since 1960." Thus, for example, the proportion of blacks in cities who completed high school rose from 43 percent in 1960 to 61 percent in 1968; unemployment rates dropped significantly between 1959 and 1967 and the median family income of blacks in cities increased from 61 percent to 68 percent of the median white family income during the same period. Also during the same period the number of persons living below the legally defined poverty level in cities declined from 11.3 million to 8.3 million.

*Source: Lawrence E. Cohen and Marcus Felson, 1979. "Social Change and Crime Rate Trends: A Routine Activity Approach," *American Sociological Review* 44(August): 588-608. Excerpted from pp. 588-591, 604-605. By permission of the publisher.
**For their comments, we thank David J. Bordua, Ross M. Stolzenberg, Christopher S. Dunn, Kenneth C. Land, Robert Schoen, Amos Hawley, and an anonymous reviewer. Funding for this study was provided by these United States Government grants: National Institute for Mental Health 1-RO1MH31117-O1; National Science Foundation, SOC77-13261; and United States Army RI/DAHC 1976 G-0016. The authors' name order is purely alphabetical.

Despite the general continuation of these trends in social and economic conditions in the United States, the *Uniform Crime Report* (FBI, 1975:49) indicates that between 1960 and 1975 reported rates of robbery, aggravated assault, forcible rape and homicide increased by 263%, 164%, 174%, and 188%, respectively. Similar property crime rate increases reported during this same period[1] (e.g., 200% for burglary rate) suggest that the paradox noted by the Violence Commission applies to nonviolent offenses as well.

In the present paper we consider these paradoxical trends in crime rates in terms of changes in the "routine activities" of everyday life. We believe the structure of such activities influences criminal opportunity and therefore affects trends in a class of crimes we refer to as *direct-contact predatory violations*. Predatory violations are defined here as illegal acts in which "someone definitely and intentionally takes or damages the person or property of another" (Glaser, 1971:4). Further, this analysis is confined to those predatory violations involving direct physical contact between at least one offender and at least one person or object which that offender attempts to take or damage.

We argue that structural changes in routine activity patterns can influence crime rates by affecting the convergence in space and time of the three minimal elements of direct-contact predatory violations: (1) motivated offenders, (2) suitable targets, and (3) the absence of capable guardians against a violation. We further argue that the lack of any one of these elements is sufficient to prevent the successful completion of a direct-contact predatory crime, and that the convergence in time and space of suitable targets and the absence of capable guardians may even lead to large increases in crime rates without necessarily requiring any increase in the structural conditions that motivate individuals to engage in crime. That is, if the proportion of motivated offenders or even suitable targets were to remain stable in a community, changes in routine activities could nonetheless alter the likelihood of their convergence in space and time, thereby creating more opportunities for crimes to occur. Control therefore becomes critical. If controls through routine activities were to decrease, illegal predatory activities could then be likely to increase. In the process of developing this explanation and evaluating its consistency with existing data, we relate our approach to classical human ecological concepts and to several earlier studies.

The Structure of Criminal Activity

Sociological knowledge of how community structure generates illegal acts has made little progress since Shaw and McKay and their colleagues (1929) published their pathbreaking work, *Delinquency Areas*.

Variations in crime rates over space long have been recognized (e.g., see Guerry, 1833; Quetelet, 1842), and current evidence indicates that the pattern of these relationships within metropolitan communities has persisted (Reiss, 1976). Although most spatial research is quite useful for describing crime rate patterns and providing post hoc explanations, these works seldom consider—conceptually or empirically—the fundamental human ecological character of illegal acts as *events* which occur at specific locations in *space* and *time,* involving specific persons and/or objects. These and related concepts can help us to develop an extension of the human ecological analysis to the problem of explaining changes in crime rates over time. Unlike many criminological inquiries, we do not examine why individuals or groups are inclined criminally, but rather we take criminal inclination as given and examine the manner in which the spatio-temporal organization of social activities helps people to translate their criminal inclinations into action. Criminal violations are treated here as routine activities which share many attributes of, and are interdependent with, other routine activities. This interdependence between the structure of illegal activities and the organization of everyday sustenance activities leads us to consider certain concepts from human ecological literature.

Selected Concepts from Hawley's Human Ecological Theory

While criminologists traditionally have concentrated on the *spatial* analysis of crime rates within metropolitan communities, they seldom have considered the *temporal* interdependence of these acts. In his classic theory of human ecology, Amos Hawley (1950) treats the community not simply as a unit of territory but rather as an organization of symbiotic and commensalistic relationships as human activities are performed over both space and time.

Hawley identified three important temporal components of community structure: (1) *rhythm,* the regular periodicity with which events occur, as with the rhythm of travel activity; (2) *tempo,* the number of events per unit of time, such as the number of criminal violations per day on a given street; and (3) *timing,* the coordination among different activities which are more or less interdependent, such as the coordination of an offender's rhythms with those of a victim (Hawley, 1950:289; the examples are ours). These components of temporal organization, often neglected in criminological research, prove useful in analyzing how illegal tasks are performed—utility which becomes more apparent after noting the spatio-temporal requirements of illegal activities.

The Minimal Elements of Direct-Contact Predatory Violations

As we previously stated, despite their great diversity, direct-contact predatory violations share some important requirements which facilitate analysis of their structure. Each successfully completed violation minimally requires an *offender* with both criminal inclinations and the ability to carry out those inclinations, a person or object providing a *suitable target* for the offender, and *absence of guardians* capable of preventing violations. We emphasize that the lack of any one of these elements normally is sufficient to prevent such violations from occurring.[2] Though guardianship is implicit in everyday life, it usually is marked by the absence of violations; hence it is easy to overlook. While police action is analyzed widely, guardianship by ordinary citizens of one another and of property as they go about routine activities may be one of the most neglected elements in sociological research on crime especially since it links seemingly unrelated social roles and relationships to the occurrence or absence of illegal acts.

The conjunction of these minimal elements can be used to assess how social structure may affect the tempo of each type of violation. That is, the probability that a violation will occur at any specific time and place might be taken as a function of the convergence of likely offenders and suitable targets in the absence of capable guardians. Through consideration of how trends and fluctuations in social conditions affect the frequency of this convergence of criminogenic circumstances, an explanation of temporal trends in crime rates can be constructed.

The Ecological Nature of Illegal Acts

This ecological analysis of direct-contact predatory violations is intended to be more than metaphorical. In the context of such violations, people, gaining and losing sustenance, struggle among themselves for property, safety, territorial hegemony, sexual outlet, physical control, and sometimes for survival itself. The interdependence between offenders and victims can be viewed as a predatory relationship between functionally dissimilar individuals or groups. Since predatory violations fail to yield any net gain in sustenance for the larger community, they can only be sustained by feeding upon other activities. As offenders cooperate to increase their efficiency at predatory violations and as potential victims organize their resistance to these violations, both groups apply the symbiotic principle to improve their sustenance position. On the other hand, potential victims of predatory crime may take evasive actions which encourage offenders to pursue targets other than their own. Since illegal activities must feed upon other activities, the spatial and temporal structure of routine legal activities should play an important role in determining the location, type and quantity of illegal acts occurring in a given community or society. Moreover, one can analyze how the structure of community organization as well as the level of technology in a society provide the circumstances under which crime can thrive. For example, technology and organization affect the capacity of persons with criminal inclinations to overcome their targets, as well as affecting the ability of guardians to contend with potential offenders by using whatever protective tools, weapons and skills they have at their disposal. Many technological advances designed for legitimate purposes—including the automobile, small power tools, hunting weapons, highways, telephones, etc.—may enable offenders to carry out their own work more effectively or may assist people in protecting their own or someone else's person or property.

Not only do routine legitimate activities often provide the wherewithal to commit offenses or to guard against others who do so, but they also provide offenders with suitable targets. Target suitability is likely to reflect such things as value (i.e., the material or symbolic desirability of a personal or property target for offenders), physical visibility, access, and the inertia of a target against illegal treatment by offenders (including the weight, size, and attached or locked features of property inhibiting its illegal removal and the physical capacity of personal victims to resist attackers with or without weapons). Routine production activities probably affect the suitability of consumer goods for illegal removal by determining their value and weight. Daily activities may affect the location of property and personal targets in visible and accessible places at particular times. These activities also may cause people to have on hand objects that can be used as weapons for criminal acts or self-protection or to be preoccupied with tasks which reduce their capacity to discourage or resist offenders.

While little is known about conditions that affect the convergence of potential offenders, targets and guardians, this is a potentially rich source of propositions about crime rates. For example daily work activities separate many people from those they trust and the property they value. Routine activities also bring together at various times of day or night persons of different backgrounds, sometimes in the presence of facilities tools or weapons which influence the commission or avoidance of illegal acts. Hence, the timing of work, schooling and leisure may be of central importance for explaining crime rates.

The ideas presented so far are not new, but they frequently are over-looked in the theoretical literature on crime. Although an investigation of the literature uncovers significant examples of descriptive and practical data related to the routine activities upon which illegal behavior feeds, these data seldom are treated within an analytical framework. . . .

DISCUSSION

In our judgment many conventional theories of crime (the adequacy of which usually is evaluated by cross-sectional data, or no data at all) have difficulty accounting for the annual changes in crime rate trends in the post-World War II United States. These theories may prove useful in explaining crime trends during other periods, within specific communities, or in particular subgroups of the population. Longitudinal aggregate data for the United States, however, indicate that the trends for many of the presumed causal variables in these theoretical structures are in a direction opposite to those hypothesized to be the causes of crime. For example, during the decade 1960-1970, the percent of the population below the low-income level declined 44% and the unemployment rate declined 186%. Central city population as a share of the whole population declined slightly, while the percent of foreign stock declined 0.1%, etc. (see USBC, 1975: 654, 19, 39).

On the other hand, the convergence in time and space of three elements (motivated offenders, suitable targets, and the absence of capable guardians) appears useful for understanding crime rate trends. The lack of any of these elements is sufficient to prevent the occurrence of a successful direct-contact predatory crime. The convergence in time and space of suitable targets and the absence of capable guardians can lead to large increases in crime rates without any increase or change in the structural conditions that motivate individuals to engage in crime. Presumably, had the social indicators of the variables hypothesized to be the causes of crime in conventional theories changed in the direction of favoring increased crime in the post-World War II United States, the increases in crime rates likely would have been even more staggering than those which were observed. In any event, it is our belief that criminologists have underemphasized the importance of the convergence of suitable targets and the absence of capable guardians in explaining recent increases in the crime rate. Furthermore, the effects of the convergence in time and space of these elements may be multiplicative rather than additive. That is, their convergence by a fixed percentage may produce increases in crime rates far greater than that fixed percentage, demonstrating how some relatively modest social trends can contribute to some relatively large changes in crime rate trends. The fact that logged variables improved our equations (moving Durbin-Watson values closer to "ideal" levels) lends support to the argument that such an interaction occurs.

Those few investigations of crosssectional data which include household indicators produce results similar to ours. For example, Roncek (1975) and Choldin and Roncek (1976) report on block-level data for San Diego, Cleveland and Peoria and indicate that the proportion of a block's households which are primary individual households consistently offers the best or nearly the best predictor of a block's crime rate. This relationship persisted after they controlled for numerous social variables, including race, density, age and poverty. Thus the association between household structure and risk of criminal victimization has been observed in individual-level and block-level crosssectional data, as well as aggregate national time-series data.

Without denying the importance of factors motivating offenders to engage in crime, we have focused specific attention upon violations themselves and the prerequisites for their occurrence. However, the routine activity approach might in the future be applied to the analysis of offenders and their inclinations as well. For example, the structure of primary group activity may affect the likelihood that cultural transmission or social control of criminal inclinations will occur, while the structure of the community may affect the tempo of criminogenic peer group activity. We also may expect that circumstances favorable for carrying out violations contribute to criminal inclinations in the long run by rewarding these inclinations.

We further suggest that the routine activity framework may prove useful in explaining why the criminal justice system, the community and the family have appeared so ineffective in exerting social control since 1960. Substantial increases in the opportunity to carry out predatory violations may have undermined society's mechanisms for social control. For example, it may be difficult for institutions seeking to increase the certainty, celerity and severity of punishment to compete with structural changes resulting in vast increases in the certainty, celerity and value of rewards to be gained from illegal predatory acts.

It is ironic that the very factors which increase the opportunity to enjoy the benefits of life also may increase the opportunity for predatory violations. For example, automobiles provide freedom of movement to offenders as well as average citizens and offer vulnerable targets for theft. College enrollment, female labor force participation, urbanization, suburbanization, vacations and new electronic durables provide various opportunities to escape the confines of the household while they increase the risk of predatory victimization. Indeed, the opportunity for predatory crime appears to be enmeshed in the opportunity structure for legitimate activities to such an extent that it might be very difficult to root out substantial amounts of crime without modifying much of our way of life. Rather than assuming that predatory crime is simply an indicator of social breakdown, one might take it as a byproduct of freedom and prosperity as they manifest themselves in the routine activities of everyday life.

ENDNOTES

1   Though official data severely underestimate crime, they at least provide a rough indicator of trends over time in the volume of several major felonies. The possibility that these data also reflect trends in rates at which offenses are reported to the police has motivated extensive victimology research (see Nettler, 1974; and Hindelang, 1976, for a review). This work consistently finds that seriousness of offense is the strongest determinant of citizen reporting to law enforcement officials (Skogan, 1976:145; Hindelang, 1976:401). Hence the upward trend in official crime rates since 1960 in the U.S. may reflect increases in *both* the volume and seriousness of offenses. Though disaggregating these two components may not be feasible, one may wish to interpret observed trends as generated largely by both.

2   The analytical distinction between target and guardian is not important in those cases where a personal target engages in self-protection from direct-contact predatory violations. We leave open for the present the question of whether a guardian is effective or ineffective in all situations. We also allow that various guardians may primarily supervise offenders, targets or both. These are questions for future examination.

REFERENCES***

Choldin, Harvey M. and Dennis W. Roncek (1976). "Density, population potential and pathology: A block-level analysis." *Public Data Use* 4:19-30.

Federal Bureau of Investigation (FBI) (1975). *Crime in the U.S.: Uniform Crime Report.* Washington, D.C.: U.S. Government Printing Office.

Federal Bureau of Investigation (1976). *Crime in the U.S.: Uniform Crime Report.* Washington, D.C.: U.S. Government Printing Office.

Glaser, Daniel (1971). *Social Deviance.* Chicago: Markham.

Guerry, A.M. (1833). "Essai sur la statistique morale de la France." *Westminister Review* 18:357.

Hawley, Amos (1950). *Human Ecology: A Theory of Community Structure.* New York: Ronald.

National Commission on the Causes and Prevention of Violence (1969). *Crimes of Violence.* Vol. 13. Washington, D.C.: U.S. Government Printing Office.

Quetelet, Adolphe (1842). *A Treatise on Man.* Edinburgh: Chambers.

***References have been reduced to those cited in the pages excerpted.

Reiss, Albert J. (1976). "Settling the frontiers of a pioneer in American criminology: Henry McKay." Pp. 64-88 in James F. Short, Jr. (ed.), *Delinquency, Crime, and Society.* Chicago: University of Chicago Press.

Roncek, Dennis (1975). "Crime Rates and Residential Densities in Two Large Cities." Ph.D. dissertation, Department of Sociology, University of Illinois, Urbana.

Shaw, Clifford R., Henry D. McKay, Frederick Zorbaugh and Leonard S. Cottrell (1929). *Delinquency Areas.* Chicago: University of Chicago Press.

U.S. Bureau of the Census (USBC) (1975-1976). *Statistical Abstract of the U.S.* Washington, D.C.: U.S. Government Printing Office.

Dorie Klein (1949-   )

Klein was born in New York, New York. She received a B.A. in sociology from the State University of New York in 1971 and a Doctorate in Criminology from the University of California, Berkeley, in 1979. Following that, Klein earned a post-doctorate fellowship at the National Institute on Drug Abuse from 1979-1981. She taught at the University of California and California State University in sociology, women's studies, and criminal justice from 1981-1983. Since then, she has worked with the Alameda County Court Services as a program specialist and director (1983-1991), and is now a senior researcher with the Public Health Institute in Berkeley, California.

The Etiology of Female Crime*
Dorie Klein**

Introduction

The criminality of women has long been a neglected subject area of criminology. Many explanations have been advanced for this, such as women's low official rate of crime and delinquency and the preponderance of male theorists in the field. Female criminality has often ended up as a footnote to works on men that purport to be works on criminality in general.

There has been, however, a small group of writings specifically concerned with women and crime. This paper will explore those works concerned with the etiology of female crime and delinquency, beginning with the turn-of-the-century writing of Lombroso and extending to the present. Writers selected to be included have been chosen either for their influence on the field, such as Lombroso, Thomas, Freud, Davis and Pollak, or because they are representative of the kinds of work being published, such as Konopka, Vedder and Somerville, and Cowie, Cowie and Slater. The emphasis is on the continuity between these works, because it is clear that, despite recognizable differences in analytical approaches and specific theories, the authors represent a tradition to a great extent. It is important to understand, therefore, the shared assumptions made by the writers that are used in laying the groundwork for their theories.

*Source: Dorie Klein, 1973. "The Etiology of Female Crime: A Review of the Literature," *Issues in Criminology* 8, 2, (Fall): 3-30. By permission of the publisher.
**I wish to acknowledge the major contributions made by the Women's Caucus of the School of Criminology, University of California, Berkeley.

The writers see criminality as the result of *individual* characteristics that are only peripherally affected by economic, social and political forces. These characteristics are of a *physiological* or *psychological* nature and are uniformly based on implicit or explicit assumptions about the *inherent nature of women.* This nature is *universal,* rather than existing within a specific historical framework.

Since criminality is seen as an individual activity, rather than as a condition built into existing structures, the focus is on biological, psychological and social factors that would turn a woman toward criminal activity. To do this, the writers create two distinct classes of women: good women who are "normal" noncriminals, and bad women who are criminals, thus taking a moral position that often masquerades as a scientific distinction. The writers, although they may be biological or social determinists to varying degrees, assume that individuals have *choices* between criminal and noncriminal activity. They see persons as atomistically moving about in a social and political vacuum; many writers use marketplace models for human interaction.

Although the theorists may differ on specific remedies for individual criminality, ranging from sterilization to psychoanalysis (but always stopping far short of social change), the basic thrust is toward *individual adjustment,* whether it be physical or mental, and the frequent model is rehabilitative therapy. Widespread environmental alterations are usually included as casual footnotes to specific plans for individual therapy. Most of the writers are concerned with *social harmony* and the welfare of the existing social structure rather than with the women involved or with women's position in general. None of the writers come from anything near a "feminist" or "radical" perspective.

In *The Female Offender,* originally published in 1903, Lombroso described female criminality as an inherent tendency produced in individuals that could be regarded as biological atavisms, similar to cranial and facial features, and one could expect a withering away of crime if the atavistic people were prohibited from breeding. At this time criminality was widely regarded as a physical ailment, like epilepsy. Today, Cowie, Cowie and Slater (1968) have identified physical traits in girls who have been classified as delinquent, and have concluded that certain traits, such as bigness, may lead to aggressiveness. This theme of physiological characteristics has been developed by a good number of writers in the last seventy years, such as Glueck and Glueck (1934). One sees at the present time a new surge of "biological" theories of criminality; for example, a study involving "violence-prone" women and menstrual cycles has recently been proposed at UCLA.[1]

Thomas, to a certain degree, and Freud extend the physiological explanation of criminality to propose a psychological theory. However, it is critical to understand that these psychological notions are based on assumptions of universal physiological traits of women, such as their reproductive instinct and passivity, that are seen as invariably producing certain psychological reactions. Women may be viewed as turning to crime as a perversion of or rebellion against their natural feminine roles. Whether their problems are biological, psychological or social-environmental, the point is always to return them to their roles. Thomas (1907, 1923), for example, points out that poverty might prevent a woman from marrying, whereby she would turn to prostitution as an alternative to carry on her feminine service role. In fact, Davis (1961) discusses prostitution as a parallel illegal institution to marriage. Pollak (1950) discusses how women extend their service roles into criminal activity due to inherent tendencies such as deceitfulness. Freud (1933; Jones, 1961) sees any kind of rebellion as the result of a failure to develop healthy feminine attitudes, such as narcissism, and Konopka (1966) and Vedder and Somerville (1970) apply Freudian thought to the problem of female delinquency.

The specific characteristics ascribed to women's nature and those critical to theories of female criminality are uniformly *sexual* in their nature. Sexuality is seen as the root of female behavior and the problem of crime. Women are defined as sexual beings, as sexual capital in many cases, physiologically, psychologically and socially. This definition *reflects* and *reinforces* the economic position of women as reproductive and domestic workers. It is mirrored in the laws themselves and in their enforcement, which penalize sexual deviations for women and may be more lenient with economic offenses committed by them, in contrast to the treatment given men. The theorists accept the sexual double standard inherent in the law, often noting that "chivalry" protects women, and many of them build notions of the universality of *sex repression* into their explanations of women's position. Women are thus the sexual backbone of civilization.

In setting hegemonic standards of conduct for all women, the theorists define *femininity,* which they equate with healthy femaleness, in classist, racist and sexist terms, using their assumptions of women's nature, specifically their sexuality, to justify what is often in reality merely a defense of the existing order. Lombroso, Thomas and Freud consider the upper-class white woman to be the highest expression of femininity, although she is inferior to the upper-class white man. These standards are adopted by later writers in discussing femininity. To most theorists, women are inherently inferior to men at masculine tasks such as thought and production, and therefore it is logical that their sphere should be reproductive.

Specific characteristics are proposed to bolster this sexual ideology, expressed for example by Freud, such as passivity, emotionalism, narcissism and deceitfulness. In the discussions of criminality, certain theorists such as Pollak, link female criminality to these traits. Others see criminality as an attempt away from femininity into masculinity, such as

Lombroso, although the specifics are often confused. Contradictions can be clearly seen, which are explained by the dual nature of "good" and "bad" women and by the fact that this is a mythology attempting to explain real behavior. Many explanations of what are obviously economically motivated offenses, such as prostitution and shoplifting, are explained in sexual terms, such as prostitution being promiscuity, and shoplifting being "kleptomania" caused by women's inexplicable mental cycles tied to menstruation. Different explanations have to be made for "masculine" crimes, *e.g.,* burglary, and for "feminine" crimes, *e.g.,* shoplifting. Although this distinction crops up consistently, the specifics differ wildly.

The problem is complicated by the lack of knowledge of the epidemiology of female crime, which allows such ideas as "hidden crime," first expressed by Pollak (1950), to take root. The problem must be considered on two levels: women, having been confined to certain tasks and socialized in certain ways, are *in fact* more likely to commit crime related to their lives which are sexually oriented; yet even nonsexual offenses are *explained* in sexual terms by the theorists. The writers ignore the problems of poor and Third World women, concentrating on affluent white standards of femininity. The experiences of these overlooked women, who *in fact* constitute a good percentage of women caught up in the criminal justice system, negate the notions of sexually motivated crime. These women have real economic needs which are not being met, and in many cases engage in illegal activities as a viable economic alternative. Furthermore, chivalry has never been extended to them.

The writers largely ignore the problems of sexism, racism and class, thus their work is sexist, racist and classist in its implications. Their concern is adjustment of the woman to society, not social change. Hence, they represent a tradition in criminology and carry along a host of assumptions about women and humanity in general. It is important to explore these assumptions and traditions in depth in order to understand what kinds of myths have been propagated around women and crime. The discussions of each writer or writers will focus on these assumptions and their relevance to criminological theories. These assumptions of universal, biological/psychological characteristics, of individual responsibility for crime, of the necessity for maintaining social harmony, and of the benevolence of the state link different theories along a continuum, transcending political labels and minor divergences. The road from Lombroso to the present is surprisingly straight.

Lombroso: "there must be some anomaly. . ."

Lombroso's work on female criminality (1920) is important to consider today despite the fact that his methodology and conclusions have long been successfully discredited. Later writings on female crime by

Thomas, Davis, Pollak and others use more sophisticated methodologies and may proffer more palatable liberal theories. However, to varying degrees they rely on those sexual ideologies based on *implicit* assumptions about the physiological and psychological nature of women that are *explicit* in Lombroso's work. Reading the work helps to achieve a better understanding of what kinds of myths have been developed for women in general and for female crime and deviance in particular.

One specific notion of women offered by Lombroso is women's physiological immobility and psychological passivity, later elaborated by Thomas, Freud and other writers. Another ascribed characteristic is the Lombrosian notion of women's adaptability to surroundings and their capacity for survival as being superior to that of men. A third idea discussed by Lombroso is women's amorality: they are cold and calculating. This is developed by Thomas (1923), who describes women's manipulation of the male sex urge for ulterior purposes; by Freud (1933), who sees women as avenging their lack of a penis on men; and by Pollak (1950), who depicts women as inherently deceitful.

When one looks at these specific traits, one sees contradictions. The myth of compassionate women clashes with their reputed coldness; their frailness belies their capacity to survive. One possible explanation for these contradictions is the duality of sexual ideology with regard to "good" and "bad" women.[2] Bad women are whores, driven by lust for money or for men, often essentially *"masculine"* in their orientation, and perhaps afflicted with a touch of penis envy. Good women are chaste, "feminine," and usually not prone to criminal activity. But when they are, they commit crime in a most *ladylike* way such as poisoning. In more sophisticated theory, all women are seen as having a bit of both tendencies in them. Therefore, women can be compassionate *and* cold, frail *and* sturdy, pious *and* amoral, depending on which path they choose to follow. They are seen as rational (although they are irrational, too!), atomistic individuals making choices in a vacuum, prompted only by personal, physiological/psychological factors. These choices relate only to the *sexual* sphere. Women have no place in any other sphere. Men, on the other hand, are not held sexually accountable, although, as Thomas notes (1907), they are held responsible in *economic* matters. Men's sexual freedom is justified by the myth of masculine, irresistible sex urges. This myth, still worshipped today, is frequently offered as a rationalization for the existence of prostitution and the double standard. As Davis maintains, this necessitates the parallel existence of classes of "good" and "bad" women.

These dual moralities for the sexes are outgrowths of the economic, political and social *realities* for men and women. Women are primarily workers within the family, a critical institution of reproduction and socialization that services such basic needs as food and shelter. Laws and codes of behavior for women thus attempt to maintain the smooth functioning of women in that role, which requires that women act as a conservative force in the continuation of the nuclear family. Women's main tasks are sexual, and the law embodies sexual limitations for women, which do not exist for men, such as the prohibition of promiscuity for girls. This explains why theorists of female criminality are not only concerned with sexual violations by female offenders, but attempt to account for even *nonsexual* offenses, such as prostitution, in sexual terms, *e.g.,* women enter prostitution for sex rather than for money. Such women are not only economic offenders but are sexual deviants, falling neatly into the category of "bad" women.

The works of Lombroso, particularly *The Female Offender* (1920), are a foremost example of the biological explanation of crime. Lombroso deals with crime as an atavism, or survival of "primitive" traits in individuals, particularly those of the female and nonwhite races. He theorizes that individuals develop differentially within sexual and racial limitations which differ hierarchically from the most highly developed, the white men, to the most primitive, the nonwhite women. Beginning with the assumption that criminals must be atavistic, he spends a good deal of time comparing the crania, moles, heights, etc. of convicted criminals and prostitutes with those of normal women. Any trait that he finds to be more common in the "criminal" group is pronounced an atavistic trait, such as moles, dark hair, etc., and women with a number of these telltale traits could be regarded as potentially criminal, since they are of the atavistic type. He specifically rejects the idea that some of these traits, for example obesity in prostitutes, could be the *result* of their activities rather than an indicator of their propensity to them. Many of the traits depicted as "anomalies," such as darkness and shortness, are characteristic of certain racial groups, such as the Sicilians, who undoubtedly comprise an oppressed group within Italy and form a large part of the imprisoned population.

Lombroso traces an overall pattern of evolution in the human species that accounts for the uneven development of groups: the white and nonwhite races, males and females, adults and children. Women, children and nonwhites share many traits in common. There are fewer variations in their mental capacities: "even the female criminal is monotonous and uniform compared with her male companion, just as in general woman is inferior to man" (*Ibid.*:122), due to her being "atavistically nearer to her origin than the male" (*Ibid.*:107). The notion of women's mediocrity, or limited range of mental possibilities, is a recurrent one in the writings of the twentieth century. Thomas and others note that women comprise "fewer geniuses, fewer lunatics and fewer morons" (Thomas, 1907:45); lacking the imagination to be at either end of the spectrum, they are conformist and dull . . . not due to social, political or economic constraints on their activities, but because of their innate physiological limitations as a sex. Lombroso attributes the lower female rate of criminality to their having fewer anomalies, which is one aspect of their closeness to the lower forms of less differentiated life.

Related characteristics of women are their passivity and conservatism. Lombroso admits that women's traditional sex roles in the family bind them to a more sedentary life. However, he insists that women's passivity can be directly traced to the "immobility of the ovule compared with the zoosperm" (1920:109), falling back on the sexual act in an interesting anticipation of Freud.

Women, like the lower races, have greater powers of endurance and resistance to mental and physical pain than men. Lombroso states: "denizens of female prisoners . . . have reached the age of 90, having lived within those walls since they were 29 without any grave injury to health" (*Ibid.*:125). Denying the humanity of women by denying their capability for suffering justifies exploitation of women's energies by arguing for their suitability to hardship. Lombroso remarks that "a duchess can adapt herself to new surroundings and become a washerwoman much more easily than a man can transform himself under analogous conditions" (*Ibid.*:272). The theme of women's adaptability to physical and social surroundings, which are male initiated, male controlled, and often expressed by saying that women are actually the "stronger" sex, is a persistent thread in writings on women.

Lombroso explains that because women are unable to feel pain, they are insensitive to the pain of others and lack moral refinement. His blunt denial of the age-old myth of women's compassion and sensitivity is modified, however, to take into account women's low crime rate:

> Women have many traits in common with children; that their moral sense is deficient; that they are revengeful, jealous . . . In ordinary case these defects are neutralized by piety, maternity, want of passion, sexual coldness, weakness and an undeveloped intelligence (*Ibid.*:151).

Although women lack the higher sensibilities of men, they are thus restrained from criminal activity in most cases by lack of intelligence and passion, qualities which criminal women possess as well as all *men*. Within this framework of biological limits of women's nature, the female offender is characterized as masculine whereas the normal woman is *feminine*. The anomalies of skull, physiognomy and brain capacity of female criminals, according to Lombroso, more closely approximate that of the man, normal or criminal, than they do those of the normal woman; the female offender often has a "virile cranium" and considerable body hair. Masculinity in women is an anomaly itself, rather than a sign of development, however. A related notion is developed by Thomas, who notes that in "civilized" nations the sexes are more physically different.

> What we look for most in the female is femininity, and when we find
> the opposite in her, we must conclude as a rule that there must be some
> anomaly . . . . Virility was one of the special features of the savage
> woman . . . In the portraits of Red Indian and Negro beauties, whom it
> is difficult to recognize for women, so huge are their jaws and cheek-
> bones, so hard and coarse their features, and the same is often the case
> in their crania and brains (*Ibid.*:112).

The more highly developed races would therefore have the most
feminized women with the requisite passivity, lack of passion, etc. This
is a *racist* and *classist* definition of femininity—just as are almost all theories of *femininity* and as, indeed, is the thing itself. The ideal of the lady
can only exist in a society built on the exploitation of labor to maintain
the woman of leisure who can be that ideal lady.

Finally, Lombroso notes women's lack of *property sense,* which contributes to their criminality.

> In their eyes theft is . . . an audacity for which account compensation is
> due to the owner . . . as an individual rather than a social crime, just as
> it was regarded in the primitive periods of human evolution and is still
> regarded by many uncivilized nations (*Ibid.*:217).

One may question this statement on several levels. Can it be assumed to
have any validity at all, or is it false that women have a different sense of
property than men? If it is valid to a degree, is it related to women's lack
of property ownership and nonparticipation in the accumulation of capitalist wealth? Indeed, as Thomas (1907) points out, women are considered property themselves. At any rate, it is an interesting point in
Lombroso's book that has only been touched on by later writers, and
always in a manner supportive of the institution of private property.

Thomas: "the stimulation she craves"

The works of W.I. Thomas are critical in that they mark a transition
from purely physiological explanations such as Lombroso's to more
sophisticated theories that embrace physiological, psychological and
social-structural factors. However, even the most sophisticated explanations of female crime rely on implicit assumptions about the *biological*
nature of women. In Thomas' *Sex and Society* (1907) and *The
Unadjusted Girl* (1923), there are important contradictions in the two
approaches that are representative of the movements during that period
between publication dates: a departure from biological Social-
Darwinian theories to complex analyses of the interaction between society and the individual, *i.e.,* societal repression and manipulation of the
"natural" wishes of persons.

In *Sex and Society* (1907), Thomas poses basic biological differences between the sexes as his starting point. Maleness is "katabolic," the animal force which is destructive of energy and allows men the possibility of creative work through this outward flow. Femaleness is "anabolic," analogous to a plant which stores energy, and is motionless and conservative. Here Thomas is offering his own version of the age-old male/female dichotomy expressed by Lombroso and elaborated on in Freud's paradigm, in the structural-functionalist "instrumental-expressive" duality, and in other analyses of the status quo. According to Thomas, the dichotomy is most highly developed in the more civilized races, due to the greater differentiation of sex roles. This statement ignores the hard physical work done by poor *white* women at home and in the factories and offices in "civilized" countries, and accepts a *ruling-class* definition of femininity.

The cause of women's relative decline in stature in more "civilized" countries is a subject on which Thomas is ambivalent. At one point he attributes it to the lack of "a superior fitness on the motor side" in women (*Ibid.*:94) at another point, he regards her loss of *sexual freedom* as critical, with the coming of monogamy and her confinement to sexual tasks such as wifehood and motherhood. He perceptively notes:

> Women were still further degraded by the development of property and its control by man, together with the habit of treating her as a piece of property, whose value was enhanced if its purity was assured (*Ibid.*:297).

However, Thomas' underlying assumptions in his explanations of the inferior status of women are *physiological* ones. He attributes to men high amounts of sexual energy, which lead them to pursue women for their sex, and he attributes to women maternal feelings devoid of sexuality, which lead *them* to exchange sex for domesticity. Thus monogamy, with chastity for women, is the *accommodation* of these basic urges, and women are domesticated while men assume leadership, in a true market exchange.

Why, then, does Thomas see problems in the position of women? It is because modern women are plagued by "irregularity, pettiness, ill health and inserviceableness" (*Ibid.*:245). Change is required to maintain *social harmony,* apart from considerations of women's needs, and women must be educated to make them better wives, a theme reiterated throughout this century by "liberals" on the subject. Correctly anticipating a threat, Thomas urges that change be made to stabilize the family, and warns that "no civilization can remain the highest if another civilization adds to the intelligence of its men the intelligence of its women" (*Ibid.*:314). Thomas is motivated by considerations of social integration. Of course, one might question how women are to be able to contribute much if they are indeed anabolic. However, due to the transitional nature of Thomas' work, there are immense contradictions in his writing.

Many of Thomas' specific assertions about the nature of women are indistinguishable from Lombroso's; they both delineate a biological hierarchy along race and sex lines.

> Man has, in short, become more somatically specialized an animal than woman, and feels more keenly any disturbance of normal conditions with which he has not the same physiological surplus as woman with which to meet the disturbance . . . It is a logical fact, however, that the lower human races, the lower classes of society, women and children show something of the same quality in their superior tolerance of surgical disease (*Ibid.*:36).

Like Lombroso, Thomas is crediting women with superior capabilities of survival because they are further down the scale in terms of evolution. It is significant that Thomas includes the lower classes in his observation; is he implying that the lower classes are in their position *because* of their natural unfitness, or perhaps that their *situation* renders them less sensitive to pain? At different times, Thomas implies both. Furthermore, he agrees with Lombroso that women are more nearly uniform than men, and says that they have a smaller percentage of "genius, insanity and idiocy" (*Ibid.*:45) than men, as well as fewer creative outbursts of energy.

Dealing with female criminality in *Sex and Society* (1907), Thomas begins to address the issue of morality, which he closely links to legality from a standpoint of maintaining social order. He discriminates between male and female morality:

> Morality as applied to men has a larger element of the contractual, representing the adjustment of his activities to those of society at large, or more particularly to the activities of the male members of society; while the morality which we think of in connection with women shows less of the contractual and more of the personal, representing her adjustment to men, more particularly the adjustment of her person to men (*Ibid.*:172).

Whereas Lombroso barely observes women's lack of participation in the institution of private property, Thomas' perception is more profound. He points out that women *are* property of men and that their conduct is subject to different codes.

> Morality, in the most general sense, represents the code under which activities are best carried on and is worked out in the school of experience. It is preeminently an adult and male system, and men are intelligent enough to realize that neither women nor children have passed through this school. It is on this account that man is merciless to woman from the standpoint of personal behavior, yet he exempts her from anything in the way of contractual morality, or views her defections in this regard with allowance and even with amusement (*Ibid.*:234).

Disregarding his remarks about intelligence, one confronts the critical point about women with respect to the law: because they occupy a *marginal* position in the productive sphere of exchange commodities outside the home, they in turn occupy a marginal position in regard to "contractual" law which regulates relations of property and production. The argument of differential treatment of men and women by the law is developed in later works by Pollak and others, who attribute it to the "chivalry" of the system which is lenient to women committing offenses. As Thomas notes, however, women are simply not a serious *threat* to property, and are treated more "leniently" because of this. Certain women do become threats by transcending (or by being denied) their traditional role, particularly many Third World women and political rebels, and they are *not* afforded chivalrous treatment! In fact, chivalry is reserved for the women who are least likely to ever come in contact with the criminal justice system: the ladies, or white middle-class women. In matters of *sexual* conduct, however, which embody the double standard, women are rigorously prosecuted by the law. As Thomas understands, this is the sphere in which women's functions *are* critical. Thus it is not a matter of "chivalry" how one is handled, but of different forms and thrusts of social control applied to men and women. Men are engaged in productive tasks and their activities in this area are strictly curtailed.

In *The Unadjusted Girl* (1923), Thomas deals with female delinquency as a "normal" response under certain social conditions, using assumptions about the nature of women which he leaves unarticulated in this work. Driven by basic "wishes," an individual is controlled by society in her activities through institutional transmission of codes and mores. Depending on how they are manipulated, wishes can be made to serve social or antisocial ends. Thomas stresses the institutions that socialize, such as the family, giving people certain "definitions of the situation." He confidently—and defiantly—asserts:

> There is no individual energy, no unrest, no type of wish, which cannot be sublimated and made socially useful. From this standpoint, the problem is not the right of society to protect itself from the disorderly and antisocial person, but the right of the disorderly and antisocial person to be made orderly and socially valuable . . . The problem of society is to produce the right attitudes in its members (*Ibid.*:232-233).

This is an important shift in perspective, from the traditional libertarian view of protecting society by punishing transgressors, to the *rehabilitative* and *preventive* perspective of crime control that seeks to control *minds* through socialization rather than to merely control behavior through punishment. The autonomy of the individual to choose is seen as the product of his environment which the state can alter. This is an important refutation of the Lombrosian biological perspective, which maintains that there are crime-prone individuals who must be locked up, sterilized or otherwise incapacitated. Today, one can see an amalgamation of the two perspectives in new theories of "behavior control" that use tactics such as conditioning and brain surgery, combining biological and environmental viewpoints.[3]

Thomas proposes the manipulation of individuals through institutions to prevent antisocial attitudes, and maintains that there is no such person as the "crime prone" individual. A hegemonic system of belief can be imposed by sublimating natural urges and by correcting the poor socialization of slum families. In this perspective, the *definition* of the situation rather than the situation *itself* is what should be changed; a situation is what someone *thinks* it is. The response to a criminal woman who is dissatisfied with her conventional sexual roles is to change not the roles, which would mean widespread social transformations, but to change her attitudes. This concept of civilization as repressive and the need to adjust is later refined by Freud.

Middle-class women, according to Thomas, commit little crime because they are socialized to sublimate their natural desires and to behave well, treasuring their chastity as an investment. The poor woman, however, "is not immoral, because this implies a loss of morality, but amoral" (*Ibid.*:98). Poor women are not objectively driven to crime; they long for it. Delinquent girls are motivated by the desire for excitement or "new experience," and forget the repressive urge of "security." However, these desires are well within Thomas' conception of *femininity:* delinquents are not rebelling against womanhood, as Lombroso suggests, but merely acting it out illegally. Davis and Pollak agree with this notion that delinquent women are not "different" from nondelinquent women.

Thomas maintains that it is not sexual desire that motivates delinquent girls, for they are no more passionate than other women, but they are *manipulating* male desires for sex to achieve their own ulterior ends.

> The beginning of delinquency in girls is usually an impulse to get amusement, adventure, pretty clothes, favorable notice, distinction, freedom in the larger world . . . The girls have usually become 'wild' before the development of sexual desire, and their casual sex relations do not usually awaken sex feeling. Their sex is used as a condition of the realization of other wishes. It is their capital (*Ibid.*:109).

Here Thomas is expanding on the myth of the manipulative woman, who is cold and scheming and vain. To him, good female sexual behavior is a protective measure—"instinctive, of course" (1907:241), whereas male behavior is uncontrollable as men are caught by helpless desires. This is the common Victorian notion of the woman as seductress which in turn perpetuates the myth of a lack of real sexuality to justify her responsibility for upholding sexual mores. Thomas uses a market analogy to female virtue: good women *keep* their bodies as capital to sell in matrimony for marriage and security, whereas bad women *trade* their bodies for excitement. One notes, of course, the familiar dichotomy. It is difficult, in this framework, to see how Thomas can make *any* moral distinctions, since morality seems to be merely good business sense. In fact, Thomas' yardstick is social harmony, necessitating *control*.

Thomas shows an insensitivity to real human relationships and needs. He also shows ignorance of economic hardships in his denial of economic factors in delinquency.

> An unattached woman has a tendency to become an adventuress not so much on economic as on psychological grounds. Life is rarely so hard that a young woman cannot earn her bread; but she cannot always live and have the stimulation she craves (*Ibid.*:241).

This is an amazing statement in an era of mass starvation and illness! He rejects economic causes as a possibility at all, denying its importance in criminal activity with as much certainty as Lombroso, Freud, Davis, Pollak and most other writers.

Freud: "beauty, charm and sweetness"

The Freudian theory of the position of women is grounded in explicit biological assumptions about their nature, expressed by the famous "Anatomy is Destiny." Built upon this foundation is a construction incorporating psychological and social-structural factors.

Freud himself sees women as anatomically inferior; they are destined to be wives and mothers, and this is admittedly an inferior destiny as befits the inferior sex. The root of this inferiority is that women's *sex organs* are inferior to those of men, a fact *universally* recognized by children in the Freudian scheme. The girl assumes that she has lost a penis as punishment, is traumatized, and grows up envious and revengeful. The boy also sees the girl as having lost a penis, fears a similar punishment himself, and dreads the girl's envy and vengeance. Feminine traits can be traced to the inferior genitals themselves, or to women's inferiority complex arising from their response to them: women are exhibitionistic, narcissistic, and attempt to compensate for their lack of a penis by being well dressed and physically beautiful. Women become mothers trying to replace the lost penis with a baby. Women are also masochistic, as Lombroso and Thomas have noted, because their *sexual* role is one of receptor, and their sexual pleasure consists of pain. This woman, Freud notes, is the *healthy* woman. In the familiar dichotomy, the men are aggressive and pain inflicting. Freud comments:

> The male pursues the female for the purposes of sexual union, seizes
> hold of her, and penetrates into her . . . by this you have precisely
> reduced the characteristic of masculinity to the factor of aggressiveness
> (Millett, 1970:189).

Freud, like Lombroso and Thomas, takes the notion of men's activity
and women's inactivity and *reduces* it to the sexual level, seeing the sexual union itself through Victorian eyes: ladies don't move.

Women are also inferior in the sense that they are concerned with
personal matters and have little social sense. Freud sees civilization as
based on repression of the sex drive, where it is the duty of men to
repress their strong instincts in order to get on with the worldly business
of civilization. Women, on the other hand,

> have little sense of justice, and this is no doubt connected with the pre-
> ponderance of envy in their mental life; for the demands of justice are a
> modification of envy; they lay down the conditions under which one is
> willing to part with it. We also say of women that their social interests
> are weaker than those of men and that their capacity for the sublima-
> tion of their instincts is less (1933:183).

Men are capable of sublimating their individual needs because they
rationally perceive the Hobbesian conflict between those urges and
social needs. Women are emotional and incapable of such an adjustment
because of their innate inability to make such rational judgments. It is
only fair then that they should have a marginal relation to production
and property.

In this framework, the deviant woman is one who is attempting to
be a *man*. She is aggressively rebellious, and her drive to accomplishment is the expression of her longing for a penis; this is a hopeless pursuit, of course, and she will only end up "neurotic." Thus the deviant
woman should be treated and helped to adjust to her sex role. Here
again, as in Thomas' writing, is the notion of individual accommodation
that repudiates the possibility of social change.

In a Victorian fashion, Freud rationalizes women's oppression by
glorifying their duties as wives and mothers:

> It is really a stillborn thought to send women into the struggle for exis-
> tence exactly the same as men. If, for instance, I imagined my sweet
> gentle girl as a competitor, it would only end in my telling her, as I did
> seventeen months ago, that I am fond of her, and I implore her to
> withdraw from the strife into the calm, uncompetitive activity of my
> home . . . Nature has determined woman's destiny through beauty,
> charm and sweetness . . . in youth an adored darling, in mature years a
> loved wife (Jones, 1961:117-118).

In speaking of femininity, Freud, like his forebearers, is speaking along racist and classist lines. Only upper- and middle-class women could possibly enjoy lives as sheltered darlings. Freud sets hegemonic standards of femininity for poor and Third World women.

It is important to understand Freudianism because it reduces categories of sexual ideology to explicit sexuality and makes these categories *scientific*. For the last fifty years, Freudianism has been a mainstay of sexist social theory. Kate Millett notes that Freud himself saw his work as stemming the tide of feminist revolution, which he constantly ridiculed:

> Coming as it did, at the peak of the sexual revolution, Freud's doctrine of penis envy is in fact a superbly timed accusation, enabling masculine sentiment to take the offensive again as it had not since the disappearance of overt misogyny when the pose of chivalry became fashionable (Millett, 1970:189).

Freudian notions of the repression of sexual instincts, the sexual passivity of women, and the sanctity of the nuclear family are conservative not only in their contemporary context, but in the context of their own time. Hitler writes:

> For her [woman's] world is her husband, her family, her children and her home . . . The man upholds the nation as the woman upholds the family. The equal rights of women consist in the fact that in the realm of life determined for her by nature, she experience the high esteem that is her due. Woman and man represent quite different types of being. Reason is dominant in man . . . Feeling, in contrast, is much more stable than reason, and woman is the feeling, and therefore the stable, element (*Ibid.*: 170).

One can mark the decline in the position of women after the 1920s through the use of various indices: by noting the progressively earlier age of marriage of women in the United States and the steady rise in the number of children born to them, culminating in the birth explosion of the late forties and fifties; by looking at the relative decline in the number of women scholars; and by seeing the failure to liberate women in the Soviet Union and the rise of fascist sexual ideology. Freudianism has had an unparalleled influence in the United States (and came at a key point to help swing the tide against the women's movement) to facilitate the return of women during the depression and postwar years to the home, out of an economy which had no room for them. Freud affected such writers on female deviance as Davis, Pollak and Konopka, who turn to concepts of sexual maladjustment and neurosis to explain women's criminality. Healthy women would now be seen as masochistic, passive and sexually indifferent. Criminal women would be seen as *sex-*

ual misfits. Most importantly, *psychological* factors would be used to explain criminal activity, and social, economic and political factors would be ignored. Explanations would seek to be *universal*, and historical possibilities of change would be refuted.

Davis: "the most convenient sexual outlet for armies . . ."

Kingsley Davis' work on prostitution (1961) is still considered a classical analysis on the subject with a structural-functionalist perspective. It employs assumptions about "the organic nature of man" and woman, many of which can be traced to ideas proffered by Thomas and Freud.

Davis sees prostitution as a structural necessity whose roots lie in the *sexual* nature of men and women; for example, female humans, unlike primates, are sexually available year-round. He asserts that prostitution is *universal* in time and place, eliminating the possibilities of historical change and ignoring critical differences in the quality and quantity of prostitution in different societies. He maintains that there will always be a class of women who will be prostitutes—the familiar class of "bad" women. The reason for the universality of prostitution is that sexual *repression,* a concept stressed by Thomas and Freud, is essential to the functioning of society. Once again there is the notion of sublimating "natural" sex urges to the overall needs of society, namely social order. Davis notes that in our society sexuality is permitted only within the structure of the nuclear family, which is an institution of stability. He does not, however, analyze in depth the economic and social functions of the family, other than to say it is a bulwark of morality.

> The norms of every society tend to harness and control the sexual appetite, and one of the ways of doing this is to link the sexual act to some stable or potentially stable social relationship . . . Men dominate women in economic, sexual and familial relationships and consider them to some extent as sexual property, to be prohibited to other males. They therefore find promiscuity on the part of women repugnant (*Ibid.*:264).

Davis is linking the concept of prostitution to promiscuity, defining it as a *sexual* crime, and calling prostitutes sexual transgressors. Its origins, he claims, lie not in economic hardship, but in the marital restraints on sexuality. As long as men seek women, prostitutes will be in demand. One wonders why sex-seeking women have not created a class of male prostitutes.

Davis sees the only possibility of eliminating prostitution in the liberalization of sexual mores, although he is pessimistic about the likelihood of total elimination. In light of the contemporary American "sexual revolution" of commercial sex, which has surely created more

prostitutes and semi-prostitutes rather than eliminating the phenomenon, and in considering the revolution in China where, despite a "puri-
tanical" outlook on sexuality, prostitution has largely been eliminated
through major economic and social change, the superficiality of Davis'
approach becomes evident. Without dealing with root economic, social
and political factors, one cannot analyze prostitution.

Davis shows Freudian pessimism about the nature of sexual repression:

> We can imagine a social system in which the motive for prostitution
> would be completely absent, but we cannot imagine that the system
> will ever come to pass. It would be a regime of absolute sexual freedom
> with intercourse practiced solely for pleasure by both parties. There
> would be no institutional control of sexual expression . . . All sexual
> desire would have to be mutually complementary . . . Since the basic
> causes of prostitution—the institutional control of sex, the unequal
> scale of attractiveness, and the presence of economic and social
> inequalities between classes and between males and females—are not
> likely to disappear, prostitution is not likely to disappear either
> (*Ibid.*:286).

By talking about "complementary desire," Davis is using a marketplace
notion of sex: two attractive or unattractive people are drawn to each
other and exchange sexual favors; people are placed on a scale of attractiveness and may be rejected by people above them on the scale; hence
they (*men*) become frustrated, and demand prostitutes. Women who
become prostitutes do so for good pay *and* sexual pleasure. Thus one
has a neat little system in which everyone benefits.

> Enabling a small number of women to take care of the needs of a large
> number of men, it is the most convenient sexual outlet for armies, for
> the legions of strangers, perverts and physically repulsive in our midst
> (*Ibid.*:288).

Prostitution "functions," therefore it must be good. Davis, like Thomas,
is motivated by concerns of social order rather than by concerns of what
the needs and desires of the women involved might be. He denies that
the women involved are economically oppressed; they are on the streets
through autonomous, *individual* choice.

> Some women physically enjoy the intercourse they sell. From a purely
> economic point of view, prostitution comes near the situation of getting
> something for nothing . . . Women's wages could scarcely be raised sig-
> nificantly without also raising men's. Men would then have more to
> spend on prostitution (*Ibid.*:277).

It is important to understand that, given a sexual interpretation of what is an *economic* crime, and given a refusal to consider widespread change (even equalization of wages, hardly a revolutionary act), Davis' conclusion is the logical technocratic solution.

In this framework, the deviant women are merely adjusting to their feminine role in an illegitimate fashion, as Thomas has theorized. They are *not* attempting to be rebels or to be "men," as Lombroso's and Freud's positions suggest. Although Davis sees the main difference between wives and prostitutes in a macrosocial sense as the difference merely between legal and illegal roles, in a personal sense he sees the women who *choose* prostitution as maladjusted and neurotic. However, given the universal necessity for prostitution, this analysis implies the necessity of having a perpetually ill and maladjusted class of women. Thus oppression is *built into* the system, and a healthy *system* makes for a sick *individual*. Here Davis is integrating Thomas' notions of social integration with Freudian perspectives on neurosis and maladjustment.

Pollak: "a different attitude toward veracity"

Otto Pollak's *The Criminality of Women* (1950) has had an outstanding influence on the field of women and crime, being the major work on the subject in the postwar years. Pollak advances the theory of "hidden" female crime to account for what he considers unreasonably low official rates for women.

A major reason for the existence of hidden crime, as he sees it, lies in the *nature* of women themselves. They are instigators rather than perpetrators of criminal activity. While Pollak admits that this role is partly a socially enforced one, he insists that women are inherently deceitful for *physiological* reasons.

> Man must achieve an erection in order to perform the sex act and will not be able to hide his failure. His lack of positive emotion in the sexual sphere must become overt to the partner, and pretense of sexual response is impossible for him, if it is lacking. [A] woman's body, however, permits such pretense to a certain degree and lack of orgasm does not prevent her ability to participate in the sex act (*Ibid.*:10).

Pollak *reduces* women's nature to the *sex* act, as Freud has done, and finds women inherently more capable of manipulation, accustomed to being sly, passive and passionless. As Thomas suggests, women can use sex for ulterior purposes. Furthermore, Pollak suggests that women are innately deceitful on yet another level:

> Our sex[ual] mores force women to conceal every four weeks the
> period of menstruation . . . They thus make concealment and misrepre-
> sentation in the eyes of women socially required and must condition
> them to a different attitude toward veracity than men (*Ibid.*:11).

Women's abilities at concealment thus allow them to successfully commit crimes in stealth.

Women are also vengeful. Menstruation, in the classic Freudian
sense, seals their doomed hopes to become men and arouses women's
desire for vengeance, especially during that time of the month. Thus
Pollak offers new rationalizations to bolster old myths.

A second factor in hidden crime is the roles played by women which
furnish them with opportunities as domestics, nurses, teachers and
housewives to commit undetectable crimes. The *kinds* of crimes women
commit reflect their nature: false accusation, for example, is an outgrowth of women's treachery, spite or fear and is a sign of neurosis;
shoplifting can be traced in many cases to a special mental disease—
kleptomania. Economic factors play a minor role; *sexual-psychological*
factors account for female criminality. Crime in women is *personalized*
and often accounted for by mental illness. Pollak notes:

> Robbery and burglary . . . are considered specifically male offenses
> since they represent the pursuit of monetary gain by overt action . . .
> Those cases of female robbery which seem to express a tendency
> toward masculinization come from . . . [areas] where social conditions
> have favored the assumptions of male pursuits by women . . . The
> female offenders usually retain some trace of femininity, however, and
> even so glaring an example of masculinization as the 'Michigan Babes,'
> an all woman gang of robbers in Chicago, shows a typically feminine
> trait in the modus operandi (*Ibid.*:29).

Pollak is defining crimes with economic motives that employ overt
action as *masculine,* and defining as *feminine* those crimes for *sexual*
activity, such as luring men as baits. Thus he is using circular reasoning
by saying that feminine crime is feminine. To fit women into the scheme
and justify the statistics, he must invent the notion of hidden crime.

It is important to recognize that, to some extent, women do adapt to
their enforced sexual roles and may be more likely to instigate, to use
sexual traps, and to conform to all the other feminine role expectations.
However, it is not accidental that theorists label women as conforming
even when they are *not;* for example, by inventing sexual motives for
what are clearly crimes of economic necessity, or by invoking "mental illness" such as kleptomania for shoplifting. It is difficult to separate the
theory from the *reality,* since the reality of female crime is largely
unknown. But it is not difficult to see that Pollak is using sexist terms and
making sexist assumptions to advance theories of hidden female crime.

Pollak, then, sees criminal women as extending their sexual role, like Davis and Thomas, by using sexuality for ulterior purposes. He suggests that the condemnation of extramarital sex has "delivered men who engage in such conduct as practically helpless victims" (*Ibid.*:152) into the hands of women blackmailers, overlooking completely the possibility of men blackmailing women, which would seem more likely, given the greater taboo on sex for women and their greater risks of being punished.

The final factor that Pollak advances as a root cause of hidden crime is that of "chivalry" in the criminal justice system. Pollak uses Thomas' observation that women are differentially treated by the law, and carries it to a sweeping conclusion based on *cultural* analyses of men's feelings toward women.

> One of the outstanding concomitants of the existing inequality . . . is chivalry, and the general protective attitude of man toward woman . . . Men hate to accuse women and thus indirectly to send them to their punishment, police officers dislike to arrest them, district attorneys to prosecute them, judges and juries to find them guilty, and so on (*Ibid.*:151).

Pollak rejects the possibility of an actual discrepancy between crime rates for men and women; therefore, he must look for factors to expand the scope of female crime. He assumes that there is chivalry in the criminal justice system that is extended to the women who come in contact with it. Yet the women involved are likely to be poor and Third World women or white middle-class women who have stepped *outside* the definitions of femininity to become hippies or political rebels, and chivalry is *not* likely to be extended to them. Chivalry is a racist and classist concept founded on the notion of women as "ladies" which applies only to wealthy white women and ignores the double sexual standard. These "ladies," however, are the least likely women to ever come in contact with the criminal justice system in the first place.[4]

The legacy of sexism

A major purpose in tracing the development and interaction of ideas pertaining to sexual ideology based on implicit assumptions of the inherent nature of women throughout the works of Lombroso, Thomas, Freud, Davis and Pollak, is to clarify their positions in relation to writers in the field today. One can see the influence their ideas still have by looking at a number of contemporary theorists on female criminality. Illuminating examples can be found in Gisela Konopka's *Adolescent Girl in Conflict* (1966), Vedder and Somenille's *The Delinquent Girl* (1970) and Cowie, Cowie and Slater's *Delinquency in Girls* (1968). The ideas in these minor works have direct roots in those already traced in this paper.

Konopka justifies her decision to study delinquency in girls rather than in boys by noting girls' influence on boys in gang fights and on future generations as mothers. This is the notion of women as instigators of men and influencers on children.

Konopka's main point is that delinquency in girls can be traced to a specific emotional response: loneliness.

> What I found in the girl in conflict was . . . loneliness accompanied by despair. Adolescent boys too often feel lonely and search for understanding and friends. Yet in general this does not seem to be the central core of their problems, not their most outspoken ache. While these girls also strive for independence, their need for dependence is unusually great (1966:40).

In this perspective, girls are driven to delinquency by an emotional problem—loneliness and dependency. There are *inherent* emotional differences between the sexes.

> Almost invariably her [the girl's] problems are deeply personalized. Whatever her offense — whether shoplifting, truancy or running away from home — it is usually accompanied by some disturbance or unfavorable behavior in the sexual area (*Ibid.*:4).

Here is the familiar resurrection of female personalism, emotionalism, and above all, *sexuality*—characteristics already described by Lombroso, Thomas, and Freud. Konopka maintains:

> The delinquent girl suffers, like many boys, from lack of success, lack of opportunity. But her drive to success is never separated from her need for people, for interpersonal involvement (*Ibid.*:41).

Boys are "instrumental" and become delinquent if they are deprived of the chance for creative success. However, girls are "expressive" and happiest dealing with people as wives, mothers, teachers, nurses or psychologists. This perspective is drawn from the theory of delinquency as a result of blocked opportunity and from the instrumental/expressive sexual dualism developed by structural-functionalists. Thus female delinquency must be dealt with on this *psychological* level, using therapy geared to their needs as future wives and mothers. They should be *adjusted* and given *opportunities* to be pretty, sociable women.

The important point is to understand how Konopka analyzes the roots of girls' feelings. It is very possible that, given women's position, girls may be in fact more concerned with dependence and sociability. One's understanding of this, however, is based on an understanding of the historical position of women and the nature of their oppression. Konopka says:

> What are the reasons for this essential loneliness in girls? Some will be found in the nature of being an adolescent girl, in her biological makeup and her particular position in her culture and time (*Ibid.*).

Coming from a Freudian perspective, Konopka's emphasis on female emotions as cause for delinquency, which ignores economic and social factors, is questionable. She employs assumptions about the *physiological* and *psychological* nature of women that very well may have led her to see only those feelings in the first place. For example, she cites menstruation as a significant event in a girl's development. Thus Konopka is rooted firmly in the tradition of Freud and, apart from sympathy, contributes little that is new to the field.[5]

Vedder and Somerville (1970) account for female delinquency in a manner similar to that of Konopka. They also feel the need to justify their attention to girls by remarking that (while female delinquency may not pose as much of a problem as that of boys) because women raise families and are critical agents of socialization, it is worth taking the time to study and control them. Vedder and Somerville also stress the dependence of girls on boys and the instigatory role girls play in boys' activities.

Like Freud and Konopka, the authors view delinquency as blocked access or maladjustment to the normal feminine role. In a blatant statement that ignores the economic and social factors that result from racism and poverty, they attribute the high rates of delinquency among black girls to their lack of "healthy" feminine narcissism, *reducing* racism to a psychological problem in totally sexist and racist terms.

> The black girl is, in fact, the antithesis of the American beauty. However loved she may be by her mother, family and community, she has no real basis of female attractiveness on which to build a sound feminine narcissism . . . Perhaps the 'black is beautiful' movement will help the Negro girl to increase her femininity and personal satisfaction as a black woman (*Ibid.*:159-160).

Again the focus is on a lack of *sexual* opportunities for women, *i.e.*, the black woman is not Miss America. *Economic* offenses such as shoplifting are explained as outlets for *sexual* frustration. Since healthy women conform, the individual delinquents should be helped to adjust, the emphasis is on the "definition of the situation" rather than on the situation.

The answer lies in *therapy*, and racism and sexism become merely psychological problems.

> Special attention should be given to girls, taking into consideration their constitutional, biological and psychological differences, and their social position in our male-dominated culture. The female offender's goal, as any woman's, is a happy and successful marriage; therefore her self-image is dependent on the establishment of satisfactory relation-

ships with the opposite sex. The double standard for sexual behavior on the part of the male and female must be recognized (*Ibid.*:153).

Like Konopka, and to some extent drawing on Thomas, the authors see female delinquents as extending femininity in an illegitimate fashion rather than rebelling against it. The assumptions made about women's goals and needs, including *biological* assumptions, lock women into a system from which there is no escape, whereby any behavior will be sexually interpreted and dealt with.

The resurgence of biological or physiological explanations of criminality in general has been noteworthy in the last several years, exemplified by the XYY chromosome controversy and the interest in brain waves in "violent" individuals.[6] In the case of women, biological explanations have *always* been prevalent; every writer has made assumptions about anatomy as destiny. Women are prey, in the literature, to cycles of reproduction, including menstruation, pregnancy, maternity and menopause; they experience emotional responses to these cycles that make them inclined to irrationality and potentially violent activity.

Cowie, Cowie and Slater (1968) propose a chromosomal explanation of female delinquency that hearkens back to the works of Lombroso and others such as Healy (1926), Edith Spaulding (1923) and the Gluecks (1934). They write:

> The chromosomal difference between the sexes starts the individual on a divergent path, leading either in a masculine or feminine direction . . . It is possible that the methods of upbringing, differing somewhat for the two sexes, may play some part in increasing the angle of this divergence (*Ibid.*:171).

This is the healthy, normal divergence for the sexes. The authors equate *masculinity* and *femininity* with *maleness* and *femaleness*, although contemporary feminists point out that the first categories are *social* and the latter ones *physical*.[7] What relationship exists between the two—how femaleness determines femininity—is dependent on the larger social structure. There is no question that a wide range of possibilities exists historically, and in a nonsexist society it is possible that "masculinity" and "femininity" would disappear, and that the sexes would differ only biologically, specifically by their sex organs. The authors, however, lack this understanding and assume an ahistorical sexist view of women, stressing the *universality* of femininity in the Freudian tradition, and of women's inferior role in the nuclear family.[8]

In this perspective, the female offender is *different* physiologically and psychologically from the "normal" girl.

The authors conclude, in the tradition of Lombroso, that female delinquents are masculine. Examining girls for physical characteristics, they note:

> Markedly masculine traits in girl delinquents have been commented on
> . . . [as well as] the frequency of homosexual tendencies . . . Energy,
> aggressiveness, enterprise and the rebelliousness that drives the individ-
> ual to break through conformist habits are thought of as being mascu-
> line . . . We can be sure that they have some physical basis (*Ibid.*:172).

The authors see crime as a *rebellion* against sex roles rather than as a maladjusted expression of them. By defining rebellion as *masculine,* they are ascribing characteristics of masculinity to any female rebel. Like Lombroso, they spend time measuring heights, weights, and other *biological* features of female delinquents with other girls.

Crime defined as masculine seems to mean violent, overt crime, whereas "ladylike" crime usually refers to sexual violations and shoplifting. Women are neatly categorized no matter *which* kind of crime they commit: if they are violent, they are "masculine" and suffer-ing from chromosomal deficiencies, penis envy, or atavisms. If they con-form, they are manipulative, sexually maladjusted, and promiscuous. The *economic* and *social* realities of crime—the fact that poor women commit crimes, and that most crimes for women are property offenses—are overlooked. Women's behavior must be *sexually* defined before it will be considered, for women count only in the sexual sphere. The theme of sexuality is a unifying thread in the various, often contradic-tory theories.

Conclusion

A good deal of the writing on women and crime being done at the present time is squarely in the tradition of the writers that have been dis-cussed. The basic assumptions and technocratic concerns of these writ-ers have produced work that is sexist, racist, and classist; assumptions that have served to maintain a repressive ideology with its extensive apparatus of control. To do a new kind of research on women and crime—one that has feminist roots and a radical orientation—it is neces-sary to understand the assumptions made by the traditional writers and to break away from them. Work that focuses on human needs, rather than those of the state, will require new definitions of criminality, women, the individual and her/his relation to the state. It is beyond the scope of this paper to develop possible areas of study, but it is nonethe-less imperative that this work be made a priority by women and men in the future.

ENDNOTES

1   Quoted from the 1973 proposal for the Center for the Study and Reduction of Violence prepared by Dr. Louis J. West, Director, Neuropsychiatric Institute, UCLA: "The question of violence in females will be examined from the point of view that females are more likely to commit acts of violence during the pre-menstrual and menstrual periods" (1973:43).

2   I am indebted to Marion Goldman for introducing me to the notion of the dual morality based on assumptions of different sexuality for men and women.

3   For a discussion of the possibilities of psychosurgery in behavior modification for "violence-prone" individuals, see Frank Ervin and Vernon Mark, *Violence and the Brain* (1970). For an eclectic view of this perspective on crime, see the proposal for the Center for the Study and Reduction of Violence (footnote #1).

4   The concept of hidden crime is reiterated in Reckless and Kay's report to the President's Commission on Law Enforcement and the Administration of Justice. They note:
> A large part of the infrequent officially acted upon involvement of women in crime can be traced to the masking effect of women's roles, effective practice on the part of women of deceit and indirection, their instigation of men to commit their crimes (the Lady Macbeth factor), and the unwillingness on the part of the public and law enforcement officials to hold women accountable for their deeds (the chivalry factor) (1967:13).

5   Bertha Payak in "Understanding the Female Offender" (1963) stresses that women offenders have poor self-concepts, feelings of insecurity and dependency, are emotionally selfish, and prey to irrationality during menstruation, pregnancy, and menopause a good deal of their life!

6   See Theodore R. Sarbin and Jeffrey E. Miller, "Demonism Revisited: The XYY Chromosomal Anomaly." *Issues in Criminology* 5(2) (Summer 1970).

7   Kate Millett (1970) notes that "sex is biological, gender psychological and therefore cultural . . . if the proper terms for sex are male and female, the corresponding terms for gender are masculine and feminine; these latter may be quite independent of biological sex" (*Ibid.*:301).

8   Zelditch (1960), a structural-functionalist, writes that the nuclear family is an inevitability and that within it, women, the "expressive" sex, will inevitably be the domestics.

References

Bishop, Cecil (1931). *Women and Crime*. London: Chatto and Windus.

Cowie, John, Valerie Cowie and Eliot Slater (1968). *Delinquency in Girls*. London: Heinemann.

Davis, Kingsley (1961). "Prostitution." *Contemporary Social Problems*. Edited by Robert K. Merton and Robert A. Nisbet. New York: Harcourt Brace and Jovanovich. Originally published as "The Sociology of Prostitution." *American Sociological Review* 2(5) (October 1937).

Ervin, Frank and Vernon Mark (1970). *Violence and the Brain*. New York: Harper and Row.

Fernalt, Mabel, Mary Hayes and Almena Dawley (1920). *A Study of Women Delinquents in New York State*. New York: Century Company.

Freud, Sigmund (1933). *New Introductory Lectures on Psychoanalysis*. New York: W.W. Norton.

Glueck, Eleanor and Sheldon (1934). *Five Hundred Delinquent Women*. New York: Alfred A. Knopf.

Healy, William and Augusta Bronner (1926). *Delinquents and Criminals: Their Making and Unmaking*. New York: Macmillan and Company.

Hemming, James (1960). *Problems of Adolescent Girls*. London: Heinemann.

Jones, Ernest (1961). *The Life and Works of Sigmund Freud*. New York: Basic Books.

Konopka, Gisela (1966). *The Adolescent Girl in Conflict*. Englewood Cliffs, New Jersey: Prentice-Hall.

Lombroso, Cesare (1920). *The Female Offender* (translation). New York: Appleton. Originally published in 1903.

Millett, Kate (1970). *Sexual Politics*. New York: Doubleday and Company.

Monahan, Florence (1941). *Women in Crime*. New York: I. Washbum.

Parsons, Talcott (1942). "Age and Sex in the Social Structure." *American Sociological Review* 7 (October).

Parsons, Talcott and Renee Fox (1960). "Illness, Therapy and the Modem 'Urban' American Family." *The Family*. Edited by Norman Bell and Ezra Vogel. Glencoe, Illinois: The Free Press.

Payak, Bertha (1963). "Understanding the Female Offender." *Federal Probation* XXVII.

Pollak, Otto (1950). *The Criminality of Women*. Philadelphia: University of Pennsylvania Press.

Reckless, Walter and Barbara Kay (1967). *The Female Offender*. Report to the President's Commission on Law Enforcement and the Administration of Justice. Washington, D.C.: U.S. Government Printing Office.

Sarbin, Theodore R. and Jeffrey E. Miller (1970). "Demonism Revisited: The XYY Chromosomal Anomaly." *Issues in Criminology* 5 (2) (Summer).

Schwendinger, Herman and Julia (1973). "The Founding Fathers: Sexists to a Man." *Sociologists of the Chair*. New York: Basic Books.

Spaulding, Edith (1923). *An Experimental Study of Psychopathic Delinquent Women*. New York: Rand McNally.

Thomas, W.I. (1907). *Sex and Society*. Boston: Little, Brown and Company.

Thomas, W.I. (1923). *The Unadjusted Girl*. New York: Harper and Row.

Vedder, Clyde and Dora Somerville (1970). *The Delinquent Girl*. Springfield, Illinois: Charles C Thomas.

West, Dr. Louis J. (1973). *Proposal for the Center for the Study and Reduction of Violence*. Neuropsychiatric Institute, UCLA (April l0).

Zelditch, Morris, Jr. (1960). "Role Differentiation in the Nuclear Family: A Comparative Study." *The Family*. Edited by Norman Bell and Ezra Vogel. Glencoe, Illinois: The Free Press.

Essay/Discussion Questions for Section VII

Note to the student: If you are able to provide thorough responses to all of the following questions, you have mastered excellent comprehension of the classic readings presented in this section.

1. Cohen and Felson's routine activities theory presumes a rational (or at least semi-rational) criminal. Why? What other perspectives are also based on rationality? (From the section introduction.)

2. Routine activities theory is based on evidence from victimization studies. Why do you think this is so, and why is this important in comparison to earlier theories? (From the section introduction.)

3. What do feminist approaches add to criminological theory? (From the section introduction.)

4. Explain the three elements of routine activities theory. Is any element more important than the others? (From the Cohen & Felson reading.)

5. What are the implications of routine activities theory for potential victims? Are there any relationships you can see with fear of crime? (From the Cohen & Felson reading.)

6. Why do you think earlier theorists ignored female criminality? (From the Klein reading.)

7. Klein writes about the "legacy of sexism." What does she mean, and how important do you think this is for today's crime and delinquency theory? (From the Klein reading.)

Index

About the Authors

Frank P. Williams III is a Professor of Criminal Justice at California State University, San Bernardino. Dr. Williams received his Ph.D. in Criminology from Florida State University. In addition to his academic experience, Dr. Williams has also served as series editor of *Contemporary Issues in Criminal Justice* and as editor of both *Presley Institute Bulletin* and *Criminal Justice Research Bulletin*. Over the years, Dr. Williams has authored several textbooks, and has authored or co-authored many articles that have appeared in professional journals. He is currently working on a grant to revise parole policing in California.

Marilyn D. McShane is the Chair and a Professor in the Criminal Justice Department at Northern Arizona University, Flagstaff, Arizona. Dr. McShane received her Ph.D. in Criminal Justice from Sam Houston State University in 1985. In addition to her assorted academic positions, Dr. McShane has also been an advisory board member of the Youth Justice Center in the San Bernardino County Probation Department, and has conducted research grants for the National Institute for Corrections, California Department of Corrections, Paroles and San Bernardino County Probation, and the Robert Presley Institute for Corrections Research and Training.